Modern romance and transformations of the novel examines the relationship between the revival of romance and the ascendancy of the novel in British literary culture between 1765 and 1850. The revival of romance as the literary form of a pre-modern cultural identity provided a metaphor of lost origins to account for the otherness of fiction to the world of historical experience. The decisive transformation of the formal repertoire, cultural status and material production of the novel, leading to its nineteenth-century heyday, took place in the historical romances of Walter Scott. Ian Duncan's innovative and illuminating study begins with the first identification of the novel with a distinct genre of romance in late eighteenth-century Gothic fiction, and moves through Scott's potent synthesis of romance and history, to the cultural relations between Scott and his successor in the role of national author, Dickens.

MODERN ROMANCE AND TRANSFORMATIONS OF THE NOVEL

MODERN ROMANCE AND TRANSFORMATIONS OF THE NOVEL

The Gothic, Scott, Dickens

IAN DUNCAN

Assistant Professor of English, Yale University

CAMBRIDGE UNIVERSITY PRESS
Cambridge, New York, Melbourne, Madrid, Cape Town, Singapore, São Paulo

Cambridge University Press
The Edinburgh Building, Cambridge CB2 2RU, UK

Published in the United States of America by Cambridge University Press, New York

www.cambridge.org
Information on this title: www.cambridge.org/9780521395359

First published 1992
This digitally printed first paperback version 2005

A catalogue record for this publication is available from the British Library

Library of Congress Cataloguing in Publication data

Duncan, Ian.
Modern romance and transformations of the novel:
the Gothic, Scott, Dickens / Ian Duncan.
p. cm.
Includes bibliographical references and index.
ISBN 0 521 39535 6 (hc)
1. English fiction – 19th century – History and criticism.
2. Romances – Adaptations – History and criticism. 3. Scott, Walter,
Sir, 1771–1832 – Criticism and interpretation. 4. Dickens, Charles,
1812–1870 – Criticism and interpretation. 5. English fiction – 18th
century – History and criticism. 6. Gothic revival (Literature) –
Great Britain. 7. Romanticism – Great Britain. 8. Scotland in
literature. I. Title.
PR868.R7D86 1992
823′.0850908 – dc20 91-43862 CIP

ISBN-13 978-0-521-39535-9 hardback
ISBN-10 0-521-39535-6 hardback

ISBN-13 978-0-521-02106-7 paperback
ISBN-10 0-521-02106-5 paperback

For Ayşe: herşey için

Contents

Acknowledgements *page* xi

Prologue: fiction as fiction 1

1 The culture of Gothic 20

2 The romance of subjection: Scott's *Waverley* 51

3 The suspension of belief 106
The end of the astrologer: *Guy Mannering* 111
Against nature: *The Bride of Lammermoor* 135
Estate of grace: *The Heart of Mid-Lothian* 146

4 Scott and Dickens: the work of the author 177

5 Scott and Dickens: the end of history 209

Notes 254

Index 287

Acknowledgements

I have drawn heavily on other people's energy, patience and goodwill in the course of this work. I am particularly indebted to those who read and criticized the manuscript in the different stages of its entirety. John Hollander and Martin Price informed its composition with the bounty of their erudition and an invigorating blend of enthusiasm and scepticism. Joseph Carroll, Scott Klein and Pat Spacks, who read early drafts, and Dick Brodhead, David Bromwich and Sara Suleri, who read the dissertation, were the most sympathetic and demanding of critics. Along the way many other colleagues and friends were generous with their commentary, discussion, advice and assistance: Marshall Brown, Jill Campbell, Tom Crawford, Al Essa, Burton Feldman, Paul Fry, Margaret Ferguson, Peter Holbrook, Thomas Greene, Elizabeth Gregory, Chuck Hatton, David Hensley, David Kaufmann, Şişko Kedi, Lewis Klausner, David Mikics, Maggie Kilgour, J. Hillis Miller, Jahan Ramazani, Helen Tartar, Gordon Turnbull, Jon Volkmer and Lynn Wardley. Special thanks are due to Norman Bryson, Giovanni Cianci, Eric Gould and John Paul Russo, who guided me to this project's place and time; and to my parents, Hamish and Maureen Duncan, who were supportive in fundamental ways. Ayşe Agiş, present at every stage, has informed and challenged my thinking on a scale I can acknowledge but not reckon.

A fellowship from the Mrs Giles H. Whiting Foundation gave me time to get most of the preliminary writing done, and a Yale College Morse Fellowship allowed me to concentrate upon revision. Bits of the work in process have been aired at recent conventions of the MLA and the North-Eastern and Midwestern MLAs, for which I am grateful to the session organizers and audience members. The students of my nineteenth-century fiction seminars at Yale have kept my wits sharper than they otherwise might have been upon these topics. Kevin Taylor, my editor at Cambridge University Press, and Christine Lyall Grant, my copy-editor, guided the manuscript through production with exemplary care and patience. Finally, this is not a book that clears the ground so much as surveys it from the tree-tops of previous criticism and scholarship. In what follows, I have tried to make them part of the view they have made available.

Prologue: fiction as fiction

> 'Let me hear her instantly,' said the boy; 'I love the lute rarely; I love it of all things, though I never heard it.'
>
> 'Then how canst thou love it, Flibbertigibbet?' said Wayland.
>
> 'As knights love ladies in old tales,' answered Dickie – 'on hearsay.'
>
> (Scott, *Kenilworth*)

I

On 6 January 1853 the citizens of Birmingham held a banquet in honour of Charles Dickens. The novelist was praised for his status 'as a national writer' and for 'the high moral purpose of his books'. At the end of the evening Dickens thanked his hosts:

> To the great compact phalanx of the people, by whose industry, perseverance, and intelligence, and their result in money-wealth such places as Birmingham, and many others like it, have arisen – to that great centre of support, that comprehensive experience, and that beating heart – Literature has turned happily from individual patrons, sometimes munificent, often sordid, always few, and has found there at once its highest purpose, its natural range of action, and its best reward.

From all the evils of patronage, Dickens went on,

> the people have set Literature free. And my creed in the exercise of that profession is, that Literature cannot be too faithful to the people in return – cannot too ardently advocate the cause of their advancement, happiness, and prosperity.[1]

Only a dozen years earlier such claims would have sounded provokingly radical: that to write novels was to own the dignity of a profession, that the novelist had a high moral purpose and that the populations of the new manufacturing towns constituted a national literary culture. Dickens's latest biographer comments upon the transformation from Boz the entertainer to the 'national writer' whose popularity was the commission of an extraordinary public authority.[2] Scarcely regarded as 'Literature' at the beginning of the century, by 1850 in Britain the novel was the ascendant form for the representation of a national cultural identity. The novel could offer a panoramic and historical imitation of the life of the people, and something more: a criticism of that life. I shall argue in these pages that such an ascendancy took place by means of the revival of romance.

Romance is the essential principle of fiction: its *difference* from a record of 'reality', of 'everyday life'. A novel could describe, by metonymy and metaphor, the shape of the world and everything in it; it could also narrate its historical formation through time. The modern formation of concepts of society and culture coincides with the great age of the novel in nineteenth-century Britain. But even as the novel began to totalize its mimetic range it reasserted fiction, and not mimesis, as its critical principle, in an elaborate commitment to plot. Fiction in these novels is the effect above all of plot, conspicuous as a grammar of formal conventions, that is, a shared cultural order distinct from material and historical contingency. To read a plot – to take part in its work of recognition – is to imagine a transformation of life and its conditions, and not their mere reproduction. Such is the rhetorical definition of romance by its modern theorists, Northrop Frye and Fredric Jameson,[3] and such is also the rhetorical agenda of the great Victorian social novels. The old commonplace of an antithetical relation between romance and reality, invoked by the novel in its own apologies of origin, produces a new, dialectical figure of romance as the fulcrum against which – positioned on its edge, between inside and out – reality can be turned around.

Yet criticism has continued to find an innate contradiction between the ambitions of an 'authentic' social representation and the elements of romance, those forms whose appearance measures the difference between the novel and reality. The major Victorian cultural critics officially ignored or condemned the novel for its status as an entertaining illusion. When Ruskin praised Scott, it was for his moral purity, as a rebuke to Dickens and Thackeray. Those essayists and reviewers who did write about fiction occupied themselves with Aristotelian canons of mimetic probability.[4] The narrative projects of high modernism claimed aesthetic dignity by repudiating that Victorian fiction that had sold itself to a mass reading public. When the novel was ushered into the academic precincts of critical thought by F. R. Leavis, it was on the strength of a high seriousness residing in social and psychological mimesis alone, although the critic's dissenting stance made him intuitively sympathetic to the transformative dynamics of romance. The Great Tradition of the English novel, a violent construct purged of all of Scott and most of Dickens, remained official until about 1970, when Dickens enjoyed promotion.[5]

No doubt the moral lens of a classical mimesis will continue to show British fiction in the likeness of one of Scott's or Dickens's dwarfs: stunted, deformed, barbaric. Franco Moretti has issued the most recent complaint of a primitive, childish, puritanical storytelling, in paradoxical coincidence with the post-revolutionary maturity of British legal institutions.[6] The high achievement of British prose fiction was, in short, one of 'romance' rather than 'the novel'. The novel, authentic, open form of the subject in history, thrives across the English channel under the title of *roman*, while the native kind, calling itself by the new name, is all the time that other from which it had striven to distinguish itself. For a historical explanation Moretti appeals to Perry Anderson's argument that, because it did not coincide with an Enlightenment culture, the British revolution failed to achieve an adequate theoretical totalization, and so could not perpetuate itself in an effective legacy of revolutionary ideology, such as a written Constitution.[7] With all of its Hellenistic bias, such a hypothesis usefully illuminates the strong persistence of 'primitive', oral and popular, forms in

British literature. It seems then that instead of a Constitution we have romance: not just the tales and ballads of the folk, urban and rural, but the English Bible, and Chaucer, Spenser, and Shakespeare, Milton and Bunyan and the novelists.

The idea of a national literature was one of the fruits of the romance revival, the major aesthetic enterprise of a broad, mixed, contentious cultural movement between 1750 and 1830 culminating in what has been called 'the invention of tradition'. Antiquarian scholars and poets redefined romance as the scattered relics of an ancestral culture that was disintegrating under the pressures of modernization. Its strangeness – its difference from modern experience – was the effect of this loss: and thus the aura of its authenticity. Romance was the *genius loci* of the last age, to be preserved in the print-medium of the modern nation-state as its native essence. Collections of folk-lyrics and ballads and scholarly editions of Spenser and Shakespeare constituted together a unified (now decisively literary) 'cultural heritage', fortified with histories and anthologies of English poetry and biographies of the poets. Poetic succession was no longer just a trope of legitimation among poets themselves but the property of an expanding reading public, and highly lucrative to booksellers.[8] After 1800 the institutions of national canon-formation began to dignify prose fiction. Popular editions of 'The British Novelists' were published from 1810 onwards, and from 1821 to 1824 Scott himself, imitating Dr Johnson, composed a series of 'Lives of the Novelists' to accompany *Ballantyne's Novelist's Library*, which he was editing. An authoritative *History of Fiction* by John Dunlop appeared in the same year as *Waverley*, 1814.

Literary historians of the period have failed, by and large, to give a persuasive account of the connections between its dominant aesthetic movement and its ascendant literary genre; a failure compounded by the persistent neglect of its major novelist, Scott. For it is Scott – antiquarian scholar and national minstrel before he became the Author of Waverley – whose transformations of romance decisively transformed the novel. The connections were sufficiently evident at the time. The entry on 'Modern Romance and Novel' in the seventh edition of the *Encyclopaedia Britannica*, a decade after Scott's death, upholds the judgement of the first reviews of *Waverley*: Scott had '[raised] the romance from the lowest level to the very highest in literature'.[9]

No doubt the nineteenth-century British novel, by George Eliot and Thomas Hardy as well as by Scott and Dickens, wears an 'archaic' mantle of folk or fairy-tale or of allegory, when one makes the comparison with Stendhal or Flaubert or Turgenev (but hardly with Balzac or Dostoevsky). This is not, however, some kind of pupal shell the creature has failed to outgrow, but its living tissue of ethical, spiritual and ideological contention: the distinctive garment of its modernity. 'The peculiarity of the English development', writes Moretti, lies 'in its unsuccessful polarization into "high" and "low" literature, testified by the abundance of "synthetic" figures such as Defoe, Richardson, Fielding, Scott and Dickens'.[10] This morphological oddity nevertheless constitutes what is most powerful in British fiction. Romance marks the novel's claim upon imaginative authenticity as the form of national life, appropriated by a middle-class hegemony (and as Moretti understands) from very different sources – from a popular culture of living speech and song and tale-telling, and from the literary culture of an aristocratic hegemony in the past. Official nationalism, 'the invention of tradition', no doubt represented a counter-revolutionary diversion of energies of protest and resistance; but at the same time it contained and expressed those energies, it kept them in circulation. As for the novel, its overlay of the mimesis of experience with a formal register of difference from it makes dialectical space for criticism as well as for idealization: the recognition that it is a fiction turns an answer (say, that of a personal and collective destiny) back into a question. This dialectic, rather than a solely mimetic imperative, generates those effects of sheer narrative capaciousness, episodic fluidity, metonymic density and metaphoric complexity, for which nineteenth-century fiction – Bakhtin's 'polyphonic novel' – is distinctive; and to which it is necessary to add the effect rather ignored by Bakhtin, an overdetermination of plot. These formal effects express a semiotic totality more purposive than that of 'the world' – the most influential contemporary term for it is 'culture' – at the same time as they chart the irregularity and accident and excess and privation that contradict any unity of purpose, unravel the order of culture.[11] The unsuccess lamented by Moretti is the effect, then, of an aesthetic strength rather than weakness. And the distracting taxonomic arguments about romance and novel, romance and realism, insofar as they are a convention of the British novel from its inception, mark at the institutional level of genre a fruitful trouble and division at the core of national cultural identity.

II

Realism is not a revelation of nature but a rhetoric and an ideology: as Martin Price has written, 'a deliberate – even militant – extension of form rather than the effort at literal representation or record'.[12] To put it this way – to emphasize conscious artifice and programme – is to correct dialectically Northrop Frye's concept of 'displacement', which would make *romance* the revelation of nature – the eternal lineaments of the human – and 'realism' one of its local precipitations. Frye's secular scripture, the totality of fictions, contains history as one of its effects: the view from a belated and ironic modernity that thinks it has nowhere to look but back, unless upward to an apocalyptic horizon. Following Schiller, Frye makes an important distinction between 'naive' and 'sentimental' romance, that is, between a 'primitive', mythic or folkloric, oral culture, its forms embedded in an archaic cosmos, and a civilized literary culture which reproduces and recombines those forms as fictions, private attempts to imagine (and so reinhabit) a cosmos from which it has fallen. Frye's anatomy is itself the ultimate sentimental romance, as Jameson has noted, even as its tendency is to apprehend *all* romance as naive: just as myth is fiction's pre-conscious body, so are myth and fiction both of Frye's lucid literary science. Together they are a collective dreamwork, an immanence of archetypes structuring those vast occult processes outside conscious agency which constitute history. For agency, rather than history, is the vanishing-point of the scheme. I wish to take the converse position made available by Frye: that all romance is sentimental, purposeful, allegorical, local in the sense that it speaks to and from particular positions; and that naive romance is a trope of sentimental romance, its own, constitutive fiction of origins. For us, romance must always be romance revival, meaning not a synchronicity of archetypes across history but an active cultural work of the discovery and invention of ancestral forms, in other words the construction of the archetype as a rhetorical figure. The novelist needs 'to re-create the myth if he is to make full use of it', in a process that is allusive rather than vatic, not so much visionary as revisionary. The relationship of an individual work to a genre 'is not one of passive membership but of active modulation'.[13] These issues are at stake, somewhat covertly, in Frye's location of Scott at the beginnings of his thought about romance. It seems that 'an abandoned essay on the Waverley novels' grew into *The Secular Scripture*. However, Frye manages an intricate evasion of Scott's activity as a writer. Scott is recovered as comforting reading for stagecoach or aeroplane: originary position redefined as etiological serial episode. Scott is interesting because his 'formulaic techniques' represent 'the uniformity of romance formulas over the centuries'.[14] In fact Scott's historical agency is very much to the point. More than anywhere else it is in *Guy Mannering*, the particular novel cited by Frye, that Scott strategically, allegorically, *invents* romance as an 'archetypal narrative structure': as I shall argue later. Like a more fortunate Frankenstein, the Author of Waverley reanimates the daemon that will be the object of Frye's anatomy.

Recent criticism has emphasized ways in which literary genre is a historical activity – only to reproduce 'history' as an effect of structures that look suspiciously like those of romance. Michael McKeon, in an impressively detailed and analytical account of the origins of the English novel, has argued that the local instance of the work of fiction takes part in a total generic historical scheme. This involves a dialectical development from 'romance idealism', encoding the aristocratic ideology of the old order; through an antithetical 'naive empiricism', the form of a 'progressive ideology', corresponding to what Ronald Paulson and others have described as anti-romance, once upon a time the proclaimed parent of the novel; to the 'conservative' counter-critique of an 'extreme skepticism'.[15] The last stage of McKeon's scheme would appear to correspond with Frye's 'sentimental romance': it is the modern stage of consciousness of the novel as a formal category, from which the earlier movements may be recognized as its own prehistory.

As a diachronic account of English cultural history the scheme is, no doubt, problematical. It does represent, however, a powerful synchronic description of the broadly hegemonic Whig historiography that informed the late-eighteenth-century romance revival: looking back to narrate its own culmination, in the rational consciousness of the present (post–1689) establishment, out of the hard contest between the *ancien régime* and revolutionary ideologies of the last age. McKeon's scheme seems particularly apt for the case of Hegel's contemporary Scott, who best personifies 'the invention of tradition' and the canonization of the novel as national cultural form, and who may have done more than anyone to put such a version of history into common currency. Much the same dialectical structure – of an obsolescent aristocratic romance idealism subjected to a rude empirical critique and resolved in a privatizing aesthetic of conservative scepticism – occupies the narrative of *Waverley*, as I shall argue in detail in my second chapter. Scott performs the grand reinvention of the novel for its nineteenth-century European heyday, a feat usually accounted for by reference to his invention of historical fiction.[16] Scott's act of reinvention relied not only upon an appeal to 'history' as authoritative subject-matter, however, but upon an appeal to the history of the genre, encoded in the alternative title of *Waverley*: *'Tis Sixty Years Since*. The year 1745 had been the moment of classical formation of the British novel, in the rivalry between Fielding and Richardson. And in this retrospect romance, the vast, mixed, ancient genealogy of vernacular European fictions, becomes visible extending back beyond the novel's moment of conscious, civilized formation. The

Waverley novels canonically represent the abstraction not only of history (as Lukács saw) but also of romance as a critical, sentimental and aesthetic category. Once the prehistoric origin against which the novel defined itself antithetically, romance may now be revived as a historical tradition – with which modern fiction is in turn to revive itself.

Scott also invented, thematically and formally, the figure of the historical ground of romance described by another eminent contemporary theorist, Fredric Jameson:

> it would seem that its ultimate condition of figuration, on which the other preconditions we have already mentioned are dependent – the category of worldness, the ideologemes of good and evil felt as magical forces, a salvational historicity – is to be found in a transitional moment in which two distinct modes of production, or moments of socioeconomic development, coexist. Their antagonism is not yet articulated in terms of the struggle of social classes, so that its resolution can be projected in the form of a nostalgic (or less often, a Utopian) harmony. Our principal experience of such transitional moments is evidently that of an organic social order in the process of penetration and subversion, reorganization and rationalization, by nascent capitalism, yet still, for another long moment, coexisting with the latter.[17]

Long indeed: Jameson's moment of a simultaneous transition and suspension is a trope that belongs to romance as much as to history, as does the register of 'experience' that yields an organic social order both in history and outside it, prior to it.[18] This 'ultimate condition' of distinct, antagonistic, overlapping cultural stages (Jameson's 'sedimentation') is the central topic of Scott's historical romance. It is at once the version of history Scott (like Marx) developed from the philosophical historians of the Scottish Enlightenment, and the condition of romance as modernity's vision of worlds it has superseded, charged with a magic of estrangement, peril and loss: a cultural uncanny.

III

One of Vladimir Nabokov's more virtuosic notes in his commentary on *Eugene Onegin* lists, after a blast against 'schoolmen', eleven senses of 'romanticism' available in the 1820s.[19]

Romance, the parent term, is if possible still more protean. In the last fifty years it has signified a courtly or chivalric fiction of the late Middle Ages, a fanciful or erotic or sentimental enhancement of a situation or event, any unlikely story, a love affair, highly conventionalized mass-marketed novels read by women, a narrative with a quest in it, four of the last plays of Shakespeare, the American novels of Poe, Hawthorne, and Melville, and a super-genre containing all fictional forms and figures that is ultimately the form and figure of a transcendental human imagination. In the first half of the eighteenth century romance meant any prose fiction in the vernacular tongue, particularly those associated with 'the last age', and more particuarly those French *romans héroïques* or *romans à longue haleine*, filled with dilemmas of love and honour and adorned with improbable exploits, written to amuse the *salons* of the age of Louis XIV. Johnson's *Dictionary* defined romance as 'a military fable of the middle ages; a tale of wild adventure in war and love', but also 'a lie; a fiction', rehearsing both historical and moral versions of a difference from present reality. The scholarship of the romance revival – particularly that of the Scottish Enlightenment literati – historicized the term so that, by the end of the century, it broadly signified the fiction of pre-modern cultures. Scott's own 'Essay on Romance' for the 1822 Supplement to the *Encyclopaedia Britannica* described 'a fictitious narrative in prose or verse; the interest of which turns upon marvellous and uncommon incidents', and went on to provide a judicious historical survey.[20] In the 'age of Romanticism' alone romance was aligned – as we shall see – with a bewildering variety of interests and positions: with an original liberty of the subject, with an ancestral patriarchy, with foreign powers of oppression and violence, with a domestic idyll, with outlaw bands, with virgin solitude. It is the stuff of the old native minstrelsy, an oriental phantasmagoria, the idle literature of the boudoir, the prophetic and allegorical sentences of protestant enthusiasm and tales of the nursery and fireside. All are ideological valences, however, of the formal version of romance established by Scott in his practice: romance as modern culture's construction of a symbolic form prior to itself.

It has been a critical commonplace that 'the rise of the novel' in eighteenth-century England took place upon the overthrow of an obsolete and inauthentic kind of fiction called 'romance'. Such literary history reproduces the etiological myth by which the novel attempted to claim respectability in the period – recent excavations have brought to light innumerable novels (many by women writers) in the century before Defoe. Available in English since 1612, *Don Quixote* was arguably the most influential work of fiction in eighteenth-century England, celebrated by critics and by novelists such as Fielding and Smollett as the first novel and the pattern of anti-romance, scourge not only of the old romances of chivalry but of the system of manners within which those had flourished. A literary equivalent of the Glorious Revolution, Cervantes' fable had exorcized overnight the baneful magic of the last age by a harmless, essentially comic power of common sense. In eighteenth-century England, however, the target of anti-romance criticism tended to be not romances of chivalry (stirring an old Jacobite to arms) but 'those voluminous works called Romances, namely, *Clelia*, *Cleopatra*, *Astraea*, *Cassandra*, the *Grand Cyrus*, and innumerable others, which contain', wrote Fielding, 'very little instruction or entertainment'.[21] These expressed more precisely a court culture of the *ancien régime*, still current over in France, the imperial rival. The question remains, however, as to why they should have remained the object of attack – a site of domestic cultural strife – as late as the middle of the eighteenth century, when the debate about fiction had intensified around the new ascendancy of the novel exemplified by Richardson and by Fielding himself. The vogue for the French romances was long gone: anti-romance parodies such as *The Mock-Clelia* (translated into English in 1678) had marked the fashion more than sixty years since. In fact the anxious focus of the debate, encoded in the choice of the French romances as the decadent type against which the modern form defined itself, was the figure of a female reader, and a feminine culture of romance.[22]

For the French romances were not just foppish and outlandish: they were written, like so many of the English novels, by and for women. Women were the occupants of a newly charged semiotic space of private life and domestic subjection which also happened to be the space of novel-reading. Official cultural anxieties about the role of women and about an expanding constituency of readers thus coalesced in the figure of the *Female Quixote.* Charlotte Lennox's novel of that name appeared at the height of the novel debate, in 1752, to the applause of Fielding, Richardson and Dr Johnson, who contributed the dedication (as well as, rumour held, its critical sermon against romance). Lennox's Arabella, a compulsive reader of ill-translated French romances, personifies the fantasy of a counter-culture of feminine desire within patriarchy, still subject to its forms and thus eventually to its discipline. (Arabella imagines herself as the imperial cynosure of an arena of male desire, but the vision of power is unstable, always broken off by a threat of rape: her fantasy of total subjectivity continues to occupy the structural position of an object.)[23] Romance-reading is pleasure without instruction, an evasion of the strict teleologies of social subjection for an interminable, repetitious play of figuration, a private, narcissistic bower of feeling. The direction of anti-romance discipline against women must be taken literally, but as we shall see the gender of the Female Quixote is a trope: the mirror of fiction may lure men too into the trance of Narcissus in which sexual as well as social identities are dissolved.

Much of the history of the novel in the latter half of the eighteenth century is occupied with the development of an ethical and aesthetic category of sensibility from (and alongside) the 'irregular' feminine subjectivity of which romance is the formal correlative. This development takes place partly through the post-Richardson female *Bildungsroman* of Burney, which retains a disciplinary strain of anti-romance moralizing, and partly through a masculine appropriation of sensibility for the type of the 'man of feeling'.[24] A critical, synthetic stage is represented by the Gothic romance of the end of the century, of which Ann Radcliffe is the grand mistress. This is the first

English prose fiction to call itself 'romance' with a certain generic intention, distinguishing itself from the novel and the representation of contemporary life. As I shall argue, Radcliffe undertakes a powerful revaluation of the term, made visible as a historical and generic category by the antiquarian revival. She replenishes romance with sensibility, emphatically reclaimed for a feminine identity. Prompted by scholarly accounts of 'Gothic' and of 'romance' as terms alien to modernity, Radcliffe defines a feminine principle of private subjectivity in antithetical relation to history, which appears as a synchronic public domain of patriarchal coercion. In other words, the Gothic setting of Radcliffe's fiction makes 'history' visible, but as an alien dimension of power and terror, enclosing and threatening private life *at the same time as it is produced by it* in a dualistic structure of sexual identities that transcends historical occasion. As the dimension of private being which is fully conscious, present to itself even in the prospective and nostalgic figurations of romance, Radcliffe's female subjectivity holds (in its very separation from narrative agency) the secret dialectical power to transform – to reduce and colonize – the antagonistic realm of historical patriarchy. A transformation, however, which the end of the romance mournfully recognizes as only imaginary after all: as romance.

Radcliffe is Scott's major immediate precursor in the British novel. Scott's recovery of romance for the representation of a public, national life involves at once its thoroughgoing historicization and its redefinition as masculine. *Waverley* narrates the sentimental education of a young man who starts off as a female quixote and encounters Gothic lures and perils in his traversal of the field of history. But Scott's novel undertakes a complex dialectical reversal of the project of anti-romance it began by rehearsing. Thematically, historical experience banishes romance illusion; but this progression is articulated by a labyrinthine formal logic of romance which secures for Waverley the tragi-comic destiny of a private life beyond historical process. From the perspective of this private life, which is that of our own reading of the novel, both history and romance become literary effects, textual figures of a dangerous activity consigned to the past and available for aesthetic contemplation. The modern, domestic subjectivity produced by the narrative remains covertly androgynous, under feminine predominance; it knows that its strength is also its impotence, its status as a romance that remains apart from historical process, in a knowledge more dialectically reflexive than Radcliffe's.

The other critical element of Scott's reinvention, fundamental to its 'historical' thematic, is the *objective* meaning of romance, as defined in the antiquarian and poetic revival. The romance revival meant the recovery of an archaic native culture, popular as well as literary, felt to be vanishing into the past. The exhumation of black-letter texts and the gathering of oral ballads nourished not only modern imitation but a literalizing attention to *place*, to local countrysides seen as haunted by their passing historical difference. The tour to regional peripheries and the poetic invocation of a *genius loci*, favourite topics of the period, are both attempts to chart a national culture and to reclaim its native spiritual essence. But the tour, exemplified by the Scotch tour in the wake of the Union and the pacification of the Highlands, is a privatized imperial ceremony which confirms the final reduction of an archaic culture and raises the *genius loci* only as a spirit of elegiac solitude.

The spells and lays of the defunct old world are recovered by the sentimental journey for aesthetic and elegiac contemplation on one's private estate – even when that estate is confined to the hire of a book and the leisure of a few hours in which to read it. Scott contains those forms within the more compendious forms of earlier sentimental romance, in particular, the national fictions of Spenser and Shakespeare. The revival of these forms confirms their power in the imperial structure of a literary tradition. The genre of naive romance evoked within sentimental romance is of course pastoral, and Scott's play with versions of pastoral is notably deft. In particular georgic, the genre of a living regional economy, gets converted into pastoral, as for example in *Guy Mannering*. 'Naive romance' tends to be dangerous insofar as it represents a live, turbulent popular enthusiasm and cultural contest in the historical present. Scott's foundation of a national fiction upon romance aligns itself with the counter-revolutionary containment of radical populist ideologies in the period. The case of those alternative romance projects ostensibly closer to popular and oral sources, such as James Hogg's remarkable version of medieval border romance, *The Three Perils of Man: War, Women and Witchcraft* (1821), may ultimately have been little different in terms of their cultural effects. Nevertheless, the form and authority of such containment – as a 'fiction', or thing which is not – is continually called into question by Scott. The romance tends to iterate its final status as an artificial exclusion from historical process, in the topos of the domestic idyll. Its only historically real space may after all be that circumscribed by the figures and materials of the text, consumed in a private leisure still contingent upon the mysterious social and economic turbulences of the commercial nation-state.

The Waverley novels represent the historical formation of the modern imperial nation-state in relation to the sentimental formation of the private individual: a homology, a synecdochic equivalence, is asserted between these processes. At the same time a tension, a contradiction, a *violence* occupies the narrative site of their conjunction – as it is one of disjunction, of dialectical contest. Romance reproduces itself as the figure of mediation and synthesis by turning contradiction into ambiguity, which provides a vital margin of refuge between fatal historical fact and extravagant spiritual impossibility. The final image of domestic and political reconciliation is the most fantastic, artful and labyrinthine of all evasions. In Scott's successor as national novelist this division between private and public life, between domestic and historical destinies, becomes an abyss. Scott had historicized romance as the form of a difference from modern life; reproducing that difference, Dickens would empty it of its historical, collective charge to make it ontological and individual.

Dickens learnt from Scott the narrative techniques of a mixed, polyphonic representation of a social totality, involving a dialogical interplay of styles and genres and a complexity of plot, fusing the real world with its romance transfiguration. In the low-mimetic language of the author's public privacy, he would call it 'the romantic side of familiar things'.[25] But for complex reasons of Dickens's own class and generation (one of the 'men of 1832') history does not appear as a category of dynamic process in his narratives: it signifies not even lives passing but only a dark, blind, dead past. Dickens recognizes no spiritual authority in prior objective formations. Hence his own historical novel, the critical task of his early career, is the site of a relentless Oedipal struggle with the culturally dominant figure of Scott. That struggle determines the thematic content of *Barnaby Rudge*. In the subsequent novels, Dickens apprehends the great world not as historical process, rationally knowable, but as an *economy*: synchronic, universal, at once material and spiritual, literal and symbolic, ubiquitous and occult. No space is left for an archaic or ancestral culture and the spiritual heritage of its passing difference. The only alternative order is disorder, that of parody or a demonic underworld.

Instead Dickens, in a revival of the Gothic dualism always incipient in Scott, domesticates romance more radically by finding it altogether within the private sensibility as an ontological faculty distinct from the public regime of exchange, work, power and sexuality. It is the fancy, the transcendental core of personal identity, preserved in the memory of its original state in childhood, and constituting an alternative psychosexual economy of its own. The literary forms of romance are those not of pre-modern historical communities but of the nursery. They recall the archaic dominion of a central male subject replenished by an all-powerful and yet subservient female presence, whose identity is fused with his own in a rapture beyond mere sexuality:

> There was a classical daughter once – perhaps – who ministered to her father in his prison as her mother had ministered to her. Little Dorrit, though of the unheroic modern stock and mere English, did much more, in comforting her father's wasted heart upon her innocent breast, and turning to it a fountain of love and fidelity that never ran dry or waned through all his years of famine.[26]

Gently supplanting the classical *exemplum* with that of modern romance, Dickens's is perhaps the most extraordinary figuration of the narrative ethos defined by Peter Brooks as an 'anticipation of retrospection'.[27] The bower of romance enfolds, as it had for the female quixote, a fantasy of androgynous sufficiency; only now more plainly a feminine subjection is the natural-magical source of a quenchless moral power that flows, across historical difference, to the male subject.

IV

Feminist critics (or rather a loose coalition of critics concerned with questions of gender) have produced the most influential recent revisions of the history of the novel in this period. Their work, after a broadly Marxist tradition of historical materialism, has done a great deal to sharpen and to enlarge our sense of the political work done by fiction in a culture, in its intersection with other discursive practices and in its production of such categories as gender, class, subjectivity and private life. In its useful but occasionally literal-minded zeal for canon-revision, however, this criticism has tended to overlook Scott, whom one would have thought should have been its central exhibit. For this is the very moment in British cultural history when (beyond a self-constituted poetic high tradition) the narrative of a heroic succession of male authors gains public currency. Ina Ferris has argued that Scott endowed the novel with 'literary authority and cultural centrality' in the eyes of the newly dominant periodical reviewers, in part because they could no longer see it 'as the confined genre of a confined gender'.[28] The use of male pseudonyms by women authors, for example, can be dated with some precision from the time of Scott's death. Scott's fables of an appropriation of female romance power also narrate the cultural position of Radcliffe as authoress, synecdoche for a generic formation in the literary market ('Gothic romance'), preparing the place to be taken over by a rich and famous (and yet anonymous) Author of Waverley. In turn the institutional example of Sir Walter Scott, personification of a new patriarchal dignity of authorship, confronted the women writers of the next generation. Through and against Scott's canonical achievement they defined their own: *Jane Eyre*, for example, reclaims romance powers with a vengeance in a showdown with (especially) *The Bride of Lammermoor*. The oppositional romance of the Brontës cannot be said, however, to have lacked critical attention, and that of a high order, in the last couple of decades.

Conversely, the historical novel after Scott offers a weaker lineage of literal imitation in the examples of Bulwer, Ainsworth and G. P. R. James. (The later exercises in the genre by Thackeray, Eliot and Dickens himself are another matter, that of an allusive reinterpretation of a form no longer dominant.) Lukács' claim, that the historical novel declined into a 'special genre' and that the true legacy of Scott's work is to be found in the mid-nineteenth-century social novel, is more to the purpose.[29] We have lacked an effective account of the transition from Scott to Dickens, or of the relation between the two most famous novelists of the age, whose careers were separated by only four years. At the time, Dickens was acclaimed as Scott's successor to the new cultural eminence of national author; it is only in our century that what was obvious has grown obscure. The appearance of such a figure, the author as hero, generates those tropes of competition, dominance and succession that have such fatal force in all the biographies of Dickens – for literary biography too (the work of Lockhart and Forster) is a part of this cultural formation. Both Scott and Dickens were to end in the manner the Victorians prescribed for their heroes: tragically.

As it turned out, the heroic station of the author as representative citizen of a national British culture was precarious and brief, although the ideal continues to enchant us today. That national culture, as a unified entity, was a fiction, perhaps the most potent fiction of all; and tensions between authentic popularity and dominant-class moral and aesthetic values haunted even Dickens's own spacious reputation. In the generation after Dickens's death, the expansion of the reading public was accompanied by its increasing fragmentation, in market specialization and a proliferation and reinforcement of class distinctions. It seemed that popular entertainment, didactic purpose and aesthetic quality were to be distinct and contradictory faculties; and 'romance' a gross commodity or an elegant abstraction. The most sophisticated defence, by Robert Louis Stevenson, anticipates modernist formalisms, and Frye himself:

> A proposition of geometry does not compete with life; and a proposition of geometry is a fair and luminous parallel for a work of art. Both are reasonable, both untrue to the crude fact; both inhere in nature, neither represents it. The novel, which is a work of art, exists, not by its resemblances to life, which are forced and material, as a shoe must still consist of leather, but by its immeasurable difference from life, which is designed and significant, and is both the method and the meaning of the work.[30]

Yet it had been the glory of the novels of Dickens that their difference from life was the measure of their competition with it.

CHAPTER I

The culture of Gothic

Who cannot be crushed with a plot?
(Shakespeare, *All's Well that Ends Well*, Act IV, sc. 3)

I

The eighteenth-century Gothic novel is the first modern British fiction to identify itself as a distinct kind under the name of 'romance'. The very first of all appeared as an antiquarian forgery: the translation, by one William Marshal, Gent., of a sixteenth-century Italian story by Onuphrio Muralto. In the preface to the second edition of *The Castle of Otranto* (1765), Horace Walpole admitted the hoax and explained that he had attempted 'to blend the two kinds of Romance, the ancient and the modern'.[1] By 'romance' Walpole meant fiction in the vernacular languages. The distinction between kinds is one between historical periods, roughly marked by the revolutionary settlement of 1689. A generation later, however, Ann Radcliffe and Matthew Lewis expanded Walpole's repertoire of figures and proclaimed as 'romance' a *fiction apart* from modern life. The opening of Radcliffe's *Romance of the Forest* (1791) announces a turbulent crossing of familiar thresholds:

> Such elegance and apparent refinement, contrasted with the desolation of the house, and the savage manners of its inhabitants, seemed to him like a romance of imagination, rather than an occurrence of real life.[2]

By the 1790s, the Gothic romance is a dominant literary genre that marks a decisive alienation of novelistic representation from its official province, 'real life and manners, and the time in which it is written'. It does not situate itself outside that province, however, so much as on its border, as if entranced in the motion of crossing. The Gothic rehearses a turn against 'real life' into the 'imagination' that never quite completes the passage into an alternative version of reality. For Radcliffe's formula retains the terms of real life and manners: her novel opens in France, the contemporary scene of revolution, and in this opening adventure a confusion of class distinctions has transformed an elegant mansion into a sinister wilderness. 'Contrast', an aesthetic principle drawn from the contemporary vocabulary of the picturesque, is the effect of a usurpation of polite property by a 'savage' underclass.[3]

In the quarter of a century since Walpole's confection, the romance revival had become a major scholarly and poetic industry. More than anything else, this romance revival involved the confrontation with cultural origins that were at once native and alien. Both 'Gothic' and 'romance' evoked a past that was other and strange: a post-classical but pre-modern European culture, problematically discontinuous with the post-revolutionary epoch of British modernity. 'Romance' had meant, originally, the demotic languages of Europe, and their songs and fables, flourishing after the fall of Rome in a rich cultural compost of imperial decay. 'Gothic' suggested, however, a more adversarial, antagonistic relation to the imperial civilization – a militant anti-classicism. By the second half of the eighteenth-century it had gained an ambiguous valence that was political as well as aesthetic. In historical terms, two myths of national constitutional foundation, and two different attitudes toward the modern revolutionary settlement, opposed one another. An unofficial, oppositional movement, populist and proto-nationalist in its appeal and with its ideological roots in the radical Whiggery of the last century, was reclaiming 'Gothic' culture as the ancient constitutional source of British liberties usurped by the Norman Conquest and subsequent aristocratic rule – including the present Whig-landlord establishment. At the same time, the establishment conception of 'Gothic' was that of barbarian forces that had overthrown a civilization, and the long cultural darkness haunted by despotism and anarchy, superstition and enthusiasm, out of which the present British dispensation, modelling itself on classical principles, had only lately emerged.[4]

On the one hand, then, 'Gothic' is the name of a northern, native, ancestral culture. But its artefacts seem alien rather than familiar to an aesthetic sensibility trained in the classical principles which continued to determine education. Gothic architecture, according to Sir Joshua Reynolds, 'though not so antient as the Grecian, is more so to our imagination'.[5] Nearer in space as well as in time, its forms embedded in a native landscape, the uncouth heritage of Gothic was already on its way towards the zenith of a national monumental style, in the century of Pugin and Ruskin. As yet, however, it appeared through a cloud of barbaric and oriental strangeness. An important debate among the scholars of the romance revival concerned the origins of romance and of Gothic art, and rival claims of a northern, native autochthony or of an influence imported from the East, in the medieval confrontation between Christian Empire and its Saracen shadow.[6] The latter view invoked the absolute, metaphysical remoteness of an archetypal antagonism: the imaginative site, for example, of Beckford's *Vathek*, an orientalist *Castle of Otranto*. In the 1760s Bishop Hurd described the passing of Gothic culture in Britain in the characteristically elegiac tones of latitudinarian or liberal-conservative compromise: 'What we have gotten by [the 1688] revolution, you will say, is a great deal of good sense. What we have lost, is a world of fine fabling.'[7] Hurd does not blame that loss on the modern Whig dispensation of 'good sense', but on the neoclassical aesthetics imported by 'our Frenchified King and his Royalists' at the Restoration (130). Elsewhere, he allows that the old romance was doomed to vanish with its historical 'world', that of feudalism (148). The contradiction, if it is that, is one we shall continue to read in Scott. The old world was fated to pass; but an artificial grafting of alien matter really finished it off. The distinction between what is foreign and what is native in history seems hard to maintain, as Hurd describes the divided sense of a past which is at the same time our own and not our own. 'Gothic' represents, in short, the crux or aporia of a myth of national culture, of 'British' historical identity – one that retains its currency to this day. In it the alien and the familiar, the natural and the unnatural or supernatural, are richly confused: neither one category nor the other is clearly stable.

Gothic names a broken historical descent, a cultural heritage grown balefully strange. The eighteenth-century Gothic romances themselves insistently thematize the structure of a dislocated origin: in the obsession with fragmented and contaminated genealogies, in plots that turn upon usurped patrimony, incest, lost relations; in characterizations of psychological repression; in settings of decayed ancestral power, the famous castles and monasteries, that still hold their aura of physical and ideological bondage, sublimated from function to 'atmosphere'; in aesthetic effects of the uncanny and the sublime. With these famous characteristics, the Gothic novel describes the malign equation between an origin we have lost and an alien force that invades our borders, haunts our mansions, possesses our souls. Strong traditions of commentary on the genre have invoked theological and psychoanalytic terms to account for this.[8]

To do so is to follow the Gothic's own major rhetorical lead, which I shall investigate presently. But first let us pursue further the myth of national secular experience, the version of history, that Gothic invokes. Clearly the tension in the cultural meaning of Gothic corresponds to the tension between its political meanings. The radical nationalist version opposed a native Gothic independence to a foreign, continental, aristocratic and prelatic oppression, of which Norman feudalism and Roman Catholicism were the most powerful institutions. It suggested that a native liberty, the ancestral birthright of every Englishman, was menaced from above by colonizing alien powers throughout history and in the present. The more conservative, Whig-establishment, classical view – powerfully revived by Burke – held that the 1689 Constitution marked the final defeat of Gothic barbarism, represented by contending forces of royalist absolutism and popular anarchy, and secured the liberty of the subject in private property-ownership. Thus

'Gothic' means the opposite of what it means in the radical myth. It stands for the alien forces of oppression, those of Pope and Pretender, and locates them in the past, or over on the continent – but not in the present historical establishment. The ideological fiction shared by both these political myths is that of 'the liberty of the subject', a native essence belonging to history yet transcending it. Conversely, both apprehend national history as the field of alien forces in resistance to which the liberty of the subject achieves its self-definition. In the fictions of Radcliffe and Lewis, the two political senses of Gothic tend to blur together to represent a middle-class subject's anxious intuitions of historical powers which are ostensibly alien to it – located in past and foreign scenes – and yet claim possession of it. Although it is the first historical novel, the eighteenth-century Gothic tends to be set not just in the past but in the foreign past, and in historically and culturally enemy territory. (The few exceptions are programmatic: Clara Reeve's *The Old English Baron* (1777), as its first title, *The Champion of Virtue*, makes explicit, domesticates the extravagances of Walpolian Gothic through a bourgeois-puritan moral discipline: it is a sort of origins of Grandison.)[9] The Gothic setting is most often Catholic – French, Spanish or Italian – marking Catholicism as a spiritual orientalism in the British Protestant imagination. Radical-protestant ideologues had described the Reformation as a second Gothic overthrow of Romish tyranny, and the anti-prelatic theme of the Gothic novel is indeed ubiquitous, as is the depiction of a tyrannical feudal aristocracy. So far, then, this might represent foreign institutions of oppression against which a native liberty of the subject might measure itself. However, the insistence of the setting *as foreign and as past* deflects, complicates, the critique of an oppressive state and ecclesiastical apparatus in the Gothic romance of the 1790s. The French peril had changed its political shape, and the radical nationalist formulation was being co-opted by establishment apologists, most authoritatively by Burke.[10] The foreign influences once again to be resisted by patriotic Britons were those of Jacobin revolution, rather than Jacobite counter-revolution. This time the contagion was not *above* but *below*.

The double meanings of Gothic – as energy of popular radical militancy, as alien oppressive power – clenched together. That regicidal revolution was an image reflected from the British past intensified the fear that it might be reflected back again, national and foreign politics shadowing one another across history. According to Burke (and Hume before him), revolutions showed that political energies of violence and tyranny flowed from the people as well as from kings and priests; more fiercely, indeed, for lacking the mediation of cultural institutions. Despotism and rebellion dialectically generate each other. In Gothic novels, aristocratic or prelatic power is a mode of lawlessness which tends to provoke popular violence, in figures such as Radcliffe's banditti or the rioting mobs of Lewis and Maturin. Despotism, rebellion and riot all run into one another because they are understood morally, as assertions of the individual passions.[11]

As well as being alien, the setting of Gothic fiction is *domestic*. The 'revolutionary' theme at the beginning of *The Romance of the Forest*, of an elegant mansion occupied by a *canaille*, is contained in an outrageous contrast between property and manners. Radcliffe's plot quickly swerves away from the material logic of the scene: instead of robbing the fine gentleman, or holding him ransom, the gang of ruffians confides a beautiful girl to his protection and bids him continue his flight. Relations between male and female, parent and child, drive the narrative, claiming its deep structure and the thematic status of 'mystery'. To note the historical myth suggested by Gothic is at once, then, to note the powerful translation of that myth onto the ground of private relations in these novels. The covert site of alien, outlaw political forces is that of the liberal subjectivity itself, ostensibly released from historical compulsion, where they take the forms of the private passions. The political archetypes we read in the Gothic are above all sexual, figures of a family romance, of a demonology of private life. Burke's most apocalyptic of contemporary accounts of the French Revolution represents that vast, complex historical event as a psychosexual myth, on the order of the late works of Freud. Its sublimity and its violence are measured, indeed, by the revelation of history so starkly in such terms. The revolution is a national family romance in which depraved subjects cannibalize their royal father and perforate with their weapons the bed of the escaping queen. The latter figure, of a lady stripped for sacrifice (cf. Spenser's Serena), invokes a familiar eighteenth-century aesthetic allegory – the dissolution of romance:

> All the pleasing illusions, which made power gentle, and obedience liberal, which harmonized the different shades of life, and which, by a bland assimilation, incorporated into politics the sentiments which beautify and soften private society, are to be dissolved by this new conquering empire of light and reason. All the decent drapery of life is to be rudely torn off.[12]

Romance, not reason, yields the liberty of the subject. Burke makes private life contingent upon a liberal space of necessary *fiction* amidst the deathly forces of history. The end of a vital imaginary harmony of politics and private society is a violent exposure of the real relation between these terms rather than their transformation. 'Reason', the reality-principle of revolutionary ideology and the historical logic that undoes romance, is thus itself irrational, a figure of violation, of power unadorned by persuasion. History is to be lived and thought not through the fatal categories of reason but in the sentimental and aesthetic terms of the imagination, articulate in myth or fable. Just so, Burke's influential early treatise upon the sublime had grounded aesthetic effects upon a psychosexual identity at once profoundly individual and 'universal'.

Gothic fiction is not then 'historical', in the sense associated with the philosophical historians of the Scottish Enlightenment and with Walter Scott; that is to say, it does not attempt a scientific depiction of past cultural stages under changing material conditions. Instead it invokes historical contingency in order to dramatize its reduction under persistent forms of sexual and familial identity. In this way, then, the other time and place is also our own. Through the strategic exoticism of costume and setting we read the figure of the present, and are bound in the spell of simultaneous familiarity and strangeness. The process is allegorical, representing ourselves, divested of our daily habits, in the 'elemental' formation of psychosexual archetypes. Political relations are the effect of this psychosexual formation, rather than of conditions in the external world. Parent and child, male and female: these become poles metaphysically charged with semiotic energies flowing from other, eclipsed sites of cultural meaning, reproducing a binary relation of the powerful (patron or oppressor) and the powerless (subject or victim). Politics, religion, economic and social relations are terms that might occur in Gothic novels, but as local effects of an everlasting sexuality. As we shall see, the *feminine child* becomes the term loaded with a desperate positive valency, as the object of all political energies, and locus of desire; and sexuality conducts the energies of utopian transformation in the novels written by a woman. In the case of Radcliffe or of Charlotte Smith the gender of the author is a more conspicuous signifier than in the case of Beckford or of Lewis – and becomes itself a figure of the romance.

II

> Vp then, vp dreary Dame, of darknesse Queene,
> Go gather up the reliques of thy race,
> Or else goe them auenge, and let be seene,
> That dreaded Night in brightest day hath place,
> And can the children of faire light deface.
>
> (Spenser, *Faerie Queene*, I.v.24)

We should not mistake the gravity of Walpole's second preface to *The Castle of Otranto* as all in jest. The mixture of tonalities, flippant and solemn together, is the problem; it will remain a feature of Gothic fictions, mostly but not all by male authors, from Walpole through Beckford, Lewis, Byron and Maturin.

Walpole describes a duality of mimetic principles behind his fiction. The synthesis of ancient and modern romance is to be one of 'imagination', that is, 'the boundless realms of invention' or absolute creative power, combined with 'common life' or 'nature', the imitation of a present (already given) register of psychology and manners. Within the representation of nature, Walpole makes a further distinction, justifying a – Shakespearian – mixture of literary kinds which represents a mixture of social classes: between the speech of 'Princes and heroes' and that of their servants. If the former suggests a classical high mimesis of epic or tragedy, we recall that the servant classes are among those licentious consumers of modern romances who aroused so much anxiety among the cultural monitors of the mid-eighteenth-century. These co-ordinates describe a tonal 'mixture of buffoonery and solemnity', instances of which, Walpole goes on,

> remind one of the Grecian sculptor, who to convey the idea of a Colossus within the dimension of a seal, inserted a little boy measuring his thumb. (9)

This figure brings us back, with a flourish, to the juxtaposition of 'the boundless realms of invention' and mere 'nature', aligned thus with an opposition between sublime, ancient and heroic magnitude, and a ridiculous, vulgar, present pettiness. The 'idea of a Colossus' takes us also to the beginning, and origin, of the tale: Walpole's famous dream of a titanic mailed hand on a banister, and the spectacle of a 'homely youth, sickly, and of no promising disposition' (15), mangled on his wedding-day beneath a giant helmet.

The fabric goes on to spell out the issue: an authentic ancestry, because it has been suppressed and scattered (the historical theme of usurpation), becomes an irresistible demonic force that returns to crush a decadent and illegitimate generation in the present. The historical dynamic is played out on a secondary, ironic level – that of the family romance – through the usurper, Manfred; he can only reincarnate ancestral *virtù* as a tyrannical paternal violence that destroys its children. The giant armoured hand of Walpole's dream would seem to have represented the mighty author of his being, a figure whose claim over 'the boundless realms of invention' is measured by its power to exclude him from that space of primal creation.

When once you have thought of big men and little men, Johnson remarked of *Gulliver's Travels*, it is very easy to do all the rest. The reader of *The Castle of Otranto* is perhaps most struck by the *literalness* of the figure at the centre of the fable and this cluster of terms, 'the idea of a Colossus' measured by a puny boy guillotined under a giant helmet. It derives, of course, from the epic topos expressing ancestral heroism as superior size and strength, decisively mediated through Milton's account of Satan's shield and spear:

> to equal which the tallest Pine
> Hewn on Norwegian hills, to be the Mast
> Of som great Ammiral, were but a wand.
>
> (*Paradise Lost*, 1.292–4)

Now the figure of the ancestral demon, epic hero-prince, giant before the flood, can only be recalled in Satanic terms. (Milton knew too that 'ammiral' has a Saracen etymology.) Milton himself straddles the great historical divide when Gothic gives way to modern: with Satan, the last of the aristocrat warrior-chieftains becomes the first Gothic villain, no longer 'colossal' so much as capriciously inflatable, and shrinkable, by an afflatus not his own. The demonic dimension of history at Otranto translates supernatural power into sheer, palpable size and weight. (Walpole surely alludes to those fragments of the giant statue of Constantine at the Roman Capitol, which he would have seen on his Grand Tour in 1740.) The heroic ancestors, once whole and spiritual in the continuum of true lineage, are grotesquely hurled into material fragments by its breach:

> He fixed his eyes on what he wished in vain to be a vision; and seemed less attentive to his loss, than buried in meditation on the stupendous object that had occasioned it. He touched, he examined the fatal casque; nor could even the bleeding, mangled remains of the young prince divert the eyes of Manfred from the portent before him. (17)

Fixed in a trance, the obsessed and arrested gaze so characteristic of a Gothic modality of seeing, knowing, reading,[13] Manfred is aghast because what should be 'visionary' (confined to the realm of imagination and figuration) is all too actual and solid. The ancestral helmet is in the most appallingly literal sense too great for the head of the false succession; the supernatural eruption that starts the narrative shocks in that it is so blatantly an *allegorical* gesture. But it is an instance of that truncated kind of allegory, described by Angus Fletcher, in which the isolation of the allegorical figure in a naturalistic mimesis, making it seem both excessively visible and solid (i.e. 'real'), and incongruous in scale or context, produces the uncanny effect of surrealism.[14] We confront the symbol as an alien effect – the opposite of a classical *prosopopoeia*, or appearance of human voice and figure in a natural scenery. Here, the loss of an original, generative allegorical system, or figural ground, makes itself felt in a disruption of the order of nature.

In the fable that follows, this disturbance takes allegorical control of the narrative. The initial rift is refigured as a recurrence or haunting, finally as an apotheosis: the scattered, empty relics of the ancestral spirit are reassembled for his final exhibition, 'dilated to an immense magnitude' (108), in a double triumph of allegory and fatality. Manfred's failure, or refusal, to read that initial 'portent' of the allegorical system has put him under its spell. From his first stupor of horror and incredulity, he passes to a violently mechanical agitation. 'Our doom is pronounced', he groans at the end, in the belated recognition that his individual will and subjectivity are an illusion, and that he is just a figure in a story that was already written from the start.

This recognition of the hollowness of the categories (promised by an empirical mimesis) of individual will and subjectivity, figured as the (etymological) reduction of 'character' to the externally inscribed letter of an allegorical scheme, constitutes the typical Gothic recognition. The narrative of *Otranto* gets under way by a parallel displacement. The allegorical charge of the emblem (giant helmet crushing puny youth) is transferred to the fable (Manfred unwittingly destroys his succession) by a sort of contagion: no sooner is Manfred rapt by the spectacle of a demonic ancestral patriarchy than he himself becomes the figure of that patriarchy, standing in relation to it much as Milton's Satan does to God. The more he strives to realize an absolute patriarchy, dramatized as tyrannical violence, incestuous desire and the ambition of immortality (he wishes to replace his extinguished son in the marriage-bed), the more he can only spell out an already written sentence. This formation of a 'Satanic' dialectic of power, whereby he who most pretends to power turns out to be most powerless, will be an important legacy from Walpole to that branch of Gothic concerned with the typology of power and sexuality.

It is important to recall that this allegorization, so terrible for its characters, takes place *after* and *against* a dominance of empirical realism in the novel, which narrates the division between an exterior surface of phenomena (objects, actions, manners, appearances) and an interior subjectivity, claiming for its symbolic work the 'imitation of nature'. Classic (i.e., for this period, *Gothic*) allegory, to paraphrase Fletcher, had represented life as a total, synchronic system of correspondences, in which spiritual and material causes and effects occupy the same symbolic space. For eighteenth-century critics, allegory was the quintessentially 'Gothic' literary mode, the almost lost and illegible principle that had articulated the extravagances of Spenserian romance. As authentic spiritual narrative, it had more recently served the radical Puritan ideology of Bunyan.[15] Walpole's 'Gothic tale', then, allegorizes its own representation as alien (*allos*): history as black-magical narrative. An occluded spiritual dimension, reduced to dispersed and broken surface forms, returns – reassembles itself – in the destructive modality of literalization. That is, we read the narrative's system of identities, relations and values in textual figures that are manifest to the fictional characters as destructive literalizations: the giant ancestral helmet that crushes his son refuses to be a 'vision' for Manfred. At the same time, it all remains visionary, that is, a set of figures, for the reader: literalization is a narrative trope, it seems that we are not the ones who are crushed.

Literalization has been the classically infernal or demonic trope of fate, absolute law, totalitarian power, in a tradition that runs from Dante through Kafka.[16] The end of this movement from the allegorical to the literal is a final loss of subjective identity and meaning, or reduction to absurdity, exteriority and automatism. Walpole acknowledges the threat, or lure, of this meaninglessness in his (pseudonymous) first-preface comment, 'I could wish [the author] had grounded his plan on a more useful moral than this: that *the sins of the fathers are visited on the children to the third and fourth generation*' (5). In other words, the allegorical theme may have turned out to be no more than the mechanical vehicle of a pointless irony. The problematical relationship of resurrected allegory, a mode of the sublime, and the deadening determinism felt to be inherent in figural schemes is measured by the tale's tonal mixture of solemnity and buffoonery. Contemporary readers found Walpole's effects equally horrid and funny. The writing mimics its own theme of degeneration into triviality, shrugging away the fable (it 'reads like a plot-summary of itself', as one critic says) as if it dare not dwell on it too closely or evoke it with a genuine intensity.[17] The tale cannot claim any of the high seriousness, ferocity or pathos of the ancestral models it invokes, only the self-conscious trifling of its antiquarian narrator. That strain of ironical trashiness, of a defensively wilful bathos, Walpole will also bequeath to subsequent Gothic authors, and Gothic and Camp remain on intimate terms today.

The rhetorical path of a fatalistic literalization, registered as a reduction of meaning and a failure of sublimity, traces the narrative turn into a private space of sexual identity defined by a psychological family romance. Its central term is the insatiable yet hollow automatism of the patriarchal will, futilely craving a lost, original and absolute state, and complemented by passive or fugitive, feminine (though not always female) victims. The point I should like to stress here is that the plotting of the history upon these private sexual archetypes *expresses itself* as a reduction, a loss, a trivialization. Walpole invokes tragedy, the Shakespearian grand genre of historical experience. But tragedy had been a socially representative, public form, not strictly domestic in its effects. Likewise, Walpole's evocation of allegory stages its own 'failure of succession', that is, a failure to comprehend large social and public themes: to be – as allegory had been for Spenser and for Bunyan – universal-historical as well as personal in the scope of its connections. (This will indeed be the task of the great nineteenth-century mythologists of the Gothic, such as Dickens and Freud).

We may read elsewhere in eighteenth-century Gothic fiction

its influential theme of patriarchy, a historical and socio logical term (denoting a pre-modern, in short 'Gothic', cultural arrangement) now fixed decisively upon the private and psychological archetype of a relentless and damned masculine will-to-power. That masculine identity achieves its archetypal status, through the return of a 'visionary' allegorical mode, but at the disastrous cost of literalization: a total loss of spiritual or subjective power, a binding to the compulsion of an external sentence, that of the private pathology: thus, to enact patriarchy is to rape and murder your children. I shall glance at two more examples, Beckford's *Vathek* and Lewis's *Monk*. Beckford's Caliph Vathek craves the possession of an ancestral, original patriarchy, troped as the knowledge that resides with 'the sceptre of the pre-adamite sultans'.[18] Vathek's quest takes him to the underground halls of Eblis, where he undergoes a typical Gothic recognition-metamorphosis: his insatiable desire is fixed forever in the character of a heart burning in quenchless flame. This ending, however, is juxtaposed with another: retreat to the bower of a perpetual, pre-pubescent narcissism, enjoyed by 'the humble, the despised Gulchenrouz' (120). Those most powerful turn out to be most powerless, while the passive and the child-like are granted their refuge from the arena of the will. It is a solution that will soon acquire more complex and definitive ideological content in the form of the domestic, that is, conjugal and heterosexual, idyll, in the romances of Radcliffe, Scott and Dickens (the lineage of the present study). Meanwhile the present idyll, covertly homosexual, is the type of a pure retreat that pretends to no transforming or colonizing effect upon the total narrative scene: a site of ('effete') class privilege, all too precarious.

Matthew Lewis's *Monk* decisively establishes the ground of Gothic themes and figures as that of sexual pathology. It does so with the guilty glee of adolescent discovery, nowhere more exuberant than in the final demonic apotheosis of the Gothic antagonist. The energies that drive Ambrosio exceed even his own ambition and appetite; they can as little be contained by his actions as within his imagination, and at last dash him to bits in a wonderfully bravura fulfilment of the logic of literalization and externalization. Once more, we read a fable plotted by the hidden relations of a suppressed narrative origin, played out in a headlong tale of perpetual crisis and blocked recognitions. Once more, the hero's satanic energies of lust, ambition and resentment exist in ironic complicity with the allegorical scheme of which he is a figure. No sooner does Ambrosio imagine his desire than its letter invades the story. He adores with a more than spiritual fervour an icon of the Virgin in his cell, invoking 'in that world which I am constrained to enter some lovely Female, lovely ... as you Madona [*sic*]!'[19] The Madonna soon appears in her carnal and original form, as Ambrosio's jilted mistress, who posed for the likeness and planted it on him to warm him up for the inevitable seduction. Now disguised as a fellow monk, she turns out by the end of the romance literally to have been a devil sent to tempt him, as is signalled by another literalization, this time of the serpent-in-the-garden figure ('concealed among the Roses ... A Serpent', 71). This figure, with the exchange of blood and poison, effects their illicit congress, so seismic an event as to break open a narrative gulf hundreds of pages wide, filled by the Raymond-and-Agnes subplot. The promptness of any image, emblem or type invoked in the text to take over in literal form gives Lewis's narrative much of its peculiar, and genuine, excitement. But perhaps the most striking of the fatal literalizations in *The Monk* occurs at the level of plot, a garish family romance of incestuous lust and violence: the victims of Ambrosio's rapacity turn out actually to be his mother and sister. I shall have more to say about this in connection with Lewis's relationship to Ann Radcliffe.

The Monk narrates with exceptional vividness the Gothic double bind of patriarchal energy, its fatal dialectic of repression and riot. A mob sacks a convent at the climax of the story, thus binding the energies of riot to psychosexual figures, epiphenomena of the career of Ambrosio himself. We read, in the Gothic, the apprehension of a (modern) totalitarian rather than (ancient) absolutist idea of power, in this very foundation of its structure on the site of private life. The effect is indeed one that captivates us. The famous setting of Gothic romance –

castle, monastery, prison, labyrinth or catacomb – occupies, as it is occupied by, our imagination. It is at once edifice of the power of a historical *ancien régime* and the model of psychological interiority, imitated, in a late work like Maturin's *Melmoth the Wanderer*, in the narrative form itself – a maze of sliding panels and secret passages to enthrall the reader.

III

Her intensest life was no longer in her dreams, where she made things to her own mind: she was moving in a world charged with forces.
(George Eliot, *Felix Holt, the Radical*)

'Is power then', complains the harassed hero of the romance of the 1790s, 'the infallible test of justice?'[20] The answer might depend on which romance you were in. The scenario of Walpolian Gothic relates a fatal and ironic bondage to a patriarchal law of antagonistic desire and crushing reaction. The connection to lost currents of identity and origin is catastrophically destructive, not liberating and fulfilling.

We find a strong revision of Gothic topographies, however, if we turn to some romances written by women. In contrast to Walpole's pseudo-forgery, Ann Radcliffe's texts were the declared productions of an 'authoress', who triumphantly named herself on the title page of *The Mysteries of Udolpho*. The first novelist to command huge fees from her publisher and the name-recognition of a middle-class reading public, Radcliffe pioneered the cultural position of the author as famous producer of a certain commodity that would be inherited by Scott and bequeathed as canonical to the nineteenth century. Here the literary genre, Gothic, defining (like a brand name) a pattern of popular consumption, coalesces into the historic figure of an individual *author*. Her prototypical situation accounts for why we probably tend (after reading, say, Dickens or Woolf) to find Radcliffe rather a minimally individualized author, and more like a generic figure: a purveyor of 'Gothic', a woman writer. It is striking that the pioneering figure should have been a woman. As Nancy Armstrong has argued, 'written representations of the self allowed the modern individual to become an economic and psychological reality; and . . . the modern individual was first and foremost a woman'.[21] Radcliffe's work reiterates the genre's preoccupation with sexual archetypes, to the extent that the gender of the author has become one of the romance's crucial literary effects. To find in Radcliffe a 'female Gothic' that distinguishes itself as such, in other words, is to note the involvement of a newly potent figure of subjectivity, the author, in the fiction of a human condition of private life determined by sexual archetypes, where the feminine is the site of 'nature'. The revision of the symbolic landscape of Walpole Gothic is thus critical. In Radcliffe's *Romance of the Forest*, the ruined abbey in the midst of the forest is at once the magnetic pole of the heroine's dread and 'a domestic asylum, and a safe refuge from the storms of power' (34).

We saw that Burke's compelling emblem of the French revolution was the violation of a woman: the stripping away of a 'decent drapery' of romance, the mob invading Marie-Antoinette's bedroom:

> A band of cruel ruffians and assassins, reeking with his blood, rushed into the chamber of the queen, and pierced with an hundred strokes of bayonets and poniards the bed, from whence this persecuted woman had but just time to fly naked.[22]

The object of the outrage is a private space sanctified as feminine. Burke draws upon traditional figures of the novel, by now the dominant genre of 'private history'. There the domestic archetype of patriarchal tyranny is the persecution of a maiden, involving rape in the worst, literal case, or the invasion, appropriation, *education* of a cultural space of feminine privacy, in sublimated, rationalized, benevolent versions that claim the status of legitimate persuasion. The great and troubling prototype is of course Richardson's *Clarissa* (1748), which narrated the path from a contingent, vulnerable, drastically limited place of the heroine's will within her father's house to exile, captivity and violation in the power of the rogue aristocrat, Lovelace. Clarissa's closet is the precariously private space of (above all) her reading and writing, also the space of our own reading of the epistolary novel; the troping of this field of discourse in terms of the fate of the heroine's body has been well described by recent criticism.[23] Exemplary of the case of legitimate cultural persuasion, Charlotte Lennox's female quixote must also suffer a decisive, but more thoroughgoing and salutary, conquest of her closet, that is, of her literary imagination; her correction is incited by fantasies, derived from romance reading, of a sensational dialectic between female sovereignty and the threat of rape.

Like Burke, Radcliffe sets in place a typological scheme of feminine romance, constituted by a dialectic of privacy and persecution. Radcliffe's Gothic fictions, the grandest of the age, mythologize a female condition in relation to a historical dimension of male power, in order to imagine the utopian transformation of their relation. The heroine's romance subjectivity, an ethical-aesthetic compound of sensibility and stoicism, is not represented as erroneous and in need of correction, but as a core of spiritual integrity, a warrant of grace. It survives, intact, to enjoy at once the withering-away of the claims of masculine tyranny and the redemptive feminization of the male hero, as he too is released from those claims. While the masculine Gothic remains obsessed with the complicity of the energies of power and eros, one of the projects of Radcliffe's fiction is their separation. The characteristic conclusion figures a division between the tragic and ironic arena of public history, and a private conjugal idyll whose genius is feminine. It will remain the prominent, counter-revolutionary resolution of nineteenth-century romance, from Scott onward.

Radcliffe's romances are in the Richardson and Burney tradition of female *Bildungsroman*; their topic is that most delicate of cultural transitions, a young lady's entrance into the world. This individual progress, more-or-less covertly middle class, is precisely what the male Gothic narrates as impossible, as either blocked or transgressive: the weakling prince crushed on his wedding day, the revenge of a patriarchal will that devours itself and its issue. Perhaps the most problematical figure for this narrative is, accordingly, female desire: that is, desire reconstructed in terms separate from a masculine will to power. On one hand, we read the suppression of an active desire on the part of heroines who, like Clarissa, wish only to be able to remain still and invisible, arrested before the threshold of sexuality, marriage, the world; or else who, under the pressure of male desire, must devote all their energies to flight and concealment. On the other hand, violent female passion is often implicated in the etiology of the Gothic fable, although as a capitulation to essentially masculine forces of ambition and license. Notable examples are the Marchesa Vivaldi in *The Italian*, whose affronted 'prejudice and pride' (122) instantly conjure up Schedoni as her satanic double of arrogance, lust and malice; and Laurentini di Udolpho, whose possession by 'all the delirium of Italian love'[24] makes her both source and ultimate victim of the mysteries of that place. Much of *The Mysteries of Udolpho* is occupied with the separation of Emily from such figures. She must find out, after much tormented doubt, that her mother is not really Laurentini after all. In the portrait Emily finds at Udolpho, Laurentini's countenance speaks 'the language of passion, rather than that of sentiment' (278). The typological distinction between the two women becomes clear at their meeting, in which Laurentini repeats the exhortations against passion, in its passive mode of excess of sensibility, that Emily has already heard from her dying father. These distinctions are aimed at the reader, rather than at Emily herself, who throughout displays impeccable prudence and rectitude. Laurentini is figured into the fable so as to exorcize doubts and questions that might otherwise attach to the heroine, in this romance of a female wish-fulfilment.[25]

The heroine's grace lies in a passive sensibility, rather than in an active desire, a will to agency. We read, instead, a romance rhetoric in which desire is sublimated to drive the plot without a visible agent, by a tropological saturation of the narrative. Its typical figure is an animation or haunting of the scene, an intensification of local atmosphere, an electricity of external energies of transformation. While the frenzied agitations of male Gothic narrative confirm only that there is nowhere to go, for the sentence is already written, the principle of Radcliffian narrative is dynamic and transformational. For Radcliffe, the term 'romance' marks an expansion and intensification of expressive register, signalled by devices such as chapter-epigraphs that textualize the theme of portent or prophecy, and the 'interspersion' of lyrics that invoke the shades of Shakespeare and Milton.[26] We also read a characteristic phenomenology and form. We have already glanced at the striking opening of *The Romance of the Forest*. The headlong sequence of flight, followed by captivity, followed by flight soon leaves behind a 'historical' framework (La Motte's financial difficulties, etc.). It establishes instead a typical structural unit, generating a hyperactivity of romance figures:

> Such elegance and apparent refinement, contrasted with the desolation of the house, and the savage manners of its inhabitants, seemed to him like a romance of imagination, rather than an occurrence of real life. (7)

> [He] ruminated on the late scene, and it appeared like a vision, or one of those improbable fictions that are exhibited in a romance. (8)

The principle of this 'visionary' transportation, in which the sensibilities of protagonist and reader are rushed across thresholds of experience, is that of dynamic 'contrast', or scenic change – soon to be defined as the narrative principle of history and of modernity in versions of romance by Scott and by Dickens. Here we read, in ascending order of narrative potency and in inverse ratio to the protagonist's agency, figures of travel, flight and kidnapping: all actually versions of each other.[27] Equally arbitrary and dreamlike, owing little or nothing to the protagonists' active enterprise, is the final delivery:

> She contemplated the past, and viewed the present, and, when she compared them, the contrast struck her with astonishment. The whole appeared like one of those sudden transitions so frequent in dreams, in which we pass from grief and despair, we know not how, to comfort and delight. (*Romance of the Forest*, 244)

> Montoni and his castle had all vanished from her mind, like the frightful vision of a necromancer, and she wandered, once more, in fairy scenes of unfading happiness. (*Udolpho*, 444)

Indeed, the narrative itself all but forgets its arch-villain, who has held so long and absolute a sway. The time simply comes when Emily can run away from Udolpho; the spell is broken. Montoni is consigned to a narrative *oubliette* until softly dispatched, in one of those rationalizing afterthoughts that seem to belong to a different kind of story.

The happy dissolution of the necromancer's spell does not mean delivery from romance illusion to an historical light of common day, as in the scheme of eighteenth-century anti-romance, but rather the delivery from one stage of romance to another. Emily's servant Annette 'almost fancied herself in an enchanted palace, and declared, that she had not met with any place, which charmed her so much, since she read the fairy tales' (*Udolpho*, 671); the narrator of *The Italian* assures us, more forthrightly, that her final scene is 'in truth, a scene of fairy-land' (412). And as in Ariosto or Spenser or Coleridge, the romance idyll (the stage of *diletto*, bliss or paradise) has to depend upon a strategic *forgetting*, encoded as a principle of narrative transition. This is nevertheless complicit with an antithetical logic of disenchantment, typical of the Whiggish rhetoric of anti-romance: that of detection, rationalization and explanation, devoted to recalling hidden plot origins in order to enlighten and demystify. The bower of delightful oblivion can only be set in place *after* the sentence of rational recollection has been spoken over the narrative.

I shall return to this divided narratology at the end of my discussion, since it has traditionally perturbed readers of Radcliffe. Meanwhile, Radcliffe's 'romance of imagination' represents a supercharged phenomenology in which moral categories, formed by submerged erotic currents of dread and desire, achieve presence. In contrast to the oscillations of frenzy and stupor that defined the male Gothic, being is heightened and intensified in these atmospheres. Narrative map and temporality are massively actual yet strangely fluid. Sudden scenic shifts and dissolutions alternate with vast stretches of 'exhausting suspense', enchantment in the dark labyrinth of forest or castle or convent (*Udolpho*, 319). While it is true that both *The Romance of the Forest* and *The Italian* display superior narrative coherence, it may be the very disarticulation of the fable, into the mode of 'suspense' and rhetorical elaboration of its visionary climates, that has made *The Mysteries of Udolpho* so compelling for readers. *Udolpho* proceeds as a sequence of scenic transformations, mapped at first by the conventions of Grand Tour journalism, later urged in more drastic devices of abduction and flight. Radcliffe makes striking use in this novel of the picturesque or sublime prospect, attached to the heroine's states of 'suspense', first on her father's estate and then at Udolpho. The prospect represents descriptively and spatially the dynamic principle of 'contrast'; it is the emblem of scenic transformation, as well as the most conspicuous of the tropes by which the narrative is suspended. In the opening chapters at La Vallée, we view the threat of a mountainous and precipitous male power that will soon overshadow the daughter's idyll of virginity. Later at Udolpho, the prospect tends to represent the sublimation of the present frightful foreground toward a visionary horizon of pure light beyond the eye's reach: no place but distance itself, the site of desire as transcendence and nostalgia. In her captivity, the prospect represents to the heroine's imagination a utopian liberty that sustains and guarantees her interior fullness, in hope for the future and regret for the past, until it realizes itself in the reconstruction of the narrative scene. The sequence follows, accordingly, the transformation of a present foreground by the prospective and retrospective mode of a background (a horizon or recess).[28]

Because the prospect is the most highly charged figure in *Udolpho's* symbolic repertoire, I shall examine a particularly elaborate instance (329–30). In this case, the rhetorical elaboration marks an intensified speculative inwardness, in ratio to the outward obscurity of the particular view: it is the Gothic and female time, night. Seeking refuge from the host of 'dismal images' and 'phantoms, that tormented her', Emily goes from bed to her window. There, the night's 'image of repose' offers a temporary stilling of 'the fierce and terrible passions' that have expanded beyond the individual human actors to saturate Udolpho itself. This serves a necessary moral distinction: Emily must not internalize, thus in turn be absorbed into, the Gothic atmosphere.

The fierce and terrible passions, too, which so often agitated the inhabitants of this edifice, seemed now hushed in sleep; – those mysterious workings, that rouse the elements of man's nature into tempest – were calm. Emily's heart was not so; but her sufferings, though deep, partook of the gentle character of her mind. Hers was a silent anguish, weeping, yet enduring; not the wild energy of passion, inflaming imagination, bearing down the barriers of reason and living in a world of its own. (329)

This set of oppositions is insistent throughout the long central narrative. As an earlier passage has made explicit, the romance turns upon its own cultural status:

Her present life appeared like the dream of a distempered imagination, or like one of those frightful fictions, in which the wild genius of the poets sometimes delighted. Reflection brought only regret, and anticipation terror. (297)

It is most urgent that Emily refuse imaginative subjection to the 'frightful fiction' she is caught in; in other words, that it not become her reality. The moral component of her ordeal, as some critics have suggested, lies in her resistance to those options of the 'distempered imagination', unruly passion or craven superstition, which are the traditional resort of oppressed and frustrated women.[29]

Emily responds to the scene in quite another way:

She remembered how often she had gazed on [the stars] with her dear father, how often he had pointed out their way in the heavens, and explained their laws. (329)

The guarantee of Emily's integrity is not a vision of 'her own' (the delirium of Laurentini) but her memory of the rational and scientific voice of her absent father.

In fact, the prospect has slipped into the mode of *retrospect*; which exercises its transforming power over the narrative scene, as we have just read ('Her present life appeared like the dream of a distempered imagination, or like one of those frightful fictions . . .'), by emptying it of its presence and reality, to mark it, precisely, as 'visionary', as 'romance':

> [These reflections] brought a retrospect of all the strange and mournful events, which had occurred since she lived at peace with her parents. And to Emily, who had been so tenderly educated, so tenderly loved, who once knew only goodness and happiness – to her, the late events and her present situation – in a foreign land – in a remote castle – surrounded by vice and violence – seemed more like the visions of a distempered imagination, than the circumstances of truth. She wept to think of what her parents would have suffered, could they have seen the events of her future life. (329)

The troubling recognition that, here and now, 'the visions of a distempered imagination' *are* 'the circumstances of truth' emerges through a blocked and broken syntax. The disturbance alerts us to the problematic plot syntax of that transition, from 'peace with her parents' (both dead; the sepulchral overtone is systematic) to the frightful fiction that constitutes her present dilemma.

The curious, recurrent figuration of Emily's romance plight in a subjunctive mode of parental foresight (prospect within retrospect within prospect) defines the causal logic of her career – from paternal estate at La Vallée to Gothic regime at Udolpho and thence back to La Vallée – in terms of a problematical relation between prospect, retrospect and present scene. The excess of the denial – her father is dead, he did not foresee the events of her future life – betrays the connection that both Emily and Radcliffe's narration avoid spelling out. It is precisely because of her father's failure to foresee her present situation, in leaving her in her aunt's custody, that Emily is here now. Meanwhile, the prospect/retrospect is sealed by a sight of that 'same planet, which she had seen in Languedoc, on the night preceding her father's death', cueing in the mysterious disembodied music that always haunts these scenes. In accord with the unusually reflective and explanatory character of this one, the music first fills Emily with 'superstitious dread', and then sounds to her, more comfortingly, 'as if her dead father had spoken to her in that strain' (330).

The soothing voice of the benevolent and rationalist father is the same that inspires Gothic dread. He, not Laurentini, enchants Udolpho and is its prime mystery. His power relies on a peculiar negativity of presence: the answer to the mysteries that thicken about his passing will always turn out to be no – he has not betrayed his marriage, there was no tryst with Laurentini of which Emily is the offspring, he is heavily absent from the secret origins of the plot. In like manner, the entire narrative of *The Mysteries of Udolpho* is fabricated upon an obliquity or displacement of the topic of parental guilt: the negligence or absence of the good father provides for the tyranny of his demonic counterpart.[30] Emily's bondage at Udolpho is the deadly literalization of a patriarchal subjection, just as Clarissa's oppression by her father was succeeded by its Gothic reversion, a wilder historical condition – ravishment by an aristocrat. For Emily to succumb to the 'distempered imagination' of the Gothic world would be quite literally to own Montoni as her father: accepting his proposed suitor, signing over her estates. As his name spells out, Montoni is the sublime figure of patriarchal power admitted in the prospects of St Aubert's estate at the foot of the Pyrenees, yet picturesquely remote. It is St Aubert, in an important early sequence, who rehearses Emily's rite of passage: conducting her into the mountains and to the first meeting with her lover, whom he wounds with a gunshot. Wild mountains presently engulf the narrative scene: prospect becomes foreground. As St Aubert's death delivers Emily into the Gothic world, so from the very beginning an incipient mortality is written into the prospects of his place of 'retirement'. The paternal domain is above all elegiac, poised at sunset, vibrant with invisible voices that already proclaim a powerful absence. Emily's prospects remain controlled by this mysterious patriarchal voice, its influence all the more decisive for the absence of St Aubert and his replacement by Montoni.

The invisible troubadour, both at La Vallée and Udolpho, turns out in the end to have been neither a ghost nor Emily's lover Valancourt but another, extra suitor, whom Emily dismisses to an extensive subplot. His name, M. Du Pont, glosses the question of the transmission of patrimony which is the cultural motive for these narrative transformations. The good father's absence opens a space of potential patriarchy around Emily's own transitional status in the world. Her situation constitutes a bridge (rather than an estate: she cannot hold property for herself) over which pass a number of prospective types. The problem of the romance then is to narrate the transition between a series of cultural archetypes, the metamorphic displacements of one another: the kind father of a sentimental ideal, the tyrannical father of a history of violent dominion and the husband new-modelled by the romance who is the figure of the heroine's desire. Valancourt is he who will court La Vallée, the synecdoche of Emily as paternal property.

The distinction among these types measures the displacement of a central Gothic fable of origins. Just so, the vast, paratactic elongation of the narrative in *The Mysteries of Udolpho* hangs over a disarticulation of plot. The comparative tightness of the plot in both *The Romance of the Forest* and *The Italian* brings those novels closer to the terrible revelation of Gothic mysteries spelt out in the tales of Walpole and Lewis: the reduction of all relations of patriarchal power to the father's violation of his children. In *The Romance of the Forest*, the ruined abbey where Adeline is persecuted by weak (treacherous) and strong (violent) parents turns out to be the site where her true father was murdered by the false one. A hairsbreadth father–daughter recognition averts the threatened incestuous rape and murder, further displaced, and made safe, by the discovery that this is not the real father but a usurping uncle. Matthew Lewis responded to *The Mysteries of Udolpho* by zealously literalizing the family-plot that Radcliffe's narrative so delicately and elaborately invokes, suspends and conjures away. Contrary to murky hints for hundreds of pages, Emily's father has not been involved in a dark secret love, and Laurentini is not her mother; for the heroine, there turn out to be no hidden origins. It is scarcely surprising that Lewis's lurid insistence upon the terms she had been most concerned to exorcize should have been profoundly obnoxious to Radcliffe. *The Italian*, her stately response to *The Monk*, reaffirms the gravity of her own version.[31] Once again, a patriarchal agent is on the point of assaulting a sleeping heroine when he recognizes his daughter. Once again, the recognition is made safe by the convention of

Schedoni's identity as wicked uncle who has done away with the true father.

The cultural ideal of a kind patriarchy is in fact a vacant throne usurped by tyrants. The heroine's romance narrates her refusal of the letter of this substitution, for to accept it is to be bound forever into the Gothic system of violence and passion, while to refuse – to delay, to hide – is to hold out for a return of the kind father's family regime. But for the actual machinery of plot-resolution, Radcliffe likes to invoke the – rational, anti-romance, authoritarian – figure of the law. In the masculine Gothic (most spectacularly, in Maturin's *Melmoth the Wanderer*), the institutions of the law are a labyrinth of mirrors: casting the violent energies of the heroic antagonist, magnified and multiplied, back upon himself. The Gothic archetype of the law, as a body of irrational yet systematic (i.e. 'organic') totalitarian power, is the Inquisition, or a secret society such as Scott's Holy Vehme.[32] As omnipotent secret apparatus, the law evokes an ethically ambiguous sublimity: its sentences are terrible yet *just*, the revelation of an order. In Radcliffe's romances, such legal institutions are impersonal forces, dreadful in appearance but benign in effect, transcending the domain of individual passion as they intervene to contain and subdue it. Adeline's wicked uncle is brought to book, and the ambiguous surrogate-parent La Motte given partial acquittal by a Parisian court at the end of *The Romance of the Forest*; the Venetian Council of Ten, which once seemed to be a quintessentially Gothic body of arbitrary rule, stamps out Montoni and his band at the end of *Udolpho*. The Inquisition in all its sinister sublimity takes over the end of *The Italian*. Reflection perhaps of the revolutionary councils of the Terror in France, 'a new view of human nature seemed to burst, at once, upon [Vivaldi's] mind' (198); but even this murky and blood-steeped tribunal endorses a reassuringly enlightened version of the law, solving mysteries and turning Schedoni's machinations back on himself. Radcliffe represents these legal bodies as informed by the same political energies of ambition, revenge and cruelty that individually drive her villains. Yet their effects, magically, transcend their human components, for the law always turns out to coincide with the providential law of the romance narrative itself. Legal process turns out to be as subordinate to this larger narrative movement as is the individual agency of human desire. The secret power which collaborates with this secular machinery of poetic justice is that of the heroine's dispersed subjectivity, fearing and mourning and yearning across the text, the engine of romance. Radcliffe's fable thus promises the political equivalent of a natural theology, by which desire subduing itself to the law will reciprocally inform its shape.

This covert, symbolic negotiation of female imagination and patriarchal apparatus is defined by the formal principle of *Udolpho*'s romance narrative mentioned earlier: the rhetorical dissymmetry, or excess, of the space of imagination with respect to its eventual regulation within the recovered and sublimated patriarchy by the letter of a rationalizing explanation that 'accounts for everything'. This we might already have noted as a local difference, between the heroine's view of her prospects – charged with an emotion (dread, nostalgia, regret, desire) that depends upon their transcendental dissolution into light, darkness, mist, clouds – and the didactic naming-and-measuring gaze of her father. More pervasive, though, is the serial disjunction of the narrative, as the fable is suspended for elaborately wrought scenes of anxiety and desire. The intensification of romance 'atmosphere', that is, figuration, is characterized by a recession of the visible and palpable, in contrast to those literal and objective confrontations of masculine Gothic that crowd out visionary possibility.

I am rehearsing here Radcliffe's own well-known distinction between the effects of terror and horror: the former a quality of indistinct suggestion, mystery, awe, the latter of proximity, explicitness and disgust.[33] Everything at Udolpho is delayed and set back to a remote horizon, cause and effect and explanation are separated by hundreds of pages, nothing can be known or seen but what is manifest in hints, traces, shadows, echoes, fragments. In this suspense, anxiety expands into a metaphysical state, in and for itself. On one hand, this is the space of the heroine's, and the reader's, consciousness – liminal, harrowed by dread, for all that authentic – and of a postponement of the crushing literalizations of persecution and violation played out in a Gothic fable. On the other, the belated rational enlightenment is simply inadequate to the expressive content of the scene of romance. Our sense of incongruity is only enhanced by the pains taken to explain absolutely everything. Romance mystery, the present-tense mode of a feminine consciousness dwelling in prospect and retrospect, and demystifying rationalism, a paternal and legal discourse that recovers past origins and connects causes with effects, describe twinned but exclusive dimensions. This mimetic disjunction, difficult for us to interpret now and problematical even for Radcliffe's contemporaries, is nevertheless a principle of the romance's genuine, considerable power.[34]

The disjunction exposes itself in two notorious figures, in which the signifier of Gothic mystery resists the text's own conventions of representation, even as it passes before the heroine's gaze. The first is the 'sentence of dreadful import' Emily reads among her father's forbidden papers; the other is that still more sensationally blank emblem of parental guilt, the figure ('no picture', i.e. not to be described) behind the black veil. The distance between these horrid effects and the explanation of their cause seems absolute. We never get to read that dreadful sentence, and Emily never gets to find out what it was she saw behind the veil. (In any case, not only has she misconstrued the sentence, but 'Laurentina's skeleton' turns out, after five hundred pages, to have been a fake.)

Radcliffe thus inverts the symbolic operation of Walpolian Gothic. But we may question how far we have come from our collaboration with the enthralled gaze of Manfred, who touched the giant helmet and wished in vain it were visionary, and with the feverish, relentless exposures of *The Monk*. Symbolic fullness and resonance, the monstrosities of meaning, are directed to the prospect, beyond the horizon, behind the veil. Terror is the apprehension of a horror not yet bared: an intensely eroticized anxiety. The condition of the subject's liberty, which is a *liberty to desire*, is bondage to a power invisible, suspended, present but in the background. Were it to show itself, it would overwhelm and crush; aesthetic pleasure lies in the knowledge that it is there but not here, not yet, and that its reality is guaranteed by its concealment. It is at such moments of an inaccessible revelation, epiphanies of the unrepresentable, that *The Mysteries of Udolpho* achieves its keenest shudders. The power of romance is that of *postponement* of the fatal sentence; so that when at last it spells itself out, it has been drained of its compulsive strength, and seems irrelevant to the richest anguishes of life and meaning. The bathos that attends the sentence of rational explanation, the disappointment of demystification, is a necessary aesthetic effect. We shall find it imitated and disavowed (its own characteristic effect) in the far more ambiguously rationalized supernatural of Scott.

Radcliffe, then, reworks a romance aesthetic of dilation and suspense, but secures it with the juxtaposition of a mode of anticlimactic rationalization that at the same time ensures its content of 'terror', that is, the knowledge of imminent dissolution, of being – all the more intensely – romance. At last, through sheer elongation, postponement is allowed to turn into escape. But the heroine's prospects, even as they enclose the narrative scene – or rather, as the scene recedes decisively into the visionary gleam of its background – are to be desired and viewed from afar, charged by distance, rather than actually inhabited. The bower of conjugal bliss remains the scene of the dead father, even as Valancourt, whose rites of legitimation have been so protracted and painful (he is twice wounded as he approaches the paternal property), takes his place. The transformation of scene has worked by a conversion of the prospect, confrontation with the sublime parent who straddles the way of experience, to a retrospect, nostalgia for the kind parent who once presided over a lost time of innocence. The new estate is a very old and familiar place, and no place at all, suffused with the sunset light of final repose. Desire has been turned into elegy – a conversion that declares itself as the romance's final logic. Radcliffe's 'happily ever after' dissolves into anxious exhortations that waver between the claims of exemplary instruction and those of romance entertainment:

> if the weak hand, that has recorded this tale, has, by its scenes, beguiled the mourner of one hour of sorrow, or, by its moral, taught him to sustain it – the effort, however humble, has not been vain, nor is the writer unrewarded. (672)

On the last page, under pressure of the return of everyday life, the author must weaken her hand, the romance declare itself void of magic. The gesture is a ritual of the genre; it refers backward to Shakespeare, forward to Scott. In the last turn of the romance, the Gothic is the real world, and the text itself has constituted an idyll of private subjectivity that must dissolve with the end of reading. This escape has been a postponement that cannot transform its conditions. The reader is returned from the bright hour of beguilement to resume the everyday duty of *mourner*: sharing, at best, the heroine's 'silent anguish, weeping, yet enduring', in a world of death.

CHAPTER 2

The romance of subjection: Scott's Waverley

I

A mild, romantic, gentle-tempered youth, bred up in dependence, and stooping patiently to the control of a sordid and tyrannical relation, had suddenly, by the rod of oppression and the spur of injured feeling, been compelled to stand forth a leader of armed men, was earnestly engaged in affairs of a public nature, had friends to animate and enemies to contend with, and felt his individual fate bound up in that of a national insurrection and revolution. It seemed as if he had at once experienced a transition from the romantic dreams of youth to the labours and cares of active manhood. All that had formerly interested him was obliterated from his memory, excepting only his attachment to Edith; and even his love seemed to have assumed a character more manly and disinterested, as it had become mingled and contrasted with other duties and feelings.

(*Old Mortality*, ch. 27)

The publication in 1814 of the anonymous novel *Waverley* was a decisive event in the institutional formation of modern narrative. As Lukács recognized, Scott's innovation was the double representation – together yet apart – of individual and collective life. The famous combination of romance and history founded itself upon a crucial division between private and public worlds. Both had hitherto coincided in the term 'history' without great semantic friction, making what would henceforth assume the more specialized title of biography: to be set alongside history and the novel in the Victorian triumvirate of official narrative forms. Scott's achievement was to define the relation between private and public meaning as the moral and formal crux that constituted these forms. In *Waverley* the public

[...]e 1745 Jacobite rebellion enlarges and complicates [...] ascendant genre of European fiction, the *Bildungsroman*, to provide its classically British and masculine form: the exemplary fable of the formation of the subject, in a coincidence of self-making and self-finding. The pattern for countless subsequent novels, young Waverley's sentimental education occupies a traversal of the field of history which defines both personal and political terms of his identity. The historical romance discovers collective life through the experience of the subject, in turn formed through – and against – the external claims of class and national allegiance. A prototypical family romance of sexual and moral development coincides with the extremity of a public crisis, civil war.[1]

Drawing from Shakespeare's history plays, Scott represented civil war as the paradigm of historical process. The difference from Shakespeare was twofold. First, the struggle was between *cultures*, different worlds of life, complex material and moral economies, more profoundly than it was between rival dynasties or parties – the vessels of individual will. Second, civil war now represented the empirical form of revolution, the catastrophically accelerated transformation of political, economic and social relations throughout society as a whole, and not merely their chaotic dissolution: in short, with the triumph of one culture and the reduction of another, a competitive and imperialist principle of progress. At the same time, the appeal to a Shakespearian model (and thus to the dominant-class property of a literary tradition) evoked the sense of revolutionary transformation as tragic and disastrous. The price of social and cultural change, whatever benefits it might claim, is the loss of ancient ties and associations that have defined personal identity within a community. The complexity of Scott's representation is structural: more radical than a mixed tonality, Whig positivism tempered by Jacobite nostalgia. These historical novels occupied their own historical moment of production and reception: felt to be one of continuous, profound, seismic crisis. The long French wars were followed at home by recession, hunger, popular unrest and harsh repression; Scott, an urban professional gentleman with a country estate, detected a 'foreign' revolutionary spectre – popular fundamentalism and militarist state absolutism – haunting the British Union's own, post-revolutionary, dispensation of legality and liberty based on property-ownership. Scott stands, with Burke and Wordsworth, for a complex transition between Whig and 'Conservative' cultural hegemonies, affirming the establishment of 1688, when domestic history was supposed to have culminated. Like the treatises of Burke, like the great national fictions of Shakespeare and Milton, Scott's first novel represents rebellion, for all the variety of motive of those involved, as a reactionary adventure – so making it more difficult to imagine in any other terms. For the ideal of 1688 was a revolution without further revolutions. Political struggle was to be confined to the past, enabling in the present a purely economic progress of agricultural and commercial 'improvement' (i.e. capitalist rationalization) without the extremity of a wholesale structural transformation of social and political relations. Even so, it seemed that such a transformation might be on the verge of happening.[2]

I shall be making the argument that the Waverley novels discover history in order to discover the horizon at which – as for the individual subject, so for the nation – history comes to a stop. Lukács has said that Scott's protagonists tend to represent a precariously neutral or middle position in the thick of objective historical conflicts, so experiencing all their points of contradiction, at the same time that successfully holding such a position makes it the figure for history's limit or end. This middle way is the ideological construction that made the Waverley novels so representative, so influential, so apt to become the official romance form of an early nineteenth-century gentry-and-middle-class cultural establishment. Alexander Welsh has shown that Scott's figure of the private subject is politically and psychologically grounded upon property. Correspondingly, it is spiritually grounded upon a domestic space set apart from public life, from politics, and (thus the logical declension) from historical process: 'home', origin and end of the story. Such a representative subjectivity – private, domestic, politically innocent – was already available culturally, as a literary figure. It was feminine, and its strong version came to Scott through Gothic romance, as I shall be arguing in the first part of this chapter. Scott's novels rewrite the historical private subject as masculine in terms already feminine; there follow two familiar effects. First: masculine subjection is composed upon, and consoled by, a further, secondary and supplementary (but actually primary), feminine subjection. Secondly, and accordingly: the character of this representative, dominant-class male subjectivity, even at its private and essential level of gender, is constituted by the same kinds of ('feminine') hesitancy, ambiguity and irrationality that define its ethical problematic, in the theme of national political allegiance.[3]

But perhaps the most vexed figure of Scott's own cultural identity is the one most advertised: nationality. Sir Walter Scott as portfolio of Victorian Scottishness, not so obsolete as we might like. It is important to recall that at its moment of production this national identity was an effect of class. Scott was born into the Edinburgh legal profession, a channel of remarkable social mobility providing the effective aristocracy and intelligentsia of a provincial capital, obliquely connected to national politics, but endowed with strong regional institutions of cultural literacy. Scott rose discreetly from solicitor's son to barrister, county magistrate and Clerk of Session; but his more spectacular acquisition of fame, estate and title came through a literary career of unprecedented triumph, first as national poet and then as the anonymous author of the Waverley novels. All the while, his official identity remained that of the powerful elite class of post-Union Scotland: Edinburgh gentleman/lawyer who had assumed (by no means atypically) the ancient dignity of Border laird. However the unofficial, covert base of Scott's fortune was not just a speculative commodity, the novel, but the imperial markets of the South: capital, credit and patronage flowing from London, site of political power as well as a huge reading public. Just as his success was supposed to have revived literary industry in Edinburgh, so Scott reinvented Scottishness for cultural export, as the local and ancient archetype of a distinctively modern condition of being British: the subject of an imperial commercial nation state. In the increasingly garish declensions of Victorian and modern nationalist mythology, this meant being a British landlord, inhabiting a local feudalism that was the adornment rather than source of wealth and power. Such Scotch Britishness was a class figure, the identity of a dominant professional class entitled not from the ground but from over it, by purchase: nevertheless claiming the legitimacy of local habitation, of native ownership, by making use of a rhetoric of cultural heritage. The troubled abstraction of the nation state in the Waverley novels replaces class difference, and erases class conflict, by an abstraction of local identity: since to be a British subject is to be middle class, to have transcended historical process in order to occupy a generic idyll of private life. At the same time, as we shall see, the Waverley novels register the historical truth revealed by Scott's financial failure in the Ballantyne–Constable crash of 1825–6, part of a national collapse of credit: that local being is a phantasm when its sources are abroad, that the revolutions of history are a vast, dispersed, impersonal machinery without regard for individual identity and its (after all but local) strategies of accommodation.[4]

The narrative discourses of collective history (of economic modes, social classes, cultural mentalities) came to Scott through the 'philosophical' or sociological historians of the Edinburgh Enlightenment.[5] The dominant genre of private history, on the other hand, was the novel, narrative above all of an 'individual accommodation'. The subtitle of *Waverley* invokes not only the matter of the 1745 rebellion but also its own British tradition of modern prose romance, flowering 'sixty years' since', and in particular *Tom Jones*. Fielding's precision-plotted 'History of a Foundling' had secured its hero's private, moral romance of legitimation by signalling the public history of the '45 rebellion – the failure of a corrupt elder dynasty's national political restoration – as a conspicuous irrelevance: noises off, source of narrative distraction and confusion, bad plotting in every sense. Legitimacy is made not a literal, genealogical but an ethical title. Tom Jones's destiny sets itself in place less with or against than to one side of the current of public affairs, in the rural backwaters of an eternal squirearchy. Nevertheless, Jones has proven his character as a loyal subject of the Hanover succession by his eagerness to enlist and in his debates with Partridge and the Man of the Hill. Such purely ethical proof seems to have absolved him from actually having to fight or take part in public life. London is the plot's generic arena of crisis and ordeal, Town as opposed to Country of moral fable, the exemplary authority of which holds over a universal range of human conduct.

However, such a commodious relation between private and public worlds is not so happily told by the end of the century. In Gothic fiction (to leap to the beginning of the present study) political struggle occupies an alien external setting and an allegory of private sexuality. In the 'Jacobin romances' of the 1790s that combined private histories with political themes, novelistic form and ideological argument tend to contradict each other. That is, their radical theme remains local, an extrinsic content added to 'aristocratic' romance conventions otherwise untransformed: producing the total ideological effect of a containment or disabling of the rational initiative of theoretical critique by deep or grammatical structures that remain impregnably in place.[6] Scott's new kind of novel, the historical romance, amplifies the project of Gothic fiction in bringing history into discourse as a *theme*, the urgent matter – even as 'another' history, the representation of a past condition – of the complex of material and political relations that determine the destiny of the subject. The categorical abstraction of this 'history' makes it possible then to imagine the relations between individual consciousness and processes represented as external to it, as alien: forces exerted by a network of origins, material and collective in their extent beyond personality. History, we recognize, is the other out of which the subject is constituted.

Correspondingly, we read in these novels the frequent thematic abstraction of 'romance'. When, at a crucial stage of his adventures, we are told that Waverley 'gave himself up to the romance of his situation', the term means something like 'psychological effect derived from imaginative literature'. Scott thus helped establish romance in its two dominant modern senses, objective and subjective: as a traditional literary form, and as a state of the imagination. As gentleman-scholar, Scott made an important contribution to the late-Enlightenment genre of antiquarian romance revival, collecting and editing native ballads and black-letter texts, the foundation of his move into 'Romantic' imitation. His own metrical and prose romances carry an enormous freight of not only historical documentation but quotation, allusion and imitation defining a canon of romance in its broadest sense: post-classical European vernacular fiction.[7] (Scott thus tropes the internationalism of Scots Renaissance and Enlightenment cultures, containing a relative English provincialism.) Scott exhibits an impressive historical attention to different kinds of romance, as the utterance of cultural mentalities within their historical moment. At the same time, they make up the texture and form of Scott's own narrative. With their (sometimes bewildering) episodic authority, they are projections of possible versions of the fiction itself. Certain models prevail: notably those capacious fictions that themselves contain a romance miscellany and define a national epos, British rather than Scottish or English, charting the limits and borders of history in their own formal complexities: Chaucer, Spenser, above all Shakespeare. In other words, a distinction between 'naive' and 'sentimental' romance, derived by Northrop Frye from Schiller, enters the novel in Scott's work, where it becomes the basis of his national fiction. In the following pages I shall describe the interplay of Ariosto, Spenser, Highland minstrelsy and antiquarian Scotch Tour narrative in *Waverley*; native and oriental, naive and sentimental romance typologies in *Guy Mannering*; the 'demonic' alienation of folk tradition, translated into Gothic narrativity, in *The Bride of Lammermoor*; and the Shakespearian mixed kind of tragi-comic romance in *The Heart of Mid-Lothian*.

Scott takes over, troping with brilliant inventiveness, the major eighteenth-century idea of romance, referred to in the previous chapter, as the narrative form of a historical otherness, a representation discontinuous with modern cultural formations. Scott derives the idea from the Scottish Enlightenment literati (Blair, Beattie and others), and indeed we find a rationalist reversal of the uncanny valence of the Gothic equation. Thus, however exotic or alien they appear, these forms are at the same time profoundly familiar. For they are the figures of our own ancestral past and of our own imagination constituted by that past. Their historical ground is that of traditional local communities now everywhere in dissolution. There are in fact two sources of romance: an antique courtly literature, and rural folk culture, even as the latter is being turned into literature in its preservation as 'romance'. This is the period of the institution of literary canons as well as of ballad 'revival'. What is lost in the present and what is found in the past are alike recovered for the individualist, class-specific act of reading. Romance, in these terms, is the aesthetic signifier of a specific historical process: the appropriation, and reinvention, of a 'common cultural heritage' as individual literary property. Not for nothing did James Hogg's mother, one of Scott's sources for the *Minstrelsy of the Scottish Border*, complain:

> there was never ane o' my sangs prentit till ye prentit them yoursell, an' ye hae spoilt them a'thegither. They war made for singing, an' no for reading; and they're nouther right spelled nor right setten down.[8]

It might seem that a romance figure of subjectivity would stand then in strong antithetical relation to progressive ideas of history, such as were promoted by the Whiggish intellectual culture of modern Edinburgh: the present imagined no longer in terms of the future but, as Hazlitt for one complained, of the past. Certainly romance signified on the one hand a cultural genealogy for the educated imagination. On the other, as literary acquisition of popular forms for aesthetic patronage, it reproduced the antique relation between gentry and folk in a 'patriarchal' culture, again as an imaginary property. Such a relation might be less remote to the experience of an educated Scottish reader than an English one in the early nineteenth century, and Scott himself could take astonishing pains to revive it practically (but still, in the end, only symbolically) on his estate at Abbotsford. The point is that the subject-position recovered in the relation is that of the gentry. The production of ancient patriarchal identity as an imaginary property, an aesthetic commodity, measured nevertheless the historical abolition of the real conditions of life – in particular, a dispersed yet 'organic' rural society of peasantry and freeholders – to which it appealed. One might speak of a kind of aesthetic enclosure movement, following hard upon the agrarian-economic one. Narrating the exemplary subjectivity of a genteel private patriarchy, Scott's novels mark the troubled fusion of culturally 'conservative' and economically 'progressive' imperatives that continues to inform capitalist state ideologies.[9]

The Waverley novels, like Scott's own autobiographical memoir, trope such a romance subjectivity (heroic Border chivalry, etc.) as an *inheritance*: claimed in the imagination of childhood and youth, naturally susceptible to the influences of legend and fable.[10] The intersection of this imaginary inheritance with the historical contingency of man's estate is the crux of the story, according to the scheme of *Bildungsroman*. In short: is that imaginary inheritance to be lost or found in 'life', in the great world? As it turns out, both. We may interpret two valences of romance in Scott, in fruitful tension with each other. First, romance signifies an individualist estrangement from real life, a puerile narcissism and egotistical delusion; in the progressive, rationalist ethos of a narrative of socialization, it is a condition to be outgrown or cured. This, the anti-romance theme of the modern novel, rhetorically governs the frame of *Waverley* and other novels. Second, however, romance signifies the heritage of a cultural identity that is lost but ethically true, an historically alienated ancestral patriarchy recalled in vision or legend. The field of the tension or contradiction between these versions of romance and history alike is the individual imagination: hence Scott's delivery of the subjective meaning of romance as map of the imagination, continent of the aesthetic and sentimental springs of a rational morality. The opposition between a 'romance of imagination' and 'real history' in the Waverley novels is thus complicated and delusive, as we shall see. Neither carries total authority, their dialectical complicity is insisted upon, they turn into each other. History is a compound of romance tropes, figures, episodes; a romance is historically embedded; just as there is no subject without a history, there can be no history without a subject. Romance and history name either side of a common border, the site of narrative experience, where identities become legible: for without borders there are no maps, and nothing to read.

A sophisticated view of Scott's grand question, such as Jane Millgate's of *Waverley*, interprets a progress from the first mode of romance to the second – from a false and individualistic to a true, communal identity – through the subject's moral and sentimental education: a tragi-comic fable of historical integration.[11] But the tenure of this scheme – its authority, precisely, to resolve its constituent oppositions – is troubled; so often do Scott's endings mark a discrepancy between the formal effects of romance closure and the other elements of the representation. The narrative logic of the relation between illusions lost and identity found tends to be obscure, tangled, devious: the 'blind roads' of Daniel Cottom's recent account. Let us glance at Scott's most thoroughgoing treatment of personal progress through civil war, *Old Mortality*, before our detailed engagement with the prototypical *Waverley*. Positivist editorial claims within the text, such as the example at the head of the present chapter, accompany the narrative of subject-formation across the field of history as an experience of radical privation, impotence, repression, with a purely ceremonial culmination, plotted as 'fortunate', or supplementary rather than teleological. The hero's entry onto the stage of public action is forced and accidental. Young Morton is rushed by the claims of others into a sequence of crises in which the loyalties and affections that bind him to a collective definition of his identity enter into harsh contradiction. In career as well as etiology ('stooping patiently to the control of a tyrannical and sordid relation ... [until provoked] by the rod of oppression and the spur of injured feeling') the hero's education consists of nothing so much as a concatenation of punishments and deprivations. In the final chapters, a fate of defeat, exile and the death of friends is belatedly turned around by a cluster of plot effects which Scott's pseudo-editorial apparatus intervenes to gloss as conventional, fictional, inauthentic, produced by the conditioned desire of readers (female, petty bourgeois) rather than by any high serious logic of history, which remains coincidental. In short: the character-revolution that marks Morton's accession to 'active manhood' redefines him in terms of an abstract cultural ideal that occupies no ground in the fierce process of the tale's 'history', save the intense but precarious position of dialectical protest; it can only preside, in a ghostly haunting, at the formal extremities of a novelistic resolution.

At the same time, let us not fail to take seriously how much more the Waverley novels do claim than the negative or antithetical recognition of historical process that such an account might suggest (F. R. Hart's 'history as fate' theme). As the turn of artistic betrayal at the end of *Old Mortality* makes mockingly explicit, their positivist charge is for our sake: a reader-subjectivity, to accommodate which the tale thus makes its romance apostasy. The end of history (with which Woolf's producer mocks her audience in *Between the Acts*) is 'the present time, ourselves'. In such terms we might begin to account for the odd, recurrent condition of the romance resolution in Scott already mentioned, a distance or disengagement marked for the reader within the text by the text's excessive closure upon its own mechanisms: the 'it's just a novel after all' effect. It is likelier that this strengthens than releases the fiction's hold. For here the act of reading itself becomes literalized as the focus of the romance project, not as a deprivation or reduction but as an elevation, a privilege. The comic recovery (or equally, as it will turn out in *The Bride of Lammermoor*, tragic loss) of a heritage tends thus to be a sentimental proposition in the strictly Schillerian sense of an imaginary relation constituted upon the loss of a real one. That is: historical being can only be rationally possessed, recognized, *as romance* – as a private aesthetic property, in the imagination, materially signified by the book we are holding. These are our stories because we have paid for them, just as their author paid for his 'ancestral' estate (but was never to stop paying for it.) Hero and heroine are to occupy a domestic scene of private life, an interior locus of moral and aesthetic feeling, separate from a field of history situated in the past. The realization of such a destiny is not so much 'in' the text, finally, as in the possession or hire of the text, according to whether one has paid the half-guinea per volume or the circulating library subscription; and in the act of reading, with the conditions of social security and economic leisure it assumes. This particular aesthetic effect is historically specific to a class of readers that could be addressed as simultaneously 'general' and privileged. In other words, the commodity status claimed so deviously and elaborately by these texts is the sign of their power over the imagination and their plenitude of meaning, rather than (as Scott's own depreciatory rhetoric might have tempted us to expect) weakness and hollowness.

Scott critics have tended to be divided between those who describe his greatness in terms of an important, if perhaps flawed, historical realism, morally valuable because it tells – however intermittently – the truth; and those who deny such truth or greatness, finding instead mere 'romance' – a self-advertising commodity, an aesthetic confection of materialism and escapism. Once more, and characteristically of Scott, both descriptions hold: only to say so is perhaps to privilege the latter – including as it does the former, rather than vice versa – as the more accurate account of a troublesome kind of artistic greatness, whereby the powerful pleasures and important truths offered by fiction are precisely those of its inauthenticity.[12]

II

In *Tom Jones* Fielding rejected the category of 'romance', no doubt because of its *ancien régime* and feminine cultural associations. In the opening chapters of *Waverley*, Scott resumes the canonical origins of modern romance in their rhetorical as well as historical aspect by engaging the principal figure – that of the erroneous reader – with which the novel had distinguished itself from a decadent fictional tradition. 'Anti-romance', as Scott knew from his reading, meant not the repudiation of fiction but the digestion of 'naive' precursor forms to constitute one's own sophistication, as in the great example of *Don Quixote*, a compound of different genres, only one among which is the chivalric romance it affects to renounce. Meanwhile, prose fiction in Scott's generation (we recall the lateness of his turn to the novel) was dominated by women authors: Maria Edgeworth, Amelia Opie, Sydney Morgan, Jane Austen, Mary Brunton, the Porter sisters (even Burney returned to print, after an eighteen-year gap, with *The Wanderer, or Female Difficulties*, in the same year as *Waverley*.) Although many of these authors were praised for their moral rectitude, it was a commonplace among the reviewers that the novel had declined into effeminacy since the golden age of Fielding and Richardson; and the stereotype of the idle reader continued to be female. We are warned early in *Waverley* that we are not about to read 'an imitation of the romance of Cervantes': the hero's imagination, insufficiently wild to transform its conditions, projects upon them more gently 'a tincture of its own romantic tone and colouring'.[13] In other words, Edward Waverley is less like Don Quixote, who rides out to force his visions on the world, than the generic type of eighteenth-century romance reader, the *female* quixote, whose imagination suspends her from intercourse with society.[14]

Scott drew upon the feminine figure of subjectivity, dominant in contemporary fiction, to resolve a cultural impasse in the representation of the virile hero, a generic problem of modern romance since its grand re-originations of the mid-eighteenth century. The problem was the combination of morally antithetical class principles of gentility and self-making. In brief, what relation should the traditional, 'heroic' figures of masculine enterprise, force and cunning, bear to the romance plot of a new dispensation – if they were not to license all kinds of subversive conduct, from social climbing to insurrection? The generous exertions of Tom Jones were exquisitely calibrated against a containing providential fable: the very artificial perfection of their relation suggests why it could not be imitated. Scott himself criticized Richardson's polemical alternative of the good man as hero, on the grounds that Grandison's social right always pre-empted the meaning of action as a basis for his character: he has never had to strive for what he has or is. Action, the commission of 'manliness', is instead sublimated into the feminine discourses of conversation and correspondence, and Sir Charles's conflicts internalized as moral dilemmas (what to do about poor Clementina, whether or not to fight duels), already determined by what and who he is. Godwin's deconstruction of the type by its code of honour in *Caleb Williams* is decisive. What is there, save good fortune, to arrest the declension of any powerful hero into the pathology of a Gothic villain?[15]

Alongside the blighted Squire Falkland we might set Ferdinand Count Fathom, Smollett's Gothic-picaresque development of the man of power as rootless, ambitious, aetiologically determined anti-hero. In *Humphry Clinker*, Smollett startles us by converting Fathom to the polar ethos of sensibility. This figure for private subjectivity, however, tended to define a textual space more radically remote from history or plot (action, politics, sexual activity), with elegiac emphasis in Mackenzie's *Man of Feeling*, and its richly prurient opposite in Sterne. With polite reverence Scott dedicated *Waverley* to Mackenzie. Donald Davie has referred Waverley to the type of the man of feeling,[16] but Scott has invigorated the chronically attenuated male with a fresher female essence, that of the romance heroine of Charlotte Smith and Ann Radcliffe. Invigorated, because of the deep, covert powers over the plot of the heroine's sensibility, so fertile to the influences of romance and so in synchrony with its providential turns: not despite but because of the restriction of her part to captivity and escape. A major concern of Scott's historical romance is the post-heroic situation of a genteel male subject within a comic destiny of private life, the genius of which has hitherto been female. In *Waverley*, the hero enjoys a feminine romance of subjectivity as the way to recovery of his patriarchal inheritance. It is an adventure made fit for heroic terms, as we shall find, by being committed decisively to the past: 'Most devoutly did he hope

. . . that it might never again be his lot to draw his sword in civil conflict' (283).

The pastness of heroic violence and the passivity of the hero of the Waverley novels, noted by Scott himself and his contemporaries, authoritatively described in our time by Alexander Welsh, are conditions of one another.[17] But that passivity means something else besides a disqualification from low-life masculine imperatives of action and ambition: it is culturally registered as a positively feminine characteristic, posed in the text just where our expectation is of an exemplary manliness. Narratorial apologies establish, as in complicity, a 'fair reader' of the narcissism and fickleness that make up the hero's 'wavering honour'. Midway in his adventure, Waverley – in figure 'rather elegant than robust' – dons the costume of the Jacobite cause:

> I hope my fair readers will excuse him if he looked at himself in the mirror more than once, and could not help acknowledging that the reflection seemed that of a very handsome young fellow . . . His blue eyes seemed of that kind,
>
> Which melted in love, and which kindled in war,
>
> and an air of bashfulness, which was in reality the effect of want of habitual intercourse with the world, gave interest to his features, without injuring their grace or intelligence.
>
> 'He's a pratty man – a very pratty man,' said Evan Dhu (now Ensign Maccombich) to Fergus's buxom landlady. (201)

Waverley is attired for 'intercourse with the world', which, as for one of Fanny Burney's maiden heroines, is about to take place at a ball, in the exchange of his own and others' admiring looks; only afterwards in battle. The looking-glass vision fixes subjectively Waverley's characteristic place, topographically as well as morally thematic in the novel and encoded in his name: being suspended on a border, a zone of 'wavering honour'. (And we recall that the eighteenth century marks the decisive shift of 'honour' from a masculine to feminine connotation.) He himself is cast as a feminine spectator (and we too, reading) admiring his own manliness, eyes looking into eyes responsive to male and female incandescence alike. The approval of the wild and hairy, bekilted Evan Dhu hits the right ironic note: an earlier remark has informed us that 'pretty' means not comely, but stout and warlike (81), but here, that meaning reflects back only – obsoletely – upon the speaker. In narcissistic and androgynous speculation, Waverley views the outward form of his own 'wavering honour', the motto of which might be, as for all of these novels: difference as the same.[18]

Such effeminate glamorization of martial address is characteristic of Waverley's youthful reading, which, although of romances of empire and chivalry, enfolds him from the world in a bower of mental bliss. Scott distinguishes his hero from the male quixotic type by describing the retirement of a vulnerable self from an alien society: 'he dreaded nothing more than the detection of such sentiments as were dictated by his musings' (18).[19] Like the female quixote's, Waverley's romance reading means a virginal suspension of the energies of selfhood in a narcissistic secrecy and solitude: desire sustains itself in the work of imagination, reflecting its energies back into itself. The early romance topic of Waverley's imagination is an 'honour' defined less by martial prowess than by erotic renunciation and sacrifice: the knight who returns from war to find his betrothed wed to her protector, the damsel who mourns a lover sacrificed (by a mother) for an imperilled Stuart prince. In fact these reflect Waverley's uncle's biography and the history to come, with its sacrifices and renunciations in the wake of a royalist lost cause. Like the female quixote's intimations of threatened and averted ravishment, they propose 'honour' as an erotic selfhood, awakened yet withheld from an external historical world characterized by its loss. Thus Waverley's adolescence:

> This secrecy became doubly precious, as he felt in advancing life the influence of the awakening passions. Female forms of exquisite grace and beauty began to mingle in his mental adventures; nor was he long without looking abroad to compare the creatures of his own imagination with the females of actual life. (19)

He doesn't find them in actual life. The exoskeletal charms of Miss Caecilia Stubbs cannot compete with his own: 'hoop, patches, frizzled locks, and a new mantua of genuine French silk, were lost upon a young officer of dragoons, who wore for the first time his gold-laced hat, boots, and broad sword' (23) (reducing the narrator of these tentative early chapters to an embarrassed chuckle of mock-heroic). A parody of one type of hero, Waverley has by internalizing the romance quest blocked it from external realization. He looks abroad for no authentic other, but the shadow of his own desire, a fetishistic completion of himself by himself, without expense of spirit in social traffic.[20]

The narrator tells us that Waverley's female quixotism occupies the failure of an education, which reflects a larger failure of patriarchal culture. Our hero has too many fathers because he lacks one, in whom biological paternity and patriarchal exemplarity might coincide. This problematical paternity rehearses the literary genealogy of the hero as female quixote. Waverley's slack youth follows, and complicates, the typical aetiology of female quixotism, that of (cf. the differently judged cases of Lennox's Arabella and Radcliffe's Emily) a paternal defection from worldly affairs. The heroine's sensibility flourishes in the rustic space of her father's retirement from public life. Waverley's blood-father Richard has deserted the family's traditional political and religious identity – all that 'Waverley honour' stands for – in the wake of its exclusion from historical power, to become the model of a modern politician. Richard Waverley consults 'reason and his own interest' to become 'an avowed Whig, and friend of the Hanover succession' (6), not as a means of elevation from low social rank but out of cadet resentment. He is the type not of a middle-class ambition, it seems, but of a dynastic betrayal of kind, like Milton's Satan or Shakespeare's Edmund: a diabolic displacement of the 'new man', then, jealous of a historical-class primogeniture. Richard Waverley's apostasy (for Scott the spirit's fall, fascinating archetype of the crossing of history and morality) signifies the loss of not just the public terms of his hereditary class identity, namely Catholicism and Royalism, but also its private quality of kindness or natural domestic affection. In the Scottish Waverley novels, human nature is almost always grounded historically in a traditional, patriarchal community of kinship and class relations. The prototype of Richard Waverley establishes a contradiction between 'honour' – one's traditional historical identity – and a rationally calculated, self-reliant devotion to the turns of historical fortune. From his father's lack of humankindness, the infant Waverley turns to his Jacobite uncle Sir Everard, who lives in retirement from public life, like St Aubert or the father of Lennox's Arabella, on the family estate of Waverley-Honour. Aetiology and setting thus define objectively the ethos of Waverley's romance-reading: an imaginary embowerment in a legendary ancestral past outside history, where 'Waverley honour' signifies not worldly power but the elegant nostalgia of its loss. Such identity is a property not of the will and action, but of imagination and feeling.

The contradiction between real and sentimental patrimony produces Waverley's character of an indeterminacy registered as feminine: a 'wavering honour', 'to one thing constant never', represented by the formal and ethical irregularities of romance. Adolescence, in the classical teleology of the *Bildungsroman*, is to be a narrative figure of change not as suspension in flux but as growth, progress, historical adjustment, into a completed destiny of manhood: Waverley honour. Most modern critics of *Waverley* have read the novel as the story of the hero's education, made homologous with a historical transition towards modernity.[21] Such a destiny is spoken for the hero, interestingly enough, by the book's impressive figure of an alternative, 'romance' and feminine deviation. Flora Mac-Ivor, local diva of ancestral honour, is also – Scott's characteristic crossing of pathos and irony – the prophetess of a post-heroic future. Waverley's 'real disposition', she notes, 'notwithstanding his dreams of tented fields and military honour, seemed exclusively domestic' (248). She advises him in the same language to seek 'a heart whose principal delight should be in augmenting your domestic felicity, and returning your affection, even to the height of romance' (135). Flora urges Waverley, in short, to recognize Waverley-Honour in rational and material terms, as a real historical place: not the romance phantasmagoria of his uncle's house, but the house itself. That rational recognition would confine the phantasmagoria to the imagination, where it belongs *as romance* – the aesthetic contemplation of a legend, comfortably indoors. The end of the hero's private history, the repossession of his heritage, will then take the proper manly form of a practical realization of the female quixote's rustic bower of pleasures of imagination:

> 'He would never have been his celebrated ancestor Sir Nigel, but only Sir Nigel's eulogist and poet. I will tell you where he will be at home, my dear, and in his place, – in the quiet circle of domestic happiness, lettered indolence, and elegant enjoyments, of Waverley-Honour. And he will refit the old library in the most exquisite Gothic taste, and garnish its shelves with the rarest and most valuable volumes; and he will draw plans and landscapes, and write verses, and rear temples, and dig grottoes; – and he will stand in a clear summer night in the colonnade before the hall, and gaze on the deer as they stray in the moonlight, or lie shadowed by the boughs of the huge old fantastic oaks; – and he will repeat verses to his beautiful wife, who will hang upon his arm; – and he will be a happy man.'
>
> 'And she will be a happy woman,' thought poor Rose. (250)

The fetishistic circle of Waverley's virginal and visionary self-absorption is to hold, enlarged into the 'quiet circle of domestic happiness' which is, like all bowers of bliss, the place of desire realized in artifice. The high stakes of military honour and dynastic politics are replaced by an aesthetic activity of scenic transformation: 'restoration', that is, as alteration no longer of an external scene of history, but of a private decor, in the mode of entertainment. The effect of this transformation is just as much as ever to exclude the world of public affairs, only now this exclusion is the sign and function of *leisure*, translated from its female-quixotic sense of vain idleness to become the emblem of a propertied gentry – no longer defined by the professionalized activities of war and politics but indeed, in Scott's case, the secret professionalization and reproduction of that leisure itself: by the writing of romances. And by the reading of them. In correspondence, Scott's readers are implicated in, and symbolically empowered by, this domain of privilege by the very ability to read, which signifies a certain education, control over one's time, access to an expensive commodity – if not (necessarily) a library of one's own. The fact that, thanks to the circulating libraries and in despite of the exorbitant cost of the

Waverley novels themselves, more and more people could share these status-markers had surely something to do with the assertion of exclusivity as well as an extraordinary 'popular' appeal.

An actual female reader may complain, like Maggie Tulliver, that she is being included out. 'Poor Rose' is figured into the scene as an ornamental detail, literally an appendage of the *beatus vir*. She figures herself into it as such: the silent insertion of her own subjectivity, 'And she will be a happy woman', takes the grammatical form of an echo, confirming it as the specular image of Waverley's, already there. The wife's function in the scene is to reflect back ('even to the height of romance') the completion of a male self. At the same time, the author writes the scene as a female fantasy, part of a conversation between Rose and Flora. Waverley's height of romance is represented to be a female project, a collaboration between Rose's dream and Flora's – let us not forget – satiric, even contemptuous utterance, in her piquant role as the sibyl of old romance allowed, by a principle of historical dialogism I shall examine later, to be the cold clear voice announcing what Alexander Welsh has called the new 'romance of property'.[22]

Property as theft: in the romance of property, Welsh argues, possession is marked off from the historical forces of its acquisition.[23] So we find possession figured as, first, aristocratic (hereditary, thus always-already) and second, feminine, where the subject is herself the thing possessed. Women cannot legally acquire property by their own deed or will; they are to be kept innocent of male historical energies of desire and ambition. At the same time they are the inhabitants of the household, it is their material, as well as symbolic, interior space. They are the genius of the property. Two of Scott's principal figures (I am modifying Welsh's romance typology of 'dark and fair' characters) are the male hero whose sensibility represents the appropriation of this domestic space of private life, and the strong women – maid and matriarch – who deliver up its spiritual essence, its romance energy, to the hero. The Victorians justly admired Scott's strong female characters; but the logic of that admiration converted the strong into the weak heroine precisely around the axis of her purity, and female strength into a demonic force.[24] What is represented as a cultural given in the Victorian novel is, as so often, represented as in historical process by Scott: women hold power (natural, magical, 'romance') in order to give it up to men. In my next chapter I shall discuss the variants of this myth in some later novels. Its dynamic constructs the famous divided-heroine convention, described by Welsh and Frye.[25] The so-called 'dark' heroine, in Scott a figure not of dalliance but of passionate moral rectitude, submits to the historical type (fair, mild) of domestic submission: in effect, donates her own magic to the domicile. Flora's encouragement of Rose evokes a contrast between a generic, classical, high-literary diva, too wild to flourish in any garden, and the local, domestic blossom of a new representation: Waverley will count the streaks on the tulip.

Rose Bradwardine is more interesting than a casual reading might grant. Her understatement betrays her secret power; Waverley's domestication, the 'height of romance' prophesied by Flora, is actually Rose's project. She comes closest to personifying the structural function of the heroine's atmospheric desire in Radcliffian romance. She manages much of our hero's progress, to the extent of arranging the spectacular rescue-kidnapping that decisively commits him to the Jacobite cause. Thus it is only the claim of a rival autonomy that separates the 'dark', visionary heroine, who must suffer exclusion, from the 'fair' feminine heroine who must (rather strenuously) position herself as the hero's mate. Both represent stations of authentic power in the narrative. Flora, so like many of Scott's maidens and matriarchs, is more virile than the hero in her strength and resolve. Scott's famous sneer at Waverley, as 'a piece of sneaking imbecility', goes on to imagine what a marriage between them would have been like: 'she would have set him up upon the chimney-piece as Count Boralaski's wife used to do with him'.[26] The fantasy, for all its jocularity, expresses a characteristic thematic anxiety of many of Scott's novels. What if the mild male hero remain, all the time, but the property of a female dominance, his passivity merely impotence? The romance-precursor looming behind these intimations is Mother Radcliffe, whose Valancourt is close kin to Waverley. The image of her own imperilled sensibility, formed by the heroine's desiring nostalgia in the ideal father's empty place – such a hero is the shadow of *her* self-completeness, disabled and tamed for the situation (Valancourt's rites of passage include wounding by gunfire). The hero may turn out after all to be the figure on the other side of the mirror: androgyny the figure of his loss rather than plenitude. The romance scheme Scott takes over has a risky valence, that of the male's anxiety about being in the passive position, even as he begins to fear that this may in fact be his true relation to historical power; that home, the mansion of a new subjectivity, may only be the cell of his subjection.

Thus Scott binds himself to the dualistic figuration of sexual archetypes from the Gothic. 'Wavering' is both figure of a hesitation between gender poles, and figure of one of them, the feminine – as the contamination, the destabilization, the diminution of the male. Any ambiguity signifies a possession by the opposite term, and it is the negative pole, the female, that has decisive effect on the hero's destiny. In *The Bride of Lammermoor*, as I shall argue, the dread of being the object of both patriarchal force and feminine sexual influence appears, garishly, as the violation of the bridegroom, in a joint figure of rape and castration.

In *Waverley* however we read Scott's normative solution, the *restoration* of romance power from women to men. In exorcism of the spectre of castration, women pour forth their natural-magical energies of healing upon the hero, disoriented and disabled at the labyrinthine centre of his adventure.[27] The complicity of women is the source of energy – the private current of romance – that flows behind the scenes of male history. Its familiar end is in self-cancellation, a consenting exclusion from those scenes, absorption into the male as its shadow. Waverley's story unveils its own official version in the last chapter, at the festive rites of the homecoming, in the form of a painting commemorating the hero's Jacobite adventure (338). It depicts a patriarchal and fraternal heroism – Waverley posed by Fergus Mac-Ivor and a background of clansmen. However, this is hardly the story we have read. Conspicuously absent is Flora, the spirit of the Cause for both men, and as such the focus of their undignified contention: the occasion of Waverley's folly, Fergus's arrogant conniving. A more accurate picture of Waverley's outlaw career might have shown him – in the thick of it – supine on his sickbed, ignorant of his place or the identities of his guardians, Rose Bradwardine, old Janet Gellatley and Alice Bean Lean. To be hero of a manly version of the romance, however, Waverley has had to become a mere image, part of the decor – just as if he had made that marriage to Flora after all. Her voice, that had prophesied his domestic triumph, is decisive in its silence.

III

History is the narrative of the loss of patriarchy, both in the objective sense of the passing of heroic, feudal or clan societies, and in the subjective sense (we shall see) of a personal recognition of impotence and mortality. At the same time the subject's recognition of himself as historically determined is to situate his security from historical contingency. 'Military honour', the nominal matter of Waverley's romance reading, is the title of an obsolescent aristocratic ideology, for owning property need no longer signify having fought for it. Scott's narrative of the '45 addresses the resurgence of that ideology into modern history; Jacobitism stands for the reversal by force of history's current, the military and political restoration of an ancient estate. As such, across the spectrum of views and motives revealed in the novel, it is at least two things: the return of an original patriarchal community, and a foreign invasion. What we read is the complex, precarious fable of the achievement of the former as a private event, across the public failure of the latter.

The revival of ancient chivalry corresponds to the revival of romance, in an allegory of genre by which the novel relates the history of its own cultural formation. Scott represents the fate of the Jacobite rising as a failure to recover military honour from romance for history. The figure becomes increasingly inauthentic as it is removed from the local ground of its original community. As the rebellion marches south – away from Highland minstrelsy, the standard at Glenfinnan, the loyalty of the clans – we discover that the subject-matter of glorious feats of arms loses its hold over the plot, until it at last disintegrates into 'a chapter of accidents', in which Fergus and Waverley are lost in a petty skirmish. 'Military honour' may achieve genuine effects of heroism and pathos, as we witness at Prestonpans, but insofar as it names an individual action, it no longer commands authority over the historical event.

Indeed, such heroism is inescapably pathetic in its bind to tableaux of valour in death or defeat. Colonel Gardiner is cut down by a rabble of Highlanders, Waverley rescues Talbot from the same fate. Military honour glows forth, as an individual and sentimental aura, only at its moment of disconnection from the logic of historical action. The story's exemplary instance of military honour is the exchange of courtesies between Waverley and Talbot across its last half. This takes place upon the protagonists' abstraction from the field of action (they are prisoners), or as a refusal of the logic of military action that works as a transcendence of its political motives. Each officer releases the other from the gravest historical consequences of his adventure, in the higher cause of domestic kindness, according to a class discourse of manners. Waverley protects Talbot because he recognizes him as 'an English officer, apparently of high rank' (225), and sets him free for the sake of his wife, suffering in childbed; while Talbot looks out for Waverley because of an old connection with his uncle. Talbot's wife lies at the source of both gestures of salvation, for she is none other than that first love over whom Sir Everard, once upon a time, renounced his claim. In short, military honour works at the service of the romance of domestic felicity, and by the novel's ideological master-trope: the articulation of a 'new', sentimental and domestic discourse of community and kinship as private property, by an 'ancient' discourse of feudal social relations. For Waverley and Talbot, class identity and private feeling together transcend the categories of national and party-political difference generated by 'modern' historical process. (This plot-figure recurs in *Old Mortality*, in the more tortuous and painful 'race of honour' between Morton and Evandale.) Waverley's strenuous good manners eventually save him; they prove that he has kept his honour because he has never really betrayed his class loyalties. Even his apostasy is based upon a generous respect for what the chauvinistic Talbot sneers at, the claims of many of these exotic, disenfranchised and impoverished Scotchmen to be gentlemen.

This private kindness is a function of a traditional class relation. We see the Jacobite cause, in contrast, as the exploitation of such relations for the dubious aggrandisement of its potentates: Fergus with his swollen Mac-Ivor retinue is the prime example. Waverley's desertion of his own tenants, far from home (the recognition of the dying Houghton, 216–19), is the gravest moral symptom of his complicity. Yet all turns out well, in piquant contrast to the fate of his father, who dies dishonoured even though he has not taken part in the rebellion. Richard Waverley, too mean to sacrifice himself for any conviction, pays the penalty at last of his original, more drastic treason, the betrayal of Waverley honour at the beginning of the story. His fate is a curious, inverted analogue of the rebellion's failure. For the great destructive irony of the Jacobite cause is that it betrays itself as soon as it becomes a historical intervention, that is, as soon as it re-enters national politics. The restoration of the elder dynasty flourishes in the forms of, precisely, 'romance revival': the nostalgic apprehension of vanishing ways of life, the glamorous relics of a fierce barbarism, in short all the stuff of Highland minstrelsy, cherished in a civilized ear. But as a historical project, that restoration is at once sustained and spoilt by short-term claims of individual ambition and opportunity.

Scott marks this revival of an ancient chivalry, mounted and betrayed by a continental, Catholic and absolutist court intrigue, with the allegory of genre, in this case Italian, specifically Ariostian romance.[28] Scott allusively revives the Renaissance mixed genre of romance epic as a formal allegory of his own project, whereby romance signifies the imaginary figures of private desire, and epic, the command of history. The Italian romance, read through British Protestant (i.e. Spenserian and Miltonic) spectacles, is purely fantastic, the marvellous glittering evasion of a history defined by the cynicism and ferocity of a Catholic court politics. Charles Edward Stuart is the 'Chevalier', 'an Italian knight-errant' (241, 274), archetype of deviation from epic and historic destiny for a delusive private quest. The novel last represents the Chevalier's history, or rather 'adventure', in a chapter of farcical muddle called 'The Confusion of King Agramant's Camp', in which we see his cause squandered upon petty quarrels and schemes for advancement, absurd punctilios of vanity and misconstrued love-plights. Charles Edward shows his royal mettle as broker and go-between. He himself is an equivocal figure, both Prince and Pretender, 'rather like a hero of romance than a calculating politician' (206), meaning that his talents lie in settling erotic intrigues and presenting a glamorous appearance. His court, however, is thoroughly political, a parody of the Hanover-rat world it seeks to replace. The principle of this romance turns out to be, as in Boiardo or Ariosto, 'intrigue', or plot in the sense of private complication: for it never translates itself into the public plot of history. The early military success at Prestonpans signifies not a political but a romance effect – the overwhelming impression made by an irregular and exotic spectacle.

Waverley, committed to the Cause, views the Jacobite army as it begins to march south out of Edinburgh. At first, as the traditional simile indicates, the spectacle suggests a mixture of romance and epic in which the latter kind's historical seriousness, marked by 'order and regularity', prevails:

> The mountaineers . . . with the hum and bustle of a confused and irregular multitude, like bees alarmed and arming in their hives, seemed to possess all the pliability of movement fitted to execute military manoeuvres. Their motions appeared spontaneous and confused, but the result was order and regularity; so that a general must have praised the conclusion, although a martinet might have ridiculed the method by which it was attained. (212)

But as the host gets moving, the formal principles of romance become insistent: it is a 'complicated medley', 'a gay and lively spectacle', 'a changing, fluctuating, and confused appearance', a 'mixed and wavering multitude'. The Chevalier displays his standard, 'a red cross upon a white ground', but he cannot be St George, only an Archimago double. The tone sinks toward burlesque: certain 'heroes', hurrying to catch up from their sojourn among 'the Circes of the High Street', contribute 'to the picturesque wildness, though not to the military regularity of the scene'. As Waverley draws near, an aesthetically impressive spectacle disintegrates into its social historical raw ingredients: 'the peasantry of the country', despite their own claims to clan gentility, have been 'forced into the field by the arbitrary authority of the chieftains under whom they hewed wood and drew water . . . sparingly fed, ill dressed, and worse armed', like Falstaff's militia:

> From this it happened, that, in bodies, the van of which were admirably well-armed in their own fashion, the rear resembled actual banditti. Here was a pole-axe, there a sword without a scabbard; here a gun without a lock, there a scythe set straight upon a pole; and some had only their dirks, and bludgeons or stakes pulled out of hedges. The grim, uncombed, and wild appearance of these men, most of whom gazed with all the admiration of ignorance upon the most ordinary productions of domestic art, created surprise in the Lowlands, but it also created terror. So little was the condition of the Highlands known at that late period, that the character and appearance of their population, while thus sallying forth as military adventurers, conveyed to the south country Lowlanders as much surprise as if an invasion of African negroes, or Esquimaux Indians, had issued forth from the northern mountains of their own native country. (214)

We read a variant of the uncanny turn of Gothic: the rebellion as a barbaric alien invasion. At the same time it is the turn of the historical real. 'Picturesque confusion' has become the image of a landless mob, a *jacquerie*, a peasant rising. (Burke in a famous passage of the *Reflections* had compared the revolutionary citizens to 'American savages'.)[29] We read, in this scene, the declension of Scott's Jacobite romance toward its own figures of 'real history', something I will return to at the end of this chapter. For conservative Britons, Republican France provided the demonology of modern historical tendencies. As the

Jacobite adventure shifts away from its native romance ground, it becomes an alien but all-too-native Jacobin rabble, more and more dependent upon French influence: it really is a foreign invasion.[30]

The rebellion's failure as a movement of the native ground is marked, then, by an alien contamination, French politics. Those politics betray it, for in politics loyalty is instrumental to party interests, as defined by the class of professional politicians. The formidable Mac-Ivor siblings, devout Jacobites, are Frenchified Scots, a sophistication of their natural sublimity of character; less so in the case of Flora, a pure woman who accepts her own, 'natural', disenfranchisement, than in that of Fergus, whose original generosity and honour, grounded in his identity as clan chieftain, are tainted by vanity and ambition. Waverley comes to view him as 'a second Lucifer of ambition and wrath' (267); while a subtler sulphurous whiff, conveyed by echoes and allusions to the first two books of *Paradise Lost*, alerts the judicious reader to the true character of the enterprise concealed behind the stag-hunt at the beginning of the second volume. A less noble and more industrious devil of the cause is the leader of the Highland banditti, Donald Bean Lean, also a Frenchified Scot, and something of an Autolycus or trickster figure. He stands for the true 'liberty' of a sort of natural politics of self-interest, a Richard Waverley on the other side of the law. At the same time, he is actually the agent of the major turns of Waverley's Jacobite career, defining it in the terms I have been describing. Waverley's involvement owes less to any authentic romance of Jacobitism on his own part than to a series of delusions, the effects of the cateran's opportunistic tricks, as the latter is bribed to gull, prompt and kidnap him along the labyrinthine track of his misallegiance.[31] This shape-shifter's effective ally is the blatant beast of slander and misprision, whose hunting-ground is party politics, on the side of the law.

The charming figure of Charles Edward Stuart has not come so far, in *Waverley*, from the offstage archetype of a fraudulent or erroneous confusion of true identity in the novels of Fielding and Smollett (Sophia mistaken for Jenny Cameron; the sinister

Count Fathom for the 'Adventurer' himself). Waverley's personal career of military honour offers a synecdoche of the Jacobite cause: a romance revival supported, and thus betrayed, by party-political aetiologies of ambition, guile and intrigue that, as romance, it cannot acknowledge.

IV

With a desire of amusement therefore, which better discipline might soon have converted into a thirst for knowledge, young Waverley drove through a sea of books, like a vessel without a pilot or rudder. (13)

In the famous narrative figure of Italian romance, Waverley's imagination is bound to no direction, but moves in and for itself, in the digression of an eternal present tense.[32] Scott names this reading with a double irony Waverley's 'education', for in fact his failure of purpose will save his neck.

As the narrative unfolds, the most frequent comment about Waverley's character identifies his inattention or 'absence' with regard to the manly ethical teleologies of duty and purpose. His progress into the Highlands literalizes the female-quixotic manner and setting of his romance-reading: it is not a 'quest', but deviation from a quest, a private retreat. The first step in a cumulative series of acts of inattention is to take a 'leave of absence' from his regiment, inspired by 'a curiosity to know something more of Scotland' (31–2). This extension of a romance pleasure-principle disconnects Waverley, stage by stage, from nominal political subjection, and from the historical terms of his 'military honour'. Adrift from familiar geographical and linguistic orders of meaning, he '[gives] himself up to the full romance of his situation' (78), yielding to a narrative principle of present diversion which will culminate in the Spenserian, and Radcliffian, sequence of abduction and rescue. Like a heroine's, his ignorance and helplessness will be the index of the purposeful agitation of his environment.

Waverley's Jacobite adventure follows the Ariostian mode of delusive enchantment and deviation from an epic plot of historic destiny, personified in the Chevalier. Scott registers the gravity of the embedded Virgilian counter-terms: such romance deviation is a surrender to the feminine and private force of eros, the flouting of an official *pietas*. Among Waverley's other favourite authors is Ariosto's English Protestant successor, Spenser, who wedded Ariostian delight to powers of instruction praised by Milton himself.[33] We might describe one of the themes of instruction in *Waverley* as that of reading according to Spenser rather than Ariosto; that is, reading *allegorically*, alert to historical and ethical figuration. The allegory of romance in *Waverley* can be plotted suggestively within the terms of *The Faerie Queene*, where the chivalric quest signifies the service of desire to state ideology. Such a theme, I shall be arguing, moves between the strict-allegorical or anti-romance model of Spenser's first and second books, in which romance yields an artificial bower of bliss that disastrously interrupts and substitutes the quest, requiring drastic disenchantment; and the romance of the sixth book, in which digression from and forgetfulness of the political arena, and sublimation of its terms in aesthetic play, recover private sources of meaning and identity in the imagination. Meanwhile, Waverley's public fate takes the form of a negotiation between the themes of Spenser's fourth and fifth books: friendship, a private virtue, and justice, the stern logic of state power and legality. We recall that Spenser's formal transfiguration of romance takes place through the great re-troping of the Ariostian romance of indirection, under the spell of eros or 'kind', in his third book, in which the transcendental origin, end and centre of being occupies the deepest narrative digression, inaccessible to all quests even as it contains them.[34] What kind of an equivalent to those gardens of Adonis might we find in *Waverley*?

Waverley's errancy involves a sequence of digressions, curiosity giving way to further curiosity. The authentic site of romance seems to fold itself multiply away from a heroic trajectory of commitment, cause and consequence. Scott makes marvellously Spenserian play with narrative topologies of beginnings and ends, middles and centres, borders and thresholds: place always turns out to be liminal rather than original or final in Scott, because it is always a stage in history. Waverley happens upon two feminine bowers, two 'original' versions of his romance imagination: Rose's parlour and garden at Tully-Veolan, and Flora's Highland glen. Each place represents a generative centre of the voice and figures of romance, tended by a female genius. The second of these, Flora's glen, seems to be the thing itself: the secret centre only attained via an involution of digressions, matrix of the wild, native spirit of romance of which Rose's parlour minstrelsy has offered but a polite relic, an ornamental replica. Flora speaks:

> 'I have given you the trouble of walking to this spot, Captain Waverley, both because I thought the scenery would interest you, and because a Highland song would suffer still more from my imperfect translation, were I to introduce it without its own wild and appropriate accompaniments. To speak in the poetical language of my country, the seat of the Celtic muse is in the mist of the secret and solitary hill, and her voice in the murmur of the mountain stream. He who wooes her must love the barren rock more than the fertile valley, and the solitude of the desert better than the festivity of the hall.'
>
> Few could have heard this lovely woman make this declaration, with a voice where harmony was exalted by pathos, without exclaiming that the muse whom she invoked could never find a more appropriate representative. But Waverley, though the thought rushed on his mind, found no courage to utter it. Indeed, the wild feeling of romantic delight with which he heard the first few notes she drew from her instrument, amounted almost to a sense of pain. He would not for worlds have quitted his place by her side; yet he almost longed for solitude, that he might decipher and examine at leisure the complication of emotions which now agitated his bosom. (106–7)

Scott makes characteristically deft play with his conventions. As Flora reminds Waverley in 1745, the spirit of romance is the spirit of solitude. The voice of the *genius loci* thrills with the pathos of an exclusion from historical life, prophesying the desolation which will overtake herself, her brother and all the people of the clans. At the same time, Flora's role as Celtic muse is directly compromised by her role as spirit of the Jacobite Cause. This is what is veiled from Waverley in the scene, and constitutes his failure to read allegorically. Waverley views Flora as 'a fair enchantress of Boiardo or Ariosto' (106), but he fails to interpret the convention his imagination has called up. Flora herself may resist the role of temptress; but Waverley's dream of an honour beyond political subjection and Fergus's suggestive management cast her in the part, for one lesson of this adventure is that few people's intentions or motives coincide with the parts they play in history. On Waverley's part, as soon as *otium* admits erotic desire, and thus the pressure of purpose, it admits ambition, it admits politics; for, as Fergus makes clear, union with Flora means union with the Cause. The *genius loci* is no longer spirit of silence and solitude, but of political ambition and foreign intrigue. The present scene of romance digression, far from being a retreat, is in the thick of the plot of history, and Waverley's 'curiosity' a sedulous inattention to political meanings. He listens to Flora's song as a purely aesthetic event; however it is not just a relict of Highland minstrelsy but a Jacobite call to arms (107–9). In the same way, as we have seen, a 'Spenserian', historical and ethical attention to the romance spectacle will convert the Prince into a Pretender, his regiment into a feral mob. Waverley's furthest digression, 'a day's journey to the northward of Glennaquoich' (116), brings him to the ceremonial theatre of Highland minstrelsy and a mode of pure recreation or diversion, signalled by a stylistic relaxation which tempts the reader into reproducing the hero's inattention. Released from the imperatives of story, the narrator extends his elbows, to claim a 'natural style of composition' in 'what scholars call the periphrastic and ambagitory, and the vulgar the circumbendibus' (116). At the same time, however, he reminds us of the ambiguous contract of authority and subjection upon which our reading depends; and the play of Miltonic allusions to the devil's party throughout the chapter invokes tactfully an allegorical alertness.

At the same time as all of this, Flora is not herself an Acrasia or Alcina but a pure woman, an authentic vessel of romance semiosis, and she speaks the truth, or rather, it speaks through her, against her knowledge. I have already mentioned her prophetic character, one of Scott's many interesting, ironical variations upon the dilemma of Cassandra: here, to speak another truth than the one she intends. As she herself admits, her song is a translation, literally, the movement of the spirit, by putting it into words, into another place: that of historical meaning. Contradiction and ambiguity haunt her speech: 'He who wooes her must love the barren rock more than the fertile valley, and the solitude of the desert more than the festivity of the hall': a simultaneous affirmation of solitude and invitation to courtship. Waverley comes to understand the latter, preferring her of the rugged glen (Flora) over her of the fertile valley and festive hall (Rose). Only by the end will the full sense become clear, that those who woo the Cause will espouse the desolation of history, in which the festive hall is lain waste.

But Waverley's desire for Flora, prompted by her scheming brother, is sophisticated, tendentious; his spontaneous intuition, responding to 'the first few notes she drew from her instrument' before he hears the 'imperfect translation', is authentic. Waverley's 'wild feeling of romantic delight' comprehends the pathos of the exclusion from history, but with the compensatory impulse of silence and retreat, converting that external solitude into an internal, private speculation, into *reading*. In other words, the pathos becomes aesthetic pleasure by the inward turn of the sensibility upon itself in the scrutiny of its own 'complication of emotions' in solitary tranquillity. This aesthetic turn is that of Waverley's narrative destination, the strategy of accommodation of his female quixotism. The spirit of romance is indeed to be recovered outside historical meaning, in the poignancy of private feeling, as a sign of the exclusion, the pastness, the death of its collective forms of life, and the corresponding detachment of the liberal subject.[35]

The scene in the glen, a height of romance that covers a depth of history, articulates then the relationship between the modes: their fateful collapse into one another. Clean of worldly ambition for her own sake, Flora embodies the fierce purity of the Cause at its romance origin, and thus also its 'tragic' historical destiny. She has always been characterized as type of 'the melancholy muse' (101; a *Penserosa* from one of Collins's romance-revival odes), and will take her place in 'the solitude of the desert', a foreign convent. Likewise, as her poem about

Captain Wogan should have warned Waverley, she can only espouse a dead hero. Her brother, to share her sublime status, has to suffer judicial dismemberment: 'She will then think of Fergus as of the heroes of our race, upon whose deeds she loved to dwell' (327). The magnificent recovery of a heroic identity takes place in the absolute exclusion from history, in death. The chieftain and his clansmen are able at last to stage their tribal honour at the Carlisle Assizes; defeat and death mark its ritual depoliticization, its purification to a condition of 'spirit'.

Heroic death for others, sedentary life for a subject who looks on: we read the elegiac structure of sentimental romance. For Waverley's absence, the ethos of romance, is just what saves him from the death sentence of historical engagement. The hero's passivity entails not a failure of action so much as one of purposeful commitment. Waverley can be pardoned because his will was never at the origin of his treasonable involvement. The anecdote of Waverley's inattention to 'the violent altercation between [Fergus Mac-Ivor] and young Corrinaschian, whether the post of honour is due to the eldest cadet of a clan or the youngest' (249), illustrates his abstraction from political discourse as such, exemplified by this type of honour, the very matter of his father's profession of politics and of the Stuart cause. The hero's romance inattention is the sign of an unworldliness that is spiritually valuable, endorsed by the providential turns of the plot. The darker purposes of Waverley's destiny are realized in their absence from conscious purpose. Scott's psychological model might be more 'primitive', but is not less complex or sophisticated, than Freud's: there is no mental unconscious – rather, its register is external, scenic and demonic, accompanied by a necessary, problematical and thus figuratively fertile denial on the part of a supposedly total rational consciousness (that of 'the narrator'). Thus, the hero's accidental, semi-voluntary participation in national rebellion results in the removal and replacement of his bad father and in his possession of the family estate, or rather, by inheritance and dowry, of two such estates.

Scott overdetermines the romance narrative more scrupulously than has his model, Radcliffe, in the emphasis of his hero's rational disconnection from the scene over the Gothic heroine's emotional saturation within it. This is evident in the narrative schemes of character doubling that support the hero's passivity. His absence at the centre of the plot is complemented by the agency and purpose of *others*, who intend, decide and act in his place. I have already described this as the principle both of the feminine achievement of a domestic bower of bliss, and of Waverley's embroilment in the Jacobite Cause: what the narrative calls its 'intrigues of love and politics' (241). There never was a synchronized coherence of will and action with the shift of events, but a quite 'accidental', 'intricate' complicity between the ubiquitous plotting of those such as Donald Bean Lean behind the scene and Waverley's disengagement within it. The history moves thus upon the narrative logic of romance: 'the mazes of the labyrinth, in which [Waverley] had been engaged' (309). Waverley is both implicated in the plot and released from it by the covert commitment of proxies: women, whose desire substitutes his in the metonymic structure of donation or influence we have already looked at; and other men, whose action substitutes his, condemning him to death but also rescuing him from it, in a metaphoric structure of sacrifice. For as Welsh's account recognizes, this means that others also die in his place. Waverley commits treason that is not really treason, parricide that is not really parricide, while around him surrogate traitors and parricides play out these roles to their harsh conclusions. Waverley's adventure is articulated upon a series of such episodes: his senior officer is cut down by his clan 'brothers' ('a parricide committed in his presence', 221), Fergus ceremonially butchered, Donald hanged. (Nor should we forget a comic surrogate parricide, Malcolm of Inch-Grabbit.) The quirkiest of these turns is the literal one, already noted, by which his own father dies for Waverley's treason – since the father, not Waverley, is the real traitor, then this is not really parricide:

– Good God! am I then a parricide? – Impossible! my father, who never shewed the affection of a father while he lived, cannot have been so much affected by my supposed death as to hasten his own; no, I will not believe it, – it were distraction to entertain for a moment such a horrible idea. But it were, if possible, worse than parricide to suffer any danger to hang over my noble and generous uncle, who has ever been more to me than a father, if such evil can be averted by any sacrifice on my part! (284)

We note the quick displacement of the literal relation, no sooner admitted than dismissed as a distraction too horrible to entertain, into a symbolic register of sentimental excess ('worse than parricide', 'more to me than a father'). The sacrifices, meanwhile, are required on the part of others.

If the novel is to yield us a figure corresponding to Spenser's Gardens of Adonis – a romance centre emblematic of the narrative itself, secret original place where a stricken, condemned youth is restored by the circulation of erotic energies – we can find it in the episode, mentioned in the first part of this chapter, of Waverley's rescue and cure.[36] Strong wild men have snatched him from captivity and carried him through the woods, mysterious women watch over him. Here, at the zero degree of his heroic career, he is reduced to a condition of pure receptivity to female donation, utterly disoriented, that is, 'innocent' of the strenuously plotted activity around him. He does not know that this confinement is the site of his real destiny, Tully-Veolan, or that the 'tutelar genius' that flits about his couch is Rose. All that is left Waverley is the elemental posture of his character, which is also that of the reader: the posture of *a stranger who looks*:

Through this minute aperture he could perceive a female form, wrapped in a plaid, in the act of conversing with Janet. But, since the days of our grandmother Eve, the gratification of inordinate curiosity has generally borne its penalty in disappointment. (180)

Surrounded by a mysterious female influence, it is Waverley who reproduces the heritage of grandmother Eve: an inordinate curiosity doomed to disappointment – but thus to final reward.

V

Ah that distance! what a magician for conjuring up scenes of joy or sorrow, smoothing all asperities, reconciling all incongruities, veiling all absurdness, softening every coarseness, doubling every effect by the influences of the imagination ... to be in the midst of the bustle is incongruous and unpleasant from the contradictions which it involves. (Scott, *Journal*, 8 April 1826)

Waverley's 'curiosity to know something more of Scotland' invokes another historically local narrative, the Highland tour. The incidence of tour figures has been well noted by commentators, who have tended to interpret them as markers of the error of the hero's vision in the first half of the story. The most striking of these figures is the picturesque prospect, also characteristic of Radcliffe romance, as described in the last chapter. We find Waverley repeatedly transfixing the scene into a view, modelled on Claude or Poussin or Salvator Rosa, of which he is the aesthetically detached spectator. As in the case of Radcliffe, this works as a suspension or repression – in pictorial terms, a *backgrounding* – of plot, in keeping with Waverley's narrative deviation from historical duty. Unlike Radcliffe, Scott gives the pictorial enactment of Waverley's romance-reading an ironic structure: the hero turns out to be most implicated in historical and political meanings just when he seems most remote and free from them. The allegorical hermeneutic becomes one, then, of penetrating the picture, apprehending its detail, engaging its figures as those of an unfolding plot.[37] However, the reader's understanding of the plot in *Waverley* tends to follow a different course, that of the temporal trope of retrospect: history as a pattern that belongs to the past. If we examine the Highland tour as a late-eighteenth-century genre occupied with the narrative relationship between romance matter and historical and regional setting, we understand a stronger exemplary force for Scott's novel, one that provides for the sentimental and elegiac turn I am describing.

The historical significance of the tour is that it marks the pacification and domestication of the Highlands, especially in the decades after 1745, when the genre began to flourish.[38] Scott, from *The Lady of the Lake* onwards, instigated something like the industrial-scale expansion of Scottish tourism; he himself, at Abbotsford, was soon a prominent feature on genteel itineraries. If the 'National Tale' of Maria Edgeworth and Sydney Owenson (Lady Morgan) made the journey to the Celtic fringe a popular novelistic device in the decade before *Waverley*, the two most striking Scottish examples are by eighteenth-century authors whom Scott particularly admired, Johnson and Smollett. The spiritual goal of the tour is to imagine the regional as the archaic: according to the philosophical historians, the Highlands are the geographical space of an earlier historical phase, of primitive and authentic types of patriarchal life, not merely (as in Defoe, agent of the Union) a desert or wild waste. Except that of course the modern Highlands are a desert – one created by human, historical, civilizing forces. With the suppression of the clans, the national-imperial emargination of local economies and the emigration of populations, the Highlands are a site beyond history because after it. Smollett's *Humphry Clinker* expedition found an aesthetic purification, beyond the social-historical mimesis of satire (register of the diseased, the 'sophisticated'), in a private Scottish feudal preserve that authenticated the figures of romance with a personal, biographical origin: that of the author himself. Johnson, visiting the Highlands *in propria persona* in search of 'an antiquated system of life', located it only in the figures and moods of romance, which signified its passing.[39] The years of the Waverley novels were marked by the acceleration of this passing: the post-war recession meant the final collapse of the old Highland economy and an intensification of the forced clearance of estates for sheep. In short, for Waverley in 1745, the Scotch tour – in contrast to an Ariostian extravagance of phantasmagoric chivalry – represents a historically progressive narrative register for the relation between real history and romance revival. As such, it constitutes the authoritative form of the hero's destiny.

Thus, we saw, the heroic manners of clan patriarchy achieve their archetypal radiance in the ceremony of state suppression. The dauntless conduct of Fergus and Evan Dhu at Carlisle proclaims a ratio of spiritual triumph and historical defeat. It is an aesthetic effect, inherent in the construction of the scene as a spectacle. ' "This is well GOT UP for a closing scene", said Fergus, smiling disdainfully as he gazed around upon the apparatus of terror' (327). The actor plays his magnificent part, but the magnificence is all for the eye of the beholder. Waverley attends the exemplary rite of history as the witness of another's death in his place: the Carlisle episode fixes, in short, the romance structure of heroic vacancy and fatal doubling described in the previous part of this chapter, and of which the tour is the 'objective' modern narrative genre. The Jacobite martyrdom is no longer a political but an aesthetic event that confirms Waverley in the role of liberal subject, who arrives, watches, sympathetically suffers – and departs. In contrast to the histrionically desolated Flora, Waverley's sympathy flows from his political and historical disengagement. The alternative, far from a disinterested tragic pathos, would have involved a queasy moral reckoning with fellow-conspirators who had embroiled him. Liberal sentiment replaces the bondage of participation: we can be 'impartial spectators' because someone else plays his part in the scene before us.[40]

The Carlisle assizes exemplify the genre of historical action as tragedy, and the spectator's part as that of a mourner, composing his sensibility upon the prospect of others' loss and death.[41] Scott's model is the most famous of English visitors, Johnson, who narrated his tour as the progress of an elegiac knowledge of history as mortality and desolation, a vision of the loss of other worlds of life, with all their savagery and tumult. But the total structure of the tour is comic: the wanderer returns home at last, to the reaffirmation of his own world of life. Waverley's last turn, rather like that of the Humphry Clinker party and of Boswell and Johnson, is through the solitude of the desert (effect of a specifically historical violence, in the 'Desolation' chapter) and into the festive hall.

Tourism means visiting a scene, moving across it, above all *being in it without belonging to it.* A historical relationship to a place is replaced with an aesthetic and commodified one. The subject circulates, changes scene. Even so, Waverley marks his freedom (the liberty of the subject) by recovering the meaning of his Jacobite adventure as an excursion, the tour's crowning 'curiosity':

> The first use which occurred to Waverley of his newly-acquired wealth, was to write to honest Farmer Jopson ... He begged him at the same time carefully to preserve for him his Highland garb and accoutrements, particularly the arms – curious in themselves, and to which the friendship of the donors gave additional value. (292)

By turning his arms into aesthetic properties, Waverley recognizes and authenticates for himself what we have been reading all along: his military adventure has been a kind of play, a private interlude. The 'real history' of the hero's life has not been that of a political rebellion, nor even a false quest or dalliance, so much as a romance of *unarming* like that of Callidore, the knight of Spenser's sixth book. Callidore both lost and found himself – with fruitful and poignant ambiguity – in idyllic diversion. This is the Spenserian prototype of the romance of tourism, the last turn from the harsh logic of historical justice.[42] Waverley's career recapitulates an unusually strenuous version of this pastoral journey. The relics of civil war are removed from historic function to private leisure, infused (however) with an 'additional value' that transcends exchange. It is an aesthetic value, constituted upon the private pathos of an intimate loss. Scott makes powerful use here of the romance convention of the renewal of a vitiated society by the return from an exotic sojourn. The most complex of Scott's models – Phaeacia in *The Odyssey*, Acidale in the sixth book of *The Faerie Queene*, Prospero's island in *The Tempest* – insist upon the fragility of the romance world in this transaction: the hero's return signifies no exchange but a subtle spiritual theft, and the desolation of the world left behind.

Waverley does not return 'home' at the end of the novel, to an English future, but to the first station of his tour. His relics make up part of the fabric of the Tayside manor of Tully-Veolan, restored – after being sacked by Hanoverian troops – to accommodate the domestic idyll. While Glennaquoich proved delusory in its character of romance origin, the conspicuous status of Tully-Veolan as restoration, already signified by Rose's drawing-room minstrelsy, is in fact its qualification to be 'the height of romance'. 'A Scottish Manor House Sixty Years Since' has been the first fully localized place in the narrative.

That is to say, it is the regional-historical figure of the novel's enabling generic retrospect of 'Sixty Years' Since', defined in the first chapter as that of imaginative possibility, of fictional life (3–5). It marks a chronological border between, and overlapping compound of, different genres, corresponding to different historical worlds: 'neither a romance of chivalry, nor a tale of modern manners', but therefore something of both. As 'place of the novel', the representation of Tully-Veolan is that of a mixed aesthetic character and a complex regional and historical situation. Its setting between Lowlands and Highlands, coping with government proscription and clan blackmail, is that of a precarious accommodation among contending historical forces: the neutral space of 'wavering' to become secured, enclosed, as a private interiority. Tully-Veolan turns out to be the secret compound of origin and end of the quest, centre of the 'labyrinth' of plot, available as home in its character as a restoration – that is, as a representation, the relation of which to history is of an aesthetically reconstituted past.[43] This romance revival makes no claim over archetypal origin, but represents itself as a fabric reassembled after ruin: collected and patched together, a new and miscellaneous combination of legal, economic and sexual arrangements. Its relics signify a past no longer to be grasped as source or cause, imitated in action, reconnected to a historic charge of violence and suffering. We do not mistake them for presences, but recognize and remember their pastness, which confirms our present life – but also our own decline into the past.[44]

Waverley's return is guaranteed by the romance logic of his digression into the Highlands. The guarantee is the trope of subjectivity I have already been describing: the aesthetic as formal or paradigmatic occasion of an inward, labyrinthine containment of feeling. We have read the trope in Waverley's response to Flora's performance in the glen, and it has affinities in the theme of Spenser's sixth book (aesthetic vision as a delicate private rite or mystery, marked by a detour). The narrative structure of the tour, unfolding this trope, converts the 'absence' of an historically engaged subjectivity, signified as a romance imagination, from an unconscious narcissism to a fully realized aesthetic consciousness. The conversion, not structural but modal, takes place by vicarious experience of an historical world of privation and death, securing the subject's return and immunity from it. In most potent private abstraction, the aesthetic functions as a psychic defence against death: no longer simply covered up, the abyss beneath a dream of presence, but figured into consciousness as its historical condition, dialectically both source and limit. Romance no longer signifies illusion, a state of false consciousness – a naive substitution for real history – but illusion sustained in self-knowledge: a play of sensibility that marks off a private space at the limits of real history. Thus it is not enough for us to stop at 'death', reinforcing its metaphysical boundary of negation: we have to read the content of that death, here in Scott the terrible abstractions of historical process and politics. For romance also confirms, in its authentic mood of an intimate elegiac pathos, the appropriation of other historical lives for our own. Scott's narratives recount again and again that aesthetic property is the last and absolute theft: a sublimation that comprehends the violence of history, all the deaths that have produced us, now reading.

VI

Romance and poetry, ivy, lichens, and wallflowers need ruin to make them grow.

(Nathaniel Hawthorne, 'Preface', *The Marble Faun*)

The story's last turn, from the public history of the '45 back toward a romance of private life, announces itself as a contrary movement for the inner life of the hero. As in the case of the female quixote, the sentence of anti-romance disenchantment – the disciplinary violation of the adolescent idyll – marks the threshold of adulthood and its true, nuptial bower. Waverley's 'real history' begins in mourning:

his mind turned to the supposed death of Fergus, to the desolate situation of Flora, and, with yet more tender recollection, to that of Rose Bradwardine, who was destitute of the devoted enthusiasm and loyalty, which, to her friend, hallowed and exalted misfortune. These reveries he was permitted to enjoy, undisturbed by queries or interruption; – and it was in many a winter walk by the shores of Ullswater, that he acquired a more complete mastery of a spirit tamed by adversity than his former experience had given him; and that he felt himself entitled to say firmly, though perhaps with a sigh, that the romance of his life was ended, and that its real history had now commenced. (283)

Waverley contemplates the desert he has, according to Flora's prophecy, sought all along: revelation of the ground of history (his own and others') as defeat, loss, death. Self-recognition comes as self-alienation, recognition of mortal limits. In Scott's strikingly reflexive formulation, self-mastery is a secondary command, over a self already mastered by historical contingency ('adversity'). In this dominion, the space of subjection, one can know a history of one's own. Waverley awakens to the tragic-ironic confirmation of his solipsism as mere solitude, a privacy that holds no fullness of being, but privation. He confronts, without visionary distraction, that absence which has signified his subjectivity all along.

Reading this passage, we are struck by the corresponding absence of any representation of subjective immediacy, by that lack of 'voice' that, perhaps more than anything else, has alienated Scott from modern reading conventions. We read, not the gestation of a consciousness, but an elaborate grammar of retrospect, an insistence of narrative as representation: 'and that he felt himself entitled to say firmly, though perhaps with a sigh . . .'. No subject speaks in the narrative apart from the editorial commentary, while the delusive promise of that 'now' fades back into its iterative construction ('it was in many a winter walk . . .'). The voice of the subject, in short, is subdued to a narrative writing through which it cannot speak in distinction. Throughout *Waverley*, as elsewhere, Scott's narrative displays its character as *composition* rather than inspired invention – that is, as a foreign rhetorical compound, eighteenth-century literary English. We read a writing that neglects to imitate a single, central, vocal subject, but exhibits itself as an assembly of other and past writings, conventions and quotations, records of absent voices, other places and times. The exemplary modern author for Scott was Johnson, whose most literary of English styles insisted upon itself as something classical, marmoreal, a monument over our temporal dissolutions. But Scott's writing is not even, as Johnson's was, the powerful sign of a personality, subduing to its self-forged inflexions the poetic canon and even the English language in the apparently humble and marginal services of commentary and lexicography. Received through instruction, not native speech, from the generation of fathers and from the nation of conquerors, it is the *Litterae imperii*. Scott's general prose is the classical English of the Edinburgh Enlightenment: a professional, institutional language, administrative and legal and academic. If Scott's mother was his personal source of romance, of a nourishing domestic culture of memory and voice, the father whose name he bore was the Writer: meaning a lawyer, and to the Signet, secular inscription of authority. Just as the Author of Waverley dissembles – scatters and masks and withdraws – his identity behind the fabric of his industry, so his writing practises a sedulous impersonality, yielding cannily to its sources and authorities, no more than its miscellany of parts preserved in a stylistic medium at once colourless and opaque.

Scott's narrative claims its imaginative life and power, that of a secular national historical mythography, in an institutional authority of narrative arrangement, rather than (privileged in our time) a local, vocal stylistic vivacity – for all the justly admired renditions of Scots speech and song. Language, spoken and written, is the constituent property of its historical scene. As such, it is articulated by the syntactic authority of the plot that commands 'history'. To read Scott well is to read a narrative syntax that sets different discourses and genres and conventions, different textual planes of narration and editorialization, in dynamic relation to one another. The revival of Renaissance romance, in other words, provides Scott with the form for what Bakhtin has called the 'polyphonic novel', the great medley of plots and worlds and languages that constitutes the more spacious nineteenth-century narratives. From its teleological horizon, that of our reading, all voices – the tumult of dialects and jargons – are contained and absorbed into the past, as literature, words printed and bound. It is tempting to interpret Scott's movement away from the Scottish novels, with their register of living languages and social differences, into historical romances based entirely on the archeology of literary sources, as a rigidification of that containment. But that is a simplification: Scott's turn from live social realism into a more abstract kind of romance also has an enlarging and liberating force as it allows his figures riskier, more sceptical allegorical play.

The characters most vividly reanimated in Scott's narrative, who seem to speak from a revived historical fullness, are those whose voices take part in the local compound of discourses among which they are set – by which produced. We note especially a series of elderly, widowed or bachelor patriarchs: the Bailie Nicol Jarvie, Major Dalgetty, the antiquary Jonathan Oldbuck, even King James I, and the present representative, the Baron Bradwardine, whose 'language and habits [are] as heterogeneous as his external appearance' (41), the mark of his identity with his historical place at Tully-Veolan: with which he shares, indeed, the name. Historical life is signified by the reassimilation of external, institutional discourses – 'writing' – to a vividly personal idiom. The elderly patriarchs are often distinguished by a humorous pedantry, represented as benign rather than otherwise. The antithetical case is that of the genuine quixote or enthusiast, deadly figure of a monomaniacal, logarchical possession by a single discourse, whether powerful like the Covenanters in *Old Mortality* or miserable like Peter Peebles in *Redgauntlet*. Such monologic possession is the figure of a death sentence. It signifies the removal of the word from its live *context*, a more important term than origin or end: for (in Burkean fashion) context means total historical community, always hierarchical and patriarchal, and origin an individualist interpretive construction, in tendency enthusiastic and fanatical. The Covenanters and Peter Peebles have alike substituted living and dense context with single, rigid text until they themselves are figures locked within it. Bradwardine and the rest are relics and survivors of history, bearing their humours like honourable scars. 'Context' has become just that: linguistic differences suspended from the determinism of historical function in a private domain, in the mode of a comedy of aesthetic difference. (I shall look at Scott's most elaborate narrative of this domain, in *The Heart of Mid-Lothian*, in the next chapter.) But for this – the idyll that is traditionally the veteran's reward – one has to have outlived one's history. It has to belong in the past.

We have seen that the 'wavering' character of the youthful romance hero is due to a lack or failure of proper historical context, reproduced as the subjective mode of his adventure. For the comic resolution of the *Bildungsroman*, we look then for the achievement of such a context: a homecoming to history. Jane Millgate has made an eloquent and finely detailed argument that *Waverley* is the narrative of a sentimental education that proceeds by the hero's recognition of other historical lives. His sympathetic response to their loss completes him as a human subject and affiliates him to their world. Elegiac pathos is, in this account, a movement of sympathy, the subject's moral grasp of a historical community and thus entry into membership with it. However, recent critical attention to 'sympathy' as a mediating term between sensibility and conduct has shown it to be a particularly vexatious trope in the discourses of eighteenth-century moral philosophy.[45] The massive overdose of subjectivity that afflicts Mackenzie's man of feeling measures the inaccessibility of not just political and sexual life, but also of the dominion of money and the law; he can but turn his mournful gaze upon a scenery laid waste by processes beyond his grasp. Elsewhere sympathy becomes effective when it signifies, usually by a donation of money, having rank and property: inclining towards the Dickensian figure of charity. It marks a political but not a practical disablement, a privatization of moral action. In Scott, this mode of sympathy tends to characterize those elderly patriarchs who have outlasted an era of political strife. Scott's most detailed account of a comic-elegiac relation between property and sentiment can be read in the portrait of the Whig laird, Jonathan Oldbuck of Monkbarns, in *The Antiquary*. The antiquary of the title, he has forged his historical identity around a powerful aesthetic and sentimental relation to the past. Monkbarns is able to reconstitute a social relationship, the feudal one between laird and tenant, by shedding tears for the drowned son of the fisherman Steenie Mucklebackit. Sensibility no longer represents the alienation of subjectivity, but, in the motions of sympathy, its reintegration into community and kinship. Mucklebackit elsewhere makes clear, in a famous speech, that sentiment is the privilege of a leisured gentry. This is by no means a critique of its authenticity. It is Monkbarns's prerogative to weep for his people, thereby laying patriarchal claim over them; he turns feeling into gesture by taking the head of the coffin. The 'natural', unalienated ground of sentiment tends to be, for Scott, a traditional, that is, feudal, structure of social relations; sentiment is a figure of repossession of this ground. Here let us note, once more, the elegiac theme of an elder generation which has outlived youth – the fisherfolk mourning their son, the elegiac tenderness of Monkbarns for the blank hero, Lovel.[46]

The relation of the young hero to this natural ground, the situation of his subjectivity, is accordingly problematic. He stands closer to the type of the man of feeling, whose sensibility is the register of a profound apartness. At the end of the novel 'Waverley-Honour' remains unlocalized, abstract and allegorical, that is, a property of the imagination: displaced by the material restoration of a house that no longer bears the hero's name. Not only does Waverley not return to any ancestral community of his own; he remains curiously absent within the description of the festival at Tully-Veolan. In fact Waverley scarcely features as a grammatical subject in the last chapter of the narrative of *Waverley*, as such disappearing altogether from the final pages. The disappearance is marked by his conversion into an object, a figure of the past: our last view of him is in the painting by the side of the dead clan chieftain, 'in their Highland dress' (338). As noted earlier, the representation is a polite fiction, and furthermore the production of 'an eminent London artist'. The hero takes his place by entering the decor, becoming one of the relics of his own adventure:

Beside this painting hung the arms which Waverley had borne in the unfortunate civil war. The whole piece was generally admired. (338)

In the culminatory ecphrastic moment of a novel so elaborately concerned with allegories of representation, Waverley is no longer the feeling viewer of the scene but an artificial figure in it, viewed by others.

Specifically, Waverley's trophies are exhibited for the landlord, the Baron Bradwardine: 'There was one addition to this fine old apartment, however, which drew tears into the Baron's eyes' (338). The comic conclusion is mediated, repeatedly, through Bradwardine's sensibility. He takes Waverley's place as narrative subject in this last chapter; he is the story's authentic heroic survivor, enjoying the triumphal restoration of his ancestral ground. The new-modelled domestic hero remains a blank term of succession, a prospective figure (as we have seen, women control romance prospects) which brings about in its stead the recovery of the ancient generation of feudal patriarchs. As in the romances of Radcliffe, prospect realizes itself as retrospect. In short, the utopian 'marriage of Scotland and England' with which *Waverley* closes turns out to be a delicate and complex exchange, in which the young, gentle Southron is the donor of revived historical possibility in the form of capital and political connection. Fresh English wealth is the romance currency that restores the real historical place, lean and battle-scarred and wily, of old Scotland. Scott, beginning a late career as a novelist (and pitching his Scottish novels to a British market), grows more like Bradwardine than the Waverley he once might have been. This narrative figure, of the douce and wayward son who brings vitality back to the veteran Scotch patriarch, will soon reach its culmination in *The Antiquary*, in which the genteel hero Lovel is the generic cipher of a backgrounded plot, and the adoptive son of the richly historical, humorously pedantic Oldbuck, who dominates the scene. The arrangement defines Scott's most elaborate authorial fiction, in the series of *Tales of My Landlord* that follows. The editorial frame combines a dead sentimental youth, a ludicrous pedantic veteran, and a shadowy figure of possession of the ground, the 'landlord' who scarcely appears beyond the generic title. The fable is posed in a structural relation of propitiation or exorcism to a sinister Gothic antitype, bound by a compulsive historical logic of father–son antagonism: best exemplified in the later 'Scotch novel' *Redgauntlet*, where feckless sons are coerced or crushed by stern fathers. As we have seen, the present comic resolution depends upon an obverse fantasy of parricide: Waverley has not killed his own father, who is not a proper father, in order to replace him with the Baron as father-in-law, at the end of a narrative sequence of donations, exchanges and substitutions. It is the Baron, accordingly, who speaks the Virgilian note of elegy finely described by Donald Davie in these scenes; for Virgil has provided the type of pathetic *pietas* in the fathers who look back in regret, fathers who mourn lost sons.[47]

Bradwardine, then, receives from Waverley the elaborate final donation of ancestral right as private property, made legitimate in the new dispensation. It seems indeed as if the main purpose of the narrative is for Waverley to have made the Baron into a father *in law*, the only true father because the one elected. And in fact the election – in the Odyssean recognition that converts feeling into gesture – is made by the Baron:

> – in the joyful surprise, a slight convulsion passed rapidly over his features as he gave way to the feelings of nature, threw his arms around Waverley's neck, and sobbed out, – 'My son, my son! if I had been to search the world, I would have made my choice here.' (316)

As landlord, Bradwardine is heritor of the natural ground of feeling. The authentic effect of patriarchy, true coincidence of love and subjection, is *loyalty*. As we have seen, state loyalty, defined purely by an abstract or opportunistic political allegiance, is a shadow. It must have a local ground, in private relations. We have found the original radiance of the virtue in the clan ethic of sacrifice that blazed through Evan Dhu's folk-rhetoric at the Carlisle assizes: eight sons of Ivor will die in place of their chief. By the sentimental transaction we have already looked at, their primitive, mythic virtue of *heroic subjection* is what Waverley brings back – preserved in spirit –

from the Highlands to Tully-Veolan. Donated to the fabric of the house, his arms and painting are its talismans.

Waverley's aesthetic and sentimental recovery of a primitive patriarchal identity – 'Friend of the Sons of Ivor' – sets the ground for the local, 'objective' restoration of feudal community at Tully-Veolan. When he returns from his adventure it is to find an exemplary loyalty and *omertà*, as soon to be proclaimed by Evan Dhu, being acted out there. According to James Boswell's tour narrative, the unfortunate Chevalier was able to become a creditable hero of romance in his exit from public history, due to the devotion of the Highlanders who covered his flight.[48] Even so the dependants of the proscribed Baron rally around and succour him, at risk to their own safety. His main supporters are the household servants, but the network of complicity, we are assured, has a broadly local extent, such 'that if the Baron were to appear instantly in public, the tenantry and villagers might become riotous in expressing their joy, and give offence to the "powers that be" ...' (314).

But this harnessing of riot to a primary feudal loyalty is entirely remote from the first, local-historical, representation of Tully-Veolan in the story. Waverley's approach at the beginning of his adventure was narrated in an unequivocally satiric mode of anti-romance. We read the ironic contradiction between the figments of a genteel leisured imagination, and the actual degradation of a feudal peasantry:

> It seemed, upon the whole, as if poverty, and indolence, its too frequent companion, were combining to depress the natural genius and acquired information of a hardy, intelligent, and reflecting peasantry. (33)

The hero moves through an objective, historical scene of neglected education that mocks his own aristocrat obsolescence: with its 'hanging gardens' and 'family dung-hill [ascending] in noble emulation', the sordid hamlet reminds us of the topic of Waverley's romance reverie (family honour), of its site (bower suspended from the world), and of its constitutive 'indolence'. We glimpse the real structural 'magic' of *rentier* privilege that has transformed its economic base into a wretched parody of its own idleness. Baronial power has declined from high historic function into mock-heroic:

> This dovecot, or *columbarium*, as the owner called it, was no small resource to a Scottish laird of that period, whose scanty rents were eked out by the contributions levied upon the farms by these light foragers, and the conscriptions exacted from the latter for the benefit of the table. (35)

But as Waverley enters the estate, his romance imagination begins to settle back into place:

> The solitude and repose of the whole scene seemed almost monastic; and Waverley, who had given his horse to his servant on entering the first gate, walked slowly down the avenue, enjoying the grateful and cooling shade, and so much pleased with the placid ideas of rest and seclusion excited by this confined and quiet scene, that he forgot the misery and dirt of the hamlet he had left behind him. (35)

The romance imagination occupies a private retreat where its function is to forget the desert that is its real historical condition: in this country of a bitter religious reformation, the historical meaning of 'monastic' is something like 'parasitic'.

In the end Scott's historical narrative too, even through the recoveries and recognitions that are the tropes of romance, performs an elaborate forgetting of this misery and dirt in order to entertain our imagination in the final idyll. The narrative takes Waverley out beyond Tully-Veolan, toward a more complete, thus delusive, romance retreat: the route which will nevertheless cleanse Tully-Veolan of its support-system of misery and dirt, and make it fit for the authentic revival of romance. Hence the function of the Highlands as 'romance territory', peripheral and archaic, in which the stresses of the present scene may be intensified, polarized and purged at their origin. The decadent domestic feudalism of Tully-Veolan gives way to its lively primitive archetype. The true feudal thieves are, not the baron, but the caterans who raid the district. This archetypal displacement of the register of 'real history' constitutes the narrative logic of the tour that animates Waverley's drift (in his moral absence of motive) toward a pure retreat and romance origin.

For the matter implicit in the first, forgotten view of Tully-Veolan, displaced by the excursion through the Jacobite rebellion, is *Jacobin* rebellion – in short, civil war not as dynastic but as class conflict, its sources not foreign but native. The oblivion of romance is not easy but troubled and fitful, sustained by persistent remindings. This matter haunts the narrative: we saw how Waverley's romantic prospect of the Jacobite host disintegrated into the gritty glimpse of a dispossessed mob, in flickering alternation with an invasion of alien savages. The strongest appearance of a theme of class war is the impressive episode of Waverley's first descent from the Highlands, in which he is almost lynched by zealous peasants; a violence contained by, but also congruent with, the legitimate state power, as he is handed over for a humiliating official interrogation. The episode is the nucleus (including some of the names) of Scott's later, full-dress treatment of civil war as a class-cultural struggle in *Old Mortality*. Here, it triggers the central romance action of *Waverley*: the rescue by outlaws, the secret female cure, Jacobite apostasy. The place of Waverley's first and rudest return to real history, Cairnvreckan is emphatically not Tully-Veolan: the secret and triple return to which marks it (and hides it) as the labyrinthine centre and end of a romance detour 'through history'.

It would not be accurate to say that we are reading, here, the figure of 'real history' as some kind of rift through which may be glimpsed the insistence of a 'political unconscious' in Scott's narrative. Scott, posed at the classical beginning of the nineteenth-century novel, is aware of far more – that is to say, these narratives are rhetorically far more comprehensive – than critical archaeology can be. (The knowledge we have that Scott lacked, that of subsequent traditions of the novel, can actually hinder us from reading his original effects.) We read here the strategic artifice of a dialectical argument between 'romance', or the form and reader-subjectivity of fiction – the shape of the imagination – and 'real history', the shape of things as they have been, are and will be. Here, the romance detour both evokes and evades an insurgence of primal historical forces that turn out to be those of raw violence and spoliation: the visiting of the desert upon the manor, the invasion of the privileged retreat by its excluded and impoverished periphery. Tully-Veolan laid waste is the most vivid view we get of the real effects of civil war: the aristocratic emblem of revolution, what F. R. Hart has called 'the fall of ancient houses'. It is at the same time the true secret place of the story, concealing within it the germs of romance plot. Here, in proscription, the Baron shares in the 'misery and dirt' of his subjects. Here, too, Waverley himself has been smuggled, hidden and healed. At the heart of both their adventures, Bradwardine and Waverley recover life in escape, secrecy, invisibility: *going to ground.* Wilt justly reproduces the centrality of this topos in her study of Scott: the outlaw prince in hiding among his subjects who reclaims the sources of his power. Truancy and evasion are the authentic modes of romance action, the faithful, magically efficacious translation of the romance imagination in the very midst of historical coercion.[49] In hiding, if escape yield a true refuge, identity is renewed by contact with its sources. Waverley is nursed back to strength by women's love, the Baron's ancient rank is warranted by the loyalty of his subjects. These essential acts of service constitute the secret magic of the pastoral mode of romance I have argued as authentic for Waverley's adventure. To go to ground in this way is to immerse oneself in a native origin deeper than history, provided by those natural springs of female and tenant-class devotion. It is to come close to death, and to be revived: hence the mythic overtones of Waverley's healing (the Gardens of Adonis, recovery of a primal relation to life-giving women, etc.). For Bradwardine, Scott's rhetoric evokes a more fundamental sinking of identity than the social in these transformations – a primal shapeshifting. The Baron in hiding is like not only St John on Patmos, mighty prophet of apocalypse, but 'the conies in Holy Scripture' (303), 'coiled up like a huge snake entering his retreat' (304), 'like an old badger with his head out of his hole' (315). (A demonic version of this is Burley at the end of *Old Mortality*.) Scott reinvents for modern fiction a powerful figure that goes back at least to Spenser's mastertrope of Faerie, a transcendental and paradigmatic dimension of imaginative life in complex allegorical relation to historical time and place: here, the figure of an essential, original, authentic British place or ground, concealed in or 'underneath' history.[50]

The restoration of the estate takes place, then, via the recovery of its pre-historic, archetypal, above all private identity, as house, as ground: as a secret interior, a refuge, a hole-in-the-earth, surrounded by a desert of strife and ruin. Its life-giving content is the devotion of others, marking the 'natural' origins of their subjection as a class, women or workers. For upon their subjection must repose that of the genteel hero. At its natural origins, of course, such subjection is a power and freedom – the spontaneous and private exercise of essential human virtues of fidelity and kindness. Thus, Bradwardine's ordeal inspires primitive impulses of sympathy among his people that confirm them – even as he enters into equality and fraternity with them – as his feudal vassals. So vivid and moving, this local odyssey (the lord in exile in his own land) is a powerful synecdoche for the narrative it closes. Its project is the recovery of 'archetypal' terms of social relation, crystallized in a revolutionary ferment. The restoration of the ancient hierarchical forms of community occupies a private patriarchal ground of natural human kindness that has resisted the oppressions of an 'external' historical process. Once more, I am not describing here the immanence of transcendental mythic archetypes in a supremely receptive tale-telling (as if – as some critics would have us believe – the character of Scott's genius were merely an exceptional porousness to cultural atmospheres),[51] but the story's cunning artifice of the very figure of the archetype. The archetype, whose matrix is the modern, private, aestheticizing imagination, is projected through historical process as a recovery from it and an exorcism of the category of history to the negative space of the other, the outside, the past. We have outlived it; it takes place somewhere else.[52]

Such then is the local operation of Scott's complex, generous and potent counter-revolutionary myth of private restoration out of historical crisis. The essence of the myth is that, at the end, social relations are not transformed, save in play or for a time; they resume their place, idealized within the imagination of the property-owner as a function of his privilege. This idealization takes the form of the sentimental transformation of economic relations of social power into 'original' domestic relations: the Baron as father of his tenants, Waverley as adoptive Son of Ivor, women as nurses of men. A world torn apart by historical forces of economic and political difference is brought together in an extended patriarchal family. But that larger community can only be situated off the page, outside the scene, beyond the story. The new hero's domestic manhood remains the theoretic project, energetically desired and sardonically prophesied, of women; his place is occupied, instead, by the ancient generation. The network of extended kinship that recovers the romance ending spreads horizontally – the exchange of manners that unites Waverley, his uncle, Talbot and the Baron – but its vertical depth remains obscure. The gravest sin of Waverley's apostasy was his desertion of his tenants, yet we do not find him among them at the end of the book. As for his other folk, we read in the Carlisle chapter that Waverley's 'memory still lives in these glens by the name of the Friend of the Sons of Ivor' (325), a curious prospective dissolution of the entire narrative scene of 'Sixty Years' Since': with whom exactly, we might ask in 1814 of the ravaged glens, might that memory still live? Waverley's return to Tully-Veolan, true to his mode of deviation, avoids the hamlet, so that it may remain forgotten. At the nuptial party, the villagers are a chorus cheering offstage. For a fuller version of the romance of private restoration we shall turn to Scott's second novel.

CHAPTER 3

The suspension of belief

There is nothing spiritual in him; all is economical, material, of the earth earthy.[1]

Carlyle complained that Scott could not be a great man because he lacked intensity of moral feeling. The modern romancer was not, himself, a hero of romance, but a literary merchant-capitalist:

He had nothing of the martyr; into no 'dark region to slay monsters for us', did he venture down: his conquests were for his own behoof mainly, conquests over common market-labour, and reckonable in good metallic coin of the realm. The thing he had faith in, except power, power of what sort soever, and even of the rudest sort, would be difficult to point out. One sees not that he believed in anything; nay he did not even disbelieve; but quietly acquiesced, and made himself at home in a world of conventionalities. (66)

The author as Laodicean: one of his own neutral heroes. Carlyle's shrewd, unforgivingly reductive sense of Scott's historical materialism hits at the paradox of his appeal to both Tory and Marxist readers. If Scott for his part declared his readiness to die for a faith, it was in terms little likely to appeal to the prophet of Ecclefechan:

I would if called upon die a martyr for the Christian religion, so completely is (in my poor opinion) its divine origin proved by its beneficial effects on the state of society.[2]

Those who claim the authority of a private revelation of that 'divine origin' are, for Scott, deadly fanatics. The worst are full of passionate intensity. We do not receive the word of truth apart from the textuality of its historical transmission; we apprehend a divine origin through the secular record of 'effects on the state of society'.

Such a position has important consequences for the status of the author and of the imagination. Scott bases his authorship on no prophetic inspiration, such as that of Carlyle's own radical-protestant romanticism, to be taken up by Dickens in the following generation: but on an interpretative, editorial work devoted to the reproduction of a historical and collective dimension of meaning. Such work will be in the strictest sense anonymous, fulfilling itself with the invisibility of its individual compiler. Its end, indeed, is to reconcile us to our historical being by making us 'at home in a world of conventionalities'. For the work will unfold a correspondence of the record of collective experience, the documents and relics of the past, with the forms of subjective meaning, the conventions which express desire and dread. In short: the romancer not as pseudo-divine maker, but as secular national mythographer.

As in the contemporary English intellectual orthodoxy of natural theology, the divine origin of secular history is to be legible in a record of 'beneficial effects': Scott has committed his faith to a providential narrative of the state of society. But what if those effects should not prevail? Two antithetical versions of public history give Scott's North British mythography its peculiar tension and complexity. First, the official story, narrated from its end: historical process is that which is over for the nation state. This articulates, as I noted at the beginning of the last chapter, a Burkean conservatism based on the finality of the 1688 Revolution and the 1707 Union of Parliaments (actually, absorption of the Scottish into the English). The catharsis of civil war and end of Scotland as a political entity have proscribed the dynamics of temporal power – that is, ambition and gain – to the private sphere of business, and to the peripheries of Empire. As in Adam Smith's idea of civil society, home is the field of purely economic forces of change as improvement, in the security of private property.

However, such security is troubled by the darker undercurrent of what one critic has aptly named a 'Tory pessimism', felt across, tugging against, the official story.[3] It is not hard to identify the suspicion – in these years of recession, credit collapse, unemployment and hunger and riot following the French wars – that historical mutation might be far from over or elsewhere. We have read the figures of contagion from the extremity of revolution that has prevailed in France, both as an alien threat and as a structural germ in the mutations of native Scottish life, invoked for purgation in *Waverley*. History may mean not the unfolding of an order but sheer temporal change, carried now by impersonal and unintelligible material forces whose end is not stable cohesion but flux and loss. The guarantee of our security and property as private subjects lies not, after all, in our coincidence with historical process, but somehow in getting outside it, in escape or transcendence. Or only in hiding the knowledge of it, in a masque of transformation that may, if kept up for long enough, become real. As Hazlitt was perhaps the first to intimate, the very brilliance of Scott's attention to past historical scenes cast the figures of futurity in the present into ominous shade. Abbotsford was the great symbol of Scott's life as such an enterprise: a private feudal estate built on the forces of the new order – quiet ambition, secret industry, invisible currents of capital. But in the end, far from commanding those forces of dissolution in the magical ceremony of preservation, 'the magic wand of the Unknown is shivered in his grasp', himself fast under their spell.[4]

Value judgements may always turn out to follow a tautology, but a value judgement is a cultural-critical trope rather than a philosphical syllogism or a scientific equation. In Scott's best work – bearing truest witness to the (exemplary) situation in which he found himself and struggled to make himself – the above apprehensions hold each other in stress: effortful utopian fable together with its cold denial. The truth of the author's lived historical situation lies not in one or the other but in their difficult occupation of the same imaginative space. To say as much is to confirm the conventional wisdom that the Scottish novels covering the period from the latter stages of the revolutionary crisis to the last generation of the eighteenth century tend to be Scott's best work: their span holds onto not only living memory, but the present establishment of kirk and state. In the preceding discussion of *Waverley*, I tried to chart the play of these versions of historical meaning against one another, in a thematic opposition of 'romance' and 'real history' that turned out to be articulated as a historical relationship among different versions of romance producing the historical model itself as a comprehensive, 'sentimental', romance containing local 'naive' elements. In this chapter, I shall consider how some of the subsequent Scottish novels pose the status of their discourse – the kind of authority, truth or meaning fiction holds – upon a radical tension between the record of historical experience and the conventional forms, derived from the miscellaneous tradition of romance, which make that experience coherent to the needs of the imagination.

In the novels after *Waverley* we find a complex relation between history, the narrative that is inexorably true, and romance, or 'Cursed Lies'.[5] The story that is 'an ower true tale' is one which relates – firmly, though perhaps with a sigh – repression, disappointment, failure, death. The fiction 'composed under the influence of an idle or foolish planet' (i.e. Mercury) limns the buoyant realization of dreams of finding a true home in the world. *Guy Mannering* yields perhaps the blithest version of Scott's historical fable, poised at a rhetorical suspension of real history and our belief. The comic and providential coincidence of the narrative categories of history and romance takes place by an absorption of the former into the latter. *Guy Mannering* is unique in the Scott canon; subsequent novels trouble its scheme of a private romance recovery by recalling the *Waverley* one of historical compromise. The typical narrative turns upon a disjunction or contradiction between romance and history, private and public destiny, conspicuous in the order of plot. The forms of a romance plot prevail in Scott through the seismic convulsion of a past, buried historical chronology, amounting to incoherence or illegibility (as in *The Antiquary*); or as a kind of subjective delirium, reducing historical forces to an incomprehensible but dangerous shadow-play behind the scenes (*Rob Roy*); or as an explicitly incongruous, ludicrous and embarrassing formal supplement to the stern narrative of historical contingency (the end of *Old Mortality*.) In these terms, I shall read *The Bride of Lammermoor* as a tragic-ironic reversal of the comedy of *Guy Mannering*, exposing the impossibility of a romance of private life transcending history. The celebrated unity of this narrative turns upon the totalization of its romance plot as 'history', an irreversible chronology of events determined by the politics of the great world. The fatalistic narration, although quite as stylized as that of *Guy Mannering*, makes the extraordinary claim of an absolute – indeed excessive – historical truth.[6]

Finally – in disruption of the chronology of the Waverley canon – I shall look at Scott's controversial revival of the mixed kind of Shakespearian tragi-comedy in *The Heart of Mid-Lothian*, which is perhaps (along with the revisionary Jacobite novel *Redgauntlet*) this author's most ambitious and complex fiction. *The Heart of Mid-Lothian* represents the relation between the mimetic modes of history and romance as a discontinuity, in the narrative modulation from one to the other rather than in their polyphonic combination. The romance estate is a result not of a historical process but of its interruption. Its occupants are not accommodated within a logic of history but delivered from it, by a miraculous grace that translates history into private terms of its own. The solution is a fiction-within-history that invokes and scatters its claims upon truth, with a rhetorical urgency exceptional among the Waverley novels. The appropriation of the letter of faith by the spirit of fiction, defining but thereby diminishing its authority in a kind of lay moralizing or secular semonizing, would constitute one of Scott's most challenging legacies to Victorian fiction.

In these three novels, set alongside the strong line of Jacobite or rebellious-son *Bildungsroman* after *Waverley* (*Old Mortality*, *Rob Roy*, *Redgauntlet*), we read an elaborate foundation of the romance of private life upon a mythography of parental and sexual roles. In the Jacobite romances this mythography tends to privilege masculine relations of political subjection, paternal authority, filial obedience and sibling rivalry and friendship, subordinating or backgrounding those of sexual difference, as I have suggested in the case of *Waverley*. In the present novels, I shall describe how the relations between formal orders of romance and history, truth and textuality, turn allegorically upon the relation between an absconded patriarchal or paternal power of origination, and a feminine, maternal force that has taken its place in nature and in history.

THE END OF THE ASTROLOGER: *GUY MANNERING*

Waverley narrated the negotiation of romance – the forms of private subjectivity – with 'real history'. I argued in the foregoing chapter that this narrative left the synchronization of real history with the hero's romance destiny, the idyll of domestic patriarchy that was the reward of his subjection, in some perplexity. Private life and public history are combined in a dialectic of mutual exclusion. *Guy Mannering*, Scott's second novel (1815), might be said to take up where *Waverley* left off. And not just chronologically: as the romance of Scott's youth, the early 1780s, years of the great flowering of the Lowlands economy and of Edinburgh bourgeois culture. Here we read a full account of the archetypal relation between romance and nature on the grounds of private life.[7]

The narrative of *Guy Mannering* is relatively unembarrassed by a chronology of public events. Instead, history is troped in terms of place or setting. One of the delights of the novel is its 'regional' mimesis of landscape, speech and custom across an extended historical community, accommodating not only the gypsies and smugglers of the Dumfrieshire coast, and the rough georgic scenery of Liddesdale, but polite Georgian Edinburgh itself. The Edinburgh chapters, felicitously described by Millgate as a 'city pastoral' (75), illustrate the rhetoric of this regional description with particular clarity. Colonel Mannering visits Edinburgh in the flush of its renaissance, 'near the end of the American war' (1776–83).[8] Scott himself was writing, a generation later, from the New Town, with which the Edinburgh professional gentry had rewarded themselves for the city's remarkable economic and cultural transformation. With its modern elegance, Hanoverian place-names and monumentalization of a classical era already passing, the New Town described a new historical order in its very topography, which divided the social classes literally by a gulf, the Nor' Loch between the old High Street and modern Princes Street. The glorious Enlightenment Edinburgh of Scott's novel is that of the Old Town, characterized by the vertical cohabitation of different classes in the towering lands or tenements: while 'the New Town on the North, since so much expanded, was just then commenced', he tells us, 'the great bulk of the better classes . . . still lived in flats or dungeons of the Old Town' (246). Scott recalls the last moment of the city, in short, as fabric of a 'natural' or 'organic' community, signified by an ancient hierarchy not yet levelled and divided. Its inhabitants, whatever their degree (*because* of their degree), are jumbled together in the same world; the lawyers receive clients in the taverns and play their traditional 'high jinks', invoking (as Millgate points out) the pastoral motif of ritual play. (An important source for Scott, once more, is *Humphry Clinker*, with its Edinburgh of a social hierarchy so stable – cf. the cawdies' banquet – that its ranks can mingle unproblematically on the golf links.)[9] The advocate Pleydell keeps up connections with the rural community, establishing a feudal familiarity with Dinmont ('your honour said before, Mr Pleydell, ye'll mind, that ye liked best to hear us hill-folk tell our ain tale by word o' mouth', 252) and listening out for the sibylline speech of Meg Merrilies. He is an idealized version of the Edinburgh lawyer as complete citizen: practising not only his profession, but, in the post-Union absence of a political aristocracy, the roles of philosopher and laird. But Pleydell is 'one of those praisers of the past time, who with ostentatious obstinacy affected the manners of a former generation' (246): with the colonial-commercial enrichment of the city, this world of life is already passing. Towards the end of the novel, Pleydell stands in for an authorial perspective that looks backward from a changed present. This vision of a natural regional community, undisplaced by historical change, can only be recognized through our own difference from it.

The novel represents, then, with loving specificity, the scenery of a vanishing order of relations, essentially rural, feudal and pre-capitalist. This is the Scottish regionalist novel described by some recent critics, the analogue of Galt's *Tales of the West* and prototype of Eliot's *Adam Bede* or the early novels of Hardy.[10] The naturalistic order of representation is articulated, however, upon a plot that has seemed to be prodigiously *un*natural, that is, artificial or contrived.[11] But such artifice is the essence of Scott's natural theology of a scenic order sustained by supernatural – providential and magical – forces. The relations among the terms of art, magic and nature that inform the plot of *Guy Mannering* constitute the rhetorical crux of the fiction. The plot, indeed, with ostentatious obstinacy affects the manners of a past generation, that is, the conventions of romance, most powerfully available in Shakespearian drama. *Guy Mannering* is a remarkable imitation, original and syncretic, of a Shakespearian romance plot. Scott's imitation reproduces the post-Augustan, romance-revival view of Shakespeare, stated forcefully by Johnson and amplified by Coleridge and Hazlitt, as the standard for the representation of nature.[12] 'Nature' here meant human nature as the exemplary and synecdochal measure of *cosmos*. Scott's 'natural-historical' or regional mimesis of scene and character makes perhaps better sense in these terms than in those of an empirical-realist aesthetic. The lively particularity of Dandie Dinmont, Dominie Sampson, Meg Merrilies, the MacGuffogs, etc. describes not an accidental and idiosyncratic individualism but their typicality within an extended social community that is the ground of this natural scene. (The polite characters are by comparison bland and interchangeable, with the partial exception of Pleydell, whose saturnalia lend him to this world.) For Scott's attention to Shakespeare, as to 'romance', is profoundly historical, and so the 'nature' of Shakespeare is historically specific (in the figure of a native genius unsophisticated by urban neoclassicisms) to a pre-modern, 'organic' and hierarchical, social order. The synchronic orders of scenic representation describe a human order embedded in the natural, the two producing one another in harmonious dialectic. This also characterizes the diachronic order of plot, which Scott has released from the coercion of public history to assume its 'natural' and 'original' shapes –

those of conventions emerging from, determined by and signifying the laws, customs and values of the old world.

Locally, the plot of *Guy Mannering* depends at every turn on the feudal imperative of an extended organic community, revealing itself in the scheme of poetic justice. Scott's romance plot thus articulates what we might call scenic identity as mythic or paradigmatic identity, ethically marked according to a scheme of grace – whether a character takes a position for or against a natural and social order based on feudal right, helping to restore the heir to his estate or obstructing and threatening him. The feudal character of these relations is described in broad, cosmic and moral rather than local, literal, economic terms. Bertram's allies include, not the Ellangowan tenantry, but a set of figures more obliquely connected with himself or his 'ground': the Dominie Sampson, a household tutor, Meg Merrilies, queen of the gypsies who used to camp on the estate, Dandie Dinmont, the honest yeoman farmer who gives him hospitality after he has helped Dinmont fight off thieves, and advocate Pleydell. It is significant that none of these pays Ellangowan rent: their loyalty consists in their affection. This qualifies their archetypal status as traditional romance plot figures. Thus, Dinmont is not only the exemplary type of the Border yeoman, but the protective giant or beast from the woodland ('resembling a huge bear erect upon his hinder legs', 361); Meg Merrilies is not only gypsy queen but both sibyl and guardian-angel of ancestral right; the pirate Hatteraick an 'elemental' devil who curses and kills by stormy weather; and so on. (The Dominie Sampson, a university-educated son of poor folk grown into a grotesque but kind-hearted pedant who twitches, mutters and dribbles his food, seems to be Scott's national revenge upon Sam Johnson.)

In this, Scott reconstructs not just specific figures and motifs from a common European tradition but the genre of Shakespearian romance in terms of a large ideological project. The romance figures are those of an archaic natural-social scenery, occupying a separate mimetic space from that of the modern state, in court or city: Frye's 'green world' and its analogues.[13] Historical time and determination by economic and political relations characterize court and civil society. Upon leaving that to enter the natural world, characterized by essential identity and daimonic influence, the characters return from historical to archetypal being, becoming allegorical figures of a synchronic order of kind only temporarily and locally displaced. The characteristic pattern of the Shakespearian romance plot is a historical loss and providential restoration of natural identity, that is, birth and kinship as signifiers of an hierarchical cosmos. The narrative tropes of diversion, disguise, ritual play and test or trial that articulate this pattern represent the synchronization of individual subjectivity with the external order of natural relations. Brilliantly in *Guy Mannering*, and perhaps for the last effectual time in British fiction, Scott inverts the typical modern narrative topography, whereby the green world is an isolated, fragile idyll enclosed by universal historical processes; here it occupies a 'total' Scottish natural-historical universe, across which the lost heir of Ellangowan wanders toward the redemption of his lapsed estate, the local blemish of a bad new dispensation.

Scott's romance revival, even as the prototype of Frye's, is specific to its cultural moment: the more specific the more it asserts otherwise, perhaps. It opposes Rousseauistic, radical or Jacobin accounts of a state of nature and natural right by representing nature as a vanishing feudal community. The present order of scenery and character, such as might be found in Wordsworth or Crabbe, and the order of an archaic tradition of narrative forms, are grounded in the unfolding of the narrative upon each other. We read a double rhetoric of the archetypalization of the natural scene and the naturalization of romance figures. The narrative turns upon the tension between these operations, which are not, in the end, equivalent: the version of nature that prevails, the empirical probability of the modern historical scene, demands the death of archetypes, the renunciation of daimonic identities.

Guy Mannering relates a utopian private history: a fuller version of the fable we have read through, and against, the narrative of public history in *Waverley*. It remains at the core of Scott's work; it defines both his own 'self-myth' and the large popular appeal of his fiction. The fable narrates a restoration, thus continuity, of ancient identity across the chasms of historical strife and loss, to secure the present scene of private life. This reconciliation takes place on the translation of the spirit of the lost archaic world and, at the same time, the exorcism of the forces that have actually done the work of displacement, most of all of those forces that have set us where we are now. The fable is dialectical in structure, in that the final dispensation requires a combination between the new law and the old natural right that transforms both into a single plenitude.

Scott's story begins with a natural scene already fallen, historical, conflicted. The collapse of the rough social contract between the gypsies' nomadic matriarchy and the feudal patriarchy of Ellangowan comes about with the accession of a weak, belated heir, Godfrey Bertram, to an estate already diminished by 'the fatality which induced the Lairds of Ellangowan to interfere with politics' (26). In hapless repetition, Godfrey attempts strict local enforcement of the new historical rule of law. The consequence is an anarchic devastation both of the old rural community and of his own line. The powerful account of the gypsy clearances and Meg Merrilies' curse is the prologue to a local, private parable of revolution, played out in the economic warfare between smugglers and excisemen and the loss of the infant heir of Ellangowan. The abduction turns out to have been managed by the opportunist upstart Glossin, taking advantage of the chaos to usurp the estate for himself. Glossin establishes a false order, based on ambition, avarice and fraudulent legality, the evil psychic energies of historical change. It is at this point, of the condensation of bad forces in a demonic figure, that history can be turned around, as myth. The romance plot determines Glossin's destiny according to a mythic and allegorical rather than historical identity. He is a type of cultivated fraud (his name means 'tongue') whose power is based on the manipulation of a double, Dirk (Dagger) Hatteraick, the type of savage and outlaw violence; the logic of their relation is worked out in their mutual destruction, a wonderfully garish set-piece.

The exorcism of the traditional figures of force and fraud,

who preside over history as fortune, accompanies the return of the true heir and the transformation of history into providence. At the same time, the restoration of ancient right is accomplished within the terms of the new historical economy: private property based on imperial merchant capital, rather than land rents. Two groups of helpers or donors, accordingly, direct the providential romance of the heir's return. First, the white witch Meg Merrilies, and her agents and ambassadors from the old world of natural magic, who turn curse into blessing. Second, the professional-class father-figures, Mannering and Pleydell, who represent the new dispensation of private property and rational legality. Pleydell, the Edinburgh advocate, stands for urbanity and the law; Mannering, the Nabob Colonel, the military–imperial arm of post-1688 commercial power. (Scott sets them in symmetrical opposition to his villains, as the legitimate versions of force and fraud: '"Very natural, Colonel," said the advocate, "that you should be interested in the ruffian, and I in the knave – that's all professional taste",' 411.) Together they represent post-Union Edinburgh as city of the law (rather than politics) and centre of East India Company patronage, the new source of wealth and advancement after the loss of America.

Yet, as we have seen, the narrative bears the recognition that the colonial enrichment of the city means the end of the old domestic community it is the romance's project to recover; as at the close of *Waverley*, the retreat to private life on the country estate defers but does not resolve the contradiction. The final set of marriages seals a compact among gentry, aristocracy and professional classes, absorbing and exorcizing the forces of individualist self-making which have, in real history, actually set them in their place. Ellangowan Old Place, site of the original patriarchy, is preserved not as a place of habitation but as a picturesque ruin, an aesthetic property signifying the continuity of historical origins and legitimate possession of the scene. The New Place, site of the degenerate descendants, is enlarged and improved for the returned heir, who marries the Nabob's daughter. Colonel Mannering himself, donor of imperial wealth, retires to a nearby 'Bungalow'. Otherwise, the new New Place rests upon the dire effects of its historical transition. The gypsies and smugglers are cleared away, the land emptied and secured for private property. The ruins at Derncleugh, former lair of the gypsies, are razed and rebuilt; a model cottage, the emblem of a pacific and deserving tenantry, fills up the Dark Cleft or Chasm, haunted relic of historical violence. Scott anticipates (as so often) a characteristic device of later nineteenth-century fiction: the displacement of class conflict into 'crime' and the solution of police work.

The lost heir's return at the end of the story figures a dialectical restoration of the usurped original order of nature and transformation of the new order of history. It is sustained both by the new historical forces of the law and imperial capital and by the old romance forces of natural magic, working together. But it is a problematical combination: fortune-seeking is morally dangerous, fortune itself something alien, dark, while natural magic, likewise alien, dark and dangerous as well as native and protective, brings about a restoration within which its banishment is complete. The question of fortune is articulated in the relationship between the homecoming narrative, in which an external, providential design assembles itself around an innocent and receptive hero, and the progress narrative, in which an enterprising hero proves himself and makes his own destiny. Representative of this is the relationship between the two sets of helpers, the natural-magical and the rational-modern, who claim authority over the providential narrative. This division of the powers of the patron is crucial: it raises the question of narrative authority, and thus of the status of 'romance', to thematic consciousness.

'Certainly Henry Bertram, heir of Ellangowan, whether possessed of the property of his ancestors or not, is a very different person from Vanbeest Brown, the son of nobody at all', pronounces Colonel Mannering (375). Bertram's social identity and his natural identity, that is, his very humanity, are both defined by his birth. (And like Odysseus the hero must be *outis*, the son of nobody at all, before he can reclaim his birthright.) But for all of Mannering's own feudal idealism, the restoration of that original identity has to be accomplished with that of the ancestral property, renewed by modern capital. This is the point of the narrative, which reconciles, in elaborate counterpoint, the restoration of natural birthright and the securing of property. The tension between two paradigmatic plots – Providence makes the hero, the hero makes his fortune – has marked the formal and moral crux of modern romance since *Tom Jones*, and we have by no means seen the last of it. Here the principles are antagonistically defined by the respective mottoes of the Bertrams and the usurper Glossin: 'Our Right Makes Our Might' and 'He Who Takes It, Makes It'.

With Glossin thwarted, the narrative of 'Ellangowan's right' insists on the old-romance model of the *nostos*, the return of the lost heir to his place of origins, rather than on the bourgeois Puritan model of the conversion or Pilgrim's Progress. In the latter, the hero's history is one of a difficult self-making, propelled by the individual will as a figure of grace, overcoming a natural origin of baseness and bondage. In that it requires a dissolution and reconstruction of the self, the conversion narrative readily accommodates the anti-romance theme of education through disenchantment. In the homecoming narrative, to the contrary, grace abounds with the recovery of an eclipsed original identity as a structure of external relations: kinship, community, place. Subjectivity, or an identity determined by will and conscience, is less at issue – a tactical rather than strategic figure.

Young Bertram's progress receives minimal psychological attention. Overall, Scott's narrative weaves itself around no central subjectivity or even a single protagonist, but a miscellany of characters and voices and discourses (young Mannering, Julia's letters, young Bertram, Colonel Mannering in Edinburgh, etc.) disposed across wide breaches of space and time; brought together not by any single human experience but by the allegorizing order of the plot. Deriving this narrative less from interlaced romance (Ariosto and Spenser) than from a Shakespearian dramatic structure of multiple locations and subplots, Scott prepares the way for the great polyphonic narratives of Victorian fiction. The hero, meanwhile, undergoes no spiritual conversion, disenchantment or self-reconstruction, but a realization of his original place in the world. His tests and trials are all based on the external confusion and loss of his identity – the repeated series of captivities, a wandering across the landscape which no longer bears the taint of moral error that it even did in *Waverley*. On the contrary: Bertram's willingness to digress, and his failure to assert the straight line of a self-willed progress, are signs of his grace, even as they were, rather more covertly, for young Waverley. For what is at stake is Bertram's *acceptance of the scene*. He asserts his identity by becoming a native of the natural order through which he moves, and thus activating the network of feudal relations that sets him in place. The stay at Charlies-hope is crucial here, as Millgate observes (and we note the Jacobite name.) Instead of following his desire across country straight to Julia, Bertram pauses to enjoy Dinmont's hospitality, and so earns his later help. In like manner, he accepts the more mysterious hospitality and assistance of Meg Merrilies. Both are enrolled as helpers and retainers in his wholly unconscious quest. Hospitality, the threshold trope of the romance of a feudal *nostos*, identifies the hero as guest in preparation for his own part as host, as landlord; it marks the transition between exile and home.

The hero's grace is defined by the readiness with which he gives himself up to the providential machinery of the romance plot: placing himself in the hands of the helpers who deliver that plot around him and secure his place. Correspondingly, he refuses to initiate a plot of his own: that is, to act according to his own desire. Bertram is more triumphantly a blank than was Waverley. He can take forceful action, but never on his own account, only in defence and as a gesture of integration in the natural scene, as when he assists Dinmont against footpads. On the occasions when Bertram does follow his individual passion, he immediately loses his way. When he at last thrusts himself in front of Julia, he gets into a fight with young Hazelwood and has to flee the country under suspicion of murder. The incident is a repetition of an earlier, more drastic episode of passion, violence and loss. Bertram's courtship of Julia in India led to a disastrous duel with her father, interrupted by an attack of native brigands; they took him prisoner, marking this episode as, in turn, a repetition of the original kidnapping and loss of identity at the climax of the petty civil war at Ellangowan. The Indian adventure reminds us, in fact, that the dynamics of fortune and self-making – those moral energies of aggression, ambition and craft that the romance is to exorcize from its account of historical transformation – have not been absent from Bertram's career. And they determine the history, not only of the heir, but of the paternal hero, Guy Mannering himself.

Although both Mannering and Bertram are endowed with gentle birth (something of a narrative safety clause: more blatant cases are the heroes of *Quentin Durward*, *The Talisman* and *Anne of Geierstein*), both also carry out careers of fortune-seeking and self-making. Mannering's military adventures secure him the capital that improves the united estates at the end. More drastically, Bertram's primal loss of identity turns him into 'Vanbeest Brown, the son of nobody at all', an archetypal adventurer who fights his way up from the ranks and chases after an heiress – a half-pay officer courting his commander's daughter. Significantly, this action takes place far away from the romance's native scene: in India.

Again, let us attend to the historical allegory. India is the new horizon of Empire: at once the source of domestic enrichment and advancement, and the arena of energies of power outlawed at home.[14] Scott's narrative equates social ambition and sexual desire in those banished energies: Brown's courtship of his Colonel's daughter brings together the motifs of male fortune-hunting by military force and of a female erotic delirium, in the dominance of her mother over Julia, a variant of the female-quixote motif. The themes of historical class conflict (oppressive aristocrat vs upstart bourgeois, cf. 96, 141) and of sexual conflict between father and son (mother and daughter are interestingly confused as objects of desire) coincide in the clash between Mannering and Bertram. The parricidal duel condenses all the demonic social and familial tensions that must be discharged for the safe operation of the providential romance. The timely distraction of the '*Looties*, a species of native banditti' (96), reflects, and thus exorcizes, the violent rapacity of British imperial fortune-hunting: the prey as monster, sanctifying the chase. For it is, precisely, Mannering's loot ('a few bags of Sicca rupees', 418) that will improve the fabric of the estate at the end of the narrative. And 'Vanbeest Brown' will end up marrying the Colonel's daughter. Both adventures will gain their objects – but at tremendous cost and delay.

These Indian adventures take place at a multiple remove from the narrative's natural scene or ground. They occupy not only an alien geographical horizon but a temporal gap in the romance plot, the seventeen-year dark 'chasm in our history' (83) following the violence at Ellangowan, from which they are recalled in a series of letters by the principals as they return to Scotland. The absence of these events from the romance narration thus signifies a different, dialectically other dimension of narrative discourse. Writes Julia Mannering:

> You will call this romantic: but consider I was born in the land of talisman and spell, and my childhood lulled by tales which you can only enjoy through the gauzy frippery of a French translation. O Matilda, I wish you could have seen the dusky visages of my Indian attendants, bending in earnest devotion round the magic narrative that flowed, half poetry, half prose, from the lips of the tale-teller! No wonder that European fiction sounds cold and meager, after the wonderful effects which I have seen the romances of the East produce upon their hearers . . . If India be the land of magic, this [Westmoreland], my dearest Matilda, is the country of romance. (120–1)

The 'family novel' imagined by her mother, her father's jealousy and the clash with Brown constitute a European fiction charged with the black-magical power of a romance of the East. Meanwhile Westmoreland, land of lakes and poets, marks a sort of generic threshold or quarantine-zone within the narrative; from here the dimension of a 'magic narrative' of turbulent fortunes can be simultaneously recalled and sealed off. Westmoreland is not, itself, part of the narrative's natural scenery, but a place taken over by fashionable aesthetics, 'the resort of walking gentlemen of all descriptions – poets, players, painters, musicians, who come to rave, and recite, and madden, about this picturesque land of ours', as old Arthur Mervyn complains (118). Julia describes the landscape with a cento of conventional tags, *avant la lettre*, from Radcliffe to Wordsworth (121).[15] And here, in 'the country of romance', the Indian matter of passion and fortune is resumed in a more covert and ambiguous manner, as Julia listens to Bertram's clandestine serenades on the lake. In short, the epistolary matter of Westmoreland both separates the perilous themes of the Indian 'magical narrative' from the novel's Scottish natural scenery, and also translates them there; fortune and magic, the risky dynamics of a dark, pure or original romance, are folded into the enlightened mimetic order of home, nature and common life, turned into the providential plot of the lost heir's return.

The distinction recalls the division of imaginative labour in the *Lyrical Ballads*. India, Westmoreland and Scotland mark a series of boundaries of genre, horizons of romance within, that is, beyond, the romance: the places of magic, artifice and nature, respectively. But the distinction, which sets fortune and magic apart from nature and providence, simultaneously asserts their continuity. This allegorical spatialization of the relationship between magical and natural grounds of romance poses the question of the status of the romance narrative as a whole. I've suggested that *Guy Mannering* is remarkable for the play of self-conscious speculation upon its own narrative procedures. By making old Mervyn complain, at Westmoreland (the place of advanced poetics in the present), in the words of Pope, Scott signals the passing of a tense Augustan reconciliation of the orders of nature, art and supernature. Archetypal figuration and peripeteia conspicuous as convention together push the logic of naturalized romance to the point where it reveals its rhetorical and artificial base: art disguised as nature equals nature revealed as art. The move invokes the question of magic, an art that commands the order of nature, and the boldest claim for a romance that has power over reality. Such a claim may be fraudulent, or such a power malignant. The recurrent figure in Scott of a romance that is both fraudulent *and* malignant marks a strong anxiety about the social and psychic energies circulating in fiction.

Scott follows scholarly orthodoxy in claiming a generic oriental origin of romance. There, 'before history', the fable is a magical speech or spell folded still in nature, with authentic power over it. For the rational and civilized British, alienated from a magical reality, the work of imagination can be grounded only on individual desire; this is the essence of Scott's critique of a romantic poetics. Its power is that of a black-magical solipsism, binding the self and others in a destructive fabric of erotic illusion. India is 'an area of darkness'.[16] Scott falls back on the conventions of anti-romance to articulate the fears that attend the magic narrative of the realization of desire. In India, Mannering's wife spins a web of female-quixotic delusion, in a deadly parody of 'the wonderful effects' her daughter has seen 'the romances of the East produce upon their hearers'. The narrator denounces

> the folly of a misjudging mother, who called her husband in her heart a tyrant until she feared him as such, and read romances until she became so enamoured of the complicated intrigues which they contain, as to assume the management of a little family novel of her own, and constitute her daughter, a girl of sixteen, the principal heroine ... Thus she frequently entered upon a scheme merely for pleasure, or perhaps for the love of contradiction, plunged deeper into it than she was aware, endeavoured to extricate herself by new arts, or to cover her error by dissimulation, became involved in meshes of her own weaving, and was forced to carry on, for fear of discovery, machinations which she had at first resorted to in mere wantonness. (124)

This is a version of Scott's favourite figure of the artist, not as Prospero but as sorcerer's apprentice, entangled within the fabric he has woven: the dupe of his own fictions, not source but object of the power he has invoked. The figure goes beyond moralizing ('Oh what a tangled web we weave / When first we practise to deceive') to question the status of the author as the origin whose individual intention controls his work. What if he himself be but the figure of a larger narrative logic? Here, as the narrative turns from India – magical source of fortune, power and passion – to its native scene, it reiterates the question. Julia's intimation is of a narrative dynamic that exceeds any personal intention:

> I feel the terrors of a child, who has, in heedless sport, put in motion some powerful piece of machinery; and, while he beholds wheels

revolving, chains clashing, cylinders rolling around him, is equally astonished at the tremendous powers which his weak agency has called into action, and terrified for the consequences which he is compelled to await, without the possibility of averting them. (209)

Julia has glimpsed her part as character in the modern romance (even as the presses roll). The vision, sublimely dreadful, identifies the romance as the representative narrative of a new industrial economy: machinery and magic together name 'tremendous powers' that exceed any individual agency or subjective meaning. Julia's vision is quickly assimilated to the motions of a providential plot, rather than a fatalist or Gothic one (such as *Melmoth the Wanderer*, to which it seems appropriate). The movement of homecoming, from India to the domestic scene of nature and custom, signifies the conversion of black-magical forces of passion and delusion to the benign unfolding of an order of grace.

As we have seen, the hero's success lies in his passiveness within this grand machinery: those who try to impose their individual direction get snagged and crushed. Both Julia and Bertram are children of romance, who abide its delivery of their destinies. She is born in India, while his birth is attended by the portents of a magic narrative. Two parental and authorial figures – deputies of the Author of Waverley – divide this mysterious, magical–mechanical force of the romance plot between them. Both claim a predictive power over the plot; both are connected, in different ways, with the oriental dimension of 'magic narrative'; both are variant figures of the artist whose originary relation to his invention is problematic. Thus, one disbelieves it, but nevertheless it comes true, while the other (or so it is suggested) feigns a part until she believes it to be true – dying of that truth. The first is Guy Mannering, the Astrologer of the subtitle. His relation to the matter of India is metonymical – an uneasy sceptic, he brings his Eastern fortune and psychic wound to the Scottish scene. The second is Meg Merrilies, 'Egyptian sibyl', who bears a more powerful, genetic relation to oriental 'talisman and spell', invoking its originary magic on British ground. (The Indian origins of the gypsies were in fact a topic of the day.)[17] In a striking parental allegory that reaches far across Scott's work and much of nineteenth-century fiction, Mannering conceives the romance plot while Meg Merrilies actually bears and delivers it. The romance is the offspring of two parents: the magical and oracular matriarchy of the old natural world, and a rational paternity associated, as we shall see, with secular forms of writing, interpretation and legality that denote separation from a supernatural origin.[18] Scott's scheme amplifies the double narratology we encountered in the fiction of Ann Radcliffe, problematically divided between a magical romance of female desire commanding the natural scene and a paternal letter of the law and of rational explanation. Both Mannering and Merrilies are present at Bertram's birth, and will be recognized by him as symbolic parents – authors of his destiny – far more powerful than his dim biological parents (who soon die). Both of them must give up their magical-parental powers for his accession to patriarchal identity. Yet the terms of their collaboration are far from equal; and the authority of each is based on the exclusion of the other. The parental allegory narrates the fragility of a romance synthesis that Scott will not achieve again.

The subtitle of *Guy Mannering* is *The Astrologer*: with this figure the book propounds the paradox of its modern romance textuality.

The story opens with young Mannering's benighted arrival at Ellangowan at the moment of the birth of the heir. He carries out a jocular promise to cast the child's horoscope, 'as well to keep up appearances, as from a sort of curiosity to know whether he yet remembered, and could practise, the imaginary science' (38). Scott makes the point that this was the real science of the old dispensation: Mannering has studied astrology at Oxford, where his tutor believed that 'the courses or emanations of the stars superseded, or, at least, were co-ordinate with, Divine Providence' (37; the ambiguity is characteristic and thematic). Throughout the eighteenth century (and afterwards) Oxford was a notorious seat of Royalist and Catholic sympathies, in marked contrast with the progressive, rationalist and Presbyterian Scotch universities. A graduate of one of the latter, the Dominie Sampson invokes Sir Isaac Newton (a Cambridge man), whose *Principia* appeared in 1687: 'the (pretended) science of astrology is altogether vain, frivolous, and unsatisfactory' (34). In the *Letters on Demonology and Witchcraft*, Scott traces the fall of 'the queen of mystic sciences' through the revolutionary era and the foundation of the Royal Society.[19] Astrology, in short, is the cosmology of romance. Both astrology and romance name the symbolic order of a prerevolutionary nature of supernatural connections and correspondences that will articulate, as plot, the natural-mimetic scenery of the narrative we are reading.

Mannering himself is irrevocably estranged from that old magical cosmos, even though he has the art to read its signs. Under the historical necessity of scientific rationalism, he renounces his prophetic art even as he performs it; indeed, he can only perform it under such renunciation. Another of Scott's figures who invoke forces that exceed their intention, he is identified with that most powerful of archetypes for the Wizard of the North: 'like Prospero, he mentally relinquished his art, and resolved, neither in jest nor earnest, ever again to practise judicial astrology' (40). This potent figure of renunciation hangs over the entire narrative: 'a second Prospero, I have broken my staff', Mannering repeats as he awaits the recognition scene, 'and drowned my book far beyond plummet depth' (352); and in the very last words of the romance, 'here ends THE ASTROLOGER' (420).

Divorced from literal belief in the old cosmos, Mannering's imaginative relationship to it, instead, is aesthetic and sentimental. He performs his art partly as a game, partly in a momentary imaginative transport. A compound of lunatic, lover and poet, he is overwhelmed by the sublime spectacle of the night sky:

> So strangely can imagination deceive even those by whose volition it has been excited, that Mannering, while gazing upon these brilliant bodies, was half inclined to believe in the influence ascribed to them over human events. But Mannering was a youthful lover, and might perhaps be influenced by the feelings so exquisitely expressed by a modern poet:

For fable is Love's world, his home, his birth-place:
Delightedly dwells he 'mong fays, and talismans,
And spirits, and delightedly believes
Divinities, being himself divine.
The intelligible forms of ancient poets,
The fair humanities of old religion,
The power, the beauty, and the majesty,
That had their haunts in dale, or piny mountains,
Or forest, by slow stream, or pebbly spring,
Or chasms of wat'ry depths – all these have vanish'd;
They live no longer in the faith of reason!
But still the heart doth need a language, still
Doth the old instinct bring back the old names.
And to yon starry world they now are gone,
Spirits or gods, that used to share this earth
With man as with their friend, and to the lover
Yonder they move, from yonder visible sky
Shoot influence down; and even at this day
'Tis Jupiter who brings whate'er is great,
And Venus who brings everything that's fair. (36–7)

Scott's verses 'exquisitely express' the poetic topos that has been called 'the de-daemonization of the landscape', the clearance of its elemental spirits: a mythological account of the destruction of natural-historical communities which is the problem of the present romance.[20] The Romantic turn towards an internal and psychologized imperative of prosopopoeia ('still the heart doth need a language, still / Doth the old instinct bring back the old names') does not correspond with the subsequent turn of Scott's narrative, away from the individual subjective imagination and towards the external, objective design of a providential power. As 'a youthful lover', in fact, Mannering is susceptible to an excitement of the imagination that reproduces, not that order of nature as grace, but an intensification of the subjective energy of his desire – everything most dangerous in this narrative. His destiny as lover lies in India, that dark chasm of a 'magic narrative' of desire and fortune: site of the fatal crisis of his marriage, the oedipal rivalry with Brown and loss of his wife.

Mannering's act of symbolic paternity – his act of love – defines him as the archetypal uncommitted father. His conception of young Bertram's history is a strange fit of passion marked by renunciation, and withdrawal from the narrative; indeed, his sexual destiny coincides with the withdrawal *of* the narrative and its forbidden themes and energies. Accordingly, the crucial fact that determines Bertram's history is the absence of the author-patriarch, of which the calamitous weakness of the pseudo-father on the historical scene, Godfrey Bertram, is only one effect. Thus, the horoscope that Mannering reads is *not* a narrative of divine providence, but the record of that absence. Its drastically limited terms are those of a sheer temporality without content, a sequence of discontinuities: 'three periods would be particularly hazardous – his *fifth* – his *tenth* – his *twenty-first* year' (39). These mark the terrible crises of young Bertram's career: its episodes of historical violence, loss of identity, sexual passion and oedipal strife, in which the author-patriarch features either as an absence or as a blocking demon. Mannering notes that his horoscope of the Ellangowan heir oddly corresponds to the one he has cast for his wife-to-be (39). In fact both tell the same story, and it is Mannering's own. He reads, without understanding, nothing but his own fortune, over and again the shadow of India, in which he figures not as the providential author-patriarch, master of magical connections, but the jealous *senex iratus*, Bertram's sexual and class rival. Mannering's refusal of belief and renunciation of prophecy have reduced his art to the solipsistic projection of his own fallen sexuality; estranged from the old order of nature as grace, his imagination can only reflect the dark energies of a purely individual desire, played out in the disastrous 'family novel'. His loss of synchrony with the providential romance, and consequent failure to control the plot, are made clear when he tries to use his Indian loot to rescue the Ellangowan estate from Glossin's clutches. Coincidence, or fortune in its negative guise of fatality, blocks the gesture; just as coincidence, in its providential aspect, will bring the right time, place and person together at the end.

Mannering's astrology expresses the enabling paradox of the work of romance itself. No longer having faith in the truth of the imaginary science, he engages it, in a complex way, as a fiction. Yet – not despite but because of that mode of engagement – all is true. The stars really do turn out to be co-ordinate with Providence. But the relation of this order to the observer's fallen will, unable to accept it, can only be ironical. Scott marvellously tropes Johnson's figure of the astrologer (in *Rasselas*); Mannering's astrology is a predictive art weakened from a prophetic mode to one of interpretation, fraught with projection and ambiguity. The astrologer, far from claiming authorial or original meaning in what he writes down, is in his solipsistic transport determined by it. The relationship, this symbolic paternity, is above all textual, in that it exposes a system already written, of which oneself, and the very act of paternity or authorship by which one enters the system, is an effect, a figure, rather than the cause or origin.

A little over half way through the novel, Mannering goes to Edinburgh to invoke the assistance of the advocate Pleydell. Adept of the codes and mysteries of the new historical order, Pleydell is the astrologer's legitimate successor. His sentimental attachment to past customs does not derange his modern citizenship so radically as does Mannering's ambiguous skill. Pleydell represents the discourse of the law, completely bound to the interpretation of words uttered and deeds committed. When he tricks Hatteraick with the clue of the footprint (401), he becomes one of the first modern literary detectives. The detective, as we shall see in Dickens and Wilkie Collins, will be an equivocal magician in the new urban romance, an anti-prophet of the law whose art lies in the reading of past deeds and thus is based upon death. Here, Pleydell deals in the textuality of traces left behind after events – his activity in the novel is entirely retrospective, rationalizing and explanatory. The objects of its revelations are letters, wills, corpses. In short, he represents 'the end of the astrologer' who renounces his art, and the redefinition of narrative authority from prophetic vision to textual hermeneutics. And as such Pleydell, more drastically than Mannering, is unable to command a plot, that is, be an author: only to interpret after an action has taken place.

Pleydell accomplishes almost nothing towards the restoration of the heir and the solution of the old mystery, despite the elaborate installation of his authority at the end of the narrative. He can only piece together the evidence once it is set in front of him. It is left to Meg Merrilies, queen of the gypsies, Galwegian sibyl and spae-wife, to realize all the providential connections. In the absence of the father who conceives and renounces, it is she who occupies the site of origins, who actually delivers the romance plot. Both alone and through her agents she tirelessly guides, instructs, saves and provides until the homecoming and recognition are fulfilled. Her power is a prophetic and performative word-of-mouth: her curse and benison direct the loss and restoration of 'Ellangowan's right'. This power consists in her presence in the natural scene, as its original denizen, ubiquitously active and influential, while Mannering and the rest must stand apart. Her voice coincides with the ballads, bans and spells of 'naive romance'. Yet that world is passing. With the completion of her work of restoration, she dies. She is the last relic of the old dispensation of natural magic; her death seals the succession of the new estate of the rational fathers.

The end of the romance rewrites the power of Providence as male and paternal. 'I trust HE, who hath restored little Harry Bertram to his friends, will not leave his work imperfect', says Dominie Sampson (378). The narrative perfects Meg's work of restoration with her death and the reassertion of rational patriarchy in the figure of Pleydell. The negotiation of the narrative between the provident natural-magical mother and the impotent rational fathers spans the radical historical chasm upon which the romance is founded, between those who inhabit the old natural world and die with its passing, and those who succeed in the new. Scott's myth of a paternal and maternal collaboration, in which the mother gives up the life she bears, and the father survives, psychically wounded, by a complex intellectual disengagement, develops the logic of romance donation we looked at in the last chapter. Meg must construe her power as subordinate to an original, natural patriarchy. Her devotion to the new heir identifies her as a loyal feudal retainer, like the other good helpers in the plot, rather than the matriarch of a competing, alternative order. However, no strong original patriarchy has figured in the narrative. We began with the historically degenerate Godfrey Bertram and the astrologer's gesture of paternity as a renunciation of power. Meg's prophetic word *creates* 'Ellangowan's right', just as it has destroyed it. Just as her curse wipes out line and house, so her blessing sets in place the ideal patriarch, who was never there before.

The transmission of Ellangowan's right is thus overdetermined: Meg's self-sacrificial act of donation coincides with a ritual of appropriation and containment of her dangerous revolutionary power on the part of the patriarchy, no harmonious and symmetrical exchange. The traditional recognition scene completes her labour of restoration. By staging this as an examination conducted by Pleydell, Scott represents the translation of the romance-work into the discourse of the law and of rational explanation. The catechism takes place in a scene of polite conversation in Mannering's drawing-room: as the Colonel nervously awaits Bertram's arrival, Pleydell regales himself on wild ducks and burgundy and flirts with the young ladies (chs. 49 and 50). The leisurely setting and pacing of the scene makes deliberate contrast with the wild woods and dark night outside, the place of frenzy and violence where Meg goes about her work. The one order – that of a rational and domestic enlightenment – has to shut out the other, even as it claims its deeds as its own.

The function of the catechism, then, is not to reveal anything – for everything has been done – but to translate the magic narrative into the safe terms of a modern natural mimesis, establishing the *nostos* as a domestic event. This requires a delicate negotiation of the subjective terms of belief or imaginative commitment, marking an embarrassment that is central and problematic to Scott's romance rhetoric. 'The witch has kept her word', says Pleydell (359): he, young Bertam and Mannering earn the fruits of her magic by an act of faith, the acceptance of the providential grace she bears. But the astrologer who has renounced prophetic art feels the dilemma most keenly: at the same time as they accept her power they cannot believe in it. Her communications are received with an urbane mockery:

'A most mystic epistle truly, and closes in a vein of poetry worthy of the Cumaean sibyl – And what have you done?'

'Why', said Mannering, rather reluctantly, 'I was loth to risk any opportunity of throwing light on this business. The woman is perhaps crazed, and these effusions may arise only from visions of her imagination; – but you were of opinion that she knew more of that strange story than she ever told.'

'And so', said Pleydell, 'you sent a carriage to the place named?'

'You will laugh at me if I own I did', replied the Colonel.

'Who, I?' replied the advocate. 'No, truly, I think it was the wisest thing you could do'. (353)

Pleydell bestows upon Meg Scott's favourite sentence of anti-romance rationalization: 'This woman has played a part till she believes it' (353).[21] The rhetoric of disenchantment pronounces, in fact, the end of Meg's power as the fathers take it over from her. Pleydell assumes her magic by reversing its dangerous energies, in burlesque and jest:

'Look ye, Dominie, if you speak another word till I give you leave, I will read three sentences out of the Black Acts, whisk my cane round my head three times, undo all the magic of this night's work, and conjure Harry Bertram back again into Vanbeest Brown'. (364)

We manage and preserve 'the magic of this night's work' by pretending *not* to believe the parts we are playing. It is an inversion of that enthusiasts' belief which is the measure of delusion. For our disbelief is a self-protective illusion: the narrative insists that the magic is alive and that those who grasp it without the glove of rational equivocation perish.

The spirit of urbane mockery and playful disengagement extends across the last chapters:

'Here is this young man come from India, after he had been supposed dead, like Aboulfouaris the great voyager to his sister Canzade and his provident brother Hour. I am wrong in the story, I believe – Canzade was his wife – but Lucy may represent the one, and the Dominie the other. And then this lively crack-brained Scotch lawyer appears like a pantomime at the end of a tragedy'. (372–3)

Julia, for one, recognizes that this is after all one of those oriental magic narratives, but that the final genre is the pantomime which reverses and repairs the tragedy. Critics who confuse seriousness with earnestness have disapproved of the end of *Guy Mannering*: the burlesque epigraph from Sheridan's *Critic* (ch. 50), Sampson's grotesque antics almost capsizing the romance into black farce (369–70), the topos of unspeakability poised a hair this side of irony – 'We shall not attempt to describe the expansion of heart and glee of this happy evening' (404). But that kind of seriousness is just what is not possible. Part of the way in which the pantomime reverses the tragedy is by dissolving its imaginative spell over us. The perilous old magic is kept safe as a game, formally intact but sealed off from the dark currents of the psyche. Such a solution comes not from anti-romance but from Shakespearian romantic comedy. Scott combines its conventions of closure: the play's turning upon its own ludic aspect, as instance of the green world of festive and ceremonious forms it represents; the final bow to the audience and renunciation of illusion-making power; the self-reflexive acknowledgement of the ideal status of romance resolutions. As the end of the romance returns us to history, it challenges not only its own status, as play or fiction, but that place in history of its production and reception: its place as our place. Millgate notes that the end of *Guy Mannering* also reproduces something of the Shakespearian sense of unresolved loss or trouble, alongside the high jinks and merry lies: if Meg Merrilies' death has been aligned with the work of justice, both Pleydell and Mannering are left to recognize their exclusion and superfluity. That this is not allowed to disturb the final tone of levity, but indeed confirms it, indicates the precariousness of the modern romance conclusion, the greater depth of the alienation upon which it rests. As usual Frye has described the convention: the last or *penseroso* phase of comedy and romance, of reflection and retreat.[22] We are left with the rational fathers, contemplating their withdrawal to solitude: and a last reiteration of that word of renunciation which, having brought the story into being, completes and terminates it – 'Here ends THE ASTROLOGER'. The romance is written upon the admission that its myth of continuity and restoration, by which it is itself able to revive the symbolic order of a lost world of life, is a fragile and once-only gesture. We raise the dead to learn – that they are dead; that we must die too.

AGAINST NATURE: *THE BRIDE OF LAMMERMOOR*

Penultimate in the great five-year sequence of 'Scotch novels', *The Bride of Lammermoor* exhibits a strict formal and thematic unity, all the more admired for its supposed untypicality.[23] The tale is likewise impressive for its grim refusals. These qualities coincide with a relentless historical determination of the action, occupying the domain of private life rather than of public events. As Hart puts it, 'a seemingly irrefutable historic fatalism may have engendered the most nearly perfect of the novels'.[24] Its narrative mode is one of an unambiguous, ritualized ironic fatality, evoking the romance models of Border ballads, Gothic fiction and (rather remote from the rhetorical texture) Shakespearian tragedy. As in *Guy Mannering*, these bodies of romance convention represent an order of nature: an utterance of the external scene or world, in the case of the ballads, the internal forces of imagination and desire in the case of Gothic fiction, the cosmic plot of their combination in the case of Shakespeare. But this is now a nature grown, as it were, *un*natural: the spirit of a lost historical world turned alien and black-magical. History names the decisive rupture of the old natural community, and the fall of its subjects through an irreversible temporality.

In the late *Letters on Demonology and Witchcraft*, Scott narrates, as it seems, a typical story, the story he tells every time: the decline of a mythic or daimonic universe, through magic and superstition, into a modern, enlightened order of civil society. Scott's anti-romance narrative turns its final irony against itself, as the author, retracing Dr Johnson's tour, spends a night in a haunted chamber only to fall heavily asleep until morning: no ghosts, but no consciousness either. Scott unfolds a mythological scheme. The progress or decline into enlightenment is but a stage of a more comprehensive narrative, one that begins with the union of heaven and earth. Scott attempts to bind together myth and history in a narrative in which both are true; magical prodigies, demonic possession, however susceptible to the empirical explanations of the present day, were real in their time and place. Once again, to historicize the idea of history, which includes one's own, is to recover romance. The fall is a historical event, indeed the beginning of history, within which all supernatural intercourse becomes diabolic, evil, 'unnatural', a crossing of alien orders. Allegory is the interpretation of separate orders in terms of one another, recognizing their apartness but joining them, thus allegory may itself have something demonic about it. The gift of vision, we saw in the case of *Guy Mannering*, may be mere fraud, or it may be a genuine, perhaps sinister, certainly dangerous possession.[25]

The Bride of Lammermoor offers a sinister reverse-image of the plot of *Guy Mannering*. We read the final obliteration of a dispossessed aristocratic line, the ghastly failure of a recuperative romance of private life. Public politics, with their private effects of ambition, avarice and betrayal, wreck the domestic romance between Edgar Ravenswood and Lucy Ashton. Even more clearly than in *Waverley*, this romance is projected as a private Treaty of Union, a formal reconciliation of a historical class (rather than national) conflict in the liberal territory of the affections. However, like the Jacobite adventure in *Waverley*, it fails to transcend the political pressures which have set it in motion and end up defining it. The romance is promoted by Lucy's father, who hopes it will consolidate his takeover of the Ravenswood estate, fatal fruit of revolutionary opportunity. Again and again, the narrator emphasizes the contingency of the romance's failure upon public politics and historical timing. The action occurs between the 1688 Revolution and the 1707 Act of Union: in Scottish history, the margin between the end of the old political order and the advent of the new.[26] This is one of Scott's liminal or transitional figures of narrative possibility, but its content here is sheerly negative, signifying impossibility. Historical process is visible in the gap between establishments as an opportunistic grabbing and dealing and quarrelling. The utopian settlement cannot take place in private life because it has not arrived in public life. Private desire cannot shape, but is utterly vulnerable to, public power; nor can it make its own refuge apart. We read no providential or progressive view of history here; it is all a matter of power and circumstance, and one's accommodation, or not, within these realities.

The novel's plot tropes this vulnerability of the private romance to public fortune as a vulnerability of character and action to circumstance. The plot's disasters take place through an intensification of narrative temporality, in which coincidences proliferate, but with effects contrary to those of the providential narrative of *Guy Mannering*. All timing is bad timing: not recognition and recovery but confusion and loss. This narrative law is illustrated in the grotesquely emblematic scene in which the coaches of Edgar's political patron, the Marquis of A——, and of his arch-foe, Lady Ashton, arrive simultaneously at Ravenswood and race each other to the house. Who gets there first is meaningless; merely their joint presence on the scene is a calamity. In the last chapters, the failure of the Edgar–Lucy engagement is dramatized as a failure of the word, both spoken troth and letter, to connect and reveal and resolve, within a disjunction of the machinery of coincidence under the pressure of narrative temporality. Edgar is absent during Lucy's time of trial, neither's messages reach the other, both of them lose faith, when he does turn up it is just at the wrong time, she fails to speak and so on.

The failure of the private romance to prevail over or alongside public history rehearses, more rigorously, the inadequacy of the figures of historical patriarchy that we found at the origin of *Waverley* and in the metafictional allegory of *Guy Mannering*. The Lord Keeper, Sir William Ashton, is another type of the weak, temporizing politician and pseudo-father, unable to fill the place he has usurped, as the emblematic scene of manners between himself and the forester makes clear.[27] In the end, like Richard Waverley and Gibbie Glossin, he is confounded within the web of political dealing and false legality he has woven ('like many cunning persons, he over-reached himself deplorably', 209). Meanwhile the true heir Edgar, Master of Ravenswood, finds himself deprived of patrimony and historic function. The dispossession condemns him to the comic-satiric register of feudal decay we find, for example, in the opening description of Tully-Veolan in *Waverley*, or in one of Scott's models, Edgeworth's *Castle Rackrent.* Edgar's straits make him a shabby parody of the hospitable feudal landlord, sustained by the desperate lies and petty thefts of his loyal steward Caleb Balderstone. Caleb continually drags Edgar's situation down from the tonalities of tragic dignity toward those of farce – the low mimesis of comic manners that will prevail in the new era. Caleb keeps up the appearance of feudal continuity by a series of monstrous shams and pranks (the last of which, ominously enough, involves the mock destruction of the castle).[28] But, after the decisive rupture marked by the 1689 settlement, authentic patrimony can only be regained by violent means. Edgar's dead father has bound him to maintain the family right in an oath of revenge – much as the ghost urges on Hamlet, or (in a later novel) Redgauntlet seeks to commit Darsie to the ancestral curse of historical opposition. Like both sons in a time out of joint, Edgar temporizes, thus meeting the smiling politician Sir William more than half way.

But in this tale we do not find the usual Waverley-novel mechanisms by which delay and evasion convert history into romance. There is no lateral expansion of the narrative into an alternative topography, no textuality of digression and dilation, in which the blocked energies of a historical dilemma can release themselves in a creative proliferation of archetypal doublings and oppositions: the space of allegorical and mythic resolution. No dark surrogate intercedes to play out the hero's rage and desire, and perish in his place. Edgar's temporizing merely surrenders him to the tyrannous logic of narrative time. Nor is Sir William replaced by any providential double, a father-substitute who might intervene to resolve the plot. At one point it seems as if the Marquis, Edgar's patron, might be such a figure, but his help is foiled by the arbitrary shift of political fortune, as the coach-race scene portends – a literal, parodic doubling signalling the bankruptcy of the trope ('*Il y en a deux*!', 223). In this novel, history itself is the site of wavering, indeterminacy, transition – but as sheer fluctuation, a condition of negative ontology in which both Edgar and Sir William are condemned to play out the logic of their roles. Sir William fails to become the father-in-law, and loses both daughter and property. The true heir fails to recover his right and suffers cancellation from the historical scene. The story converges upon the violation of the woman who should have been the figure of mediation, the exchange of title and property between them.

Unlike the Jacobite novels, with their series of parental and filial doubles ranged on the nether side of history and the law, *The Bride of Lammermoor* supplies the absence of strong masculine types with female substitutes. And unlike Meg Merrilies in *Guy Mannering*, these women do not represent a providential logic of the donation and historical continuity of natural right. Here, female occupation of the abdicated terms of male power signifies a usurpation, a malign inversion. The women are demonic parodies of the strong patriarch, passionate lover, avenging warrior: Lady Ashton, who rules the family in her pride of 'rank and temporal greatness' (42), and her daughter Lucy, who carries out the bloody violation at the catastrophe.

With Lucy Ashton Scott returns the figure of sensibility to its feminine ground, completing the motion we traced in *Waverley*. She is a type, just this side of parody, of the romance-reading female quixote who falls into the role of Gothic heroine. The narrative first represents Lucy by a song, overheard by her father, in which a submerged pun connects 'idyll' with 'idle', that is, (literally) vacant. The idyll is the absence from history that will remain absent from this history:

> Look not thou on beauty's charming, –
> Sit thou still when kings are arming, –
> Taste not when the wine-cup glistens, –
> Speak not when the people listens, –
> Stop thine ear against the singer, –
> From the red gold keep thy finger, –
> Vacant heart, and hand, and eye, –
> Easy live and quiet die. (39)

'The words she had chosen seemed particularly adapted to her character', says the narrator. He invokes a characteristic romance tradition for her embowered fancy:

> Left to the impulse of her own taste and feelings, Lucy Ashton was peculiarly accessible to those of a romantic cast. Her secret delight was in the old legendary tales of ardent devotion and unalterable affection, chequered as they so often are with strange adventures and supernatural horrors. This was her favoured fairy realm, and here she erected her aerial palaces. But it was only in secret that she laboured at this delusive, though delightful architecture. In her retired chamber, or in the woodland bower which she had chosen for her own, and called after her name, she was in fancy distributing the prizes at the tournament, or raining down influence from her eyes on the valiant combatants; or she was wandering in the wilderness with Una, under escort of the generous lion; or she was identifying herself with the simple, yet noble-minded Miranda, in the isle of wonder and enchantment. (40)

But these romance maidens – vessels of patriarchal grace – are all figures of a lost cultural past. Scott promptly makes the hard sceptical point that the female quixote is the modern archetype of female *powerlessness*: 'in her exterior relations to things of this world, Lucy willingly received the ruling impulse from those around her'. Her imaginative sensibility is not a source of inner strength but precisely her vulnerable feature:

> We have described her in the outset of our story as of a romantic disposition, delighting in tales of love and wonder, and readily identifying herself with the situation of those legendary heroines, with whose adventures, for want of better reading, her memory had become stocked. The fairy wand, with which in her solitude she had delighted to raise visions of enchantment, became now the rod of a magician, the bond slave of evil genii, serving only to invoke spectres at which the exorcist trembled. She felt herself the object of suspicion, of scorn, of dislike at least, if not of hatred, to her own family; and it seemed to her that she was abandoned by the very person on whose account she was exposed to the enmity of all around her. (296)

We may be no more than what circumstances allow. Unlike the exemplary heroines of Richardson or Radcliffe, Lucy's sensibility does not encode an inner integrity, the spiritual preserve of an honour lapsed in the world at large. On the contrary: the patriarchal rule of the old romance, emptied – in the removal from its historical context of values – of intrinsic 'morality' (now the figure of individual choice), reinforces her submission in the present. 'The fairy wand . . . became now the rod of a magician, the bond slave of evil genii.'

Lucy's collapse under persuasion follows the narrative logic of a failure of romance doubling. The blonde heroine of sensibility, with no fierce twin to assume and release her stifled desire, turns into that twin – the madwoman in the bedchamber.

> Here they found the unfortunate girl, seated, or rather couched like a hare upon its form – her head-gear dishevelled; her night-clothes torn and dabbled with blood, – her eyes glazed, and her features convulsed into a wild paroxysm of insanity. When she saw herself discovered, she gibbered, made mouths, and pointed at them with her bloody fingers, with the frantic gestures of an exulting demoniac. (323)

We read the wavering of sexual identity, not 'resolved' but fixed in monstrous deviancy. Lucy has wounded by stabbing the husband who is (like her father) her lover's substitute; Edgar's failure to act has cast her in the double masculine parts of ravisher and revenger. Scott's rhetoric, however, discovers the scene with Lucy in the part of the victim – cowering, traumatized, bloody. We read the violation of her private room, of her body (as it seems), and of her spirit (in fact): encoding her 'possession' in all three senses – legal, sexual and demoniac.

The Bride of Lammermoor poses, then, a gruesome conservative and materialist critique of the idealism of individual subjectivity of Richardson and Radcliffe. Radcliffian Gothic, the modern romance of a 'past' (i.e. transhistorical) subjectivism, is more specifically at issue in Scott's novel, which narrates the persistence of structures of domination in history. Cagey about Radcliffe's influence in his own prefaces, Scott took much from her: the feminine-passive hero, the rationalized supernatural, and overall the recovery of romance for the representation of a domestic and sentimental retreat from the coercions of historical power.[29] Among Scott's revisions perhaps the one here most troublesome for Victorian novelists is the de-idealization of the heroine. Or rather, not so much a de-idealization as an emptying-out of the spirit of femininity, to retain its letter: mild, soft, passive, etc. For alongside Lucy is ranged a demonic series of powerful women. Whereas Radcliffe's novels showed their heroines oppressed by satanic fathers, Scott describes the fallen historical patriarchy as a female usurpation. The plot turns on a mother–daughter relationship (nearly always disastrous in Scott, as in *Guy Mannering* and *The Pirate*, to name two other novels with witches in them). Here, the breaking of the female quixote is women's work. Proud Lady Ashton reconstitutes by herself the patriarchal authority in abeyance, as a Gothic machinery of captivity, surveillance and persuasion: a domestic Inquisition. Scott's model here is the Marchesa Vivaldi in *The Italian*, but this terrible mother, 'deeply skilled . . . in the recesses of the human heart' (293), plays her own Schedoni. She finally breaks her daughter's will by enlisting Ailsie Gourlay, 'the Wise Woman of Bowden'. The witch is at once the fatal obverse of Lucy's fantasy-self as 'legendary heroine', and the archetypal projection of her mother: much as Lady Macbeth tapped the spiritual energy of weird sisters out of doors.

Here, too, a demonic matriarchy presides out of doors. The domestic narrative of Lucy's persuasion is framed by the prophecies, spells and portents of the old natural world, pronouncing the destiny of the Ravenswood line. Blind Alice Gray by her ruined cottage is a potential Meg Merrilies, at once Wordsworthian relic and sibylline guardian of a vanishing way of life ('the last retainer of the house of Ravenswood', 237). Counselling Lucy, rebuking the Lord Keeper and warning young Ravenswood, she might prove a benign alternative to Lady Ashton. But her oracles are the doom-laden bans of the old Border ballads, whose spell over the narrative is deadly. She sits by a 'Gothic fount ruined and demolished' (56), mythical site (i.e. social-as-natural figure) of an original breach of kind, the fatal union of an ancestral Ravenswood and a water-nymph: 'From this period the house of Ravenswood was supposed to have dated its decay' (58).[30] Desire for the nymph at the fountain, like the oath of the ghostly father, marks a deadly force of repetition: here Edgar becomes fascinated by

Lucy, and here, after plighting his troth, he sees old Alice's ghost. Her passing signifies the decisive turn of the novel's matriarchal figures from possible donors of ancestral patriarchy into demons who usurp it. Alice Gray is immediately translated into black-magical (thus anagrammatical) Ailsie Gourlay, 'female agent of hell' (301), who takes her place as Lady Ashton's familiar in the diabolical possession of the 'Lammermoor Shepherdess'.

Scott's ghost scene, while signalling the end of the ambiguity of prophetic female figures in the narrative, is itself ambiguous, in a marvellous equivocation upon the Radcliffian naturalized supernatural. The apparition hovers between magic and illusion, objective and subjective effect; both accounts are true of the moment, which retains its present mystery, in contrast to Radcliffe's solution of retrospective rationalization. This phenomenological wavering occupies the crisis of Ravenswood's destiny, the fulcrum of the plot, marking its turn toward final, fatal resolution. The distinction between apparition and hallucination is not fixed because it does not matter, as everything from now on is fixed: no more wavering for plot or hero. The spectre marks Edgar's complete dislocation from his ancestral origin. That origin's influence is to be felt as no natural continuity but an alien haunting. History is the chronicle of an irreversible breach of the old natural theology: its magic is malign, its relation baleful. If the narrative yields no alternative romance space of a natural scenery outside the law and daylight reason, it is because this is already, as I have suggested, its historical condition: the gap between Revolution and Union is a twilit moment of transition as pure discontinuity and flux. The powerlessness of individuals to command this transition is represented by their fixation into archetypes, but the term now identifies a literalism, sclerosis and deadness, not life and potency.

After the vision by the fountain Edgar falls under a Gothic narrative rhetoric, in which he is figured less and less as an individual who may internalize his conflicts as a matter of conscience and choice, increasingly as the external character of an allegory of loss of historical place and identity. In contrast to the monstrous excess or condensation of sexual figures upon Lucy's fate, Ravenswood's is the site of increasing narrative displacements: excluded from the bedchamber scenario and every other, he is more drastically than Waverley the hero as figure of his own absence. His activity at the end of the novel literalizes a 'historical' belatedness, a fossilization. He returns in time to witness Lucy's wedding, an ineffectual stone guest whose grim posturing raises fewer and fewer hackles. He is compared with 'one returned from the dead' (307), 'a demon dismissed by the exorcist' (315), and 'a marble bust' (307). The last simile combines patriarchal monumentality and inviolate female honour, both here defeated; its cold rigidity mocks the failure of the Waverley hero's covertly androgynous ideal of flexibility. In Ravenswood's final failure to keep his appointment for a duel, 'accident', the contingency of world or place and time, voids the last, decisive ritual of masculine honour – after all, even Lovelace was allowed to 'expiate' that way. Instead, Edgar is absorbed into the Kelpie's Flow. A magical-natural ground that is at once a 'feminine' region of flux and margin between solid and liquid elements, the quicksand is a topographical figure of the 'natural supernatural', upon which we read the wavering of identity as its final cancellation. Here at the terminal site of prophetic utterance is no rising of the Genius but a weird *sinking*:

> The prophecy at once rushed on Balderstone's mind, that the Lord of Ravenswood should perish on the Kelpie's Flow, which lay half way betwixt the tower and the links, or sand knolls, to the northward of Wolf's-hope. He saw him accordingly reach the fatal spot, but he never saw him pass further.
>
> Colonel Ashton, frantic for revenge, was already in the field, pacing the turf with eagerness, and looking with impatience towards the tower for the arrival of his antagonist. The sun had now risen, and showed its broad disk above the eastern sea, so that he could easily discern the horseman who rode towards him with speed which argued impatience equal to his own. At once the figure became invisible, as if it had melted into the air. (332)

We read a last failure of synchrony as the line of the Ravenswoods disappears from the historical scene: we see-but-don't-see his death, the startling literalization of a characterological absence, not just once but twice.

Scott's tragic narrative is worth comparing with later essays in the genre by Hardy, who admired *The Bride of Lammermoor* as 'a perfect specimen of form'.[31] Hardy's novels invoke a Victorian canon of tragedy, Hebraic, classical and Shakespearian. The final retreat of Tess and Henchard from the arena of social and historical life turns them into wanderers across a natural landscape, connecting them with that tragic canon and bringing at the last moment an 'elemental' or archetypal grandeur – an enlargement of their individual human identities. For Scott, there is no human dimension beyond the historical and social community. His narrative relates not expansion and intensification into sublimity, but limitation, constriction, impoverishment, the loss of power and life and meaning. Henchard's last testament ('& that no man remember me / To this I put my name') recovers a magnificent assertion of subjectivity in the very sentence of its negation, quite unlike the weird bathos of Ravenswood's vanishing.[32] Scott's Shakespeare is contextualized by the stark and linear Border ballads – 'before' its moment of a classical, heroic subjectivity – and Gothic fiction, 'afterward', in its modern deliquescence. We read a narrative that makes itself more and more schematic, reducing its characters to allegorical signs and thus to their erasure. Scott's much-admired formal *askesis* represents itself as an insistence of narrative as mechanism – hollow, perfunctory, sardonic: 'tragedy' offering no fullness or dignity of its own, but reversal unredeemed by recognition, a failure of life and possibility.

This rhetoric extends to the novel's self-representation. As the end closes in, the fiction dissolves itself into the letter, or rather the deed, of historical fact:

> I have myself seen the fatal deed, and in the distinct characters in which the name of Lucy Ashton is traced on each page, there is only a very slight tremulous irregularity, indicative of her state of mind at the time of the subscription. But the last signature is incomplete, defaced and blotted; for, while her hand was employed in tracing it, the hasty tramp of a horse was heard at the gate, succeeded by a step

in the outer gallery, and a voice, which, in a commanding tone, bore down the opposition of the menials. The pen dropped from Lucy's fingers, as she exclaimed with a faint shriek – 'He is come – he is come!' (306)

In a wonderful turn, the very incompleteness of the historical record brings back the romance imagination in a last pressure of diversion that, however, fails to bear out its promise of reversal, of rescue or escape. The deed is done, that is, written. The narrative makes its final claim, extraordinarily, in an epilogue inserted in the body of the narrative *before* Ravenswood meets his end – as if marking the latter's supplementary status:

By many readers this may be deemed overstrained, romantic, and composed by the wild imagination of an author, desirous of gratifying the popular appetite for the horrible; but those who are read in the private family history of Scotland during the period in which the scene is laid, will readily discover, through the disguise of borrowed names, and added incidents, the leading participants of AN OWER TRUE TALE. (326)

Another gloss on the figure of the natural supernatural, this sentence inverts the typical mediatory rhetoric of Scott's comic conclusions, which tends to highlight their fictive status. Here, the negativity of the ending allows the narrator to claim a strange double excess. His tale is 'ower true', not just true but all too true, and such excessive historical truth is the measure of an excessive romance affect of the incredible, irrational, horrible. 'Tales of ghosts and demonology are out of date at forty years and upwards', wrote Scott, who had become an author of historical novels at forty-three.[33]

ESTATE OF GRACE: *THE HEART OF MID-LOTHIAN*

A third rogue writes to tell me . . . that he approves of the first three volumes of the H. of Midlothian but totally condemns the fourth. Doubtless he thinks his opinion worth the sevenpence Sterling which his letter costs. (Scott, *Journal*, 10 December 1825)

What to believe, in the course of his reading, was Mr Boffin's chief literary difficulty indeed; for some time he was divided in his mind between half, all, or none; at length, when he decided, as a moderate man, to compound with half, the question still remained, which half? (Dickens, *Our Mutual Friend*)

The tale previous to *The Bride of Lammermoor* is Scott's most ambitious and comprehensive. More than any of the other Waverley novels *The Heart of Mid-Lothian* (1818) – its very name suggestive of centrality and amplitude – invents for nineteenth-century fiction the universal representation of a national society that exceeds and contains any particular local, public or domestic scene. This is a world far more troublesomely extensive and miscellaneous than the regional ecology of town and country in *Guy Mannering*: a world socially, politically, psychologically and morally rifted by the differentiating expansions of historical time and national–imperial geography – and at the same time interconnected by private, secret, outlaw channels of power and negotiation. The novel takes in not only Edinburgh and its countryside, but London, seat of post-Union power, Lincolnshire and the Argyll Highlands; three generations of parents and children; and an immense social range, including Queen and Duke, city lawyers and burgesses, country lairds and puritan tenants, thieves and thief-takers. Scott's narrative represents this social-historical panorama, fragmented in so many ways, as nevertheless a total, complex system. The law – the textual codification of power and social relations – claims to unify this world as a nation state but is in fact the medium of its disunity, of political and moral contradictions between regions, classes and the sexes, and between public and private life. The meaningful structures of connection and identity are instead occult, unofficial, underneath or above the law. Allegorical interpretation is required to uncover them.

The Heart of Mid-Lothian exhibits a narratorial self-consciousness, posed in its gaps and starts, different from the tentativeness that marked the early chapters of *Waverley*. After the fast, fierce description of the Porteous riots the narrative seems to pause and begin again at its eighth chapter, with an elaborate description of the prospect of Edinburgh from Salisbury Crags. The harrassed vision of young Reuben Butler, jostled along with the mob, is replaced by the detached view of the modern connoisseur, to whose 'romantic imagination' the ancient city might resemble a dragon.[34] The allegorical interpretation – that the old town, steeped in the violence of history, is a type of Leviathan – bides just beneath the surface of aesthetic contemplation. Scott directs the reader to a total representation which, in order to comprehend this, is at once *panoramic*, like a view of the city, and *historical*, occupied with a sequence of events. For this, he repeatedly interrupts the linear current of narration to invoke another point in time and space. These different points are all co-ordinates in a larger dimension of narrative – not a diachronic line, one thing after another, but a *text*, a fabric of synchronic patterns. The more scattered the narrative, the more proof of a larger form filled by its scattering. The narrator appeals to the generic authority of sentimental romance:

> Like the digressive poet Ariosto, I find myself under the necessity of connecting the branches of my story, by taking up the adventures of another of the characters, and bringing them down to the point at which we have left those of Jeanie Deans. It is not, perhaps, the most artificial way of telling a story, but it has the advantage of sparing the necessity of resuming what a knitter (if stocking-looms have left such a person in the land) might call our 'dropped stitches'; a labour in which the author generally toils much, without getting credit for his pains. (158)

Where Dickens will speak in quite a domestic-pastoral manner of 'the story-weaver at his loom', sixty-six years hence,[35] Scott raises the figure as a conceit intricately inflected by its historical moment: the novel is an instance of domestic labour even as the new industrial technologies are taking it away from this site. The nature of a domestic pastoral economy and the gender of the agent, carefully indeterminate here (at what point in the process is the cottage industry womens' work?), will prove to be the romance's central theme, as the identity of its protagonist already hints.

Scott's modern romance involves something more, not less, than the imitation of a real historical sociology, which it contains among other elements. As critics have lately noted, *The Heart of Mid-Lothian* is a wonderful compendium of vernacular genres: documentary history, folk-tale, ballad and lyric, Cameronian oratory and Puritan allegory, Gothic and pastoral romance, proto-Newgate novel, demotic and professional jargons. And as always in Scott, the medley of local genres makes for more than local colour. It is plotted; it articulates, as it is articulated by, a dynamic and transformational narrative order. Glaringly, the entire novel shifts its shape from history to romance, beginning as one kind of story and ending as another. This has made it something of a critical scandal, and the touchstone of Scott's modern reputation. For a long time it was orthodox to praise the first two or three volumes for their sober account of historical events and ethical dilemmas, and to deplore in the fourth the resurgence of Scott's worst vices of frivolous and melodramatic contrivance. More recently, the utopian logic of the fourth volume has been acknowledged by critics who describe its pastoral romance as the last, prescriptive stage in a fable of national regeneration. These readings (represented by Crawford, Gifford and Kerr) have tended to interpret the nationalist romance back across the first part of the novel – a strategy which has the merit of following the author's intention.[36]

The novel remains compelling for its confident shifts and disruptions, the Beethovenian boldness of its modulations. The strategies of narrative transformation constitute Scott's influential development of the formal and thematic repertoire of national and historical fiction for the most ambitious kind of nineteenth-century novel. As we read, we follow a complex series of changes, from the public historical narrative of the Porteous riots, through a historically contingent private dilemma (Effie Deans will be hanged, unjustly it seems, for infanticide; her sister, thanks to a rigorous Puritan upbringing, will not tell a lie to save her), towards the solutions of romance (the scrupulous sister walks to London to see the queen). Jeanie Deans's ethical initiative is the fulcrum upon which the narrative turns. The dramatically vivid, historical-documentary, 'ower true' register of the Porteous riots and the infanticide trial takes its place retrospectively within a broader, allegorical range of narrative discourses. Jeanie's pilgrimage fills in the allegorical connections that give the sisters' private dilemma its universal, representative, archetypal status, allowing us to interpret the complaint of post-Union Scotland as a failure or absence of patriarchy, within which women have acquired a problematical, transgressive presence and power. In turn the historical condition, so abstracted, becomes itself the problem to be left behind. The priority of a social-historical realism in the first half of the novel turns out, as we read on, to be purely serial or episodic. The figures and devices of romance carry the story from Edinburgh, domain of the letter of the law, to an idyllic promised land where justice is poetic – ideal, in other words, but also a fiction. The Heart of Mid-Lothian is restored, in the facetious terms of the novel's epilogue, on the *right* side of the body, in a West Highland Arcadia rather than in the quotidian and unruly city. In the end, Scott's romance solution evades a prophetic register of truth and belief for an aesthetic irony that recognizes, and mocks, what regression might be claimed from progress.

In *The Heart of Mid-Lothian*, then, Scott amplifies the historical romance of *Waverley* to create the capacious form of the mid-Victorian apocalyptic social allegory of Dickens, Thackeray, Gaskell, Eliot and Trollope. The dynamic relation between individual and social life expands across a multiplicity of worlds and conditions, represented by a mixture of registers and genres. It is symphonic rather than, to invoke Bakhtin's Renaissance model, polyphonic: Scott's narrative moves on a diatonic axis from the minor mode of historical conflict to the major mode of idyllic repose. The combination of a complex imitation of social-historical life with its romance transformation constitutes the profound influence of *The Heart of Mid-Lothian* perhaps still more than the other Waverley novels. Scott's epochal invention is not simply that of an enlarged social-historical mimesis, in short; it involves the allegorical ordering of that mimesis according to its cultural mixture of genres. In Dickens's most ambitious novels, *Dombey and Son*, *Bleak House*, *Little Dorrit*, and *Our Mutual Friend*, the fractured surfaces and dark correspondences of life in the imperial capital are charted in a bewildering narrative phantasmagoria which casts the shadows of an apocalyptic horizon of transcendence: from the tumult of the city emerge romance figures of providential, demonic and redemptive agency, wandering maidens and patriarchal wizards above the law, witches and brigands beneath it, fools and lunatics outside it.

Like its extensive progeny of Victorian novels about erring and redemptive daughters, *The Heart of Mid-Lothian* is composed of 'a typical ballad-plot' with 'many fairy-tale and folk-elements', as Thomas Crawford notes.[37] Those folk-elements identify the cultural place of Effie and Jeanie and Madge Wildfire: they are among the terms by which the young peasant women interpret their destinies. Once again Scott comprehends these local folk romance kinds, more or less ironically, within a larger, literary and 'sentimental' form. Once again, his authority is Shakespeare, in this case the Shakespeare of the so-called problem comedies, which turn upon the rhetorical embarrassments of romance in real history. Tragi-comedy – from its inception in Italian Renaissance fiction, an experimental mixture of genres – dramatizes a philosophical discontinuity between historical experience, composed of ironic and fatal contradictions, and fictional forms, which represent an imaginary order of justice.[38] Tragedy is the genre of politics and the passions, expressing the destructive tendency of an autonomous social and psychological dynamic of the will; comedy, conversely, projects upon human nature an ideal cultural order, consisting (in a secular mimesis) of artificial convention and figuration: literature, in short, and the law, insofar as the law is a written representation of justice. Thus the Shakespeare of *Measure for Measure*, not only allusively conspicuous in the legal drama of the first half of *The Heart of Mid-Lothian*, but the formal model for its midway swerve from a naturalistic set of dilemmas of duty, conscience and feeling to an artificial narrative in which a female suppliant is assisted by an omnipotent Duke whose stage-management turns aside the sentence of the law for that of justice: poetic justice. Scott's imitation (as usual syncretic) also takes in elements from *The Winter's Tale*, the action of which crosses more dimensions than space and time, from the tragic arena of a woman's trial to a romance world of children lost, disguised and found again; and *The Tempest*, whose sovereign-wizard is the type of the miracle-managing Duke and the author whose ghost he is. Simplifying the dramatic form, Scott breaks his tragi-comical prose romance into a prologue (the Porteous riot) and three acts (the events surrounding Effie's trial in Edinburgh; Jeanie's pilgrimage to London; the return to the Highland Arcadia).

In reviving the Shakespearian form, Scott had to reckon with its historically complex Royalist ideology: the problematical vision of a sovereign incarnation of divine authority, whose absence is now supplied by the destructively limited literality of law and contract. Scott's reproduction of this ideology for his post-revolutionary, North British tale is as little naive, as carefully revisionary, as his revival of the romance form. As we have read in *Waverley*, the literal, military and political return of such a sovereignty into national history is an impossible fancy, a chimera – the Gothic sublime, horrid, ridiculous and factitious, of Jacobite reaction. Such a vision is to be translated instead into the historical dispensation of law and property; Scott's narrative unfolds not some apocalypse of Bonapartist absolutism but the solution of a private feudal domain guaranteed by the king's *dis*appearance. Absent in public politics, monarchical authority proliferates across the realm of private life as a kind of divine right of property, to inform what is at least in part the author's personal myth of self-empowerment. The 'fable of national regeneration' ends up, in fact, turning away from the political idea of the nation and concentrating upon the domestic and moral economy of a private estate whose virtue consists in its seclusion from a hopelessly chaotic external world. Knocktarlitie and Abbotsford are two attempts to fabricate a destiny outside and against the currents of public history.

More than other Scott novels, *The Heart of Mid-Lothian* grants a measure of interpretative power to a Whig–Presbyterian myth of the defeat of radical revolution, the political failure of a national spiritual transfiguration, in imagining the fallen historical scene of post-Union Scotland. A generation after the great lost fortune of a Covenant on earth, we read of the decline of the Deans and Butler families into poverty and impotence in the grasp of the Lairds of Dumbiedikes. Scott narrates this decline as a repetition of class conflict, no longer in epic feats of civil war (cf. *Old Mortality*), but on the diminished, satirical scale of a regional comedy of manners (cf. Maria Edgeworth's *Castle Rackrent*). The male members of the families are contrasting types of incapacity in the new establishment, unable to prosecute an authentic heroic struggle. The principled rigour of the patriarchal survivor, David Deans, has petrified into fanaticism, capable of a terrible pathos. The grandson of Bible Butler, hero of Monk's army, is 'a pale, thin, feeble, sickly boy, and somewhat lame, from an accident in early youth', unable to sustain the role of Waverley hero allotted him in the opening chapters (83). (Monk himself is another, historical type of the wavering apostate or turncoat.) The death of Porteous before Butler's helpless, horrified gaze puts on ceremonious public display the end of a certain possibility of masculine character – modern, 'mixed', 'fey' or fatally determined, its claim of heroic agency resulting only in senseless violence: 'by the red and dusky light of the torches, he could discern a figure wavering and struggling as it hung suspended above the heads of the multitude' (71).

It is the womenfolk who then bear the great issues of the story. As some critics have noted, Jeanie Deans is a radical variant of the Waverley protagonist[39] who brings about the romance transformation – not for her wretched sister, but for the family: the deposed generation of patriarchs. Her virtue is her patrimony; her father's disciplinary affection, expressed in his Presbyterian creed and its allegorical vehicles, distinguishes her from the fallen daughters, her sister Effie and Madge Wildfire. 'Thou hast redeemed our captivity – brought back the honour of our house', cries her father at their reunion (407), which takes place, not at the old home, 'the hard and sterile soil of those "parts and portions" of the lands of Dumbiedikes which it [had been] their lot to occupy' (83), but in the dukedom of Argyle. The important work of the romance transformation is a change of estate, accomplished by Jeanie's invocation of the power of a new landlord, a feudal patriarch who (Daedalus-like) 'soars above' the tumults of political dissension. In *The Heart of Mid-Lothian*, Scott undertakes an ambitious allegorical synthesis: accommodating the utopian energies of a Whig-Presbyterian folk or tenants' romance within the formal solution of a Tory landlord's romance, where the economic relations of a regional economy are changed into something rich and strange. Jeanie's pilgrimage and the romance forms of popular Puritanism – in particular, the personal allegory of election – authenticate one another. Deliverance from the place of bondage by a providential power of grace follows the model, alluded to here, of the Pilgrim's Progress, the individual life as heroic spiritual journey: elsewhere so troublesome for Scott's young men, under narrative compulsion to digress from their quests, but here accomplished by the female hero. And yet the grace that intervenes at the climax of Jeanie Deans's quest turns out to be the idealized return of an absconded feudal chief: 'your Lordship's Grace . . . Mind to say your Grace' (347).

The ludicrous and pathetic appearance of old Deans at his daughter's trial makes it all too clear that the radical vision of a Covenant of Grace has failed the historical imagination. Scott tells us that 'the mob of Edinburgh were at that time jacobitically disposed, probably because that was the line of sentiment most dramatically opposed to existing authority' (212): so much for popular political loyalties. This is Edinburgh a generation after the Union: city no longer of national sovereignty but of the law. That is, the law is a textual system (Scots law, unlike the English, is based on Roman law) covering the loss of the monarch whose presence, according to pre-revolutionary Stuart ideology, embodied divine authority. (Yet already that doctrine, formulated after the Union of Crowns, craved what in history it secretly knew it had lost.) As Edinburgh is the city of Scots law, so the heart of decapitated Midlothian is the law's prison-house, symbolic centre, as it will be still more systematically in Dickens, of the narrative's historical scene. Scott narrates the rule of law as a bizarre sequence of contradictions and inversions, beginning with the lurid spectacle of its overthrow in the Porteous riots, which mark the public, 'masculine' theme of the allegory of authority. Captain Porteous enforces the absent sovereignty of which he is a delegate by illegal violence, firing on an unruly crowd; that absent sovereignty asserts itself, in turn, by a breach of statute, pardoning Porteous of murder; the mob rises up, breaks upon the Edinburgh gaol, and lynches Porteous, in the name of an abrogated justice. The conduct of the riot, Scott emphasizes, displays a scrupulous discipline, in contrast to the licentious cruelty of the police.

Then, in a remarkable and complex displacement, the narrative begins again – in the eighth chapter – with a new topic: the capital conviction of Effie Deans upon a charge of infanticide. In other words, the problem of the law – the relation between legality and justice, letter and spirit, in the absence of the divine presence of the sovereign – turns from public to private and domestic life, and the object at its centre: the body of a woman. 'Riot' not as tumult in the streets, the exhibition of death, but as a mystery of the bedchamber, not sex even, but childbirth. 'The horrid delict of bringing forth children in secret' shares with smuggling the distinction of being a murder made by the law, that is, a capital penalty imposed from Westminster for reasons of state: Effie is to die under a 'William and Mary Act' for the discipline of a refractory Scotch capital. 'The heart of Mid-Lothian' means other things besides the prison: notably, a female space of private life to be filled by the heroine.

The turn from public to private life sets off a full-scale allegorical revision of the narrative – a retrospective reordering of its terms – from history to romance. The riot, emblem of popular power, turns out to be at the service of the private motives of the romance plot that engrosses the narrative after its historical-documentary opening chapters. George Staunton leads the mob, first, to avenge his comrade, butchered for defying the hated English excise ('an unjust aggression upon their ancient liberties', 28); and second, which becomes first, to rescue his mistress Effie. The botched rescue, narrated at first as a side-effect of the public revenge upon Porteous, becomes, as the narrative moves away from Edinburgh, the main enterprise for which the riot was just a cloak. Elsewhere Scott tells us of riots that turn out to be staged for the darker purposes of a romance plot: the rescue of Brown from Portanferry gaol in *Guy Mannering*, the kidnapping of Darsie at the fishing-riot in *Redgauntlet*. Popular risings, in other words, cannot happen alone through local motivation, but are always promoted by a (foreign, upper-class) plot. As the plot of Effie's transgression unfolds, it completely assimilates the theme of the Porteous riot, drawing off the sublime energies of mass insurrection to contain them in intelligible and manageable forms. The two topics haunt each other across the story. By the time of Jeanie's audience with the Queen, it is clear that Effie has become something of a scapegoat for the Porteous affair. Shadows of the riot recur throughout the narrative, but figured into the allegorical-romance design: separated into distinct elements of, on the one hand, organized banditry – Meg Murdockson's gang kidnaps Jeanie on the road to London – and, on the other, senseless mob cruelty – such as Madge Wildfire suffers, simultaneously with Meg's execution, on Jeanie's return North through turbulent countryside. Both episodes, carefully symmetrical in their placement, enclose the figure of riot within that of maternity, according to the scheme I shall describe in a moment.

In the last quarter of the novel, the idyll at Inverary signifies a retirement from the pressures of real history. We read here a curious dialectic of retreat and containment: the romance describes a private enclosure that, as it were, keeps history out, and at the same time readmits historical forces within its terms, as conventions of the genre, local colour. The energies of riot erupt once more, but as formal effects of the romance plot, void of any historical charge. Argyle's politics of transcendence convert the '45 rebellion into the offstage pretext for a series of conventional alarms: the pastoral topos of an attack of wild men or brigands, the Gothic one of parricide, etc. Scott marks this return of early disorder as, quite literally, a textual event: Jeanie turns up the broadside containing the 'Newgate narrative' of Meg Murdockson's confession, a last explanation of plot origins. With this, the novel has reversed the generic hierarchy of its opening: we have moved from the proto-Newgate novel identified in Pattieson's introductory chapter of *The Heart of Mid-Lothian*, containing Jeanie's quest as a romance fancy, to the romance idyll that now in turn contains the prison-narrative as mere literature, the shadow of a world elsewhere.

Finally, in a striking reduction to archetype, rebellion joins its origin in the act of parricide. George Staunton, Effie's seducer and leader of the Porteous riot in the guise of Madge Wildfire, falls by the hand of 'the Whistler'. This savage is, of course, the lost child of the occult union of Staunton and Effie/Madge: the figure at the origin of Effie's trial, Jeanie's quest and the Porteous riot itself. The bloody-handed wild child recedes from the narrative in a repetitious sequence of revolts and parricides, echoes of historical and social violence at last scattering back to their element, natural anarchy at the edge of Empire. (He joins the Indians in America: Scott's answer to the noble savage theme in radical romances by Charlotte Smith and Robert Bage.)[40] 'Outlaw' names no longer revolutionary anarchy or the law's overthrow (in the law's name); nor a criminal society 'under' the law; but, in allegorical topography, the wilderness outside civil society.

As the narrative closes with a parricide, reducing the matter of rebellion from historical to archetypal event, so its problem – its allegorical key – has been that familiar one of the failure of patriarchy. *The Heart of Mid-Lothian* is the most complex fable of this topic among Scott's fictions. James VI/I himself had identified state and household together as site of his authority in the role of *pater patriae*. Just so, Scotland's loss of sovereignty coincides, in private and legal homology, with the loss of a father (who will turn out to be a renegade English aristocrat); to be precise, with paternity as the term of the father's absence. Hence the peculiar contradictions of Effie's dilemma. She is a woman who has given birth but can show neither father nor son. If at first she is condemned because the child cannot be found, it later becomes clear that she is to die in the place of the missing father, Robertson/Staunton, leader of the Porteous mob. Paternity, it becomes clear, is not even a legal fiction. In the trial, Effie will not speak the father's name. The novel's lawyers, professional and amateur, are quick to point out the cruel anomaly of the statute that makes the *absence* of the *corpus delicti* the point of conviction (233). Technically, Effie is condemned not for murder of her child but for concealment of its birth. The burden of proof lies upon her *not* having committed a deed which is a crime because no traces of it remain. The crux of the trial is a failure to 'communicate her situation': under interrogation, her sister can only answer, 'Nothing' (231). Effie's guilt rests upon a sequence of silences, denials, concealments, gaps in memory and consciousness. Its substance is maternity itself, the act of birth, in which the presence of a female body is total and signifies the powerlessness or absence of the male. 'He might be in a lying-in hospital, and ne'er find out what the women cam there for' (53): Mrs Saddletree's joke about her husband only exaggerates a disability that extends to include the narrator's own stance. His determinately masculine view of Effie's condition expresses a weird conflation of eroticism and death: 'the disfigured shape, loose dress, and pale cheeks of the once beautiful and still interesting girl' (104). The actual childbirth is not exposed to this view. Instead we hear of a nightmarish transaction of passion, delirium and violence among women, fitfully and indirectly recalled in the formal incantations of the Court of Session:

> Interrogated, declares, that among the ill-language the woman gave her, she did say sure enough that the declarant had hurt the bairn when she was in the brain-fever; but that the declarant does not believe that she said this from any other cause than to frighten her, and make her be silent. Interrogated, what else the woman said to her? Declares, that when the declarant cried loud for her bairn, and was like to raise the neighbours, the woman threatened her, that they could stop the wean's skirling would stop hers, if she did not keep a' the lounder. (225–6)

This primal scene is only exorcized with the parricidal union of lost son and absent father in the final pages.[41]

The translation of the narrative from its historical, legal, documentary register to that of romance turns, above all, upon a systematic insertion of the figure of maternity, by a kind of analogical proliferation, at the origins of the theme of riot, defining the mother's body as the space outside the law. After Jock Porteous has been hung up in the Grassmarket like a tradesman's sign, women become the novel's victims of madness, murder, judicial and mob violence. A typical romance-allegorical scheme of doubling and shadowing connects Effie's transgressive motherhood-without-male terms to a series of mad and bad mothers, occupants of a night-world of suffering and death. Her dark double is Madge Wildfire, ballad-archetype of the seduced and abandoned country lass. With the exchange of children, Effie's maternity is not so much a close repetition of Madge's as its substitution or translation, completed with Madge's death in her narrative stead: Staunton's mistress, mother of a lost son, is sentenced to die in this story. The female scapegoat is further doubled in the spectral figure of Ailie Muschat, who rises beyond Madge as archetype of female victim – this time of uxoricide. Muschat's Cairn is one of the terminal sites, or centres of symbolic energy, in the book's allegorical topography: as usual in Scott, it is marked by a powerful narrative digression. It lies on the other side of the Heart of Mid-Lothian from the Grassmarket, place of public execution (in the Puritan phrase, 'justification'). Outside the city walls in a nocturnal waste, the site of murder, Jeanie Deans seeks a tryst with her sister's demon lover, and Madge croons to Ailie's ghost in the glimmer of 'Lady Moon'. Madge's 'raving discourse' evokes female eroticism in its wild state, that of an eerie, glamorous narcissism:

> But the moon, and the dew, and the night-wind, they are just like a caller kail-blade laid on my brow; and whiles I think the moon just shines on purpose to pleasure me, when naebody sees her but mysell. (174)

This is a primitive, oral-culture version of the female quixote. Madge's possession by the ballads and lyrics of folk romance signifies her delusion, her aptness for seduction: both she and Effie are victims of the charming but falsehearted gentlemanly interloper, one of the conventions of that folk romance. And while Madge's lunacy grants her access to the novel's register of prophetic and allegorical meaning, this is now the sign of her pathetic powerlessness. Just as with folksong, she utters the sentences of Puritan allegory – Christiana and Mercy at the Interpreter's House – without the benefit of ethical power over it. Her last words are the famous song of Proud Maisie, beautiful in its truth about a maiden whose love knows no man, only death.

Behind both Effie and Madge stoops the criminal hag Meg Murdockson, 'Our Mother', 'Mother Blood', the demon mother of mothers who destroys children, for whom birth is the giving not of life but of death. As archetypal condensation of maternity, unregenerate nature and death, Old Meg is revealed to be the ultimate source of crime in the novel: she nursed Staunton, procured his mistresses, assisted at their lying-in, disposed of the children. Together, Madge and Meg divide the figure of transgressive maternity into guilt-crazed victim and sinister witch, respectively, a division formally completed with the double exorcism of the demon mother from the tale. At the same time as poor Madge is beaten up by the mob, Mother Meg suffers judicial execution. In formal repetition of Butler's sight of the masculine transaction of the Porteous affair, a female view completes the rite as Jeanie and her companion (Mrs Dutton) watch from a distance:

> the outline of the gallows-tree, relieved against the clear sky, the dark shade formed by the persons of the executioner and the criminal upon the light rounds of the tall aerial ladder, until one of the objects, launched into the air, gave unequivocal signs of mortal agony, though appearing in the air not larger than a spider dependent at the extremity of his invisible thread, while the remaining form descended from its elevated situation, and regained with all speed an undistinguished place among the crowd ... The sight of a female culprit caught in the act of undergoing the fatal punishment from which her beloved sister had been so recently rescued, was too much, not perhaps for [Jeanie's] nerves, but for her mind and feelings. (390)

Alexander Welsh, in a fine insight, writes about the abstract character of the law in Scott's narrative, in that it represents reality as a textual system of relations.[42] The odd rhetoric of the passage here, with its wrong-end-of-the-telescope reduction of the scene to a scheme of shapes and contrasts, confirms the coincidence of the sentence of the law with that of the romance allegory, now that Jeanie has made her romance intercession; we 'see', that is, we read, an abstract conventional rigour, a formal play of substitutions: poetic justice.

If Effie Deans, as secret mother, belongs to this night-world, she has another identity for the world of fashion, Lady Staunton of Willingham. As her dark double is Madge Wildfire, her daylight double is Lady Suffolk, bad passionate wife. Mother Meg's daylight counterpart is 'Queen Carline' herself (48), who, with 'the masculine soul of the other sex . . . loved the real possession of power, rather than the show of it' (360), and is yet another delinquent mother. Effie stands for the symbolic complicity of these court beauties with the secret, black and midnight hags. As in the next novel, *The Bride of Lammermoor*, female power is produced by an absence of patriarchy which it in turn reproduces; the mothers have usurped their place at the origin of life. Queen Caroline wields power in the absence of her husband, abroad in his native Germany: configuration of the absence of a native Scottish dynasty. In private-life counterpart, the termagant Mrs Balchristie, 'the favourite sultana of the last Laird' (252), holds sway in 'the castle of the sluggard', the younger Dumbiedikes. Both Reuben Butler and George Staunton are the poor products of excessive mothering, laid up sick throughout the critical middle of the narrative. Reuben inherits his mother's sickly temperament and is brought up by 'a doting grandmother' (83), while George, offspring of an ineffectual 'rigid censor' of a father and a 'doting', 'beautiful and wilful' mother (341), can do little more than rant over his own ineptitude as parent and Gothic antagonist alike ('like a crushed snake, writhing with impatience at my incapacity of motion', 322: cf. Genesis 3:15). Nursed in his infancy by Meg Murdockson, he is only able to assume the scene of action by becoming her daughter (also his mistress) when he raises the Porteous mob in the costume of Madge Wildfire. Even then he fails to rescue Effie; men can only destroy, not save. Masculine power effectually asserts itself, in dialectical reaction, as a terrible violence against women, who turn out to be powerless after all.

These are the terms of the narrative scheme within which Jeanie Deans, 'cruelly sted between God's laws and man's laws' (197), takes the place of romance hero. Scott carefully sets her in opposition to her excessively feminine sister Effie, undisciplined 'child of nature' (99), along with Effie's night-double Madge: and alongside her lover, Butler, whose share of physical vigour she assumes (84). A rational forthrightness defines the love between herself and Butler ('rather affecting from its simple sincerity than from its uncommon vehemence of feeling', 423), and divides her from the Gothic tendencies of female sensibility. Unlike the lunatic-prophetic Madge or her sister, 'gifted in every particular with a higher degree of imagination ... an admirer of the beauties of nature' (508), Jeanie is triumphantly literal-minded. (This is the point about her answers both to the High Court of Justiciary and to Queen Caroline; 'friends' means, in Scots usage, blood relations.) Her religious patrimony makes her immune to the charms and terrors of romance, and grants her a power over her words all the greater for being unwitting. Having, as a good Puritan daughter, internalized the letter of New Testament law imparted by her father, Jeanie receives the spirit beyond it, in exclusion of secular and personal fancies. Her lack of imagination, that faculty of fallen desire, is a quality of her election. When the narrator comments that Jeanie 'was no heroine of romance' (251), but that 'there was something of romance in [her] venturous resolution' (268), it is to distinguish her from the Gothic type of female quixote. Thus, she is not so much a romance heroine as a *female hero*, 'like the second Calender ... like the said prince errant' (252), in contrast to the Edward Waverley type of male heroine. She is the most effective of those androgynous figures who are to resolve the historical-cultural impasse of gender roles and preside over the domestic idyll. The pious and literal-minded – 'innocent' – romance daughter will be a central figure in Dickensian fiction, though rather without Jeanie's folk vitality. Such a figure can pursue the romance of property with a vigour and a clarity denied to men, if only because the law ensures that the daughter's destiny does not admit property on her own account.

Jeanie's quest 'to work out her sister's deliverance' (180) brings her into contact with the nocturnal romance world and its female demons; she is the vessel, her enterprise the medium, through which these lawless energies and the thwarted powers of paternal sanction can wholesomely combine. The journey has a double hermeneutical and ideological function, as the sojourn with Madge at 'the House of the Interpreter' lets us know. Here we understand the full conversion of the narrative to allegorical romance, as the secret system of plot connections and causes is uncovered, and public events are given their private explanations. And here the dark mothers who lie at the hidden origins of the tale are conjured up for exorcism. As the narrative sequence that reproduces doubles and archetypes, the quest begins to fulfil the promise of romance: that everything turns up, that all that is lost shall be found. In ideological terms, this process totalizes the theme of a loss and restoration of patriarchal virtue across the text. Jeanie is 'more flexible in manner, though no less upright in principle' than her father (248), and her combination of feminine flexibility of manner and paternal rectitude of principle accounts for her power over the spirit of the law. She prays to her father at moments of crisis, and is careful to obtain his blessing for her journey, though by a 'flexible' sleight of letter. Judith Wilt, whose account of the pilgrimage I am following here, describes how Jeanie's agency is at every point sanctioned by paternal proxies: she moves with the aid of Daddie Rat's underworld passport, Dumbiedikes's 'siller', Mr Staunton's coach, the Butlers' hereditary credit with the Campbells; while at the royal interview, power is referred to, and managed by, the male figures of Argyle and the absent George II.[43] Scott frames Jeanie's appeal to the monarch with a symbolic re-containment of female misrule within the terms of patriarchy. Jeanie inadvertently reminds Queen Caroline that she is an 'unkind' mother, and Lady Suffolk that she is an adulteress (367). To name their transgression is to identify them as mortal women, like Effie Deans. Caroline answers Jeanie's plea by recognizing herself in Jeanie's role of suppliant, thus bowing to the authority of the absent king: '*I* cannot grant a pardon to your sister – but you shall not want my warm intercession with his Majesty. Take this housewife case ...' (370). The queen's donation redefines the term of female power: not the sovereign word of grace that turns death to life, but the 'housewife case' that is to be Jeanie's romance destiny, and the historical destiny of women, the role of ('warm') spiritual intermediary within a renewed patriarchy.

For, after all, the crucial theological point of Jeanie's pilgrim's progress is that she receive grace, not for her sister, but for herself – that is, for her father's house, since it is to this that she has always referred her identity. The pardon comes to seem more and more of a formality as the narrative proceeds – neither Effie nor George are saved, in the allegorical scheme of things, but are condemned to play out the logic of their roles in a career of barrenness and fraud, to Gothic conclusions. Perhaps Effie's penitential retirement to a Catholic convent is the last, ironical trace of her sister's work of intercession on her behalf. Otherwise, the operation of grace shows a Calvinist rigour and precision. Jeanie saves herself, because she has always been saved, and because she does not strive for her own salvation: 'You seem to me to think of everyone before yourself', remarks the embodiment of that grace, the Duke of Argyle (350).

The end of this progress is not the pilgrim's conversion so much, again, as one of the narrative scene. Jeanie's romance destiny accommodates her father and husband; the good mother and housewife is the central, constitutive figure of a new domestic patriarchy. Thus the significant patron that stands at the end of Jeanie's quest is not the queen, but the lost overlord: 'I will seek the king's face that gies grace' (246). His Grace John, Duke of Argyle, is the representative of that sovereign presence, whom Jeanie's pilgrimage calls into the narrative. He is the answer to the question she performs, and the relation between them is more important than any other here. It is a feudal relation, one that exorcizes its modern, Gothic reversion, that of Richardson's Clarissa and Lovelace,

Radcliffe's Emily and Montoni, or Effie Deans and George Staunton:

> Encouraged as she was by the courteous manners of her noble countryman, it was not without a feeling of something like terror that Jeanie felt herself in a place apparently so lonely, with a man of such high rank . . . A romantic heroine might have suspected and dreaded the power of her own charms; but Jeanie was too wise to let such a silly thought intrude on her mind. (359)

Jeanie's romance role is that of the suppliant woman, whose petition invokes, and indeed creates, the overlord as patriarchal protector. Like Shakespeare's maiden heroines, she becomes the vessel of the sovereignty it is her mission to restore. Jeanie knows a letter will not suffice to turn aside the law's sentence: 'it's word of mouth maun do it, or naething' (267). But unlike that of the matriarchal sibyls of other novels, Jeanie's 'word of mouth' represents no rival order of power. On the contrary, as we have seen, it speaks from a peculiarly familial posture of submission, that of daughter to father. She sets out to recover a relation between sovereign and subject available no more in South than in North Britain: 'the kings nowadays do not sit in the gate to administer justice, as in patriarchal times' (266), Butler warns her on her way. Like all pilgrim-questers, Jeanie dons allegorical armour: she approaches Argyle in the typical costume of his subject countrywoman. If Jeanie personifies 'nature' and the common or everyday life of the people, then, it is for a revival of traditional feudal relations. She thus appoints the Duke her landlord, the local representative of sovereign authority, and as such head of the family as well as her protector and intermediary: an appointment fulfilled with the translation of Jeanie and her menfolk to the Duke's country. The meaning of this translation is rehearsed in the chastisement of Mrs Dutton by the 'wholesome violence' of the Duke's Highlanders – an assertion of patriarchal ascendancy which is now entirely jolly (403–5).

It is true that through Jeanie Deans Scott invokes, with wonderful sympathy in this year before Peterloo, popular energies: but in order to contain those energies within a traditional structure of submission, the ground for which is found in the domestic relation of father and daughter. We shall read in Dickens the remarkable influence of this ideological solution upon the Victorian novelists. Jeanie's quest and Argyle's intercession represent a reversion of historical relations, an extraordinary movement out of history to grasp a lost cultural formation in the psychically charged space of private life. This movement does not coincide with public history; no king reasserts his divine right at Westminster, or at Holyrood. Scott describes Argyle's power as a miraculous individual survival, a political transcendence. Its source is the renunciation of ambition for the 'course more safe and more honourable' dreamt of by every Waverley hero – the middle way as a triumphant *altitudo*:

> He was alike free from the ordinary vices of statesmen, falsehood, namely, and dissimulation; and from those of warriors, inordinate and violent thirst after self-aggrandisement ... Soaring above the petty distinctions of faction, his voice was raised, whether in office or opposition, for those measures which were at once just and lenient. (344)

– a splendid transformation of the Gothic spectacle of Porteous's fate, where we saw the violent officer of the law suspended above a turbulent crowd. Argyle best serves Scotland by working with the Hanover regime, while never submitting to be a party man. He is the obverse of the type of the politician, represented by Sir William Ashton in *The Bride of Lammermoor* ('a skilful fisher in the troubled waters of a state divided by factions', 28). Argyle himself stands for the return of that sovereign authority that no scion of the house of Stuart, soiled with ambition and resentment, could ever incarnate. If he is, as Mrs Glass calls him, 'the Prince of Scotland', it is because he is not officially a prince, and not in Scotland. When Jeanie calls him a law-maker, he replies that power over the law lies not in his 'individual capacity' but in his membership 'of a large body' – the proper constitutional answer (349). In 'the Duke's country', however, his authority is absolute. Argyle is a monarch of private property and local genius of divine right, an absolute landlord: even in his absence, a quality he shares with his aetiological shadow, the renegade English aristocrat Staunton. What kind of a *national* identity might be represented in the last volume of the novel is an interesting question. *The Heart of Mid-Lothian* finds authentic identity not in the national, corporate, public domain, but in private life, a separation that paradoxically must be managed by the most astute political address. In Argyle, Scott foreshadows those philanthropic wizards of early Dickensian romance who bring grace by charity, or money sanctified by love, but whose relationship to public life is obscure or ambiguous. The novel ends, as it has begun, with the flow of power and identity by unofficial, underground, extraterritorial conduits, with the difference that its heroine has been able to tap into them.

O Meliboee, deus nobis haec otia fecit. [O Meliboeus, a god has made this idyll for us.] [Virgil, *Ecloga* 1]

The 'Highland Arcadia' unfurled in the last volume of *The Heart of Mid-Lothian* is Scott's most elaborate version of private patriarchy: a domestic idyll enclosed within a private feudal estate. Here we read a fable of property accumulation and class ascent: the progress of a family of the elect from tenantry to freehold, under benign ducal patronage.[44] The wizard-landlord's subjects inhabit the double dream of colonial settlement within a promised land and of private autonomy within the household. Jeanie's apotheosis is that of the first Angel in the House of nineteenth-century fiction.

Scott sets the domestic idyll in familiar imaginative territory – at once 'on the verge' and 'beyond the bounds':

> Living on the verge of the Highlands, she might, indeed, be said to be out of Scotland, that is, beyond the bounds of ordinary law and civilisation. (410)

The final scene of the novel is an elaborate romance allegorization of historical themes. As we remarked earlier, the Waverley topos of violent upheaval, the '45, is converted into a set of blatantly fictional figures. The '45 (a date, historical fact *par excellence*) is itself a figure, then, for something else: the later Highland chronology toward which the end of *The Heart of*

Mid-Lothian gestures, namely, an interminable aftermath of impoverishment, dispossession, emigration and cultural destruction, taking a turn for the worse in Scott's present. Thomas Crawford has pointed out that Scott draws upon the eighteenth-century record of the Campbells as progressive landlords, who supported their tenants and instituted agricultural improvements during the period. It seems that the Campbells were conspicuous, however, for resisting the settlement of Lowland farmers within Highland estates, which is what we find here. The Duchy of Argyle represents a curious domestic or interior frontier of colonization for the tribe of Deans and Butler: a sort of reverse emigration, stabilized with the final pacification of the natives after the '45. We read, in short, less a historical representation of agricultural improvement than an imaginary, private anticipation and reversal of the public theme of emigration. Scott was writing in the midst of a particularly nasty phase of forced clearances of Highland land for sheep. The Marquess of Stafford's factor had lately been acquitted of atrocities at Strathnaver in 1814, and a few months after the publication of *The Heart of Mid-Lothian*, at the end of 1818, the evictions would start up again on the Sutherland estates.[45]

Once more, Scott's troping of his literary traditions lies in wait for the allegorically alert reader. Raymond Williams recalls succinctly that 'the contrast within Virgilian pastoral is between the pleasures of rural settlement and the threat of loss and eviction', connected, as here, with 'the disturbance of civil war and the political chaos of cities'. Thomas More had proposed the literal, historical-material ground of the archetypal *Utopia* as a malefic (anti-georgic) pastoral in which the greed of landlords, expropriating land for sheep, drove peasant populations into exile, vagrancy, robbery.[46] Thus, the Highland Arcadia might represent a utopian prescription for the present historical scene, a vision of an ideal feudality undertaken by the private means of wealthy landlords, using a new economic power to recover an ancient historic function. However, Scott's historical placement of the romance idyll on the edge of the collapse of the Highland economy and culture does not address it to a present reality so much as make absolute its separation from it. Argyle being an ideal though absent landlord, the connection between his class and the banditry of the displaced clansmen is obscured: for all that Scott's readers might have remembered the variations upon that theme descanted by his earlier heroic outlaws, Roderick Dhu and Rob Roy. In fact, the call for a paternalist programme of Highland recolonization and cultivation is a commonplace of late-eighteenth-century tour narratives, surveying the desert a generation after the '45.[47]

Accordingly, the scenery of the idyll is composed of no sociological or natural-historical register of empirical observation, but an anthology of the romance topoi invoked by Highland tour literature. Its temporal pull is toward a mythic ancestral past rather than any historical future. Here is that Phaeacia of domestic virtues in the midst of the desert, momentarily found by Johnson at Raasay and Inch Kenneth; we witness the end of those banditti, reduced in Johnson to legend and editorial margin. Here is also, some miles westward of Smollett's native Cameron, the 'Scotch Arcadia' of the *Humphry Clinker* expedition, a preserve cleared of historical turbulence not for tourism now, but settlement. We even read celebratory lyrics, 'the description of a forgotten Scottish poet' (Alexander Ross, *The Fortunate Shepherdess*: 431–2), rather more charming than Smollett's piffling 'Ode to Leven-Water'.[48] Here, in the perpetually mild and medicinal climate (406) of 'a goodly and pleasant land, [that] sloped bonnily to the western sun' (409), the imagination may dwell 'in our fathers' times' (406). Or, in a pun that conflates the aesthetic of romance with the excise-free economy of a pre-Union Scotland (and we recall the origins of the Porteous affair), 'those happy times without duty' (439).

The romance rhetoric of the patriarchal fief also defines its domestic interior. The sign of Jeanie's grace is a magical transcendence of labour, in her housework:

Notwithstanding her strict attention to all domestic affairs, she always appeared the clean well-dressed mistress of the house, never the sordid household drudge. When complimented on this occasion by Duncan Knock, who swore 'that he thought the fairies must help her, since her house was always clean, and nobody ever saw anybody sweeping it', she modestly replied, 'That much might be dune by timing ane's turns.' (448)

Once more, we appear to be outside a historical economy. Jeanie appeals instead to the old romance secret of providential synchrony: timing one's turns. Her serious work is her mediation between her menfolk – keeping the strife between her radical-reactionary father and liberal-conservative husband, relic of the great religious themes of civil war, within the comic precinct of domestic manners. The tragic themes and identities of the earlier part of the story are repeated, but as harmless comedy. Butler complains, 'I cannot be persecuting old women for witches, or ferreting out matter of scandal among the young ones, which might otherwise have remained concealed': for concealment is now the special wisdom of pastoral (449).

Jeanie herself identifies the genre of romance as both joke and necessary illusion:

'Surely', said Mr Butler, when he had again counted over the money, as if to assure himself that the notes were real, 'there was never man in the world had a wife like mine – a blessing seems to follow her.'

'Never', said Jeanie, 'since the enchanted princess in the bairns' fairy tale, that kamed gold nobles out o' the tae side of her haffit locks, and Dutch dollars out o' the t'other'. (466)

With this evasion, Jeanie identifies the kind of story she is in. The romance rhetoric marks a generic evasion: that of a 'new' kind of mimesis of real history, the bourgeois-household comedy of manners. 'To name the various articles [of domestic furniture and apparel Jeanie receives from the female Campbells] by their appropriate names, would be to attempt things unattempted yet in prose or rhyme' (365), shrugs the narrator, and refers us out of the text to 'my kind friend, Martha Buskbody', custodian of the embarrassments of modern romance since the conclusion of *Old Mortality*. A gentleman is, by definition, ill-equipped to realize what George Eliot will call the domestic epic: even though this is now his property. The first-rank novelists of daily life and manners are all women, Scott writes in the preface to *St Ronan's Well*. Wrapping himself in the mantle of Prospero at the end of the third series of *Tales of My Landlord*, he will feign farewell to his art and hail a new adept, 'the author of the very lively work entitled *Marriage*' (Susan Ferrier).

Thus, the insistence of a romance rhetoric at the end of *The Heart of Mid-Lothian* accompanies the refusal of a feminine bourgeois-domestic realism. Scott cleaves to that invention of farewell, the magical patriarch, with the recognition that he does not, after all, belong to any new dispensation. Argyle embodies a kind of patronage that was on the way out as Scott was writing – perhaps he is an ideal version of Scott's old friend and early helper, the long-omnipotent Scotch Manager Lord Melville – 'King Harry the Ninth' of Scotland, impeached in 1806. Two systems of advancement mapped the division of Scott's own identity: that of the old patronage, upon which Sir Walter relied for jobs for himself and his family, and that of a new international marketplace – the secret public domain of the Author of Waverley, who dedicated these *Tales of My Landlord* 'to the people of Scotland'. As Argyle wields his grace he reveals himself as no historical character but a 'benevolent enchanter, whose power had transplanted [Jeanie's] father from the Crags of St Leonard's to the banks of Gare-Loch' (412). Like Prospero, like the author of the tale himself: with whom, at last, Argyle's powers of intercession and transformation are identified.

With this discovery, the wizard withdraws from the scene. After all, not so much has changed, in the structure of the transformed patriarchy that enfolds Jeanie's new home – its sovereign remains absent. A problematical deputy oversees the estate. Duncan of Knockdunder is himself a walking emblem of the reconciliation of historical and cultural differences, 'beyond the bounds of ordinary law and civilisation':

> [He] was a stout short man about fifty, whose pleasure it was to unite in his own person the dress of the Highlands and Lowlands, wearing on his head a black tie-wig, surmounted by a fierce cocked-hat, deeply guarded with gold lace, while the rest of his dress consisted of the plaid and philabeg. Duncan superintended a district which was partly Highland, partly Lowland, and therefore might be supposed to

> combine their national habits, in order to show his impartiality to Trojan or Tyrian. The incongruity, however, had a whimsical and ludicrous effect, as it made his head and body look as if belonging to different individuals; or, as some one said who had seen the execution of the insurgent prisoners in 1715, it seemed as if some Jacobite enchanter, having recalled the sufferers to life, had clapped, in his haste, an Englishman's head on a Highlander's body. (427)

Knockdunder is a rather tiresome burlesque of his master, and of the Waverley romance ideal of national reconciliation; he parodies that ideal as no organic synthesis, but a botched-together chimera that never lived in history or in nature. (It is difficult, here, not to think forward four years, to the pageant Scott would organize around George IV's state visit to Edinburgh, and its richly embarrassing centrepiece of the monarch's pantomime of a Highland chief.)[49] The hasty project of the Jacobite enchanter is the author's own, reviving historical sufferers for a factitious re-membering that only mocks the contradictory mixture, Jacobite heart and Hanover head, of his own historical being. The actual violence of historical process is announced rather than concealed, in the essentially grotesque mixture of history and romance, at the same time as the modulation from tragic reality to comic fiction is its point.

The overseer is just the most 'whimsical and ludicrous' of the set of incongruities that fills up this final romance. Scott's wonderful farrago of genre episodes, from the Knockdunderish heavy comedy of regional humours (out of Smollett and Edgeworth) to the Gothic and sublime set-pieces of Effie's return and the adventures with robbers, refuses an organic or harmonious co-ordination. In part, the disjunction reveals the Presbyterian-theological scheme noted above: narrative preterition takes place by a relentless mechanical logic of pure plot, while the elect inhabit a timeless bourgeois comedy distinguished by the reiteration of character as humour. But the utopian order of an estate of grace is no new horizon of reality: instead, it reads like an old tale still. In short, romance – knocked-under, de-idealized – signifies as incongruity, both in its relation to the history, past and present, of which it is the transformation, and within itself, as literary form. 'It was too wonderful to be believed – too much like a happy dream to have the stable feeling of reality' (407): the narrative invites the embarrassment many of its serious readers have obligingly reproduced. Or, rather, have failed to entertain but turned to impatience. Let us cultivate a salutary queasiness. The issue is indeed one of what, how much, we can swallow; of the kind of imaginative assent claimed by a fiction that has invoked the forms of historical chronicle and religious Providence in order, it seems, to confirm its secular character as something else that is neither – as fiction.

The formal pressures of this embarrassment can be read in the extraordinary multiple ending of *The Heart of Mid-Lothian*, which I shall quote in full. Ever more forceful gestures of formal and doctrinal closure, as if striving for repose upon some final simplicity, give way to a wry editorial mockery. The last narrative event is Effie's penitential retirement to a Catholic convent:

> Jeanie had so much of her father's spirit as to sorrow bitterly for this apostasy, and Butler joined in her regret. 'Yet any religion, however imperfect', he said, 'was better than cold scepticism, or the hurrying din of dissipation, which fills the ears of worldlings, until they care for none of these things'.
>
> Meanwhile, happy in each other, in the prosperity of their family, and the love and honour of all who knew them, this simple pair lived beloved, and died lamented.
>
> READER – This tale will not be told in vain, if it shall be found to illustrate the great truth, that guilt, though it may attain temporal splendour, can never confer real happiness; that the evil consequences of our crimes long survive their commission, and, like the ghosts of the murdered, for ever haunt the steps of the malefactor; and that the paths of virtue, though seldom those of worldly greatness, are always those of pleasantness and peace.
>
> L'ENVOY, BY JEDEDIAH CLEISHBOTHAM
>
> THUS concludeth the Tale of 'THE HEART OF MID-LOTHIAN', which hath filled more pages than I opined. The Heart of Mid-Lothian is now no more, or rather it is transferred to the extreme side of the city, even as the Sieur Jean Baptiste Poquelin hath it, in his pleasant comedy called *Le Medecin Malgre lui*, where the simulated doctor wittily replieth to a charge, that he had placed the heart on the right side,

instead of the left, '*Cela étoit autrefois ainsi, mais nous avons changé tout cela*'. Of which witty speech, if any reader shall demand the purport, I have only to respond, that I teach the French as well as the Classical tongues, at the easy rate of five shillings per quarter, as my advertisements are periodically making known to the public. (507–8)

Effie's apostasy and Butler's liberal rationale pose explicitly the question of religious belief in secular history: how may we recognize truth, what are its forms, is any version better than none? The formulaic cadence of a fable of private destinies follows to neutralize the problem. Fictional solutions occupy the space of ideal form, are true to the logic of their own conventions. But this provokes, in turn, the startling direct address to the reader, whereby an authorial voice breaks with doctrinal and literary formal mediations to rescue the story for a universal, human and moral 'great truth'. Such a rhetorical move, unprecedented in Scott, amplifies the stress upon the end of the narrative of the question of its generic and ideological status. The homily, so inadequate an account of the five hundred pages we have read, is just as formulaic – just as much a reflex of convention – as the romance conclusion it follows.

Nor does the book close here. The intervention of Jedediah Cleishbotham, fictive editor of the series of tales of which *The Heart of Mid-Lothian* is one instalment, breaks the illusion of an unmediated authorial voice reaching across the narrative frame. That disconcerting sincerity was the property of another satirically located editorial figure, the late sentimental enthusiast Peter Pattieson, whom we had forgotten. Old Jedediah, as last envoy of the author, dashes the cold waters of an elaborate self-mockery on the didactic posture of the author, or editor, as purveyor of truth. 'The Heart of Mid-Lothian is now no more', he announces with the pedant's literalness of mind: not gone, but translated, in a grotesque conflation of historical change to the dexterous bungling of the 'simulated doctor', who seems to be another version of the Jacobite enchanter. (Scott marks another author's private name even as he masks his own.) Textual 'purport' is likewise a matter of translation, the letter that is moved and bought and sold like any other commodity. 'The time is gone of sages who travelled to collect wisdom as well as heroes to reap honour', grimaced the ruined, ailing Scott in his journal: 'Men think and fight for money'. And write for it too, he knew with the bitter knowledge of an interminable, public indebtedness.[50]

Scott's puritan critics, from Carlyle to Leavis and Levine, have viewed the figure of the materialistic and literal-minded author-as-editor, paradoxically identical with a naive well-spring of pure 'story', with a certain shrewd clarity. But they have let themselves be taken into taking literally this genteel hack: Scott's closest mask was that of the fate he most wished to fend off and most dreaded as actual. He knew how deeply, how absolutely he was committed to his historical moment, now a secret turbulence of capital and credit, not crowns and parties. 'The great truth' is the claim of the dead man of imagination and sentiment; the survivor is the pedant who fleers and obfuscates. For Scott, belief is mortality, truth is death, as surely as are their opposites: disengagement is the difficult, desperate figure of life. The vitality of many of his characters lies in a spontaneous, unreflexive orthodoxy, the atmosphere of their native scene, and when that dissolves in the blast of historical conflict, in their capacity, equally spontaneous and unreflexive, to follow the tossings of the tempest rather than holding any straight course through it. The title of the great novel of religious and political commitments is *Old Mortality*. In the same way, the aesthetic solemnities of the ends of late Shakespeare romance – in which we seem to be present at a tense conjunction of fictional form and spiritual truth, as in the complex claim made at the end of *The Winter's Tale* on magical and sacramental functions of art – these would be as epochally belated, as false, after two revolutionary centuries, as Jacobite reaction or Catholic apostasy. The romance is not a rite of sympathetic magic that turns history, the place of our reading, into its form; it is not the word that invokes a divine and sovereign grace, but (as we now say) a literary text, the very condition of which is that untransformed site of the imagination, to resume as soon as we close the book. The difficulty of Scott lies in an aesthetic of disappointment nowhere stronger than at the end of this, his best novel. It stands for a last refusal to sublimate its own fictional form, its own textual materials: thus the assertion of form returns us to our history, that real history the narrative had set out to replace. We can admire this aesthetic, I think, as the crux of Scott's artistic greatness, by recognizing the rhetorical seduction of idealizing a de-idealization – a morose delectation if ever there were – at work in these endings. Scott privileges us to read the historical artifice of modern habits of reading, including the precious liberal-conservative space of neutrality, ambiguity, figural play, which may last no longer than the tale. The arch-patriarch's display of his powers is thus his own disappearing-act, a dissolve, grotesque rather than pathetic, to his own textual tricks and mechanisms. If he cannot be sovereign or divine then he is nobody but the author, himself just a series of shadows of our reading. 'A shadow – and an impersonal author is nothing better – can cast no shade'.[51] It would become the task of the great Victorian novelists to imagine an authentic ghost in the allegorical machinery of romance representation that Scott bequeathed to them in *The Heart of Mid-Lothian*.

CHAPTER 4

Scott and Dickens: the work of the author

> [The] book ends after Mr Pickwick has taken a house in the neighbourhood of Dulwich. But we know he did not stop there. We know he broke out, that he took again the road of the high adventures; we know that if we take it ourselves in any acre of England, we may come suddenly upon him in a lane.
>
> (G. K. Chesterton, *Charles Dickens*, 1906)

> It is the man rather than the writer that still haunts his own Border, like an emanation from its changeless hills and waters, so that on some forgotten drove-road in Ettrick one almost looks to see in an autumn gloaming his ruddy face and silvery hair, and to hear the kindly burr of his speech. It has been given to him to conquer the world, and yet remain the tutelary genius of his native glens.
>
> (John Buchan, *Sir Walter Scott*, 1932)

I

'*I fought for my own hand*,' said the Smith indifferently, and the expression is still proverbial in Scotland. [Meaning, I did such a thing for my own pleasure, not for your profit: *Scott's Note*.] (Scott, *The Fair Maid of Perth*)

In 1847 Charles Dickens, who had served on the London committee to raise funds for a monument to Sir Walter Scott in his native city, came to have a look at the result. Dickens did not like the new monument; it resembled 'the spire of a Gothic church taken off and stuck in the ground'.[1] Up until now, monuments to poets and men of letters had usually been placed *inside* churches. The exception was post-classical Edinburgh, where Burns and Dugald Stewart (who had been Scott's teacher) were commemorated by elegant model temples around the slopes of Calton Hill. There is certainly nothing neoclassical or discreet about the Scott monument, which exhibits a statue of the author himself framed by a vast Gothic tower in the heart of the city. A romantic allusion to the Old Town on the brink of the commercial New, the monument reproduces the historical and cultural situation of modern romance. Here, Scott constitutes his own temple, one that dominates the civic scene. The author as private country gentleman, beloved wolfhound at his feet, is enclosed by the fantastic canopy of his literary achievement; for the monument is at once an interior, a shrine for the figure brooding at its base, and an exterior, a pedestal exalting the characters of the Waverley novels to the city skyline. The author has given them the resemblance of life, and they give him in return their own immortality of effigy or figure.

It has been said that Scott's life, still more than his works, constituted his mythic prominence in the Victorian imagination.[2] That 'Life', however, is one more narrative in a larger institutional text, the romance of an official national culture that continued to unfold in the wake of the Waverley novels. With Sir Walter Scott, the cultural figure of the author achieves its modern canonical integrity, its monumental weight, in the public imagination. The Waverley novels had done much to define that figure of a unified public imagination – a society brought together in the act of reading the same book – as they charted an expanding and modernizing literary market. In this, they won not just wealth but honours for their author. For it is important to emphasize that Scott redefined the reading public in terms not only of magnitude but of quality, that is, social and political respectability. The official honours – the baronetcy, a personal association with George IV culminating in the dedication of the collected works – reflected in turn upon a popular readership that had been the occasion of persistent ruling-class anxiety throughout the latter half of the eighteenth century. The consumers of a toxic diet of pornographic chapbooks and Jacobin pamphlets were now absorbing, it could be presumed, a modern national mythology that bore the equivalent of the royal warrant of purveyance.

As they gained it dignity, the Waverley novels defined the publication format of fiction for the rest of the century. Richard Altick has emphasized that their immediate impact, in the long post-war recession, was retrogressive, driving prices up to unprecedented heights and establishing the novel as a luxury commodity. The publication in 1821 of *Kenilworth* in three post octavo volumes at a guinea and a half the set fixed a ceiling that publishers and circulating libraries together would prop up for the next seventy years.[3] Hence a certain paradox, already mentioned. The Waverley novels, soliciting a 'universal' reading public, definitively establish the 'popular' form of an expanding national literacy, at the same time as they mark off a class boundary in economic terms. That boundary turns out to be of the familiar Waverley type: policed but shifting and permeable. For if few private subjects could afford to own Waverley novels, rather more could rent them. The circulating libraries enlarged Scott's reading public to include the lower middle classes of the provinces as well as Edinburgh and London. Miss Martha Buskbody, the mantua-maker, is the typical consumer of modern romances within the Waverley novels, and Scott's conclusion of *Old Mortality* acknowledges even as it mocks her predominance.

At this point, it is worth recalling the collective enterprise of which the Waverley novels were the centre. The author's collaborators – his amanuensis Laidlaw, his printers, partners and promoters John and James Ballantyne, and Constable, truly a revolutionary figure – played their decisive parts in a production process in which the distinction between the purely artistic and the merely technological is often difficult to maintain. It was Constable, publisher not only of *Waverley* but of the *Edinburgh Review*, who dreamt of an industrially mass-produced cheap reprint series of respectable literature for the huge market of readers who could not afford to pay 10 shillings and sixpence per volume. The formal principle of that industrial mass-production was to be the serial miscellany: a family library on hire-purchase. In the event, the 1826 crash left the conquest of this new market to others. One immediate legacy of Constable's scheme, however, was the so-called *Magnum Opus* edition of the Waverley novels (1829–33), revised and annotated by the author and (through use of state-of-the-industry publishing technologies) retailing at only 5 shillings a volume. Here was a literary equivalent of the extension of suffrage, enabling householders of respectable but moderate means to acquire a national cultural heritage for their own possession instead of having to rent it, one book at a time.[4]

Scott's last edition represented not only a cheap, high-quality serial reprint format as influential as had been the gentrifying inflation of the first editions, but, as Jane Millgate's valuable study has recently made clear, a new and just as influential model of the novelist's *œuvre.* The dignity of the novel was sealed by a new generic formation, the collected works.[5] The cohesive principle of this formation was the supervising presence of the author as his own editor, revising and annotating to clarify the retrospective shape of a career – a life in writing. Literary production now represented itself as a new relation between life and works, exceeding the sum of the parts. It was an organic totality, a dynamic presence; it was life itself, recovered in the act of reading. The author sat at the chronological origin of this animating circuit and the reader at its end. All that was wanting was the formal complement of a 'Life', such as those Scott himself had written for the *Ballantyne's Novelist's Library* collection: raising, like Dr Johnson, the dignity of his craft.

Five years after Scott's death, in the year of Victoria's accession, that want was provided. Lockhart's *Life of Scott*, justly recognized to be the most important British literary biography after Boswell's *Life of Johnson*, redefined its genre as the official monument of a new hero of civilian culture, modernity's distinctive figure of a transcendental subject, at once unique and universal. Lockhart's seven volumes (1837–8) constitute the most impressive article in the national canonization of Scott that, already under way in his lifetime, was solemnized in the decade after his death. This is the period of the Scott monument (1840–4) as well as of Carlyle's celebration of the man of letters as modern hero. 'Universal History, the history of what man has accomplished in the world, is at bottom the History of the Great Men who have worked here', Carlyle declared.[6] It would thus be the special function of biography, established in Lockhart's *Scott* and followed in examples such as Forster's *Dickens*, to furnish the 'Life' as the origin, completion and ground of the author's works, containing them as its allegorical types and figures. It would turn out to be the life that imitated the works, however, in order to maintain its paradigmatic form.[7]

Scott powerfully reinvented romance, as the narrative of individual lives in a collective experience of history. Just so, the Waverley novels inaugurate not only a heroic age of the author but a heroic age of literary character. The nineteenth-century acclaim of both Scott and Dickens appealed to their invention of a secular mythology – a kind of national and domestic pageant – of *characters*, produced by history yet transcending and incorporating it, to form a living tradition reaching back to Shakespeare and Chaucer. Character was the genius that animated the national literary tradition: its image of the eternal subject.[8] The figure of the author occupied a potent, ambiguous position with respect to this register. He was at once its origin and its effect, the sign of his mastery being his very status as one of his own inventions: his own greatest character. In such a way the Scott monument represents the Author of Waverley in terms of a dialectical relation between life and works that is also one between internal and external, private and public sites of character. The national, official dimension of this self-making might now seem quaintly or grotesquely 'Victorian', since the figure of the author in modern capitalist cultures has become more radically privatized. The reveries cited at the head of this chapter, turning their modernist and late-imperial nostalgias back upon the age, invoke phantasms of just such a transcendental subject; more subtly in the case of Chesterton, for whom Mr Pickwick is the Genius of Dickens, delivered from the dark city. By now, the authorial daimon has become unofficial, covert, cultic rather than institutional: a *genius loci* that dodges history, not its trophy. The modern romance topos of a submerged authentic Britain, signified by a lost rural economy and described earlier as Scott's particular contribution to the novel, coincides with an idea of reading as solitary consolation and refuge.

The presence of the man before the work, as the genius of romance, is the central rhetorical claim of literary biography. It is also the commonplace of Scott's reputation, pronounced by debunking critics from Carlyle to Leavis as well as by admirers such as Buchan. Such is the impressive achievement of Lockhart's great work. Its prototype, the *Life of Johnson*, had made personality, rather than literary work, the location of its subject's essential identity. Boswell had celebrated the hero as man of letters, but in difficult relation to a literary production all too visible as labour, at odds with the institutional systems of patronage and the market. Johnson's heroic character was to be found in that aspect of his life represented as sublimating his work: a moral integrity revealed above all in private conversation.[9] Boswell's book was scandalous (to us, most modern) in its programmatic breaching of the boundaries between private and public life. However, it enabled Lockhart to make his version upon that very breach, even as he saved dignity by refusing to report gossip. The situation is in most ways a commodious one, for unlike Johnson Scott had enjoyed the due rewards of his genius in fortune, fame and title. Lockhart voluminously records Scott's popularity, honours and intercourse with the great, mingled with a private register of the domestic manners of the Laird of Abbotsford. With its unfailing graciousness, exhuberant hospitality and *ad hoc* revivals of ancient ceremony, this latter composes the image of a private life in inextricable unity with the public. F. R. Hart has written finely of Lockhart's 'romantic' project of representing an organic unity of imagination and life. It has to be added that this exemplary integrity represents above all a national cultural ideal, that of the historical allegory of the Waverley novels; and a class ethos, that of the bourgeois gentleman, in whom property, power and moral kindness may harmonize and guarantee one another. The author himself personifies the romance of private patriarchy unfolded in his literary works.[10]

Applying to Scott his own principle of domestic morality, Lockhart insists that the essence of the great man is the good man. To that end, it seems that some of the story's pious highlights, such as Scott's deathbed exhortation to 'be virtuous – be religious – be a good man', were forged or at any rate embellished by the biographer. But if 'most truly might it be said that the gentleman survived the genius' then the dimension occupied by the genius is problematical.[11] For Lockhart continually represents the Laird of Abbotsford *rather than* the Author of Waverley. The author's work gets done, spontaneously, enigmatically, in the interstices of the crowded day of the Laird, and Sherriff and Clerk of Session: early before breakfast, or when he is ill (dictating *The Bride of Lammermoor* in a delirious trance). Reproducing itself in the reader's romance ethos of delight over duty, this is the effect, perhaps, of an 'aristocratic' leisure rather than labour – as in Scott's own fable of the composition of *Waverley*, serendipitously resumed via a quest for fishing-tackle.[12] It is more accurate, however, to say that Scott's life exemplifies, not merely industry, but something more sublimated, a characteristic – once more prototypically 'Victorian' – *energy*. Genius is present as the haunting of so restless a life: to risk anachronism, an early figure of the unconscious, a mental force alien to the life it inhabits (we recall that the pre-Freudian psychoanalyst is called an *alienist*.) Closeted away, ultimately private, the work of writing is a mysterious, impersonal process, at once a kind of magical power and merely mechanical reproduction. Or so Lockhart represents it, in his striking anecdote of the Author of Waverley at work as a hand writing by itself, disembodied and indefatigable. In the summer of 1814, Lockhart joins a party of Edinburgh law students:

After carousing here for an hour or more, I observed that a shade had come over the aspect of my friend, who happened to be placed immediately opposite to myself, and said something that intimated a fear of his being unwell. 'No,' said he, 'I shall be well enough presently, if you will only let me sit where you are, and take my chair; for there is a confounded hand in sight of me here, which has often bothered me before, and now it won't let me fill my glass with a good

> will.' I rose to change places with him accordingly, and he pointed out to me this hand which, like the writing on Belshazzar's wall, disturbed his hour of hilarity. 'Since we sat down,' he said, 'I have been watching it – it fascinates my eye – it never stops – page after page is finished and thrown on the heap of MS., and still it goes on unwearied – and so it will be till candles are brought in, and God knows how long after that. It is the same every night – I can't stand a sight of it when I am not at my books.' – 'Some stupid, dogged, engrossing clerk, probably,' exclaimed myself, or some other giddy youth in our society. 'No, boys,' said our host, 'I well know what hand it is – 'tis Walter Scott's.'[13]

The anecdote – once more, it seems, fictionalized by Lockhart – makes visible an emblem of Scott's writing, but as an ambiguous display, a secret activity spied on.[14] This emblem condenses the terms of anonymity, fame, industry and magic. Writing divorced from personal identity, lacking a face although not a name (''tis Walter Scott's'), is at once an image of romance magic, the power of an enchanter, and of an alienated and reified mechanical toil, the hand of a clerk, a metonymic extension of the Ballantyne presses. Adam Smith's famous metaphor for market forces has been disclosed as the content of a Gothic recognition.

As usual, the authority of the biography consists in the fidelity with which it transmits its subject's own tropes of authority. Lockhart reproduces here the Author of Waverley's self-representation in terms of a faculty or function separate from personality, from 'life', in an ontological division of labour: the eidolon figure invoked in the prefaces to *The Fortunes of Nigel* (1822), *Peveril of the Peak* (1822) and *Tales of the Crusaders* (1825). The last is the most elaborate: 'the Eidolon of the Author of Waverley' chairs an assembly of his characters and editorial avatars in order to discuss the incorporation of the Waverley novels as a joint-stock company. (After a fever of such incorporations, the year would close with the Constable–Ballantyne crash). The symposium soon turns into an industrial dispute. Dousterswivel, the foreign trickster-entrepreneur of *The Antiquary*, proposes the composition of future novels by a steam-engine which would mechanically recombine the repertoire of romance commonplaces, thus saving altogether the labour of an author. The meeting disintegrates into uproar as the characters protest that all these technologies of modernization actually mean that the author is trying to accumulate despotic power over them, and he in turn threatens to 'unbeget' them all by forsaking romance for real history – an advertisement for the forthcoming *Life of Napoleon Buonaparte.* The author's recourse to a Napoleonic authoritarianism can only take the form of a bluff, the hollow threat of a self-unmaking, for his own, economic Waterloo awaits him; he will not be able to give up writing novels.

The most conspicuous trope of this complicated and self-divided authorship was, of course, Scott's celebrated anonymity, which he maintained with tortuous ceremony for over a decade. The 'secret' (that everyone knew) was a condition of the author's unprecedented cultural visibility, a mask that advertised itself. The function of the 'anonymity game', following recent, sophisticated accounts, seems to have been apotropaic, self-defensive at a superstitious level, as much as it was a reasoned cleaving to gentility.[15] Thus it was that the publication of Scott's private name came at last with the wreck of his fortunes – that larger revelation of the rift upon which, it now appeared, the identity was founded all along. Lockhart's deconstructive emblem of the writing hand foreshadows the ruin in its uncanny figuration of authorship as a radical dismemberment, rather than as a whole person or speaking visage. The romance of private patriarchy, magically transcendent within a modern historical economy, had turned out to be a delusion: fiction in the trivial, literal sense. In his strongest poetic insight, Lockhart glosses Scott as the dupe of his own baronial inventions, a romance wizard whose Abbotsford phantasmagoria fatally eclipsed a knowledge of economic realities (the state of his accounts with the Ballantynes and Constable). Once more, the image derives from Scott's own writings. In the journal he had begun to keep on the verge of his ruin, Scott put a tragical turn upon the persona of Prospero he had so often inhabited: condemned now to a bleak disenchantment, his broken spell the revelation of a self-betrayal.[16] The biographical romance, in short, recapitulates the broad theme and allegorical motive of the Waverley novels. They, rather than 'Scott's Life', generate the tropes of Lockhart's biography, even those of an ironic, sceptical exposure of the relation between life and writing. The Author of Waverley was always a figure produced by his own romance production.

As Millgate has argued, the *Magnum Opus* edition, the major project of financial recovery out of the abyss of debt, reconstitutes 'Sir Walter Scott' as 'the author of the Waverley novels', both in the definite shape of a unified *corpus* and in the systematic insertion of the author as autobiographical subject by the editorial apparatus (a technique Scott had already employed in his poems). In an analogous strategy, Lockhart's great last volume (1838) completes Scott's *Journal* in its narration of a strong moral self-recovery upon the ruins of health and fortune. Here the *Life* obeys a sterner anti-romance logic than had the novels. Yet, once more, the collapse of a romance identity generates its proof and restoration. We read the dour ethical sublime of an authentic, private honour refined by endurance, sacrifice, 'vassalage' (Scott's term) to creditors.[17] It redeems the chivalric character of a gentleman in the historically real, that is, economic, identity of author, unmasked and named, as labourer after all. Yet what is real, his work, is his bondage; it possesses him, the opposite of a free creating spirit; he is written to death, in mechanical drudgery. The catastrophe was not so much that the professional gentleman had turned out to be a popular author, as that the author turned out to be a failed speculator in his own commodities: his industry – the resources of his genius – bound to, and by, an invisible and intangible network of hollow credit, of which writer, printer and publisher formed just one node. Such a machinery appeared to confound a middle-class ethos of work and reward still more than it did an 'aristocratic' one of leisurely independence. Scott's fall represented the failure of a bourgeois romance of ambition, for which the reverie of a noble estate had been the extravagant cover.

The example of Scott's hard *askesis* spoke through Lockhart to inform the dominant ethical solution of Victorian fiction: the redemption of a fall or disgrace through a self-repressive, stoical course of work and duty.[18] The figure bears a cautionary charge in relation to the authors themselves, who would have to fend off Scott's fate even as they claimed the station he had instituted. While the conventions of romance might contrive the rescue of fortune even in the loss by which honour is proven, Scott had only redeemed his debts with his death, a dark conclusion. At the same time, the triumph of the Waverley novels held out the promise of gentility and title, in addition to wealth and fame, as the rewards that could be won from a huge new literary market, not just British but international in its extent.

Scott's example was thus problematic and controversial even while it was pioneering and authoritative. Carlyle's review of Lockhart, as we have seen, denied Scott the transcendental quality of heroism he would shortly proclaim for the poet and man of letters. Despite Carlylean disapproval of the novel in general, however, it was now widely recognized as the representative literary form of an era of industrial, demographic and electoral expansion. The case is put with particular force by one of the ambitious young novelists in Scott's wake, Bulwer-Lytton, in a 'condition of England' tract published in the year after the Reform Act:

> As with the increase of the crowd, appeals to passion become more successful, so in the enlargement of the reading public I see one great cause in the unprecedented success of fiction. Some inconsiderate critics prophesy that the taste for novels and romances will wear itself out; it is, on the contrary, more likely to increase as the circle of the public widens. Fiction, with its graphic delineation and appeals to the familiar emotions, is adapted to the crowd – for it is the oratory of literature.[19]

Bulwer-Lytton looks forward from Scott, who after all had abhorred reform, to a democratic proliferation of Scott's example. Novelists will actually occupy the platform of the man-of-letters hero. Even so, the appearance of the *Life of Scott* in 1837 overlapped with a more clamorous, and revolutionary, publishing event. The universal ecstasy over *The Posthumous Papers of the Pickwick Club* acclaimed Scott's successor as master of a national reading public. At the same time, it established the democratizing innovation of format, the serial miscellany in parts, of which Constable had been the prophet.

Kathryn Chittick has recently made the forceful revisionary argument that the wildly successful Dickens of the 1830s was not yet, by the canons of official literary culture, an author of novels. *Pickwick* was received, excerpted and reviewed as a series of sketches, a 'magazine consisting only of one article', a 'popular periodical'; and Boz was 'a monthly producer of public entertainments', more than one of which would be running at any given moment. Only after serialization would the text be bound and sold as a book. At the same time as Dickens inhabits this journalistic and episodic form, however, he aspires toward the superior status of the novelist as professional man of letters – the dignity established and exemplified by Scott.[20] It would be crucial for this aspiration that the new 'miscellany', however diverse its elements, should be unified by a single narrative line and a single author.

II

In 1832 – four years before *Pickwick* – Dickens had been jotting shorthand in the Press Gallery of the House of Commons, reporting the debates over the Reform legislation so sternly resented by Scott, who lay dying at Abbotsford. By 1838 he would hear his title to 'the throne of letters vacated by Scott' conceded by a formidable rival – Harrison Ainsworth, the feted and dandified author of *Rookwood*.[21] In just two years Dickens had acquired a literary career, wife and household, and national fame. Flushed with these initiations, he read Lockhart's *Life of Scott* as each volume appeared, and contemplated the summit of ambition upon the profession of letters.

The role model in Dickens's life had up till now been another Edinburgh literary gentleman: George Hogarth, a respected music critic, and currently editor of the new London paper the *Evening Chronicle*. Modern biographers emphasize Dickens's esteem for the social achievement of this son of a well-to-do Lothian farmer, who encouraged the tyro journalist and helped him publish his early sketches. In April 1836 Dickens confirmed a filial relationship with Hogarth by marrying his daughter Catherine. Edgar Johnson has suggested that the father-in-law was as important a part of the match as was the bride.[22] In any case, the talismanic ingredient of Hogarth's appeal seems to have been a personal connection with the great North British romancer. At this delicate stage of his fortunes, Dickens would boast that his prospective father-in-law had been 'the most intimate friend and companion of Sir Walter Scott, and one of the most eminent of the literati of Edinburgh'.[23] On both accounts he was exaggerating somewhat. In 1815, Scott's printer James Ballantyne had wanted to marry Hogarth's sister; in order to satisfy the family of his credit he had to renegotiate his (secret) partnership with Scott, and it was young George who worked out the terms of the new arrangement. At Scott's ruin in 1826, Hogarth was one of the committee that helped draft the terms of his debt repayment, and he remained an important financial adviser. Dickens also liked to claim that Hogarth had introduced Scott to his own literary son-in-law, Lockhart.[24]

Hogarth, in sum, was a local avatar of Scott, the late Monarch of Olympus. Dickens's relation to both figures evokes an intricate pattern of authors and publishers and fathers-in-law, a network of patriarchal and professional contracts mediated by the exchange of women. These relations are conduits of symbolic power: Sir Walter's magic is to descend now, via the editor, to the ambitious son-in-law at the start of his career. Scott is thus the ideal shadow or archetype of the father-in-law, a figure whose professional and ceremonial, symbolic patriarchy is far more impressive than any actual, personal, mortal father, the type of ruinous weakness and improvidence in Dickens's life and fiction.[25] The official ceremony of succession took place, accordingly, in the summer of 1841, when Dickens visited the Hogarths' native country. Dickens later described the banquet in his honour in Edinburgh as 'the first public recognition and encouragement which I ever received'. Professor Wilson ('Christopher North') and other representatives of the powerful Edinburgh literary establishment toasted the young Englishman as the heir of

Burns and Scott; it was Scotland's prerogative to pass on the laurels of national authorship to this cockney son-in-law.[26]

By now Dickens was at work on his own, long-meditated imitation of the Scott historical romance, and his Scottish triumph (preceding by a few months the more strenuous American tour) marked a turning-point in the obsessive interest with which he recurred to the senior author's career between about 1838 and 1842. Dickens announces a sometimes fulsome reverence for Scott's achievement, addressed less to specific works or matters of literary technique than to Sir Walter as representative of the profession of novelist. The context of these references is almost always discussions of publication, reader-reception, sales and contracts; matters that the reading of Lockhart would have brought into particular focus. Scott's relations with his publishers dominate *The Life of Scott*, forming the essential plot of authorial identity. The story impressed Dickens at a period when his own relations with his publishers were at their most turbulent. Here, indeed, we can read Dickens's shifting and developing sense of his professional identity with particular clarity, as he strove to revise the terms of his contracts from journalistic dependence toward economic and legal control over his work. The story is familiar: first the struggle to establish artistic priority in *Pickwick*, and then the devious and acrimonious negotiations with Macrone and with Bentley, with whom successively Dickens fought to dissolve contracts he claimed were disadvantageous. These local, bitter clashes mark the author's progress toward a state of literary professionalism as yet unarticulated because scarcely formed in the culture at large. As fiction becomes fully established as a mass-produced commodity, so the author strives to distinguish himself from – by claiming a relation of command over – a complex machinery of commodification in which are included his publishers.[27]

In a series of anonymous reviews published in Forster's *Examiner* between September 1838 and September 1839, Dickens intervened in the public quarrel that had broken out between the Ballantyne family and Lockhart over the latter's account of Scott's ruin. Dickens takes the side of Lockhart against his father-in-law's kinsfolk, arguing vigorously that the Ballantyne brothers owed everything to Scott, and were in effect his creatures. Dickens seems to have had some special knowledge from that same George Hogarth who had more than once arranged terms between author and printer; even as Dickens was now becoming, in turn, the patron of his own father-in-law and former editor. Dickens concludes his defence of Scott with a panegyric to the genius who was worthy of the most extravagant claims to fortune and estate. Dickens's hyperbole marks a striking departure from the conventional responses to Lockhart's account of the ruin, which tended to moralize upon Sir Walter the overreacher.[28]

In the two or three years following his reading of Lockhart's last volume, Dickens recurs to Scott as the model of prolific industry and popularity he himself is overtopping. But it is, as we have seen, a dangerous model, and Dickens reads warning there: despite 'a sale wholly unprecedented and unknown, even in Scott's time', he worries about 'making myself too cheap'.[29] This meant something else besides overproduction. Scott's popular success had been the ironical measure of his failure to control the economic infrastructure of his literary production. The hard lesson of that career was that the destiny of the author was determined in the marketplace by fluctuations of capital and credit. As Wilt points out, the part of Lockhart's narrative that most impressed Dickens and his contemporaries was its catastrophe. In his ruin the author lost all he had gained by his inventive powers, including his own copyrights – the property of the work itself. 'Poor Scott' became, for Dickens, a colossus sunken in the quicksands of the market; the type of a failure as impressive as was his success. The 1841 Scottish tour provided Dickens with the unforgettable emblem of this failure – as if, in the moment of his own coronation, as he was claiming the patrimony of historical fiction for himself, Dickens had to contemplate his precursor's fall. 'When I was at Abbotsford', he recalled nine years later,

> I saw in a vile glass case the old clothes Scott wore. Among them an old white hat, which seemed to be tumbled and bent and broken by the uneasy, purposeless wandering hither and thither of his heavy

head. It so embodied Lockhart's pathetic description of him when he tried to write, and laid down his pen and cried, that it associated itself in my mind with broken powers and mental weakness from that hour.[30]

The sublime father-in-law had turned out to be as frail and vulnerable as an actual mortal father, after all.

The success of the Waverley novels defined not just a British but an international literary market. The ruin of their author accordingly came to represent, for Dickens, the necessity of gaining legal and economic control over his own work worldwide. During the brawl over international copyright that vexed his first US tour, in 1842, Dickens kept using Scott as a cudgel to beat the American literary industry. Ruined, exhausted, dying at Abbotsford, Scott might yet have been revived by the income from his American popularity. In an extraordinary, ceremonial public passion, the young novelist brandished the name of his fallen predecessor:

I wish you could have seen the faces that I saw, down both sides of the table at Hartford, when I began to speak about Scott. I wish you could have heard how I gave it out. My blood so boiled as I thought of the monstrous injustice that I felt as if I were twelve feet high when I thrust it down their throats.[31]

Scott's fate inspires Dickens with a tremendous resentful energy. The 'monstrous injustice' that reduced his precursor to a senile apoplexy makes him, instead, titanic.

Scott had fallen, according to Lockhart, because he had kept himself ignorant of the commercial conditions of his authorship. Now, where Scott had been weak, Dickens would be mighty. Where the Author of Waverley's lack of control over his work was signified by the genteel concealment of his own name and an editorial diffusion of identity, we shall find in Dickens a fierce concentration of functions – not just author but journal editor, public speaker and advocate for the rights of authors – in a famous public name, identifying itself proudly in the midst of the marketplace. Dickens's involvement in the copyright issue (occupying Parliament, on and off, between 1837 and 1844) showed him more than ready to wield his celebrity in the struggle for professional status.[32] Sir Walter

Scott's considerable public distinction had required the novelist to lie unacknowledged because it accompanied a professional status already established. Now, thanks to Scott's dignifying example, Dickens could rise to an eminence scarcely accessible, to a man without a university education, in politics or the law.

By the early 1850s Dickens would be able to claim such professional status, however singular or problematic (as Feltes and Poovey argue) its economic and cultural terms might actually have been. He would at last have founded a successful periodical of his own, *Household Words* (1850). His novels were being reissued in a 'Cheap Edition' dedicated to 'the English people' with new prefaces emphasizing social issues and responsibilities (1847–). He would be tireless in organizing such activities as a lobby of eminent fellow authors against the Booksellers' Association monopoly (1852) and (with Bulwer-Lytton) a 'Guild of Literature and Art', by this time (1850) 'a Branch Insurance and Provident Society, solely for the Professors of Literature and of Art', in other words a prototypical professional organization.[33] And, famously, Dickens would have mythologized his vocation in one of his most successful works: the autobiographical romance *David Copperfield* (1850).

III

In forging a unified identity of author as public figure, Dickens's writing insists upon itself as the idiom of a personal presence. It is always 'Charles Dickens' who 'speaks to us', whatever the occasion, as though face to face. Chittick points out that the volume publication of *Nicholas Nickleby* (1839) not only shed 'Boz' to reveal the author's true name, but affixed as frontispiece his portrait by Maclise.[34] A facsimile of the author's signature appears beneath his countenance. It is, in short, a healing of that fatal dismemberment of work from name, of face from hand, evoked in Lockhart's anecdote of the Author of Waverley writing. Under such a sign the author's work becomes something more than composition or imitation: it is a present voice, the medium of a spirit. The contemporary theorist of such a claim is Carlyle, whose influence is ascendant in the years following Dickens's reading of Lockhart. Dickens's rhetorical self-making as authorial subject may be expressed very schematically as a negotiation between the dominant cultural models of Scott and Carlyle. If Scott personifies the material authority of a social institution – the author, the novel – then Carlyle represents that institution's spiritual reformation.

Dickens met Carlyle in 1840, the year of the lectures *On Heroes, Hero-Worship, and the Heroic in History*. These claim for the man of letters a powerful type of public presence: that of prophet in a modern secular culture. The individual will achieves its authentic and authoritative expression by engaging the institutions of the age in a purposeful dialectical contest, wresting to itself their spirit as it jettisons their forms:

> He that can write a true Book, to persuade England, is he not the Bishop and Archbishop, the Primate of England and of all England? I many a time say, the writers of Newspapers, Pamphlets, Poems, Books, these *are* the real working effective Church of a modern country.[35]

And its academy, and Parliament and justiciary: since the scope of a true book is to persuade the entire nation. Refusing to subordinate itself, in this radical-protestant claim, to established cultural institutions and ideological formations, writing is a mode of individual power that will eclipse the decayed influences of church and state, to convert and reform – to *educate* – a new republic of readers.[36]

To intervene in the public domain is thus to enter into a relation of opposition and competition – a *market* relation – with (rather than simply within) its discursive institutions. Again, it is necessary to insist on the importance of social class here. For Scott, public office and authorship were to have occupied coincident but exclusive dimensions; but for Carlyle and Dickens, authorship was the only means to public influence and authority, as well as to professional distinction. Public life was for them an alien social dimension, and their only access to it was by the sale of their labour in the marketplace. This double redefinition of the public domain – as *alien* and as a *marketplace* – is critical, not least because it entails a corresponding redefinition of the private, as the home of an original, authentic identity, distinct from the market and its machinery of exchange.

Prophetic force – the moral authority of an individual 'voice' – inheres then in an address *across* the discursive field of public exhange, reaching to and from an inalienable private core of identity. In the rhetorical circuit between author and reader the integrity of the subject is forged. For Dickens, this private, symbolic and transcendental economy is constituted by pathos or sentiment, the essential energy of domestic intimacy rather than of a radical individualism. Love, not money, binds author and reader together in the text, troped not (as in Scott) as a material process but as an organic psychic dynamism of production and reception. In the idealization of a sympathetic communion we may read Dickens's allegiance to his precursors in the Enlightenment novel and familiar essay (including Scott) rather than to Carlyle, who remained mistrustful of sentiment as another inauthentic social delusion, and preferred to stay up in the pulpit if not – like some Covenanting forebear – to take to the hills. As we shall see, Dickens presses sympathy and sentiment much further than his precursors toward 'deep' or 'primitive' psychic drives that are pre- or anti-social in their narrative logic.[37]

In the prefaces to the different editions of Dickens's early novels, we can follow the attempt to formulate the relationship between the author and his public. They are friends, host and guest, fellow-travellers. Publication in monthly serial numbers, the most thoroughly commodified of forms, is claimed to be the site of a 'freedom of intimacy' and 'cordiality of friendship', based on 'the feelings of the day' and 'the language which those feelings have prompted': in the volume preface to *Nicholas Nickleby* Dickens quotes the man of feeling himself, Henry Mackenzie, and finds precedent in the periodical essay, rather than any more grandiose novelistic precedent, such as the arch-literary, pompous and self-mocking prefaces of Fielding and Scott.[38] Through the most rigorous of 'professional' conditions, the journalist's deadline, Dickens produces the language of an 'amateurism' that reaches etymologically back through gentlemanly leisure to love. In serial production, writing and reading share a single duration of imaginative activity, generating one another by a dialectical pathetic force. Rather than the bound volume of a book the fiction is a fluid circulation of affective energies, broadcasting the author as a speaking presence – particularly if he is being read aloud at the hearthside.[39] Yet of course he is not really 'here': what is materially exchanged between author and reader is a printed text and a money payment. The evidence of the 'participation in feeling' that authenticates *The Old Curiosity Shop* is its sales figures (100,000 purchasers).[40] In a commodity system no property is valuable in and for itself, but according to its valence for exchange with others. Poovey describes serial publication as 'an absolute standardization' of format in which 'the writer was constructed not as an individual, much less a "genius," but as just one instance of labor, an interchangeable part, in a fully industrialized process'.[41] It needs no denial of Dickens's 'genius' – the fact that he offered better work than his competitors – to appreciate the fragility of the asset, that is, of the figure of personal identity *as* an asset – one's only real asset. In a recurrent theme in these prefaces up until *David Copperfield*, the private exchange of pathos between author and reader is called upon to bear a transcendental relation to its public analogue, market exchange.

The relation between author and reader receives its perfected statement with *David Copperfield*, the author's romance of his own identity. Appropriately, the rhetoric is that of an extraordinary, confessional sincerity. Dickens's tropes blend together composition, publication and reading in a single natural process: an organic expansion of the author's self in a relation of sentimental intimacy with his public:

> I cannot close this Volume more agreeably to myself, than with a hopeful glance towards the time when I shall again put forth my two green leaves once a month, and with a faithful remembrance of the genial sun and showers that have fallen on these leaves of David Copperfield, and made me happy.[42]

(The green leaves are the distinctive covers of the 1 shilling part issue format.) Yet the author speaks from a shadowy margin *between* literary works, in a mixture of anticipation and retrospect. The topos of Dickens's prefaces has become an increasingly ritualized gesture of parting from his work and his public. The utterance of authorial identity is valedictory and elegiac: 'sentimental' in the full-blown sense of a relation which exists only as a representation. Although situated before the novelistic text, on the threshold of our reading, the prefaces announce a process that is already finished for the author: publication as a book at the end of serial production.

> I do not find it easy to get sufficiently far away from this Book, in the first sensations of having finished it, to refer to it with the composure which this formal heading would seem to require. My interest in it, is so recent and strong; and my mind is so divided between pleasure and regret – pleasure in the achievement of a long design, regret in the separation from so many companions – that I am in danger of wearying the reader whom I love, with personal confidences, and private emotions . . .
>
> It would concern the reader little, perhaps, to know, how sorrowfully the pen is laid down at the close of a two-years' imaginative task; or how an Author feels as if he were dismissing some portion of himself into the shadowy world, when a crowd of the creatures of his brain are going from him for ever. Yet, I have nothing else to tell; unless, indeed, I were to confess (which might be of less moment still) that no one can ever believe this Narrative, in the reading, more than I have believed it in the writing. (47)

The divided sensation of pleasure and dejection defines a paternal cadence of creation: post-coital rather than post-natal. To part with the creatures of the author's brain is to part with something of himself, private and essential: the 'shadowy world' is not, as we might expect, the author's imagination, but the outside public world into which that imagination (more real, substantial, vital) has discharged itself. The imagination's life has not consisted, however, in any prior, self-contained wholeness, but in the transaction of composition and reception, the psychic intercourse afforded by serial publication. It is with the book that Dickens writes this epitaph upon his work. As he bids farewell to the children of his fancy, the author records the pang of disengagement from an intimate embrace. He and his reader have converged in a shared pathos, the spiritual simultaneity of 'belief', or authentic imaginative life. But how equal is the relation? What is exchanged, what life flows back to the author? The structural uncertainty of the reciprocation of this pathos – for if it is not returned, how can it be real? – makes the author claim for himself the prior, more powerful position. Literary work is defined by a surplus value which is one of *feeling*: the work's origin, the author's inalienable property. Our belief, however passionate, will always be secondary, a reproduction or shadow of the author's – always 'there', in the text, before us: the ghost in his own machine.

IV

If you mark Alexander's life well, Harry of Monmouth's life is come after it indifferent well; for there is figures in all things.

(Shakespeare, *Henry V*, IV.vii)

'And to think of a man's killing himself for such a miserable place as Abbotsford', Dickens remarked to Richard Henry Dana at the beginning of his American tour.[43] Abbotsford, after all, had been a bad bargain. It was the false idyll of a retirement from the public market that meant no more than the failure of the author, bamboozled by the glamour of a moribund feudalism, to balance his accounts. In the post-American satire of *Martin Chuzzlewit* (where it is the essential ingredient of a nation-wide credit swindle) gentility becomes the choice figure of identity as self-deception or conscious fraud in Dickens's fiction. Sir Walter Scott might have rested his claim of aristocracy upon a typically Scotch sentimental obsession with genealogies, but his title and his property alike were the fruits of industry, not inheritance. Carlyle's critique of (Lockhart's) Scott, as we have seen, denounced the Laird of Abbotsford for being a property-accumulating bourgeois, and no true peer of romance. For Dickens, who would leave an estate worth £97,000, the problem could rather be stated the other way around. Scott's fortune was inauthentic because of the pretence that it was aristocratic. In contrast to the example of the Author of Waverley, wasting his substance on fantastic romance-ancestral estates (Thomas the Rhymer's glen), Dickens would rehearse a simple democratic fable of the conquest of class boundaries: the author buys the big house his father showed him when he was a little boy.[44]

Dickens recognized that fable and myth constitute the body of biography, whatever its circumstantial dress. For the account of his identity as author he turned to romance. 'Whether I shall turn out to be the hero of my own life, or whether that station will be held by anybody else, these pages must show.' The famous opening sentence of *David Copperfield* (49) elects the author as the subject of the romance representation by confiding that identity to its forms: no consciousness may proclaim itself above or apart from 'these pages'. At a critical early stage of the narrative, as in *Waverley* and the anti-romance tradition it recapitulates, we come upon a scene of reading which encodes the young hero's romance identity. Scott had built the scene of reading upon elegiac conventions of historical class obsolescence and patriarchal retirement. Dickens's version locates a more radical alienation within the bourgeois nuclear family, narrating the loss of class status as a proto-Freudian psychosexual fall. The absence of a strong gentle father remains the condition of the scene. His father's headstone overlooks David's infant idyll with his widowed mother; when the 'crocodile' Murdstone claims her, David apprehends first that she has gone to join his father in the graveyard, and then that his father has risen from the dead (92). The Murdstones, dissenters and in trade, subject David, the son of a gentleman, to a puritanical regime of privation, labour, punishment, arithmetic and guilt, in preparation for his expulsion to the city. 'I believe I should have been almost stupefied but for one circumstance', he recalls:

> It was this. My father had left a small collection of books in a little room upstairs, to which I had access (for it enjoined my own) and which nobody else in our house ever troubled. From that blessed little room Roderick Random, Peregrine Pickle, Humphry Clinker, Tom Jones, the Vicar of Wakefield, Don Quixote, Gil Blas, and Robinson Crusoe, came out, a glorious host, to keep me company. They kept

> alive my fancy, and my hope of something beyond that place and time, – they, and the *Arabian Nights*, and the *Tales of the Genii*, – and did me no harm; for whatever harm was in some of them was not there for me; I knew nothing of it. (105)

For all its bower-like situation, David's reading is informed by Protestant and middle-class themes of self-improvement and social ascent, in contrast to the imaginative truancy that characterized Waverley and the female quixote. What David and Waverley have in common is a secretly magical virginal narcissism. Romance, here, is the promise of 'something beyond that place and time'. The mirror of the reader's destiny is an apocalyptic future rather than a heroic past. Its promise is redeemed by the worldly progress traced in the book *we* are reading, a combination of romance and spiritual autobiography, which is its own material evidence. The luminous glimpse (as in one of Blake's lyrics) of 'a summer evening, the boys at play in the churchyard, and I sitting on my bed, reading as if for life' (106) divides the author from his happy, heedless generation in a lonely glory of election. The promised land beyond his bondage is David's (and Dickens's) present triumph as an author of novels, a man of property and public eminence, a husband and father himself. The dead father's library represents then a radically individualist, psychologized patrimony, the material condition of which is estrangement and privation: the impulse to set forth 'on my own account'.

When David describes himself, late in the story, as looking back from his last horizon, it is to mark the archetypal figure of his progress as 'a ragged way-worn boy', pilgrim on the Dover road (937). Notoriously, the 'real' or economic content of that progress – how David does his work, the conversions of fancy into industry into profit – has consistently been refused explicit representation. Authorship as material process of production, as labour and sale, is never *shown* to the reader. Authorship is rather an energy of sublimation: just as its teleological horizon, as Alexander Welsh has insisted, seems not just domestic but otherworldly ('this tranquillity', 937; 'when realities are melting from me, like the shadows which I now dismiss', 950.) Throughout, David's worldly status is continually, systematically blurred, in part by a series of marvellous reversals, making him struggling orphan yet attended with flights of guardians, who themselves oscillate mysteriously between wealth and ruin. He is at once ambitious, industrious self-maker and douce gentleman.

This plot rhetoric corresponds to a principle of narrative doubling, present in Dickens's work from his first 'progress' romance, *Oliver Twist*, onwards. Well noted by critics, it is a formal topos of modern romance, and its strong derivation is through Scott and Gothic fiction.[45] It encodes the familiar ethical problem of the patrimony that must be earned. Such a plot, as we have seen, provides for a congruence between individual ambition, fraught with moral prohibitions against the getting of power and property, and providential donation, discredited as decadent *ancien régime* privilege. Now each authenticates the other as though cancelling its ideological contingency. Such a plot is schizophrenic, or doubled through and through, over and over; it is haunted by repetitions, foreshadowings, foretellings, it swarms with wraiths and shapeshifters, it is often at least two plots. In *Oliver Twist* the parish boy's progress across the institutional territory of the underclass, menaced by thieves who represent the bad potential of his fate, is rather clumsily juxtaposed with a different story, that of the recovery of the lost aristocratic heir, menaced by a reactionary usurping half-brother (whose name, Monks, identifies his Gothic provenance). David Copperfield's career is nothing if not one of second chances, endowing him with at least two doomed childhood idylls; two schools; two marriages; and a host of parental, sibling and sexual doubles. The chronological principle of this duality is a temporal sequence of discontinuities. The narrative sets forth discrete historical stages, in metaphoric correspondence with its serial publication: the transition from one to another is total and revolutionary. As the prior stage is superseded all at once so it is cancelled. Dickens's plot tends to represent a radical-protestant conception of temporality not as a continuous, organic development but as a sequence of ontological transformations. It is marked here by the frequency with which the hero is renamed and by the conspicuous technical figure of the 'Retrospect' chapters. These impressionistic evocations punctuate the chronological narrative in order to dissolve it for an extraordinary access of authorial feeling, charged with visionary, wishful, plot-shaping power. Here we find, for example, the convenient death of a Dora who has outlasted her stage, and the work's beatific and self-elegiac consummation.[46]

The problematic moral term of David's progress, identifying this structural crux as an ethical theme, is the 'innocence' the hero claims throughout, disavowing energies of desire that are economic and political as well as erotic. David insists that the bower of reading is secured by his innocence: 'whatever harm was in some of them was not there for me; I knew nothing of it'. The magic of virginity lies precisely in its sublime narcissism: for the book can show the reader nothing that, already and potentially, he is not. Identity has a fixed moral core, and a book cannot corrupt, it can only prompt. All the same, the conventional topic of the scene remains the quixotic infection of the fancy by a logic of imitation. As it happens many of the stories David cites are prototypes of the one we are reading, stories of a young man's ambitious-and-providential rise from dearth to fortune. The bower of reading is what it has been – canonically, covertly – in *Waverley*: one of instruction as well as pleasure. What pleasure, however, occupies the present scene and constitutes its pretext? The 'harm' of romance would seem to lurk in what many influential Victorian critics censured as the libertine example of a Fielding or Smollett hero.[47] There is something worse, though, than the 'undisciplined heart' which David will later rebuke as his principle fault. The literary presence that dominates his childhood reading appears to be Smollett's, and among Smollett's heroes licentiousness is only exceeded by a stubborn and brutal vindictiveness. In them, the evil spirit of masculine bourgeois romance – its complex of lust, ambition and resentment – is most violent. David dwells fondly on plots of revenge against his oppressors:

It is curious to me how I could ever have consoled myself under my small troubles (which were great troubles to me), by impersonating my favourite characters in them – as I did – and by putting Mr and

Miss Murdstone into all the bad ones – which I did too. I have been Tom Jones (a child's Tom Jones, a harmless creature) for a week together. I have sustained my own idea of Roderick Random for a month at a stretch, I verily believe. (105–6)

Within a page or two, we find David biting his step-father's hand, in imitation of Tom Jones's more manly and spectacular bout of fisticuffs with Thwackum, or Roderick Random's sadistic, premeditated revenges (he smashes the teeth of his cousin's tutor and instigates the flogging of his own dominie). 'It sets my teeth on edge to think of it' (108): the sensuous intensity of the revolt is one with its anguish. It marks a repetition of, a binding into, a prior, paternal logic of jealous violence.[48]

David's revolt provokes his exile to London, first as a pupil at Salem House and then as 'a little labouring hind at the service of Murdstone and Grinby' (208). His own story-making begins in captivity at Salem House, where it signifies not just, as he tells us, a 'romantic and dreamy' disposition, but an energy of survival: for with his fancy David enchants the formidable Steerforth, just as Scheherezade was able to captivate her tyrant:

Whatever I had within me that was romantic and dreamy, was encouraged by so much story-telling in the dark; and in that respect the pursuit may not have been very profitable to me. But the being cherished as a kind of plaything in my room, and the consciousness that this accomplishment of mine was bruited about among the boys, and attracted a good deal of notice to me though I was the youngest there, stimulated me to exertion. (146)

A will to power, in feminine disguise, is the inheritance secreted in David's romance imagination. This is the instruction disavowed by the claim of innocence, which invokes a 'dark' and 'unprofitable' aesthetic of feminine oneiric bliss – and so justifies the conjugal idyll of private patriarchy. We read, in short, the apology for romance. Its demonic power of instruction (harm or error) is contingent upon its being read innocently, as a child reads.

Yet how can the author, whose authority is his experience, continue to imagine in such terms, without bad faith? The claim of innocence can be sustained without terrific perplexity throughout the narrative of childhood, or for so long as the protagonist, like little Oliver, remains quite powerless, 'a kind of plaything'. Yet it appears that David is to be the hero of his own life. What would his idea of Tom Jones or Roderick Random look like, with the libertinism and resentment censored out? Dickens's striking solution is to factor out the masculine vices to a set of doubles: a careless squirely libertinism to Steerforth, a petty-bourgeois will-to-power to Uriah Heep.[49] With the exorcism of both figures from his story, David may retain for himself their respective virtues – frankness and earnestness – purified of their class origins. (Traddles, meanwhile, is the apotropaic double of David's innocence as unworldly naivety at the heart of a feminine domestic regime.) The ethical imperative of the hero's innocence entails, in other words, within or rather against the autobiographical ideal of a grace earned 'from within', the narrative of one produced externally by a providential plot and a daimonic figuration of character. Anything else (or rather everyone else) *except* David's 'genius' seems to be driving the plot. The other characters take part in his progress insofar as they exert *influence*, promoting or obstructing his destiny, standing in for and blocking off its alternative possibilities: Good and Bad Angels (the title of chapter 25). The plot turns upon the interventions of such figures rather than any play of conscience, the moral arena of psychic and ideological contradiction, within David. Hence the odd sententious blankness (there is nothing else quite like it in Dickens) of the late sequence of the hero's spiritual crisis, pilgrimage and conversion – elsewhere the crucial matter of spiritual autobiography.[50] The mixed-plot narrative, notoriously, loses vital tension as its schemes of doubling solidify into plot-lines distinct from David's own sensibility, which is to say, as he has too little to do with his doubles in their roles as mediators of his own desire. The logic of censorship that separates him from them, once they have become legible in their functions, fulfills itself all too well.

Many critics have found that the synchronization of David's progress with the author's present triumph brings about an aesthetic collapse. The notorious emblem of that bathos is Agnes, presiding over the narrative's last rites. Dickens's solution to the schizophrenic impasse of masculine bourgeois romance is to make David Copperfield's women the figures of his destiny, standing for the completion of his identity and thus (standing *in* for it) its persistent lack ('that old unhappy want of something'). Many have observed that Agnes is David's muse, personifying what the romance of the author's life has refused to describe, his literary labour. Mary Poovey has argued convincingly that, in taking the blank place of David's 'genius', Agnes typifies the foundation of the patriarchal conjugal idyll upon the regulative energies of feminine subjection.[51] The series of stages articulating David's progress has indeed presented an erotic and domestic rather than public and professional career, in which the woman alternates with the male doubles to mirror the masculine self as other, its own always missing complement, its essence. The first of these is of course David's mother, whose original position confers upon her the burden of archetypal status. Her betrayal of David marks his knowledge of gendered sexuality, hers and his own, as the term that divides them. But David is able to overcome that division, in an extraordinary visionary transaction, upon the simultaneous death of his mother and usurping half-brother:

> In her death she winged her way back to her calm untroubled youth, and cancelled all the rest.
>
> The mother who lay in the grave, was the mother of my infancy; the little creature in her arms, was myself, as I had once been, hushed forever on her bosom. (187)

The lullingly ambiguous reference of the last clause typifies the novel's temporal rhetoric of transcendence by stages that revise and cancel one another, as also its typological rhetoric of doubling. David's fancy that the dead child is himself converts a rival into a donor; the death becomes an exchange in which he is born again, or (rather) less a gift or exchange than an appropriation, not of life but of innocence. For innocence is the character of infancy, or in-fancy, the inward imaginative core of being. 'The mother of my infancy', purified by death into a spirit of the memory and of the symbolic imagination, becomes the teleological influence of David's progress, guiding him to Dover. Dora is her false avatar because Dora represents a carnal and literal repetition, thus captivity to an earlier stage, and a sterile and parodic 'innocence' that is only the useless mirror of David's own. Her true avatar is Agnes, for Agnes represents pure 'influence', or the magical presence of the mother's absence, a completed sublimation, as the final term of the author's identity.

The object of this sublimation is the author's own origin. 'I am born', announced the first chapter, quietly and tactfully disposing of the distracting example of *Tristram Shandy*. For the subject's life begins at birth rather than at conception; his narration is determined not by a father's emission, the word of another, and thus the infinite regressions of textuality, but by his own present *consciousness*. Yet 'I am born' is an impossible utterance, and David is the absent centre of that wonderful first chapter. The most provocative homage to his absence is paid by Aunt Betsy Trotwood, a kind of domesticated Meg Merrilies, for whom the son of an absent father must be an absent daughter. It seems from the start that David's authentic self, his 'genius', is another, shadowy female presence, a phantom sister. It is not only that romance power, once again, wears the *déshabille* of a feminine seduction, and that literary labour, as Poovey argues, is displaced onto the feminine cultural site of domestic economy. To these accountings must be added the eschatological dynamic identified by Hillis Miller and Welsh:[52]

> My lamp burns low, and I have written far into the night; but the dear presence, without which I were nothing, bears me company.
>
> O Agnes, O my soul, so may thy face be by me when I close my life indeed; so may I, when realities are melting from me, like the shadows which I now dismiss, still find thee near me, pointing upward! (950)

Agnes's 'pointing upward' signifies a transcendental destination, but also her function as a fetish of the phallic desire and social ambition so strenuously excluded from David's own narrating consciousness. Hers is the emblematic stance of erection and *excelsior*: John Carey was right to remark that she is pointing the way upstairs to the bedroom.[53] That is, David may welcome home the alienated majesty of his own sexual and social energies; his own, yet separate from him, they occupy the emblem of innocence; his sublime (sublimated and essential) self is not someone he *is* but someone he *has*. The author imagines the embrace of his genius in a narcissistic rapture.

The rapture is cast in a mood of prophetic elegy, characteristic of Dickens's sentimental sublime (cf. Sydney Carton's thoughts from the scaffold, evoked subjunctively after his execution at the end of *A Tale of Two Cities*). In a powerful variant of the valedictory convention of the prefaces, the presence of the author signals the death of the author at the end of *David Copperfield*. In the dimension of reading that will outlast his lifetime, after all, the author has no existence beyond the text. David's opening hesitation over who might be the hero of his own life is thus not only coy; Agnes might, properly speaking, be that hero, with David's other doubles ranked beside her; but in fact the question is deferred to the showing of 'these pages'. The identity of the author is inextricable from his narrative in a far from trivial tautology. The author coincides with the material and symbolic forms of his romance, for he is their symbolic product as well as their material producer. The famous absence of a representation of literary work in the novel marks, in these terms, the vanishing point where the literary work does not reflect itself because it coincides with itself. The absence in which the author finds his identity may then express not so much a 'repression' as a punctilious tact towards the reader, who is expected to be a discriminating as well as enthusiastic reader of novels, a connoisseur of romance devices. The vanishing point is occupied then by an allegorical figure who is herself the figure of allegory, that is, of an anagogic horizon of completion (of spiritual meaning) beyond the last letter of the text: hence not only her pointing upward but the schematic blankness that signifies her alienness within the tropical vitality of Dickensian mimesis.

Spiritual autobiography is occupied by romance form, the most proximate and powerful example of which is Scott's.[54] *David Copperfield* relies intimately on the providential mixed and multiple plotting, articulated by schemes of doubling, that Scott had developed from the eighteenth-century novelists by the creative imitation of Renaissance romance. As in Scott, these forms constitute the narrative subject, an equation Dickens makes radical by writing romance as the author's self-representation. This literal precipitation of author as romance enables the spiritual register of a bold transcendentalism, in which the romance is the ideal form of the author's destiny – not just works but grace. The domain of the fiction is entirely, intensely, that of 'private life', animated by a psychosexual allegory more elaborate (in the range of its types, in its groundings upon individual sensation and upon infancy) than any in Scott. In Dickens, Freud's parent, the family resemblances of Gothic are strongly marked. But what of Scott's other narrative innovation, history? It is time to turn to Dickens's direct literary engagement with his official precursor.

CHAPTER 5

Scott and Dickens: the end of history

'Thinking of the fields,' the turnkey said once, after watching her, 'ain't you?'

'Where are they?' she inquired.

'Why, they're – over there, my dear,' said the turnkey, with a vague flourish of his key. 'Just about there.'

'Does anybody open them, and shut them? Are they locked?'

(Charles Dickens, *Little Dorrit*)

It might have been thought by any other than a sternly tentative philosopher, that the denial of their natural food to human feelings would have provoked a reactionary desire for it; and that the dreariness of the street would have been gilded by dreams of pastoral felicity. Experience has shown the fact to be otherwise; the thoroughly trained Londonder can enjoy no other excitement than that to which he has been accumstomed, but asks for *that* in continually more ardent or more virulent concentration; and the ultimate power of fiction to entertain him is by varying to his fancy the modes, and defining for his dulness the horrors, of Death.

(John Ruskin, *Fiction, Fair and Foul*)

I

Dickens's friend Percy Fitzgerald recalled Dickens's fondness and admiration for Scott, 'the first of all the novelists'.[1] Scott does not appear, however, among the eighteenth-century canon of novels and tales that nourished the author's childhood fancy, according to the autobiographical scene of reading in *David Copperfield*. In the 1820s Scott would have been too contemporary, thus expensive, to have featured in Dickens's father's small library of cheap editions. Dickens probably read the *Magnum Opus* edition of the Waverley novels, almost certainly in London in the early 1830s, the period of his self-education and journalistic apprenticeship. Scott belongs, in short, to the imagination of Dickens's early manhood rather than of his childhood.[2]

Dickens's references to Scott, crowded in the frantic first half-dozen years of his novelistic career, express an enthusiastic and wary identification with the senior author's achievement. In standing for literature as a social institution, Scott exemplified not only novel-writing as a profession but also novelistic discourse in its full technical repertory of forms and topics. The influence of Scott, in this institutional character, was of a different kind from that usually reckoned in Dickens's reading by his critics and biographers. The classic eighteenth-century English novels and the chapbook nursery tales, *The Arabian Nights* and *The Terrific Register*, melodrama and pantomime and comic song: all of these comprised for Dickens, by their very status as the stuff of childhood imagination, a naive-romance register of comic, pathetic and sensational effects. They yield the primitive, irrational archetypes of desire and dread. They are Dickens's oral tradition, the folklore of the urban middle and working classes. Paul Schlicke notes that this popular culture too was changing, so that for Dickens its familiar forms signified an imaginative origin located not in an ancient past but in childhood.[3] If childhood reading and popular culture rendered the primitive elements of romance – images of appetite, violence, hilarity, terror, loss, longing and marvellous transformation – then Scott provided a comprehensive principle of design, a literary architecture, in short, the model of sentimental romance. Imitation of the Waverley novels frames the first stage of Dickens's career, which begins with the genteel aspiration to write a three-volume historical novel and closes with the exceptionally studied and laborious production of *Barnaby Rudge*.

Meanwhile, Dickens found himself racing to popular acclaim upon a serial and miscellaneous narrative of comic sketches, which he was quick to harness with the old protestant folk-romance design of an allegory of providential progress. As we shall see, the traditional ideology of that allegorical design tended to fight against the worldly and vagabond affections of the fancy, Dickens's principle of narrative invention. Writing a historical novel in competitive imitation of Scott, Dickens was to acquire a more flexible and complex narrative technique, capable of a 'visionary' or synchronic representation of a total social world which was theoretically precise as well as synecdochally vivid. For Scott offered his fellow novelist a far more exact, comprehensive and subtle model of social representation, in the mixed narrative forms of modern romance, than did Carlyle – however important the latter was for ideological content.

In Scott, 'romance' stood for the relation of a subjectivity both to a historical scene and to a representation, encoding an imaginary transformation under its spell. Dickens intimates the individual imagination's priority over its occasions. Its principle is no external scene or text but a private, inward estrangement: the self finds its origin in a feeling of being *elsewhere than itself.* The fancy is the gleam of 'something beyond that place and time', an energy of change, of progress. Before it acquires the allegorical and transcendental direction of the pilgrimage, however, it is sheer peripatetic seriality, narrative as a perpetual motion machine. In the early novels, *Pickwick*, *Oliver Twist*, *Nicholas Nickleby* and *The Old Curiosity Shop*, highway and city street are the sites of narrative representation, always in circulation, always (in the theatrical language of *Nicholas Nickleby*) changing scene. As for settling anywhere, the threat of a prison or a grave is more vivid than the promise, fading into an idyllic haze, of home; or rather, when home becomes a goal rather than a place to fly from, it turns out to be an absolute kind of elsewhere, very like a grave.

That serial production and circulation are the vital principles of narrative is the thematic as well as institutional commonplace of *Pickwick*. As we saw in the last chapter, Dickens himself represented literary producation as an organic rather than mechanical process. The serial narrative is fruitfully entwined in everyday life, not just with its readers' feelings but with the journalistic matter of its contemporaneity, from which it draws idiom and texture. In the course of publication, the story comes into synchrony with 'real time', and shares volume-space with those quintessentially temporal texts, advertisements.[4] At the same time seriality, in the traditional topographical figure of the journey, is the thematic occasion for narration. The Pickwickians (a club of which the reader is a member) go about gathering data for its own sake, however trivial or miscellaneous.[5] This activity can be benignly comic because it is supposed to be innocent of political or economic utility. It is absurd, whimsical and liberating, an 'amateurism' exalted beyond the crotchets of antiquarian lairds to a boyish middle-class reverie of perpetual holidays. The pure lustre of gentility – without guilt of power and money – in the middle-class imagination is leisure; and so Dickens inaugurates the Victorian equation of pastoral with *nonsense*, a blissful (yet anxious) freedom from the world of work and commerce.

Like the Sherriff-Deputy of Selkirk riding after border ballads, the Pickwickians are keen above all to collect narratives. Their peregrinations produce not only the episodes of their own misadventures but a series of typical scenes in which a tale is told and received. Dickens alludes to the prototype of ballad-gathering at the end of the fifteenth number, when he reproduces a 'wild and beautiful legend' sung by Sam Weller. Under the generic title of 'Romance', it celebrates an episode in the career of 'the bold Turpin'. This, however, is not Ariosto's or Boiardo's warlike bishop, chronicler of the feats of Roland, but the British highwayman, who blows bishops away. 'Romance' is the rubric of parody and outlawry. Scott's self-mockery of the conventions of scholarly editing is turned into a rather fierce derision: 'We would beg to call particular attention to the monosyllable at the end of the second and fourth lines, which not only enables the singer to take breath at those points, but greatly assists the metre':

> Bold Turpin vunce, on Hounslow Heath,
> His bold mare Bess bestrode – er.

The romance chronicler hints at his adult familiar name, with a rude phallic swagger, in the Chorus:

> But Dick put a couple of balls in his nob,
> And perwailed on him to stop.[6]

Outrageous violence, so effervescent in the conceits of the servant Sam and the pretender Jingle, is otherwise contained – muddy and curdled – in the interpolated stories. The contrast between their Gothic and oedipal heaviness and the geniality of the main narrative has been well remarked by readers. Dickens, in other words, has reversed the traditional generic ratio of modern romance, and herein lies the wonderful appeal of *Pickwick*. The naive idyll is sustained in the serial episodic mode of the main narrative, as the way of the world, while the matter of anxiety is locked up in a sequence of artificial enclosures – only threatening the hero when he is himself *arrested*. Pickwick's incarceration for debt redefines the outlaw status of his liberty at the same time as it forces him into a fully institutional condition of social experience.[7]

Dick Turpin, as it happens, is the life and soul of Harrison Ainsworth's immensely popular *Rookwood* (1834), and the 'knight of the road' is the generic anti-hero of the so-called Newgate novel, instituted with Bulwer-Lytton's *Paul Clifford* (1830). Ainsworth himself invoked 'the bygone style of Mrs Radcliffe', along with Walpole, Lewis and Maturin, for his British romance ancestry; but *Rookwood*, with its variety of character parts and its intricate inheritance plot, derives most from Scott, as Philip Collins has noted. Both Ainsworth and Bulwer-Lytton, acclaimed as epigones of Scott in the years immediately following his death, undertook what might be called a re-gothicization of historical romance, already prepared by Scott in his own novels written after 1820, especially those featuring London: 'the grand central point of intrigues of every description, [which] had now attracted within its dark and shadowy region the greater number of the personages whom we have had occasion to mention'.[8] This tendency suggests that 'history' – the public affairs of great folks – is a glossy but empty pageantry, and the fiery currents of life flow underground, in populous warrens and secret labyrinths. Historical romance in the two decades from Peterloo through the 1840s, to risk a generalization, apprehends a subject of history more vast, inchoate and subterranean than the private professional gentleman of feeling: the people, source of a vitality not just demotic but demonic, criminal. Personifying this double nature, Ainsworth's Turpin refreshes the tawdry melodrama of the aristocratic-Gothic overplot with a sprightly vernacular of thieves' cant.

Oliver Twist, which began to appear well before *Pickwick* was over, was quickly associated with the Newgate school, partly because it overlapped with Ainsworth's *Jack Sheppard* in *Bentley's Miscellany*.[9] In what would turn out to be Dickens's second novel, the streets through which the hero wanders are now an urban criminal wilderness. As we shall see, Dickens extends the late-Scott and Newgate manner of Gothic revival, but for the important matter of the fable he draws upon the *Bildungsroman* model of the Scotch novels. Again we read about a young hero's formative but unwitting quest through outlaw territory, populated by uncanny familiars, foes and patrons, in the course of which his legal identity is threatened and affirmed. But while Scott's bandits and conspirators are remnants of a primitive patriarchal order, reduced to outlawry by economic emargination and political proscription, Dickens's are decisively *criminal*, now an ontological rather than historical category. The Dickensian wilderness of public experience occupies no border between different historical economies but an underworld, at the heart or rather depth of the city. It is its nocturnal aspect, synchronic and pervasive. Dickens represents this world as an economy structurally congruent with the official, legal one, but in a relation to it of shadow and parody. The division is metaphysical rather than contingent: adult criminal types such as Sikes and Fagin are authentically demonic. The epiphany of crime unfolded towards the end of the tale touches not property but life itself. Beginning with *Oliver Twist*, Dickens characteristically represents murder as an apocalyptic event: a chaotic explosion of violence illuminating the final order of the plot. Alexander Welsh has commented upon the typological prominence of Cain, the founder of the city as well as the first murderer, in Dickens's fiction. It is as if, for Dickens, the original sin – the creation of death – is not subaltern ambition, but a 'civilizing' and family-splitting violence of social competition. The sacred bond lies not between landlord and vassal but between brothers and sisters. Dickens's remythologization coincides with a well-known set of historical events, namely, the abolition of almost all capital statutes except those applying to homicide, which was thus promoted to the status of a unique category of crime, and the formal institution of a metropolitan police. Dickens expresses killing as a supremely private act, 'passionate' rather than 'political', involving a metaphysical intensification of irrational and sensational effects. It is a fatal transaction of power between individuals, fixing them in an archetypal relation outside social meaning. In Scott, on the other hand, killing tends to remain a historical and political event. Far from kindling a sensational or a visionary blaze, it brings a cooling editorial sententiousness or irony.[10]

Contemptible as are its institutional representatives, the law gains a spiritual charge in Dickens's plot. The progress of the hero, claimed alternately by thieves and pious householders, compassionated and suspected in turn, has a starker allegorical relief than ever it did in Scott. As a child, Oliver can be a more generic and universal pilgrim than Scott's young people, who are to acquire historical, social and sexual definition on their journeys. *The Parish Boy's Progress* is the first of many novels across Dickens's career to map an exemplary individual history of childhood and youth anagogically onto a vertical class structure, making it an ascent from the abyss. Downward and upward social mobility alike are not part of a collective historical process, but stations of an individual apocalypse. Oliver's journey toward legitimacy and (as it turns out) gentility is menaced by demons of the underclass so that his ontological difference from them can be confirmed. However, 'Progress' carries a double allusive and generic charge in Dickens's title. On the one hand, to be sure, it invokes Bunyan, and a promise of grace: Oliver will not be corrupted by thieves because of a virtue innate in him. On the other, it invokes the satirical model of Hogarth, and an ironical logic of worldly contingency: the child will be twisted into an Artful Dodger by privation and bad company. This duality expresses itself in the functional division of the plot that I mentioned in the last chapter. For resolution, Dickens resorts to the old-romance trope of election as gentle birth; Oliver's origins and the thwarting of Monks take over from Fagin's influence as the problem of the plot (its mystery) in its latter stages.

As the narrative moves into its latter stages, and the romance plot takes over with the recovery of Oliver's origins, the note of his end reverberates in an otherworldly as well as secular key. Oliver's second birth is shadowed by the death of another child, called Dick, the near-death of Rose Maylie and intimations of his own 'immortality'. This transcendental key dominates *The Old Curiosity Shop*, the central fable of which concerns a girl's pilgrimage towards a grace which turns out to be death. With greater thematic emphasis than in *Oliver Twist*, *The Old Curiosity Shop* arranges a repertoire of figures from popular and nursery romance (dwarfs, giants, Mr Punch, etc.) in an allegory of spiritual progress. In this case, Dickens's decision to extend his weekly sketch, the 'Little Child Story', meant the development of an emblematic suggestion:

> We are so much in the habit of allowing impressions to be made upon us by external objects, which should be produced by reflection alone, but which, without such visible aids, often escape us; that I am not sure I should have been so thoroughly possessed by this one subject, but for the heaps of fantastic things I had seen huddled together in the curiosity-dealer's warehouse. These, crowding upon my mind, in connection with the child, and gathering round her, as it were, brought her condition palpably before me. I had her image, without any effort of imagination, surrounded and beset by everything that was foreign to its nature, and furthest removed from the sympathies of her sex and age . . . As it was, she seemed to exist in a kind of allegory; and having these shapes about her, claimed my interest so strongly, that (as I have already remarked) I could not dismiss her from my recollection, do what I would.
>
> 'It would be a curious speculation,' said I, after some restless turns across and across the room, 'to imagine her in her future life, holding

her solitary way among a crowd of wild grotesque companions; the only pure, fresh, youthful object in the throng.'[11]

The passage offers one of Dickens's fullest accounts of the process of imaginative invention. It begins with an involuntary, spontaneous possession of the subjectivity by the world of objects, a 'crowding upon my mind' which suggests that this 'fantastic' is particularly an urban effect. The intimation of 'a kind of allegory' *produces* the work of the imagination: it is prior to it, and provokes it into the 'curious speculation' of a progress tale. The work of imagination, in other words, is the turning into narrative of impressions made by a pre-existing structure of meaning. Allegory, the appearance of this meaning, is the form of the difference between a heterogeneous, crowded, 'fantastic' urban scene and (in Dickens's verbal ambiguity) both the narrator's imagination and the little girl: 'I had her image, without any effort of imagination, surrounded and beset by everything that was foreign to its nature . . .' His mind is crowded upon by the vision of the little girl crowded upon by fantastic things: the content of this allegorical structure is differential and negative. Its theme is its own division between an uncanny miscellany of external objects and one 'pure, fresh, youthful object' constituted by its separateness from the rest of the heap.

And so we find in the course of the fable. The child Nell flies from the monstrous old curiosity shop of all London, in which materiality, commerce and desire are inextricably confused. Not only Quilp, its wicked genius, but the figures of 'popular entertainment' encountered on the road are part of its stock; they all try in some way or another to turn Nell into a commodity, even the relatively benign Mrs Jarley. Yet they are the author's stock-in-trade too; he is the keeper of the Old Curiosity Shop. All the refuge and alternative the country affords is a cold pastoral of late-eighteenth-century literary conventions: country churchyards and deserted villages. Steven Marcus aptly remarks on the novel's 'frustrated or failed idyll', for within modernity, the mode of pastoral is elegiac. There is no longer any alternative historical economy or world of life outside the imperial metropolis, save in the past, the realm of figures and of death, of the disembodied. Dickensian 'sentimentality', in this instance, represents a disconcerting rhetorical amplification and logical reduction of the traditional thematics of sentiment, or feeling spent upon loss or absence. Nell's characteristic blankness, her crucial difference from the grotesque materiality of the curiosity shop, is made absolute by her death, which defines her purity – the term of grace – once and for all as sexual: an absence of the body. In these terms (notwithstanding her first appearance in Covent Garden market) she cannot be bought or sold, at the same time that almost everyone in the tale wants to claim her. The splendid irony is that this very loss reserves her as *Dickens's* most valuable commodity: 'killed for the market', as Ruskin put it, 'as a butcher kills a lamb'.[12]

Dickens represents no other historical way of life in dialectical, transforming relation to the material and symbolic economies of the modern metropolis. The journey to the country discovers only abstract, ritualized, obsolescent figures and forms, whose contact with 'nature' is by their decay: a literal resolution into the ground. As the wonderful exchange between Little Dorrit and the turnkey recognizes, 'the country' is a sentimental convention produced within the city – a memory and velleity of elsewhere: another, softer image of that Death that Ruskin saw as the universal topic of metropolitan modernity. From Scott to Dickens, then, we can track a shift from 'folk culture' to 'mass culture' as the popular source of romance, the national collective body of imaginary forms. Both authors are close to popular life, from which they draw characteristic strengths; they share this closeness with Shakespeare, the archetypal writer for both of them. Scott's relation to popular culture however is mediated by the classicizing terms of a professional education, to be one of scholarly patronage and feudal revival. A popular minstrelsy is identified with an ancestral rural economy, passing but still accessible to modern memory and the aestheticizing gaze of the Border laird who is foremost an Edinburgh lawyer. Here we can read an important cultural difference between provincial Edinburgh ('classical', antique even in its urbanity) and metropolitan London, from which the historical distance of an archaic rural world is generations greater than the reach of memory. For Dickens, popular culture is entirely urban, modern and pullulating. Its otherness to an official elite culture is a synchronic difference of class, intensified – in the antithetical figure of the 'outlaw' – into a difference of parody, not just illicit but criminal in its appropriation of genteel forms. The apprehension is at least as old as the 'Newgate pastoral' of *The Beggar's Opera*, and Dickens will develop it beyond the work-as-game ethic of Fagin's thieves' college to the mock-pastoral sarcasms about Lincoln's Inn Fields in *Bleak House*, where the pastures of crime and those of the law comprise one total, dark, intricate estate. And as we read later Dickens novels, we find a systematically satirical representation of what this description has already suggested: that the criminal underworld is not confined to a particular frontier, but extends throughout the whole of urban civilization. It defines the infernal figure of an abyss, underlying and shadowing the world's legitimate, daylight forms and institutions. Even so (the 'sociological insight' provided by the figure) an underclass becomes an essential feature of a class structure under industrial capitalism: an illegitimate, privative, deviant state into which fall those dislodged by the febrile throes of the official economy. Thus the demonic character of Dickens's villains is expressed in their preternatural ubiquity: Fagin and Monks vexing Oliver's trance at the Maylie cottage, Quilp rising from the earth to Nell's dismay. Again, Scott's outlaws share some of this uncanny skill of appearance and disappearance. The apprehension of an alternative secret order or power, lurking beneath daylight forms and haunting them, is quintessentially Gothic. It has made an extraordinary appearance as the Vehmic tribunal in a late Scott romance, *Anne of Geierstein*, as well as in guardian-fairy figures such as the heroine of that novel. And as in Scott, the hero is involved in this dark order; his extrication from it will become increasingly difficult in Dickens's late novels, for no one represents the usurpation of genteel forms by popular energies more blatantly than does their author. In short,

Dickens totalizes a Gothic romance principle developed before him by Scott, whereby daily life is a surface articulated by occult nodes of connection, and animated by illegitimate outlaw or supernatural – energies of transformation, the sources of which are not only alternative but oppositional, seditious, demonic.

Dickens, then, makes Scott's historical imagination of modernity into a synchronic, schematic vision of a present totality. Provincial mixed ecology has achieved its climactic, imperial stage of metropolitan universe. The principle of romance – the fancy – is radically divided; it is generated by the phenomenological confusion of the city, but as an intimation of alienness to it, theorized as grace in a narrative of election. Its site is either *outside the world*, literally, that is, spiritually; or else, in secular, carnal and material form, it inhabits an underworld of illicit, parodic, grotesque (*grottesco*) formations. For a more complex kind of narrative Dickens would turn to the Waverley novels; to perfect his own version, as it turned out, in Scott's romance rather than his history.

II

The most elaborate project of Dickens's early career was an essay in the genre of novel that commanded the highest contemporary prestige, the three-volume Waverley historical romance. In May 1836, just two months after beginning *Pickwick* (and before the era of its triumph), Dickens contracted to write just such a novel, *Gabriel Vardon, the Locksmith of London*, which he may have thought of as early as 1833. It would not begin to appear, however, until February 1841. In the five years since committing himself to *Barnaby Rudge*, as it was now called, Dickens had completed four other novels and broken off relations with two publishers. So retarded, so long-intended a production is unique in Dickens's literary career. Critics have ascribed it to a reluctance (Johnson) or determination (Tillotson) to come to grips with the project. These are not contradictory motives. *Barnaby Rudge* can be understood as its author's first real *novel*: for most writers of Dickens's generation, writing a historical romance was a professional rite of passage, mastering the dominant (masculine) cultural model and measuring oneself against its formidable parent. As it turned out, *Barnaby Rudge* is a tense combination of attitudes: formal reverence in a paralytic clench with furious revolt.[13]

By the time *Barnaby Rudge* came out Dickens could boast that he was more popular than Scott had ever been, and cast back upon his friends their former admonitions that serials were 'a low, cheap form of publication'. Not only had he earned wealth and fame by the form, but he would make it accommodate the most respectable kind of fiction, and compose a full-scale historical novel in not just monthly but *weekly* instalments. After the enormous popular and pathetic success of *The Old Curiosity Shop, Barnaby Rudge* constituted (whatever else) a virtuosic technical feat, that of *composing* the complex matter of the high genre in the periodical mode. Nor did Dickens merely reproduce the bastard version of his contemporaries. He returned to Scott's more theoretically ambitious original to refashion it for himself, and if the result shares some of the lowering Gothic features of Newgate fiction, it has drawn them from the parent for its own allegorical purpose.[14]

Dickens had begun *Master Humphrey's Clock*, the periodical vehicle of both *The Old Curiosity Shop* and *Barnaby Rudge*, as a linked series of tales with historical settings, in imitation of Scott's own irregular volume series, the *Tales of My Landlord* and *Chronicles of the Canongate*. This was an ambitious extension of the young writer's range. Yet the double antiquarian–mythopoeic framework – the tale-telling circle of Master Humphrey and the chronicles of the Guildhall giants – and the enclosed stories themselves represent failed, wasted and neglected lives, in a tonality of grotesque and morbid pathos. Critics have interpreted a regressive turn in Dickens's imagination at this stage of his career. Whatever the case, the representation had a performative or self-fulfilling effect. After the success of *The Old Curiosity Shop* readers began to turn away, and Dickens abandoned the editorial framework, complaining that the weekly format cramped *Barnaby Rudge*. The work had cost its author more labour than any hitherto, and it did not reproduce his earlier triumph. It was during the composition of *Barnaby Rudge* that Dickens visited Scotland to be hailed as Scott's successor. But even as he claimed the trophies of the great enchanter, he gazed upon the image of his ruin. What if the author's fall were a portion of his fortune? Dickens would follow the historical novel with an unprecedented pause in his literary production: a 'creative moratorium' occupied by the strenuous American tour.[15]

If the triumphal procession of Dickens's early career stumbled at *Barnaby Rudge*, it was because the Waverley novels were the turning-point of modern fiction – for Dickens no less crucially than for his contemporaries. Scott had reinvented the novel by using a sentimental-romance mode of multiple episodes, plots and genres to represent a mixed historical universe of experience and desire. The formal principle of this doubled and multiplied representation is analogy, which implies a unified semiotic field informing the dispersed registers and episodes of the narrative, charted by the intricate connections of the plot. In *Barnaby Rudge* Dickens applied systematically, for the first time, such an analogical method of narrative composition. It marked an important advance over his earlier allegorical technique, which had tended to split the field of representation with a dualistic scheme, relentless in its totalization. The Waverley novels offered a more flexible and worldly use of analogical patterns: polyphonic, to use Bakhtinian language, dialectical rather than dualistic. As we shall see, Dickens misread Scott's technique even as he applied it, and only in the turn from 'history', and the burden of literal and agonistic imitation, to 'romance' would he make it fully his own.[16]

Dickens's imitation of Scott in *Barnaby Rudge* reproduces a major thematic as well as structural pattern: a correspondence between public and private disorders of rebellion and parricide. As Steven Marcus has shown, Dickens's narrative turns about a quintet of tormented relations between father and son, established during the first two-fifths of the novel, well before its tremendous collective action gets under way.[17] Scott had made this traditional (Shakespearian) equation his own, above all in the Jacobite romances. There are important differences in the pattern, however. Scott's fathers, whether themselves pious or wayward, tend to be ineffectual governors of their sons, who resist the paternal will by romantic evasion. At best, the son achieves a certain wilful integrity of his own by holding out against the persuasions of a quixotic father-figure who nevertheless embroils him in seditious plots (as in *Old Mortality* and *Redgauntlet*). In Dickens we find an altogether starker antagonism, for which the parent is unequivocally to blame. A set of degenerate fathers, variously corrupt, violent and stupid, exerts a despotic authority over its sons. Their official cultural forms include the brutal and inane backwoods Toryism of old Willett, the landlord of the Maypole, and the depraved, nihilistic urbanity of Mr Chester, the enlightened fine gentleman. The only fathers in the novel who are at all admirable, and reminiscent of the worthy patriarchal types in Scott, are Varden, the bluff locksmith, and Haredale, the melancholy Catholic, who are fathers of daughters – that is, fathers in law. Even in these cases, a broken or disorderly house marks a certain failure of authority, political in Haredale's case, domestic in Varden's. Varden's disastrous relationship with Sim Tappertit is the only instance in the quintet where the blame is on the side of the junior party, and it is significant that they are not literally father and son, but master and apprentice. Even here, Sim's resentment, a compound of thwarted social and sexual ambition, is nourished by the locksmith's failure (despite his name and title) to regulate the psychosexual energies in his household, blatant among unruly women.

The brave, earnest sons who survive at the end of the tale are those who have made an open and principled breach with their fathers and left home of their own free will. For Edward Chester and Joe Willet, this antithetical recognition is a necessary moral discipline. Conversely, the sons who fail to accomplish it suffer the worst damage. Barnaby and Hugh fall under the diabolic thrall of lost, secret fathers who return to haunt them. Unable to define a moral identity in opposition to the wicked parent, the child is condemned to an unconscious, reactive and slavish relation to him. Significantly, both these sons are figures in the novel's allegory of blindness (as expounded by its literal representative, the sinister beggar Stagg).[18] Hugh's illiteracy is a consequence of his utter neglect, while Barnaby's 'blindness of the intellect' is the deformation of an originary paternal violence:

> with his unearthly aspect, and his half-formed mind, he seemed to the murderer a creature who had sprung into existence from his victim's blood. (622)

Morally, however, Barnaby is rescued by his infirmity. In a sardonic gloss on the grace of the Waverley hero, it signifies a saving lack of the social and sexual aggressiveness of the rational masculine will. The altogether-too-virile Hugh, in contrast, goes to the gallows. In the funniest, also cruellest, version of these punishments and castrations the presumptuous Sim loses both his legs, the idols of a phallic narcissism ('If they're a dream ... let sculptors have such wisions, and chisel 'em out when they wake', 307).

As things turn out, only the genteel hero, Edward Chester, survives the novel with all his members and faculties intact. Since he is a pallid diagram of the Scott prototype, belonging to an upper-class plot-line reproduced with a minimum of creative variation, he scarcely has flesh and blood to spend anyway.[19] The nice lad Joe Willett weds the locksmith's daughter, and nasty Sim Tappertit does not, but both suffer amputations, even though Joe's is less drastic than Sim's (an arm instead of both legs). Joe is reconciled with his father, but by now the old man is lobotomized by the shock of historical experience. The sons' exercise of moral judgement, in short, reduces but does not avert the sentence of oedipal damage. In the Waverley novels, the devices of narrative dilation – topographical diversion and figural doubling – sustain the filial ethos of romance evasion. Oedipal strife is waged covertly, in retreat and by proxy, so that its crisis may be deferred, displaced, diffused, until it suspend itself upon a transformed historic ground where struggle is no longer necessary. Actual violence between fathers and children tends to be confined to a Gothic ancestral past. In cleaving to the superior authority of modern civil society, the son is able to transcend the obsolescent loyalties of ancient patriarchy, discarding its historical letter of oppression and revolt and claiming its spirit as an aesthetic property. In *Barnaby Rudge*, however, no such transcendence is possible. The analogical multiplication of the father–son relation has the effect of making the conflict overdetermined. It is always the same because Dickens affords no space of historical difference: no ambiguous cultural border upon which identities may endure, and enjoy, creative metamorphosis. We read, instead, the inevitability of a universal psychic structure, and an unstable difference between 'order' and 'chaos'. For patrimony is both of these: the tyrannical identity of a psychic formation, clear and unyielding in its outline, founded on division, repudiation and repression.

History, such as it is, is the product of this psychic law. In the case of the apprentice Sim Tappertit, Dickens makes the predominant motive of his *ressentiment* sexual, as if – fixed forever in an infantile lust – he can only aspire to a grotesque enactment of his name ('Tappertit'). Riot, for Sim, is a fantasy of rape rather than revolution. The professional relationship between him and his master provides the novel's crucial mediating term between private and public life. He is one of the conspirators riding upon, rather than leading, the mass insurrection. As in the folk-romance cases of the 'naturals', Hugh and Barnaby, a private psychic violence overflows in the public deluge of the riots merely to repeat the original violence of the father on a universal scale, and so to confirm his archetypal power. In this respect, Dickens's Gordon riots are more like the spontaneous mob frenzy at the end of *The Monk* than the Porteous riots (so deliberate in their aim and execution) at the beginning of *The Heart of Mid-Lothian.* They reveal that Gothic dialectic in which repression and revolt can only perpetuate one another, just as the very origination of the collective forms of historical life in private psychology is the sentence of Gothic. Dickens's representation of the riots as the performance of a universal pathology amplifies the rhetoric of criminality described earlier in this chapter. Private malice is translated into public action in a kind of sympathetic black magic, a psychic diffusion which threatens to obliterate all individual identity in the violence of a universal schematization. For as Wallace Stevens's connoisseur of chaos will put it, a violent order is disorder, and a great disorder is an order: these two things are one. The contingent, amorphous, serial life of the city streets is drawn into formation as though by a magnetic current:

> Each tumult took shape and form from the circumstances of the moment; sober workmen, going home from their day's labour, were seen to cast down their baskets of tools and become rioters in an instant; mere boys on errands did the like. In a word, a moral plague ran through the city. The noise, the hurry, and excitement, had for hundreds and hundreds an attraction they had no firmness to resist. The contagion spread like a dread fever: an infectious madness, as yet not near its height, seized on new victims every hour, and society began to tremble at their ravings. (484)

The riots are like a fever; both are among Dickens's figures for a sinister totalization of the mysterious collectivity of urban life, a system of myriad connections and currents that has a strange vast occult energy of its own, overwhelming individual meaning.

A great disorder is an order. The book's most ambitious rhetoric invests the riots with apocalyptic force. They are a demonic possession of the city, revealing its fallen character. The first impressive prose in *Barnaby Rudge* describes the approach to London as a shifting of perspectives between the city of darkness visible, a type of Pandemonium, and the material town of causes and phenomena, of irregular architecture and bad lighting:

> And, now, he approached the great city, which lay outstretched before him like a dark shadow on the ground, reddening the sluggish air with a deep dull light, that told of labyrinths of public ways and shops, and swarms of busy people. Approaching nearer and nearer yet, this halo began to fade, and the causes which produced it slowly to develop themselves. Long lines of poorly lighted streets might be faintly traced, with here and there a lighter spot, where lamps were clustered round a square or market, or round some great building; after a time these grew more distinct, and the lamps themselves were visible; slight yellow specks, that seemed to be rapidly snuffed out, one by one, as intervening obstacles hid them from the sight. Then, sounds arose – the striking of church clocks, the distant bark of dogs,

the hum of traffic in the streets; these outlines might be traced – tall steeples looming in the air, and piles of unequal roofs oppressed by chimneys; then, the noise swelled into a louder sound, and forms grew more distinct and numerous still, and London – visible in the darkness by its own faint light, and not by that of Heaven – was at hand. (71)

Red is the colour of riot. The prospect's latent infernal energy is released in the hot midst of the city:

Thus – a vision of coarse faces, with here and there a blot of flaring, smoky light; a dream of demon heads and savage eyes, and sticks and iron bars uplifted in the air, and whirled about; a bewildering horror, in which so much was seen, and yet so little, which seemed so long, and yet so short, in which there were so many phantoms, not to be forgotten all through life, and yet so many things that could not be observed in one distracting glimpse – it flitted onward, and was gone. (465)

The visionary glimpse represents a sublime intensification of that *sensation* which is the subjective correlative of the massed life of the city – disintegrating the rational co-ordinates of space and time in 'a bewildering horror'. From excessive vision, universal blindness. The city skies flaring red,

as though the last day had come and the whole universe were burning; the dust, and smoke, and drift of fiery particles, scorching and kindling all it fell upon; the hot unwholesome vapour, the blight on everything; the stars, and moon, and very sky, obliterated; – made up such a sum of dreariness and ruin, that it seemed as if the face of Heaven were blotted out, and night, in its rest and quiet, and softened light, never could look upon the earth again. (618)

The lesson of Dickens's apocalyptic allegory seems to be that mass activity, the mobilization of the collective underground life of the city, brings a disastrous annihilation of individual meaning and identity. The rioters are demoniacally possessed, plague-stricken, idiots, madmen. The only historical, public figure among the ringleaders, Lord Gordon himself, is a deranged Scotch Puritan. After a few token bows toward Scott's prototypical rhetoric of Presbyterian fanaticism ('A malignant . . . unworthy such a wife', 345), Dickens represents him somewhat desultorily as foolish and weak, a ruling-class shadow of poor Barnaby, the dupe of diabolical associates behind the scenes who manipulate him out of their private lust and spite. The 'No Popery' riots lack the historically specific political motivation that Scott suggests for even such a bizarre episode as the Oates conspiracy in *Peveril of the Peak*, let alone for the Puritan insurrectionary movements in *Old Mortality* and *Woodstock*. Here, popular rebellion means not a clarification of historical meaning but its chaotic disintegration – in, to be sure, a titanic and thrilling spectacle. The convulsion of the public streets ends as arbitrarily as it began. The riots consume their agents, dissolved into a mortal senselessness, in which the Gothic trope of a terminal literalization is elevated into a conceit worthy of *Bleak House*. Sublimity leaves behind only ashes:

> On the last night of the great riots – for the last night it was – the wretched victims of a senseless outcry, became themselves the dust and ashes of the flames they had kindled, and strewed the public streets of London. (618)

As though they have no opportunity to strew ashes on themselves in public penitence, because they are themselves those ashes: so much for 'No Popery'.

The 'moral plague' of the riots brings to a crisis by threatening to terminate the characters' private lives, thus completing a distinction between them and public history. They are to work out their destinies in individual ethical terms, measured by the degree of their absorption in the riots. In Dickens's fiction the division between political agency and private integrity, already representative in Scott, gains a more lurid emphasis, and becomes a set of dualistic oppositions between depth and surface, past and future, death and life. Where Scott describes a conflict between different historical worlds producing an emerging modern polarity between private and public life, Dickens reveals a schism between private and public 'worlds' as such.

Dickens compounds a variety of Scott models in *Barnaby Rudge*, much as Scott himself had synthesized elements from Shakespeare and other authors and poets of romance. (Indeed, that very technique forms part of Dickens's imitation, as we see in the studied deployment of Shakespearian echoes, themes and characters here and in subsequent novels.)[20] If the storming of Newgate is like the storming of the Heart of Midlothian and Barnaby is a scion of Madge Wildfire and Davie Gellatly, the opening scene in the inn imitates that of *Kenilworth*, as does the theme of a weak lord manipulated by parasites. The 'No Popery' riots, as suggested, have precedent in *Peveril of the Peak*. In its general ethos Dickens's historical novel is closer to the later, Gothic Waverley novels than to the earlier Scotch ones. There, strife within family relations tends indeed to become overdetermined and ineluctable. The amputations at the close of *Barnaby Rudge* are reminiscent of an obsessive topic in *The Fair Maid of Perth*, a novel filled with literal and metaphoric mutilations and sons destroyed for their failure to embrace a patriarchal code. The triangle of Gabriel Varden, Sim Tappertit and Joe Willet reproduces that of old Simon Glover, his fierce apprentice Conachar and the armourer Henry Smith. Conachar is a genuine outlaw chief, whose cowardice expresses a fatal historical belatedness. The sons who resist the patriarchal ethic, whether of tribal warrior prowess or (in the case of Rothsay) court politics, are represented as decadent, pathetic and doomed. The bourgeois progressive energy of the survivor and son-in-law, Henry Smith, is identified with his zestful mechanical talent for violence – despite all his vows of renunciation, he cannot help chopping people up out of sheer exuberance. There is no public space for a modern, civilian pacifist morality. It remains a poignant velleity, only available as a feminine, domestic property, in the person of the eponymous Fair Maid. Nevertheless, Scott's late, bleak, sardonic revision of his own Waverley myth (already at work in *The Bride of Lammermoor*) still allows for the utopian horizon of historical allegory. In the cultural struggle between the warrior clans (manipulated into making a polite spectacle out of butchering themselves), the royal court (rotten with factional intrigue) and the free borough of trades and crafts, there appears the dialectical possibility of a future, politically unified civil order, guaranteeing a free space of private life. Fragile and precariously situated as it is in a turbulent era of historical transition, Perth is nevertheless the one local society that does not devour its own children. At the same time, the novel also expresses the intuition that all historical eras are eras of transition. Thus, to keep as well as win the order of a domestic peace, the sons of civil society must be not merely able but willing to be violent – inspired by those very reasons of private life, the personal passions. The 'feminine virtues' of civil society, sympathy and meekness, remain confined to women, in a wonderfully influential reassertion of that traditional division of labour.[21]

Across the last numbers of *Barnaby Rudge* Dickens flourishes an array of romance closure conventions: such rites of poetic justice as executions, a reprieve, a duel, a retreat to the cloister, happy and punitive marriages. This final order confirms a private moral logic but no historical allegory, since Dickens has represented no historical difference of economy or culture among the novel's range of social worlds, classes and households. All are figurations of each other in a homologous field of power grounded on the psychosexual identities of an archetypal nuclear family. In this case, the women too are figures of unruliness, rather than the vestals of an alternative, transcendental spirit of subjection. Varden, the admirable patriarch, is finally restored (in the capacity of father-in-law) to 'the centre of the system . . . in the bright household world' (714), but only because the riots have scared his refractory womenfolk into submission. Neither they nor the spotless, indeed blank, heroine of the upper-class plot-line, Emma Haredale, represent any positive ethical energy that might be available for some progressive historical horizon, however remote or utopian. Simply, the threat of wild masculine force has administered wholesome chastisement: rapists in the street justify the custody of a kind father, the locksmith of London.

As the novel's critics have observed, none of its conflicts achieves ethical resolution; there is no reconciliation, no moment of mutual sympathy and assent. The novel lacks any figure of a vigorous and complacent bourgeois victor, such as Scott's Henry Smith; it also lacks the dialectical compensation of ethical consciousness that Scott gives his 'passive' subjected heroes such as Waverley. There, as we saw, a rational conscience is invoked at the moment of submission, defining the historical place of the subject: identity means the coincidence of consciousness and subjection, that is, the knowledge of one's own historical formation as a subject. In Dickens, the moment of moral consciousness tends to be fiery and spasmodic, synchronized with the motion of revolt, filled with the virulent negative energy of resentment. Revolt, like crime, is passionate and sensational. Dickensian moral assertions often take the form of a righteousness excited by revulsion: Nicholas Nickleby thrashing Mr Squeers, David Copperfield biting Mr Murdstone. Even in Scott, I have argued, the negative knowledge at the core of subjection persists within the comic pomp of homecoming, restoration and marriage. In *Barnaby Rudge* it is still less clear how the gains outweigh the losses, or how they can be measured in each other's terms, in the nevertheless inescapable, thrilling, but damnable uprising against paternal authority and its institutions.[22]

Critics who judge *Barnaby Rudge* to be a failure, such as Lukács and Caserio, have indeed complained that its private conflicts do not deliver any collectively significant issue, ethical or political. Lukács accounts for this as a historical failure to reproduce the cultural conditions of Scott's success, Caserio as a resistance to Scott's influence.[23] It remains curious that Dickens's failure or resistance should have coincided with so explicit and literal an imitation of the Scott model. Alone among the earlier Dickens novels *Barnaby Rudge* draws attention to itself as an example of a given genre, elects the Scott historical romance as a source of 'influence', and confronts an authoritative cultural form in the light of a conscious discipline. In other words, the novel's analogical theme of a conflict between fathers and sons and a revolt against law informs its own position in its author's career as the novel which recognizes and challenges a precursor. The production of *Barnaby Rudge* coincides with the turbulent formative stage of Dickens's vocation, and with his concern with the figure of Scott, at one moment the master of the profession and at the next a helpless effigy wrecked upon the machinery of his trade. The Scott historical novel as form of national *Bildungsroman*, combining the private crisis of psycho-sexual formation with the public matter of vocation and rank, has already composed this material into a unified narrative topic. It is little wonder then that *Barnaby Rudge* makes Scott's particular achievement the site of an overdetermined oedipal struggle: necessary, arduous and ultimately barren, as the ethical recognition of authority and subjection consists of nothing but the struggle itself.

III

Barnaby Rudge rejects the ethical content of subjection in Scott's historical *Bildungsroman*, even as it reproduces its form. The story locates moral energy not in reconciliation and compromise but in resentment and contest. Both public and domestic social orders are determined by power, the twin forms of which are discipline and riot. It might seem, then, as if Dickens combined a strong appropriation of form and technique from Scott's novels with a refusal of what had become their political meaning (which is not necessarily that of their own time and place, or of their author's intentions). Such a combination of aesthetic admiration with ideological disagreement recalls its classicial statement, Hazlitt's essay on Scott in *The Spirit of the Age*.

But the relation is more complicated and paradoxical than that. For even as the 'Radical' Dickens takes over the 'Tory' Scott's novelistic form, he reproduces its cultural ideological formation. Both versions represent rebellion not only as reactionary in motive and chaotic in effect, but as a grand illusion, a fantasia, an occultation or disintegration of a normative everyday reality – and at the same time, as a visionary trance in which lost, buried, archetypal forms might be recalled, the true shapes of reality glimpsed. As much as its Waverley prototype, *Barnaby Rudge* defines the centre of a middle-class domestic order threatened from above and below (or from left and right) by a conspiracy between aristocrat despotism and underclass anarchy:

'No Popery, brother!' cried the hangman.
'No Property, brother!' responded Hugh.
'Popery, Popery,' said the secretary with his usual mildness.
'It's all the same!' cried Dennis 'It's all right. Down with him, Muster Gashford. Down with everybody, down with everything! Hurrah for the Protestant religion!' (359–60)

Commentators have pointed out the rhetorical alliance between the radical wings of Chartism and dissenting Protestantism in the 1840s; while Dickens's own Radicalism was aligned with the Reform establishment rather than with the labour mass movement.[24] The political difference between Scott and Dickens is that of a historical rather than synchronic class position, and it is signified by the date of Scott's death, 1832. Dickens belonged to the class of new men empowered by Reform, which reaffirmed the constitutional origin of a peaceful middle way of British history as a bloodless, legal revolution carried out by middle-class management. Nevertheless, even though its justification was that it had saved the nation from the double pest of anarchy and reaction, that historical movement – at once conservative and progressive – was an act of usurpation. Its moral aetiology, ambitious and aggressive, is the same as that of insurrection: discipline and the law mark the difference between them. It is a critical commonplace that the mob scenes in *Barnaby Rudge* are the heart of the book's imaginative life; that the demonic and destructive energies of mass revolt coincide with the creative energies of the author. It is less a matter of Dickens's 'sympathy' with the mob, more one of a moral economy in which the riots are where fantasy is, because everywhere else is discipline. Riot is irrational, visceral, compelling and therefore must be repressed; in Scott we find less (if any) passionate identification with mass movements (they compel the imagination in subtler ways) and consequently a greater measure of rational sympathy for those caught up in them. So it is that the radical Dickens makes a more reactionary representation than the conservative Scott.[25]

To note the historical difference between the two novelists is to note Dickens's own address to the category of 'history' in defining his political antipathies. Dickens rejects the version of history, associated with Scott, that finds in the past a source of positively meaningful difference from the present. Instead, difference is a negative quality, and only identity has positive signification, in the mode of moral homology. In his journalism, speeches, letters and private bookcases as well as in his fiction Dickens expressed sarcastic contempt for the Good Old Times, feudalism, all the articles of faith of the literalizations of Scott's medievalism by Young England, the Oxford Movement, etc. He composed *A Child's History of England* to warn his eldest son off Tory and high-church principles; it was Scott who had made the children's history something of a novelists' sinecure with the *Tales of a Grandfather*, one of the happier tasks of his ruin. Scott cheerfully involves his young reader with a picturesque ancestry of malice and violence. Moralizing asides, in the name of providential equity, are urbanely perfunctory. Dickens's *Child's History* is far more rigorously a sort of negative conduct book, a fierce and sardonic gallery of moral grotesques: 'that history full of pugnacious ethics and of nothing else', Chesterton called it.[26] Our relationship to the past is not genetic, but analogical. It is not a tradition but a repository of examples, most of which are to be refused rather than imitated: once more, indeed, the vital moral action to be imitated is that of refusal. The preface to *Barnaby Rudge*, which appeared in the final number of *Master Humphrey's Clock*, makes just such a claim for the didactic importance of history. History is significant not because it has formed us, but insofar as it provides a cautionary register of examples by which we can *form ourselves*:

> It is unnecessary to say, that those shameful tumults, while they reflect indelible disgrace upon the time in which they occurred, and all who had act or part in them, teach a good lesson. That what we falsely call a religious cry is easily raised by men who have no religion . . . all History teaches us. But perhaps we do not know it in our hearts too well, to profit by even so humble an example as the 'No Popery' riots of Seventeen Hundred and Eighty. (40)

With all its rather aggressive humility, the text makes grand claims upon a truth rescued from false prophets.

The opening of the narrative itself establishes (as critics have noted) the reach of 'Sixty Years Since' so carefully formulated by Scott as the enabling generic perspective of *Waverley*.

In the year 1775, there stood upon the borders of Epping Forest, at a distance of about twelve miles from London – measuring from the Standard in Cornhill, or rather from the spot on or near to which the Standard used to be in days of yore – a house of public entertainment called the Maypole; which fact was demonstrated to all such travellers as could neither read nor write (and sixty-six years ago a vast number both of travellers and stay-at-homes were in this condition) by the emblem reared on the roadside over against the house, which, if not one of those goodly proportions that Maypoles were wont to present in olden times, was a fair young ash, thirty feet in height, and straight as any arrow that ever English yeoman drew. (43)

Dickens's 'sixty-six years ago' does not fix the kind of tension, at once ironic and providential, that pervades *Waverley*. The very phrase flattens Scott's incantation, a phonetic palindrome, into a journalistic matter-of-factness, which is immediately blurred by the superimposed rhetoric of a quite different kind (not degree) of historical distance, taken from another, different kind of Scott novel. 'The year 1775' is set against an archaic depth of 'days of yore' and 'olden times', with all the matter of the greenwood, maypoles and straight-shooting yeomen, familiar from *Ivanhoe*; which has become the Victorian type of a more fantastic, medievalist romance associated (however erroneously) with a visionary, lost, original Britain. However, Dickens's rhetoric evokes a generic pastness divided between, rather than comprehended by, the historical and mythic modes of retrospect. The relationship between the modes and the nature of the continuity between past and present are problematic. Decisive data of historical situation – 1775, twelve miles from London – quiver into uncertainty: is there or is there not a Standard in 1775, and when were those days of yore to which measurement is referred ('on or near to which')? It seems both present and past lack a Standard, property of an indefinitely remoter past. And is there or not a maypole? The 'emblem' of a mythic generation is no sign, as we expect, but an actual tree; but to measure it, now, is to register its diminutiveness, at the same time as to recall the deeds and proportions of a heroic age.

Nevertheless it is young, strong, growing: it may in time achieve that proportion. In short, the past as mythic plenitude and as source of empirical 'standards' is pushed back to some indeterminate prehistory, overshadowing the historical scene. At the same time, the relation between our present and the past is one of a qualitative superiority, of progress, improvement, *education*, defined in our very act of reading. The pseudo-maypole is a sign for the ignorant and illiterate. The delusive character of its authority will be demonstrated in the story when that same constituency, the mob, chops it down. The inn named after the maypole accommodates the false idyll of a stagnant, oppressive patriarchy which breeds its own overthrow.

Dickens's historical scene is a negative zone between an oppressively fictive anterior fullness and a future possibility of improvement. Our relation to the past is of a radical *dis*continuity, marked by the difference between reading and illiteracy, in the allegorical senses of reading as vision and knowledge. The figure of illiteracy circulates throughout the novel, from the hermeneutical murk of its opening to the literal and spiritual darkness that covers eighteenth-century London (for Dickens, the Enlightenment is just another of the Dark Ages), and in the theme of blindness mentioned earlier. We ourselves, it seems (the text is our witness), can read: yet what is it to read? Dickens's rhetoric disallows both the mythical and the historical modes for another, the allegorical, and the dark side of this conceit is that we too are the past we read, or it is us. In the 1780s Dickens's grandparents were domestic servants: the glass of history showed him no illustrious ancestors, but obscure and anonymous lives, that might well have been swallowed in the mob. The past represents, then, the menace of a reversion to a social underworld of privation and criminality, blighted by a dominance of fathers. The 'real' correspondence of the historical novel is the present social crisis: illiteracy and hunger, a darkness and poverty of the spirit, a senseless alternation of mass revolt and official repression, the disintegration of the liberal cultural hierarchy that the act of reading itself would encode. Thus, it is by no means easy to read this opening paragraph: to fix the allegorical perspective, identify ourselves in relation to that other time and space by which we would read ourselves, distinguish ourselves from our benighted circumstantial origins. The past's dark, as well as its light, is ours.[27]

IV

Dealings with the Firm of Dombey and Son: Dickens's title identifies patrimony as a public, economic institution. His plot reveals it to be also a delusion and a curse. Patriarchal succession is blocked, bankrupt, self-devouring: the cultural system of the father extinguishes the son, and it is a daughter who redeems him with a natural patience and love. Dickens elaborately associates this solution with the theme of romance, which for the first time in his novels represents a magic at once worldly, beneficent and true.

At the same time, it is a critical commonplace that *Dombey and Son* is Dickens's first carefully organized novel, a unity of conception and construction.[28] Perhaps a more specific way of expressing this claim, which otherwise confines itself to the shadowy realm of authorial intention, is to observe that Dickens highlights the figures of romance with allusive reflection upon their generic status, making 'romance' one of the allegorical themes in the text. The effect is qualitatively different from the naive, 'spontaneous', appearance of such figures in *Oliver Twist*, or their oppositional arrangement in the allegory in *The Old Curiosity Shop* so that the fiction is divided between its own principles. Here, the allusive identification of romance archetypes makes them the basis of the allegorical system. Mr Dombey's 'romantic and unlikely' suspicion that the working-class nurse might exchange his son for her own[29] gets its comeuppance in the typology of romance:

[Paul] was childish and sportive enough at times, and not of a sullen disposition; but he had a strange, old-fashioned, thoughtful way, at other times, of sitting brooding in his miniature armchair, when he looked (and talked) like one of those terrible little Beings in the Fairy tales, who, at a hundred and fifty or two hundred years of age, fantastically represent the children for whom they have been substituted. (151)

It is the public identity of 'Dombey and Son', fixed and everlasting, that substitutes the fancy – the private inward nature and very life of the child. He is only one of the novel's changelings, and the romance allusion identifies a thematic pattern in this novel obsessed with social change, commercial exchange, moral conversion and marvellous transformation. Elsewhere, among many such allusions and identifications, Mrs Pipchin is an ogress, Mrs Brown a witch or gipsy, Solomon Gills 'a magician disguised in a Welsh wig and a suit of coffee colour', Mr Dombey himself 'the Caliph Haroun Alraschid', Carker a cat, spider and 'scaly monster of the deep', and Florence and Captain Cuttle 'a wandering princess and a good monster in a story-book' (776). Dickens's allusive register extends beyond individual figures to include typical episodes, notably the sequence of the sea-voyage, shipwreck and miraculous return of the 'Son and Heir'. He even reproduces, with beautiful comic tact, the convention of the narration that restores a lost loved one to life, whereby the fiction wishes upon a thaumaturgy of its own (782–4).[30]

The narrative also advertises the abstract structural devices of sentimental romance plotting, giving them a ceremonial visibility. Conspicuous among these is the scheme of character doubling. The disgraced John Carker tells his successful brother James that he sees in the young Walter Gay his 'other self': 'Not as I am, but as I was when I first came here too; . . . full of the same qualities, fraught with the same capacity of leading on to good or evil' (247). His ability to make moral reflections upon the story he is in informs us that he is actually the good brother and the Manager the wicked one. In other words, the scheme is brought into consciousness in acquiring an ethical valency. Mrs Skewton and Edith encounter the crone Mrs Brown and the harlot Alice Marwood, shadows of their moral selves and potential fates: Phiz's illustration (663) emphasizes the artificial symmetry at work. The highlighting of the formal principle of opposition and analogy is thus accompanied by the claim of an ethical function: this is how we are to read, tracing the mutations of our own virtual and potential images across the text. The allegory is more elaborate and more conceited that it has been in previous Dickens novels – more Spenserian than Bunyanesque. Indeed Kathleen Tillotson, after listing many of the romance allusions, comments that *Dombey and Son* 'could be broken up like a book of *The Faerie Queene*'.[31]

Scott had revived a Spenserian as well as Shakespearian romance poetics for the novel; and what was grim discipline in *Barnaby Rudge* is splendid mastery in Dickens's allegory of pride, *Dombey and Son*. The election of romance as archetypal figure is reminiscent of *Guy Mannering*, except that its origins are in childhood, rather than in an old ecology of town and country. The difference is crucial: in his systematic evocation of the nursery, and not the cultural past, as the matrix of romance, Dickens commits his fiction to modernity. The impasse of the historical novel allowed Dickens to comprehend his difference from Scott in terms of a failure of history, and he proceeds to reinvent Scott's genre as his own by drawing upon the transformation of it most potent ('radical') in the 1840s: not Newgate fiction or 'tushery' romances such as Bulwer-Lytton's *Harold* (1848), but the social or condition-of-England novel, which may be understood as the historical romance of the present moment. Disraeli's is only the most egregious attempt to take over the political thematic as well as the form of the Waverley novel by infusing it with a matter as emphatically contemporary as Scott's was the reverse. *Dombey and Son* represents a contemporary social universe, as Scott had a past one, as a multiplicity of scenes and communities and classes brought together in a totalizing mutual relation of transition and transformation. We saw that *The Heart of Mid-Lothian*, which is also close thematically to *Dombey and Son*, achieved what might be called a proto-Victorian representation of a whole national society, connected dynamically across a social–geographic range and a mixed register of literary genres. Scott's trope of a knitted or woven text, and a synchronic narrative order, reappears in Dickens, once again given explicit moral force:

Were this miserable mother, and this miserable daughter, only the reduction to their lowest grade, of certain social vices sometimes prevailing higher up? In this round world of many circles within circles, do we make a weary journey from the high grade to the low, to find at last that they lie close together, that the two extremes touch, and that our journey's end is but our starting-place? Allowing for great difference of stuff and texture, was the pattern of this woof repeated among gentle blood at all? (579)

This rhetoric will be developed in *Bleak House* and *Little Dorrit*, novels of mysterious systems, patterns and connections still more extensive and intricate. Dickens reflects upon the global reach of an archetypal moral order; and upon its circulatory logic, which abolishes the merely serial and temporal differences of history, rendered here in the pilgrimage metaphor as those of individual history and social class. Scott's synchronic vision was qualified by its historical content, and vice versa: the dynamic of change and struggle was between worlds that were passing and worlds to come. But Dickens's vision is more thoroughly panoramic: it sees an entire universe, in the order and disorder of its changing, all at once. Everything is simultaneously present, and the present faces the future, its transitional dynamic accelerating toward the apocalyptic horizon of a total transformation.

Dickens represents the great imperial capital as a vast spatial miscellany of sites, things, forces, accumulated in a dynamic adjacency. This heterogeneity of forms with its latent vitality of metamorphosis generates 'romance' as an antithetical quality within it:

Though the offices of Dombey and Son were within the liberties of the City of London, and within hearing of Bow Bells, when their clashing voices were not drowned by the uproar in the streets, yet there were hints of romantic and adventurous story to be observed in some of their adjacent objects. Gog and Magog held their state within ten minutes' walk; the Royal Exchange was close at hand; the Bank of England, with its vaults of gold and silver 'down among the dead men' underground, was their magnificent neighbour. Just around the corner stood the rich East India House, teeming with suggestions of precious stuffs and stones, tigers, elephants, howdahs, hookahs, umbrellas, palm trees, palanquins, and gorgeous princes of a brown complexion sitting on carpets, with their slippers very much turned up at the toes. Anywhere in the immediate vicinity there might be seen pictures of ships speeding away full sail to all parts of the world; outfitting warehouses ready to pack off anybody anywhere, fully equipped in half an hour; and little timber midshipmen in obsolete naval uniforms, eternally employed outside the shop doors of nautical Instrument-makers in taking observations of the hackney carriages. (87–8)

Dickens begins by opposing the 'hints of adventurous and romantic story' to the Dombey offices, a nerve-centre of capital accumulation, and to the quotidian uproar of the streets; romance seems to belong to traces of antiquity, as in Scott, and as in Dickens's late imitations of Scott in *Master Humphrey's Clock*. But Dickens's very rhetoric of 'the adjacent objects' moves on from this faded formula to the present institutions of the imperial capital, registering the glow of a magic behind the scenes: down among the dead men underground, overseas in India. The magic is that of an *economy* that binds together the diversity of scenes and objects in its immense, complex, universal field.

The panoramic impetus of the description takes us to the place that will constitute the novel's official idyll, the Instrument-maker's shop of Solomon Gills. Here are fun and innocence, a kindly grotesquerie, the charm of unworldliness. It is set up as a refuge from the world: for Florence, rescued from sinister streets and in flight from her father's house; for Walter, setting out on and returning from his marvellous voyage; and for the 'good monster' Captain Cuttle, hiding from ferocious widows. This pastoral space occupies ambiguous co-ordinates in the symbolic geography of Dickens's metropolis. As we saw, it is produced by the imperial economy; at the same time, it is excluded by it. Once upon a time, explains Uncle Sol, 'fortunes were to be made':

But competition, competition – new invention, new invention – alteration, alteration – the world's gone past me. I hardly know where I am myself; much less where my customers are . . . Tradesmen are not the same as they used to be, apprentices are not the same, business commodities are not the same. Seven-eighths of my stock is old-fashioned. I am an old-fashioned man in an old-fashioned shop, in a street that is not the same as I remember it. I am fallen behind the time, and am too old to catch it again. Even the noise it makes a long way ahead, confuses me. (93–4)

'The world', 'the time': potent terms for a global energy system that devours and wastes, producing obsolesence: a universal economy. As the plot unfolds, the Instrument-maker's business is progressively disconnected from the world, a process culminating in bankruptcy – an economic dismantling that sanctifies its status as pastoral retreat. Dickens charges his idyll with its romance virtue by setting it at once inside and outside the world, a pocket of old time overtaken by the world's energies of change. The difference from Scott is that its 'old fashion' does not represent a different historical economy and culture. It is a purely private, psychological and domestic space of life within an already total modern economy, discarded by that same economy's internal dynamic of competition, new invention, alteration.

In Uncle Sol's old-fashioned perspective (the changeling Paul is also old-fashioned) 'the time' has become a confusing uproar 'a long way ahead'. At the horizon or rather epicentre of 'alteration', the modern economy is an invisible force that tears apart the fabric of the city:

The first shock of a great earthquake had, just at that period, rent the whole neighbourhood to its centre. Traces of its course were visible on every side. Houses were knocked down; streets broken through and stopped; deep pits and trenches dug in the ground; enormous heaps of earth and clay thrown up; buildings that were undermined and shaking, propped by great beams of wood. Here, a chaos of carts, overthrown and jumbled together, lay topsy-turvy at the bottom of a steep unnatural hill; there, confused treasures of iron soaked and rusted in something that had accidentally become a pond. Everywhere were bridges that led nowhere; thoroughfares that were wholly impassable; Babel towers of chimneys, wanting half their height; temporary wooden houses and enclosures, in the most unlikely situations; carcases of ragged tenements, and fragments of unfinished walls and arches, and piles of scaffolding, and wildernesses of bricks, and giant forms of cranes, and tripods straddling above nothing. There were a hundred thousand shapes and substances of incompleteness, wildly mingled out of their places, upside down, burrowing in the earth, aspiring in the air, mouldering in the water, and unintelligible as any dream. Hot springs and fiery eruptions, the usual attendants upon earthquakes, lent their contributions of confusion to the scene. Boiling water hissed and heaved within dilapidated walls; whence, also, the glare and roar of flames came issuing forth; and mounds of ashes blocked up rights of way, and wholly changed the law and custom of the neighbourhood.

In short, the yet unfinished and unopened Railroad was in progress; and, from the very core of all this dire disorder, trailed smoothly away, upon its mighty course of civilisation and improvement. (120–1)

In Dickens's apocalyptic formula, the tremendous chaos of the present is the unfolding of a tremendous order in the future. The convulsion of the scene releases that signifying, metonymical energy that seems most characteristically 'Dickensian' – an attention to jumbled material details that charges them with an electricity of strangeness. In the mangling of the city's ancient circuits, this energy vibrates between observer and scene. It is the sheer structural energy of city life without social form or moral content, for 'law and custom' are shattered along with the walls and streets.

The language of Dickens's description, appalled and exhilarated, recalls that of the riots in *Barnaby Rudge*. This revolutionary landscape is infernal, as well as chaotic; that is, we might be viewing an essential rather than temporary aspect of the city. And at the same time as Dickens promises the modern order of the railway, he describes its 'mighty course of civilisation and improvement' as receding 'smoothly away' from 'the very core of this dire disorder' – as if disorder is history's centre and origin, the essence of 'the time'. When the narrative returns to Staggs's Gardens, it is to survey 'civilisation and improvement' as a present order – formed upon a surface wiped clean. 'There was no such place as Staggs's Gardens. It had vanished from the earth' (289). The former chaos can now be identified in retrospect as a *decay* – 'old rotten summer-houses', 'miserable waste-ground' and heaps of 'refuse-matter', 'carcasses of houses'. It has given way to a prosperous, planned and packaged, mechanically synchronized community:

> There were railway hotels, office-houses, lodging-houses, boarding-houses; railway plans, maps, views, wrappers, bottles, sandwich-boxes, and time-tables; railway hackney-coach and cab-stands; railway omnibuses, railway streets and buildings, railway hangers-ons and parasites, and flatterers out of all calculation. There was even railway time observed in clocks, as if the sun itself had given in. (290)

This vision of a universal economic order is entirely cheerful; Dickens's ironies are pointed against 'human nature' rather than the order as such. For the point seems to be that the order as such, rather than people, is in control – happy as they might be, they are its dependents. The economic energies hypostatized in the railway are consistently represented as sublimely impersonal, a force of nature exceeding human agency. Which means that they exceed, also, the human order they inform:

> Night and day the conquering engines rumbled at their distant work, or, advancing smoothly to their journey's end, and gliding like tame dragons into the allotted corners grooved out to the inch for their reception, stood bubbling and trembling there, making the walls quake, as if they were dilating with the secret knowledge of great powers yet unsuspected in them, and strong purposes yet unachieved. (290)

The social order might not fully contain the energies of change that produced it; it is vibrant with the possibility of further dissolutions and transformations – fire brewing in the bowels of an obedient leviathan.

Mr Dombey himself is the novel's personification of economic forces, and he exemplifies the tragic distortion of a private, essential human nature, possessed by the powers and properties that it had thought to possess. The connection between an individual moral destiny and a collective social and material condition occupies the crux of the novel: Dickens has learnt from Scott the narration of individual subject and social–economic order as concrete entities, life-forms at different levels of organization, that inform one another. When Dickens brings their connection into explicit, editorial focus, he is careful to resist formulating it as simply a categorical opposition. Dombey, in mourning for his son, rides the railway, and 'the power that forced itself upon its iron way' is hailed as 'a type of the triumphant monster, Death' (355–6). The journey reveals, panoramically, the darkness and misery of urban slums as if they are trappings of this universal progress of death, but the narrator intervenes to limit such an interpretation to Dombey's own morbid fixation. The question remains as to a larger interpretation of the scene, the one available to the reader. Its answer lies in Mr Dombey's rejected daughter, Florence:

[He] knew full well, in his own breast, as he stood there, tinging the scene of transition before him with the morbid colours of his own mind, and making it a ruin and a picture of decay, instead of hopeful change, and promise of better things, that life had quite as much to do with his complainings as death. One child was gone, and one left. (356)

Hopeful change turns out to be aligned with the girl-child and the domestic affections: not so much in addition to as *rather than* economic and social processes. Mr Dombey's morbidity derives from his total devotion to a public and economic identity. We are left with a moral topography in which private life and the public economy occupy separate realms, and while the division is diagnosed as Mr Dombey's complaint, it goes on to determine the romance resolution, as if a reunification were unimaginable.

In a much-discussed passage towards the end of the novel,[32] Dickens invokes the figure of romance to convert the panoramic description of an 'unnatural' society into a prophetic and performative cry:

Oh for a good spirit who would take the house-tops off, with a more potent and benignant hand than the lame demon in the tale, and show a Christian people what dark shapes issue from amidst their homes, to swell the retinue of the Destroying Angel as he moves forth among them! For only one night's view of the pale phantoms rising from the scenes of our too-long neglect; and from the thick and sullen air where Vice and Fever propagate together, raining the tremendous social retributions which are ever pouring down, and ever coming thicker! Bright and blest the morning that should rise on such a night: for men, delayed no more by stumbling-blocks of their own making, which are but specks of dust upon the path between them and eternity, would then apply themselves, like creatures of one common

> origin, owing one duty to the Father of one family, and tending to one common end, to make the world a better place!
>
> Not the less bright and blest would that day be for rousing some who never have looked out upon the world of human life around them, to a knowledge of their own relation to it, and for making them acquainted with a perversion of nature in their own contracted sympathies and estimates; as great, and yet as natural in its development when once begun, as the lowest degradation known. (739)

The 'good spirit', an angelic counterpart of LeSage's satirical imp Asmodeus, is an emblem for Dickens's own romance in its instructive capacity, showing us the world of human life around us and our own relation to it. Dickens harnesses the apocalyptic process of social change at the rhetorical level of gesture and effect: to take off the house-tops, to reveal a ruinous and haunted cityscape, will generate the future, higher order of one universal household. Dickens's exhortation 'to make the world a better place' delicately elides society, the thick, fermenting, public and political hotchpotch of communities and their claims, as a site for moral agency, even though his vision has conjured it up. It has become visible as a disease, 'a dense black cloud' spreading across the city from the poor quarters to the rich: to disappear again with the cure. The end of the fiction's didactic work is a transcendental patriarchal household luminous with lack of social content and locked in by a homogenization and coincidence of 'origin' and 'end': birth and death are the points of universal human equality. Just so, the site for the fiction's work, the site of moral agency, is the domestic affections: understanding one's individual relation to the world will bring an expansion of 'sympathies and estimates', and the charitable activism Dickens himself practised so energetically. The individual conversion of Mr Dombey is to correspond with a conversion of the reader of the book. Thus Dickens invokes, cannily rather than otherwise, the institutional limit as well as power of his art: his mass public is constituted by readers, individual sensibilities under separate rooftops. If 'the Father of one family' should be reading these pages aloud to his women and children at the hearthside, then all the more appropriately does he become the medium for the author himself, in this cautionary novel about the arrogations of paternity.

The novel's redemptive transformation is a moral and sentimental conversion, grounded on private family relations, emphatically disconnected from the forces of social and economic progress. The 'nature' that reclaims Mr Dombey is feminine. Florence's example consecrates romance in the novel as figure of a beneficent magic, rejected by the harsh and fatal disciplines of paternity but therefore able (the repressed returns) to save it. Her moral power is earned by submission; the equation that could not be made in *Barnaby Rudge* becomes possible when the son's place is taken by a daughter. Dickens reproduces the fable of Scott's most Victorian novel, *The Heart of Mid-Lothian*. There, however, romance and nature inspired a dangerous, erroneous female self-sufficiency, personified by the fallen daughters Effie and Madge. In *Dombey and Son* Florence personifies romance and nature, but as a *child* first and a woman second. Insofar as they remain segregated from the public world, women better preserve those qualities of innocence, meekness, sympathy and purity of the affections that constitute (according to this scheme) the grace of childhood: a lack of physical power, exclusion from the work- and marketplace, and an absence of 'pride'. The significant, ontological division of moral identity in Dickens is not so much then between masculine and feminine as between child and adult. Sexual identity measures the depth of a fall from childhood.

Mr Dombey, at his worst moment, turns on his daughter:

> in his frenzy, he lifted up his cruel arm, and struck her, crosswise, with that heaviness, that she tottered on the marble floor; and as he dealt the blow, he told her what Edith was, and bade her follow her, since they had always been in league. (757)

As when Othello strikes Desdemona, the venting of a sexual rage upon the innocent constitutes the shock. Adult sexuality in the novel is a fatal force, a kind of demonic possession, an overwhelmingly phallic transformation of both men and women. Only readers blinkered by literality can complain of a lack of sexuality in Dickens: in *Dombey and Son* it is abundant, if perverse. Dombey and Edith are fit partners, images of one another, and their intercourse is charged with a sado-masochistic frenzy:

> The very diamonds – a marriage gift – that rose and fell impatiently upon her bosom, seemed to pant to break the chain that clasped them, and roll down on the floor where she might tread upon them. . . . His insolence of self-importance dilated as he saw this alteration in her. Swollen no less by her past scorn of him, and his so recent feeling of disadvantage, than by her present submission (as he took it to be), it became too mighty for his breast, and burst all bounds. Why, who could long resist his lofty will and pleasure! . . . She had changed her attitude before he arrived at these words, and now sat – still looking at him fixedly – turning a bracelet round and round upon her arm; not winding it about with a light, womanly touch, but pressing and dragging it over the smooth skin, until the white limb showed a bar of red. (652–3)

Bondage and fetishism are the trappings of a commodification of natural affection. The adult sexual will, with its phallicism and pride, is part of the larger economy of power and traffic. Paradoxically, its ends are frigidity, impotence, sterility. The upstart Carker stalks Edith 'with his gleaming teeth, through the dark rooms, like a mouth', himself the emblem of the *vagina dentata*. When she defies him 'uprearing her proud form', he is correspondingly unmanned:

> He would have sold his soul to root her, in her beauty, to the floor, and make her arms drop at her sides, and have her at his mercy. But he could not look at her, and not be afraid of her. He saw a strength within her that was resistless. (860)

In the political economy of sexuality, the partners exchange their identities in the mirror of each other's pride, and are both turned to stone. At last Carker is devoured by a railway-train before Mr Dombey's eyes; the plot confirms the locomotive as indeed the type of the triumphant monster, Death, and agent of the onlooker's vengeance. The distance between the protagonist's morbid psychology and the allegory is closed. Ambition, guilt, sexuality, death and the objective forces of the new economy all combine into the one tremendous emblem of the

Manager smashed by the railway in front of the elder sinner his bad deeds have eclipsed.

Romance is innocence: 'naiveté' a moral category. Florence is obliged to shudder in the presence of Carker, recoil from Edith as from pollution and fly from her father's house bearing the stain of his hand upon her breast. Quite early in the story, her adventure with Good Mrs Brown constitutes the romance episode that fixes her in her allegorical identity as the gentle child in the mean streets, the changeling princess in the modern city. The episode grows narratively out of the first description of Staggs's Gardens. The moment-by-moment tumult of the streets – Rob the Grinder mobbed by urchins, an alarm of a mad bull – claims Florence for the essential urban state of confused, helpless solitude. The sinister old woman drags the trusting child into her lair and makes her strip, a command fraught with the unspoken, unspeakable threat of a sexual molestation. The type of the woman in the streets is the prostitute. But Florence, exchanging her finery for rags, can impersonate the wandering princess of romance, of *The Faerie Queene* or *The Winter's Tale*.

The crucial subjectivity that interprets its desire by the romance archetype is young Walter Gay's. He is characterized by a 'spice of romance and love of the marvellous', associated at first with subaltern ambition as his Uncle and Captain Cuttle comically urge upon him the example of Dick Whittington (172). The authority of the nursery tale guarantees, however, that these naive reveries of fortune lack policy: just as Dick Whittington's success was assured when he turned his back on London. Walter's rescue of the lost Florence is highly delicate. The ragged girl he has picked up from the street happens to be the boss's daughter, compounding the risk of suspicion for an ambitious as well as a sexual motive:

Yet Walter so idealised the pretty child whom he had found wandering in the rough streets, and so identified her with her innocent gratitude of that night and the simplicity and truth of its expression, that he blushed for himself as a libeller when he argued that she could ever grow proud. On the other hand, his meditations were of that fantastic order that it seemed hardly less libellous in him to imagine her grown a woman: to think of her as anything but the same artless, gentle, winning little creature, that she had been in the days of Good Mrs Brown. In a word, Walter found out that to reason with himself about Florence at all, was to become very unreasonable indeed; and that he could do no better than preserve her image in his mind as something precious, unattainable, unchangeable, and indefinite – indefinite in all but its power of giving him pleasure, and restraining him like an angel's hand from anything unworthy. (287–8)

We read here Dickens's manifesto for romance: it is a mode of imagining in which desire is disconnected from 'reason', that is, from an economy of definite objects endlessly attainable and exchangeable, for a pure receptivity of pleasure that seems to consist in the contemplation of an image of one's own simplicity and vulnerability in childhood. Walter's purity of motive sanctifies his progress; he is not aspiring for the hand of his master's daughter, his fortune-hunting expedition to the imperial periphery consists of exile and shipwreck and when he returns his desire must be subject to exquisite negotiation (both of them, but especially she, are penniless; she and not he makes the proposal) before he can become the son and heir and have his princess.

In *The Old Curiosity Shop*, Dickens had identified the contrast between the innocent child and the grotesque heterogeneity of her surroundings as the germinal principle of his allegory. In *Dombey and Son* he develops the same device, giving it a more complex positive valence, by making romance the figure of a moral discipline. First, Florence in the rough streets becomes an emblem to regulate a young man's fancy. Later, towards the middle of the story, Florence earns that romance identity as a virtue for herself, in the Tennysonian set-piece description of her solitude in the 'wilderness' of her father's house. The rhythms, rhymes and repetitions of Dickens's refrain mimic a heavy stasis:

Florence lived alone in the great dreary house, and day succeeded day, and still she lived alone; and the blank walls looked down upon her with a vacant stare, as if they had a Gorgon-like mind to stare her youth and beauty into stone. (393)

However, 'Florence bloomed there, like the king's fair daughter in the story' (395). She represents a natural vitality that does *not* reflect the morbid, petrifying speculation of its surroundings. The wonderful description of the house itself suggests, not an unchanging stasis out of time, but rather the reverse: the process of time and change as a decay, an occult reanimation of the world:

Damp started on the walls, and as the stains came out, the pictures seemed to go in and secrete themselves. Mildew and mould began to lurk in closets. Fungus trees grew in corners of the cellars. Dust accumulated, nobody knew whence nor how; spiders, moths, and grubs were heard of every day. An exploratory blackbeetle now and then was found immovable upon the stairs, or in an upper room, as wondering how he got there. Rats began to squeak and scuffle in the night time, through dark galleries they mined behind the panelling. (394)

The waste house succumbs to the secret colonizing order of a counter-life, with its own unwholesome citizens and gardens. Florence, on the other hand, finds a source of life out of time, in the medium of the fancy: a haunting of memories and imaginary possibilities:

Shadowy company attended Florence up and down the echoing house, and sat with her in the dismantled rooms. As if her life were an enchanted vision, there arose out of her solitude ministering thoughts, that made it fanciful and unreal. She imagined so often what her life would have been if her father could have loved her and she had been a favourite child, that sometimes, for the moment, she almost believed it so, and, borne on by the current of that pensive fiction, seemed to remember how they had watched her brother in his grave together; how they had freely shared his heart between them; how they were united in the dear remembrance of him; how they often spoke about him yet; and her kind father, looking at her gently, told her of their common hope and trust in God. At other times she pictured to herself her mother yet alive. (396)

Something else than the sinister life of mortality quickens about Florence as she submits to the memory of her childhood affections, and imagines a family with herself at the hub of its currents of love. Except that each of those relations is unreal: her brother and mother are dead, her father rejects her, the reunion at the graveside never happened. In the grammar of the fancy the past turns into the subjunctive – but then, as the narrative completes itself, into the optative and future too. Florence's ministering thoughts of her father's love become 'the purpose of her life' (397). In the conversion from retrospect to prospect that asserts a narrative order transcending mere chronology, Dickens develops the romance figure powerfully rendered by Mrs Radcliffe in Emily's reveries at Udolpho, which also expresses an essentially modern solitude within the socially diminished, psychically intensified community of the nuclear family. This wilderness is reclaimed by a daughter's submissive yearning for the kindness of an authoritarian father. Unlike Nell, unlike her brother Paul, but like Tiny Tim – and much more positively – Florence does NOT die. Becoming once more the maiden in the streets, 'like the survivor on a lonely shore from the wreck of a great vessel' (758), she can conjure Walter back from his more literal shipwreck.

Dombey and Son is a revolutionary narrative: we read about the overthrow of a dynasty, the replacement of the sombre donkey by the squire of gaiety. Exept that, once more, the new order is set apart from forces of collective transformation represented as fatal and sublime in their impersonality. Raymond Williams observes that the strategic ambiguity of Dickens's representation responds to 'the real contradiction – the power for life or death; for disintegration, order and false order – of the new social and economic forces of his time', and that the author's great concern 'is to keep human recognition and human kindness alive, through these unprecedented strains, and within this unrecognizable altered landscape'.[33] By the end of the novel Dickens's plot has resolved that the new social and economic forces, grasped as global and inhuman in their scale, do not correspond with 'human recognition and human kindness'. The one space where such qualities flourish – Sol Gills's shop – has been left behind by economic development. Even so, we learn at last that

> some of Mr Gills's old investments are coming out wonderfully well; and that instead of being behind the time in those respects, as he supposed, he was, in truth, a little before it, and had to wait the fulness of the time and the design. (971)

By now the meaning of 'the time' has been transformed to coincide with the allegorical 'design' of the romance as a process at once natural and providential. I have said that Dickens's technique in *Dombey and Son* is remarkably close to Scott's in *Guy Mannering*, for all the contrast of setting. The difference between their plots (in other ways so alike) is that here the father's fall constitutes the catastrophe, and the son and heir remains a Vanbeest Brown by birth. So, not being noble, Walter is not even tempted by a course of self-assertion. Anyone may be a gentleman except, on the whole, gentlemen; all that is needed is a Florence, since chivalry has been emphatically redefined as a quality of subjection to an idealized woman, who has earned that idealization by a superior subjection of her own. Which ends up being the position, also, of the father, broken and converted into a grateful subject of the new order like Pu Yi in *The Last Emperor*. But where Pu Yi acquired the spiritual recompense of serenity and self-sufficiency in his release from history, Mr Dombey remains without moral power – a miser of love:

> The child herself almost wonders at a certain secrecy he keeps in [his affection for her]. He hoards her in his heart. He cannot bear to see a cloud upon her face. He cannot bear to see her sit apart. He fancies that she feels a slight, when there is none. He steals away to look at her, in her sleep. (975)

Notes

PROLOGUE: FICTION AS FICTION

1 K. J. Fielding, ed., *The Speeches of Charles Dickens* (Oxford: Clarendon Press, 1960), pp. 154–7.

2 Peter Ackroyd, *Dickens* (New York: HarperCollins, 1990), pp. 666–7. The position remained highly controversial: cf. the 'dignity of literature' dispute that took place, not without acrimony, between Thackeray and Forster in 1847: Gordon N. Ray, *Thackeray: The Age of Wisdom 1847–1863* (New York: McGraw-Hill, 1958), pp. 114–15, 136–8, 150–3.

3 Frye: 'the search of the libido or desiring self for a fulfilment that will deliver it from the anxieties of reality but still contain that reality', *Anatomy of Criticism: Four Essays* (Princeton: Princeton University Press, 1957), p. 193. Jameson: 'the possibility of sensing other historical rhythms, and of demonic or Utopian transformations of a real now unshakably set in place', *The Political Unconscious: Narrative as a Socially Symbolic Act* (Ithaca: Cornell University Press, 1981), pp. 104, 110. On the importance of plot as (in Pat Spacks's phrase) the medium of 'desire and truth' in fiction: Robert Caserio, *Plot, Story and the Novel: From Dickens to Poe to the Modern Period* (Princeton: Princeton University Press, 1979). Peter Brooks, *Reading for the Plot: Design and Intention in Narrative* (New York: Knopf, 1984). Patrician Meyer Spacks, *Desire and Truth: Functions of Plot in Eighteenth-Century English Novels* (Chicago: University of Chicago Press, 1990).

4 Edwin M. Eigner and George J. Worth, eds., *Victorian Criticism of the Novel* (Cambridge: Cambridge University Press, 1985), pp. 2–13. James T. Hillhouse, *The Waverley Novels and Their Critics* (Minneapolis: University of Minnesota Press, 1936), pp. 188–228. Joseph Carroll, *The Cultural Theory of Matthew Arnold* (Berkeley: University of California Press, 1982), p. 157. For Carlyle and Scott and Dickens, see below, chapters 3 and 4.

5 The academic revaluation of Dickens was largely a North American project, through Edgar Johnson's biography (1952) and criticism by Edmund Wilson, Dorothy Van Ghent, J. Hillis Miller and Steven Marcus. The Leavises took part in the centennial honours but fiercely repudiated any American contribution: F. R. Leavis and Q. D. Leavis, *Dickens the Novelist* (London: Chatto & Windus, 1970), pp. ix–x.

6 Moretti: 'the worst novel of the West, and the boldest culture of justice'; 'one long fairytale with a happy ending, far more elementary and limited than its continental counterparts': *The Way of the World: The Bildungsroman in European Culture* (London: Verso, 1987), pp. 213–14.

7 Moretti, *Way of the World*, p. 198. For Anderson, 'Origins of the Present Crisis', *New Left Review* 23 (1964), 28, 30.

8 E. J. Hobsbawm and Terence Ranger, *The Invention of Tradition* (Cambridge: Cambridge University Press, 1983). Arthur Johnston, *Enchanted Ground: The Study of Medieval Romance in the Eighteenth Century* (London: Oxford University Press, 1964). Geoffrey Hartman, *Beyond Formalism: Literary Essays 1958–1970* (New Haven: Yale University Press, 1970), pp. 310, 311–36. Lawrence Lipking, *The Ordering of the Arts in Eighteenth-Century England* (Princeton: Princeton University Press, 1970). Raymond Williams, *Keywords: A Vocabulary of Culture and Society* (New York: Oxford University Press, 1976), pp. 15–54. Stuart Curran, *Poetic Form and British Romanticism* (New York: Oxford University Press, 1986), pp. 18–28, 128–32. Arthur Sherbo, *The Birth of Shakespeare Studies* (East Lansing: Colleagues Press, 1986). Gerald Newman, *The Rise of English Nationalism: A Cultural History, 1720–1830* (New York: St Martin's, 1987), pp. 109–19. Alvin B. Kernan, *Printing Technology, Letters, and Samuel Johnson* (Princeton: Princeton University Press, 1987), pp. 268–82.

9 George Moir, 1842, reprinted in Eigner and Worth, eds., *Victorian Criticism of the Novel*, p. 54. On the reception of *Waverley*: Ina Ferris, 'Re-positioning the Novel: *Waverley* and the Gender of Fiction', *Studies in Romanticism* 28 (Summer 1989), 291–301. On the canonization of the novel: Nancy Armstrong, *Desire and Domestic Fiction: A Political History of the Novel* (New York: Oxford University Press, 1987), pp. 37–8, 267 n. 10 (citing an unpublished ms. by Homer Obed Brown).

10 Moretti, *Way of the World*, p. 251 n. 55.

11 For a recent, incisive critique of the nineteenth-century holistic myth of culture: Christopher Herbert, *Culture and Anomie: Ethnographic Imagination in the Nineteenth Century* (Chicago: University of

Chicago Press, 1991), pp. 4–21. The canonical statement of this view of the nineteenth-century novel's rhetoric of form (as a dialectic of order and incoherence) is by J. Hillis Miller, e.g.: *Fiction and Repetition: Seven English Novels* (Cambridge, Mass.: Harvard University Press, 1982).

12 Martin Price, *Forms of Life: Character and Moral Imagination in the Novel* (New Haven: Yale University Press, 1983), p. 27.

13 Price, *Forms of Life*, p. 15. Alastair Fowler, *Kinds of Literature: An Introduction to the Theory of Genres and Modes* (Cambridge, Mass.: Harvard University Press, 1982), p. 20. Northrop Frye, *The Secular Scripture: A Study of the Structure of Romance* (Cambridge, Mass.: Harvard University Press, 1976), pp. 3, 36. Jameson, *Political Unconscious*, p. 130. On Frye as Enlightenment romance revivalist: Hartman, *Beyond Formalism*, pp. 24–41. Criticisms of Frye for 'excluding history' perhaps tend to take too literally the synchronicity of his schemes: Frank Lentricchia, *After the New Criticism* (Chicago: University of Chicago Press, 1980), pp. 2–27. Michael McKeon, *The Origins of the English Novel 1600–1740* (Baltimore: Johns Hopkins University Press, 1987), pp. 4–10. Fowler concedes that 'Frye is historical in spite of his theory', *Kinds of Literature*, p. 243.

14 Frye, *Secular Scripture*, pp. 2–4.

15 McKeon, *Origins of the English Novel*, pp. 20–2 and *passim*. Paulson, *Satire and the Novel in Eighteenth-Century England* (New Haven: Yale University Press, 1967), pp. 23–40, 110–14. Paul Salzman, *English Prose Fiction 1558–1700: A Critical History* (Oxford: Clarendon Press, 1985), pp. 270–82. See also, canonically, Ian Watt, *The Rise of the Novel: Studies in Defoe, Fielding and Richardson* (Berkeley: University of California Press, 1957), pp. 9–34.

16 Canonically, by Georg Lukács: *The Historical Novel* (Lincoln: University of Nebraska Press, 1983), pp. 19–63.

17 Jameson, *Political Unconscious*, p. 148.

18 Patricia Parker makes it the constitutive, metalinguistic, trope of romance: *Inescapable Romance: Studies in the Poetics of a Mode* (Princeton: Princeton University Press, 1979), pp. 6–15 and *passim*.

19 Aleksandr Pushkin, *Eugene Onegin*, translated from the Russian, with a commentary, by Vladimir Nabokov (Princeton: Princeton University Press, 1964), III, 32–6.

20 On 'romance' and English fiction before 1800: Salzman, *English Prose Fiction 1558–1700*, pp. 177–200, 265–91, 338–46 (Salzman's recuperation of the mightily abused French heroic romance, pp. 177–200, is especially valuable). McKeon, *Origins of the English*

Novel, pp. 52–64, 212–314, etc. A useful anthology of contemporary statements is Ioan Williams, ed., *Novel and Romance, 1700–1800: A Documentary Record* (New York: Barnes & Noble, 1970).

21 Henry Fielding, *Joseph Andrews*, Author's Preface. Williams, ed., *Novel and Romance*, pp. 120, 127–8, 319–20.

22 Salzman, *English Prose Fiction 1558–1700*, pp. 177–9, 277. Jane Spencer, *The Rise of the Woman Novelist: From Aphra Behn to Jane Austen* (Oxford: Basil Blackwell, 1986), pp. 23, 182–7.

23 On *The Female Quixote*: Spencer, *Rise of the Woman Novelist*, pp. 187–92. Paulson, *Satire and the Novel*, pp. 274–8. Patricia Meyer Spacks, *The Adolescent Idea: Myths of Youth in the Adult Imagination* (New York: Basic Books, 1981), pp. 129–35, and *Desire and Truth*, pp. 12–33.

24 Cf. Spacks, *Desire and Truth*, pp. 114–46. The distinctive contribution of the Scots Enlightenment (from Smith to Mackenzie) to the discourse of 'moral sentiment' – more mobile, robust, and complex in its inflexions – must be acknowledged here.

25 Dickens, *Bleak House*, preface to the first edition (1853). I am using Bakhtin's terms, although Scott's mixed forms are symphonic rather than polyphonic: see chapters 2 and 3, below. M. M. Bakhtin, *The Dialogic Imagination: Four Essays*, trans. Michael Holquist and Caryl Emerson (Austin: University of Texas Press, 1980), pp. 259–422.

26 Charles Dickens, *Little Dorrit* (Harmondsworth: Penguin, 1967), pp. 273–4; see also p. 825.

27 Peter Brooks, *Reading for the Plot*, p. 23.

28 Ferris, 'Re-positioning the Novel', 298–301. For the new history of the novel: Patricia Meyer Spacks, *The Female Imagination* (New York: Knopf, 1975) and *Desire and Truth*. Elaine Showalter, *A Literature of Their Own: British Women Novelists from Bronte to Lessing* (Princeton: Princeton University Press, 1977). Sandra Gilbert and Susan Gubar, *The Madwoman in the Attic: The Woman Writer and the Nineteenth-Century Literary Imagination* (New Haven: Yale University Press, 1979). Margaret Homans, *Bearing the Word: Language and Female Experience in Nineteenth-Century Women's Writing* (Chicago: University of Chicago Press, 1986). Nancy Armstrong, *Desire and Domestic Fiction*. (Ferris notes the 'gap' constituted by Scott in Armstrong's account: see p. 280 n. 1.) Mary Poovey, *The Proper Lady and the Woman Writer: Ideology as Style in the Works of Mary Wollstonecraft, Mary Shelley, and Jane Austen* (Chicago: University of Chicago Press, 1984) and *Uneven Developments: The Ideological Work of Gender in Mid-Victorian England* (Chicago: University of Chicago Press, 1988).

29 Lukács, *The Historical Novel*, pp. 242–4. On Scott's successors: Andrew Sanders, *The Victorian Historical Novel, 1840–1880* (London: Macmillan, 1978), pp. 14–31.

30 Robert Louis Stevenson, 'A Humble Remonstrance' (1884), reprinted in Eigner and Worth, eds., *Victorian Criticism of the Novel*, p. 217.

1 THE CULTURE OF GOTHIC

1 Horace Walpole, *The Castle of Otranto: A Gothic Story* (Oxford: Oxford University Press, 1964), p. 7. Future references to this edition will be given in the text.

2 Ann Radcliffe, *The Romance of the Forest* (Oxford: Oxford University Press, 1986), p. 7. Future references to this edition will be given in the text.

3 The formula is Clara Reeve's, in *The Progress of Romance* (1785; repr. New York: Facsimile Text Society, 1930), I. 111. The full titles of these works are, Radcliffe: *A Sicilian Romance* (1790), *The Romance of the Forest* (1791), *The Mysteries of Udolpho: A Romance* (1794), *The Italian, or the Confessional of the Black Penitents, A Romance* (1797); and Lewis: *The Monk, A Romance* (1796).

4 On eighteenth-century Gothic revival: Paul Frankl, *The Gothic: Literary Sources and Interpretations Through Eight Centuries* (Princeton: Princeton University Press, 1960), pp. 372–96, 402–7. Maurice Levy, *Le Roman 'Gothique' Anglais, 1764–1824* (Toulouse, 1968), pp. 7–76. Montague Summers, *The Gothic Quest* (London: Fortune Press, 1930), pp. 37–43. The classic contemporary account is Richard Hurd's *Letters on Chivalry and Romance* (1762; repr. London: Henry Frowde, 1911), which identifies 'Gothic' as the historical matrix of 'Romance'. For the radical mythology of a Gothic constitution, see Samuel Kliger, *The Goths in England: A Study in Seventeenth and Eighteenth Century Thought* (Cambridge, Mass.: Harvard University Press, 1952), pp. 6–28, 3–111. Gerald Newman, *The Rise of English Nationalism: A Cultural History, 1720–1830* (New York: St Martin's, 1987), pp. 179–91.

5 Sir Joshua Reynolds, *Discourses on Art*, ed. Robert R. Wark (New Haven: Yale University Press), p. 242.

6 Kliger, *The Goths in England*, pp. 211–17, 223–39. John Dunlop, *The History of Fiction: Being a Critical Account of the Most Celebrated Prose Works of Fiction from the Earliest Greek Romances to the Novels of the Present Day* (1814; repr. Philadelphia: Carey & Hart, 1842), pp. 119–30.

7 Hurd, *Letters on Chivalry and Romance*, p. 154. Future references will be given in the text.

8 For the Gothic as religious or theological allegory: Devendra P. Varma, *The Gothic Flame* (London: Arthur Barker, 1957). Joel Porte, 'In the Hands of an Angry God: Religious Terror in Gothic Fiction', in G. R. Thompson, ed., *The Gothic Imagination: Essays in Dark Romanticism* (Pullman, Wash.: Washington State University Press, 1974), pp. 42–64. Most imaginatively (as 'heretical' mythography), Judith K. Wilt, *Ghosts of the Gothic: Austen, Eliot and Lawrence* (Princeton: Princeton University Press, 1980), pp. 12–24. For psychoanalytically informed accounts: Levy, *Le Roman 'Gothique' Anglais*. William Patrick Day, *In the Circles of Fear and Desire: A Study of Gothic Fantasy* (Chicago: Chicago University Press, 1985).

9 On Reeve, see Levy, *Le Roman 'Gothique' Anglais*, pp. 170–7. J. M. S. Tompkins, *The Popular Novel in England, 1770–1800* (1932; repr. Lincoln: University of Nebraska Press, 1961), pp. 229–31.

10 Newman, *The Rise of English Nationalism*, pp. 228–32.

11 The Marquis de Sade was the first to make the connection between Gothic fiction and contemporary anxieties about the French Revolution: 'Reflections on the Novel', in *The 120 Days of Sodom and Other Writings*, tr. and ed. A. Wainhouse and R. Seaver (New York: Grove Press, 1966), p. 109. For a lucid account of the Gothic as bourgeois ideology: David Punter, *The Literature of Terror* (London: Longman, 1980): 'In Gothic the middle class displaces the hidden violence of present social structures, conjures them up again as past, and falls promptly under their spell', p. 418.

12 Edmund Burke, *Reflections on the Revolution in France* (Harmondsworth: Penguin, 1968), pp. 170–1.

13 Eve Kosofsky Sedgwick, 'The Character in the Veil: Imagery of the Surface in the Gothic Novel', *PMLA* 96 (1981), 255–70, discusses the 'ocular contagion' of fixation, repetition and death, p. 265; Day, *In the Circles of Fear and Desire*, describes how the reader takes part in the Gothic text's modality of 'enthrallment', pp. 63–9.

14 Angus Fletcher, *Allegory: The Theory of a Symbolic Mode* (Ithaca: Cornell University Press, 1964), pp. 100–8 (and on a Gothic aesthetic, pp. 262–3). Scott complained that 'the supernatural occurrences of *The Castle of Otranto* are brought forward into too strong daylight, and marked by an over degree of distinction and accuracy of outline', *Sir Walter Scott on Novelists and Fiction*, ed. Ioan Williams (New York: Barnes & Noble, 1968), p. 91. On the

Gothic and surrealism: Summers, *Gothic Quest*, pp. 382–412, and Varma, *Gothic Flame*, pp. 233–4.

15 Fletcher, *Allegory*. Hurd's account of *The Faerie Queene* as 'a Gothic, not a Classical poem' (p. 115) defends its 'unity of *design*' according to '*Allegorical*' principles (pp. 125–7). Elsewhere, though, Hurd finds the origins of allegory in a late, embattled stage of romance, as 'a sort of apology, for the absurdity of the literal story' (*Letters on Chivalry and Romance*, pp. 151–4). Thomas Warton describes allegory as the characteristic mode of a Gothic culture, *Observations on the Fairy Queen of Spenser* 2 vols. (1762; repr. New York: Greenwood Press, 1968), II, pp. 89–113. On allegorical and novelistic or romance modes in Bunyan: Leopold Damrosch, *God's Plot and Man's Stories: Studies in the Fictional Imagination from Milton to Fielding* (Chicago: Chicago University Press, 1985), pp. 170–86; Michael McKeon, *The Origins of the English Novel 1600–1740* (Baltimore: Johns Hopkins University Press, 1987), pp. 295–314.

16 Cf. John Freccero, *Dante: The Poetics of Conversion* (Cambridge: Harvard University Press, 1986), esp. pp. 93–109, 119–35.

17 Elizabeth MacAndrew, *The Gothic Tradition in Fiction* (New York: Columbia University Press, 1979), p. 9. In the preface to *The Old English Baron*, Clara Reeve complained: 'When your expectation is wound up to the highest pitch, these circumstances take it down with a witness, destroy the work of imagination, and, instead of attention, excite laughter'. Peter Sabor, ed., *Horace Walpole: The Critical Heritage* (London: Routledge and Kegan Paul, 1987), p. 77.

18 William Beckford, *Vathek* (Oxford: Oxford University Press, 1983), p. 93. Future references to this edition will be given in the text.

19 Matthew Lewis, *The Monk* (Oxford: Oxford University Press, 1973), p. 40. Future references to this edition will be given in the text.

20 Vivaldi, in Radcliffe's *The Italian*, p. 121.

21 Nancy Armstrong, *Desire and Domestic Fiction: A Political History of the Novel* (New York: Oxford University Press, 1987), p. 8.

22 Burke, *Reflections on the Revolution in France*, p. 164.

23 See, among numerous examples, Rachel M. Brownstein, *Becoming a Heroine: Reading about Women in Novels* (New York: Viking, 1982), pp. 40–77; Terry Castle, *Clarissa's Ciphers: Meaning and Disruption in Richardson's 'Clarissa'* (Ithaca: Cornell University Press, 1982).

24 Ann Radcliffe, *The Mysteries of Udolpho* (Oxford: Oxford Univer-

sity Press, 1966), p. 656. Future references to this edition will be given in the text.

25 On the heroine's 'disciplined subjectivity' as 'the central signifying and structural principle in Radcliffe's novels, as in Burney's': Gary Kelly, *English Fiction of the Romantic Period, 1789–1830* (London: Longman, 1989), pp. 50–5.

26 Jay Macpherson describes this rhetorical expansion in *The Spirit of Solitude: Conventions and Continuities in Late Romance* (New Haven: Yale University Press, 1982), pp. 54–5. Cf. Kelly, *English Fiction of the Romantic Period*, p. 54.

27 Radcliffe adapted the most forceful of these terms from Richardson, whose heroines, Pamela, Clarissa and Harriet Byron, are each kidnapped toward a romance transformation of their lot, whether successful or (for Clarissa) failed; in Harriet's case, the 'quixotic' counter-abduction of her chevalier Grandison delivers her to a 'society of angels'.

28 My account of the positivity of Radcliffe's representation is indebted to recent feminist accounts of the 'Female Gothic': Ellen Moers, *Literary Women: The Great Writers* (New York: Doubleday, 1976), pp. 122–40. Cynthia Griffin Wolff, 'The Radcliffean Gothic Model: A Form for Feminine Sexuality', in Juliann E. Fleenor, ed., *The Female Gothic* (Montreal: Eden Press, 1983), pp. 207–23. Kate Ellis, *The Contested Castle: Gothic Novels and the Subversion of Domestic Ideology* (Urbana: University of Illinois Press, 1989). Eugenia C. DeLamotte, *Perils of the Night: A Feminist Study of Nineteenth-Century Gothic* (New York: Oxford University Press, 1990), pp. 29–35, 149–92.

29 Cf. Punter, *Literature of Terror*, pp. 75–6, and MacAndrew, *Gothic Tradition in Fiction*, pp. 131–5, on Emily's sentimental education at Udolpho.

30 Patricia Meyer Spacks, *Desire and Truth: Functions of Plot in Eighteenth-Century English Novels* (Chicago: University of Chicago Press, 1990), pp. 147–74, discusses Radcliffe's articulation of a 'new kind of plot' upon the father–daughter relation.

31 Punter describes *The Italian* as 'a kind of de-parodisation of *The Monk*', *The Literature of Terror*, p. 70.

32 In *Anne of Geierstein*. J. M. S. Tompkins describes the Gothic topos of the Secret Society, *Popular Novel*, pp. 281–3.

33 In an article published posthumously in the *New Monthly Magazine* (vol. 7, 1826), under the title 'On the Supernatural in Poetry'; cited in Bonamy Dobrée's Introduction to *The Mysteries of Udolpho*, p. ix. 'Terror and horror are so far opposite, that the first

expands the soul, and awakens the faculties to a high degree of life; the other contracts, freezes, and nearly annihilates them.' Radcliffe cites Burke as her theoretical, Shakespeare and Milton as her poetic sources.

34 Thus Mrs Barbauld's objections: '[The mysteries] are not always, however, *well* accounted for; and the mind experiences a sort of disappointment and shame at having felt so much from appearances which had nothing in them beyond this "visible diurnal sphere" ' (*British Novelists*, 1810, XLIII, preface, p. iv). Scott, who would make complex use of precisely this disjunction in his own romances, acknowledged that 'some feeling of disappointment and displeasure attends most readers' (*Sir Walter Scott on Novelists and Fiction*, pp. 115–18). Tompkins asserts, however, 'it was this compromise, so unsatisfactory to later generations, that was most popular in its own' (*Popular Novel*, pp. 291 and n. 1).

2 THE ROMANCE OF SUBJECTION: SCOTT'S *WAVERLEY*

1 Scott's fiction thus exemplifies two major European ideas of literary genre at the beginning of the nineteenth century: what Georg Lukács calls 'the classical form of the historical novel', *The Historical Novel* (Lincoln: University of Nebraska Press, 1983), pp. 19–88; and the *Bildungsroman*, what Franco Moretti calls 'the "symbolic form" of modernity', *The Way of the World: The Bildungsroman in European Culture* (London: Verso, 1987), p. 5.

2 James Hogg, a critical as well as sympathetic witness, actually blamed Scott's death on the Reform ascendancy: *Memoirs of the Author's Life and Familiar Anecdotes of Sir Walter Scott*, ed. Douglas Mack (New York: Barnes & Noble, 1972), pp. 132, 134. For Scott's politics: Graham McMaster, *Scott and Society* (Cambridge: Cambridge University Press, 1981). P. H. Scott, 'The Politics of Sir Walter Scott', in J. H. Alexander and David Hewitt, eds., *Scott and His Influence* (Aberdeen: Association for Scottish Literary Studies, 1983), pp. 208–19.

3 Lukács, *The Historical Novel*, pp. 30–63. An influential account of the middle way as a figure of historical compromise, following Lukács, was David Daiches' 1951 essay 'Scott's Achievement as a Novelist' (reprinted in *Modern Judgements: Walter Scott*, ed. D. D. Devlin (London: Macmillan, 1969), pp. 33–62). Alexander Welsh, *The Hero of the Waverley Novels* (New Haven: Yale University Press, 1963). On the 'moderate' position of the subject as a site

of tragic consciousness within history: John P. Farrell, *Revolution as Tragedy: The Dilemma of the Moderate from Scott to Arnold* (Ithaca: Cornell University Press, 1980), pp. 38–63.

4 On landowners and lawyers in post-Union Scotland: T. C. Smout, *A History of the Scottish People 1560–1830* (New York: Scribner's, 1969), pp. 280–301, 373–7. For a vivid evocation of the type: Karl Miller, *Cockburn's Millenium* (Cambridge, Mass.: Harvard University Press, 1976). On Scott and Edinburgh literary culture: J. G. Lockhart, *Peter's Letters to his Kinsfolk*, 1819; ed. William Ruddick (Edinburgh: Scottish Academic Press, 1977), pp. 90–1, 147. On Scott as figure of a 'burden of the past' in Scottish literature: Edwin Muir, *Scott and Scotland* (London: Routledge, 1936). David Craig, *Scottish Literature and the Scottish People 1680–1830* (London: Chatto & Windus, 1961), is briskly hostile towards Scott, as agent of a pernicious cultural anglicization and gentrification. P. H. Scott, *Walter Scott and Scotland* (Edinburgh: Blackwood, 1981), offers a defence that rather confirms the opposition's case, but usefully gathers the relevant information on Scott's own sense of national identity. A balanced view is Thomas Crawford, *Sir Walter Scott* (Edinburgh: Scottish Academic Press, 1982). For Scott as author of a British nationalism: Gary Kelly, *English Fiction of the Romantic Period, 1789–1830* (London: Longman, 1989), pp. 140–1.

5 For Scott's debt to the Scottish Enlightenment historians: Duncan Forbes, 'The Rationalism of Sir Walter Scott', in *Cambridge Journal* 7 (1953), 20–35. McMaster, *Scott and Society*, pp. 59–68; more thoroughly, P. D. Garside, 'Scott and the "Philosophical" Historians', in *The Journal of the History of Ideas* 36 (1975), 497–512; P. H. Scott, *Walter Scott and Scotland*, pp. 58–68, and 'The Politics of Sir Walter Scott'. Kathryn Sutherland, 'Fictional Economies: Adam Smith, Walter Scott, and the Nineteenth-Century Novel', *ELH* 54:1 (1987), 97–127. Scott attended the lectures of Dugald Stewart, a student of Smith, at Edinburgh University.

6 Thus Marilyn Butler's critique, *Jane Austen and the War of Ideas* (Oxford: Clarendon Press, 1975), pp. 29–87 – a confirmation of Scott's own views of (e.g.) Godwin and Bage: *Sir Walter Scott on Novelists and Fiction*, ed. Ioan Williams (New York: Barnes & Noble, 1968), pp. 138–45, 193–203. For a full account of the genre, Gary Kelly, *The English Jacobin Novel 1780–1805* (Oxford: Oxford University Press, 1976).

7 On Scott as antiquarian scholar: Arthur Johnston, *Enchanted Ground: The Study of Medieval Romance in the Eighteenth Century*

(London: Oxford University Press, 1964), pp. 171–94. Jane Millgate describes Scott's progress from antiquarian editor to romancer, *Walter Scott: The Making of the Novelist* (Toronto: University of Toronto Press, 1984), pp. 3–35. On Scott as verse romancer: Stuart Curran, *Poetic Form and British Romanticism* (New York: Oxford University Press, 1986), pp. 135–40. Nancy M. Goslee, *Scott the Rhymer* (Lexington: University of Kentucky Press, 1988). On Scott's knowledge of, and debt to, medieval literature: Jerome Mitchell, *Scott, Chaucer and Medieval Romance* (Lexington: University of Kentucky Press, 1987). Cf. Scott's own 'Essay on Romance' written for the 1822 Supplement to the *Encyclopaedia Britannica*.

8 Hogg, *Memoirs of the Author's Life*, p. 62.

9 William Hazlitt, 'Sir Walter Scott', in *The Spirit of the Age* (London: Dent, 1967), pp. 223–34. Gary Kelly succinctly describes Scott's achievement: 'the new literary institution of the novel as the main element of a new kind of national culture based on print', *English Fiction of the Romantic Period*, p. 140.

10 Scott, 'Memoir of His Early Years Written by Himself', in *Scott on Himself: A Selection of the Autobiographical Writings of Sir Walter Scott*, ed. David Hewitt (Edinburgh: Scottish Academic Press, 1981), pp. 1–13.

11 Millgate, *Walter Scott*, pp. 35–58. Commentary on Scott has followed the author's own thematic concern with tensions between 'romance' and 'reality'. Among modern accounts I am particularly indebted to those that have tried to recover the dialectical strength of the category of romance: Alexander Welsh, *The Hero of the Waverley Novels*, pp. 1–29. F. R. Hart, *Scott's Novels: The Plotting of Historic Survival* (Charlottesville: University Press of Virginia, 1966) and *The Scottish Novel from Smollett to Spark* (Cambridge, Mass.: Harvard University Press, 1978), pp. 19–22. McMaster, *Scott and Society*. Millgate, *Walter Scott*. Judith Wilt, *Secret Leaves: the Novels of Walter Scott* (Chicago: Chicago University Press, 1985). Daniel Cottom, *The Civilized Imagination: A Study of Ann Radcliffe, Jane Austen, and Sir Walter Scott* (Cambridge: Cambridge University Press, 1985), pp. 127–70. Joseph Valente, 'Upon the Braes: History and Hermeneutics in *Waverley*', *Studies in Romanticism* 25 (1986), 251–76. James Kerr, *Fiction Against History: Sir Walter Scott as Story-Teller* (Cambridge: Cambridge University Press, 1989).

12 Critics who defend Scott the historical realist: following Lukács, Robert C. Gordon, *Under Which King? A Study of the Scottish Waverley Novels* (Edinburgh: Oliver & Boyd, 1969). David Brown,

Walter Scott and the Historical Imagination (London: Routledge & Kegan Paul, 1979). Harry E. Shaw, *The Forms of Historical Fiction: Sir Walter Scott and His Successors* (Ithaca: Cornell University Press, 1983). Thomas Carlyle initiated the attack on Scott as a shallow entertainer, reviewing Lockhart's biography for the *London and Westminster Review* in 1838 (reprinted in *Essays: Scottish and Other Miscellanies* (London: Dent, 1967), pp. 54–111). The keenest recent criticism in the Carlyle mode is George Levine, *The Realistic Imagination* (Chicago: University of Chicago Press, 1981), pp. 81–130.

13 Sir Walter Scott, *Waverley; or, 'Tis Sixty Years Since*, ed. Claire Lamont (Oxford: Oxford University Press, 1986), p. 18. Future references to this edition will be given in the text.

14 For the contemporary view of the novel as constituted by a feminine circuit of writing and reading, see Ina Ferris, 'Re-positioning the Novel: *Waverley* and the Gender of Fiction', *Studies in Romanticism* 28 (Summer 1989). Ferris shows that the reviews of *Waverley* acknowledged its redefinition of the genre as masculine, public and 'literary'. For the female quixote, see prologue, above.

15 A contemporary notice of Tom Jones's problematical exemplarity is Mrs Barbauld's, in her *British Novelists* edition preface (1810; vol. XVI, viii). An effective recent statement is Damrosch, *God's Plot and Man's Stories; Studies in the Fictional Imagination from Milton to Fielding* (Chicago: Chicago University Press, 1985), pp. 263–303. Scott's criticism of *Grandison* (from his *Ballantyne's Novels* preface) is reprinted in *Sir Walter Scott on Novelists and Fiction*, pp. 32–4. Paulson, *Satire and the Novel in Eighteenth-Century England* (New Haven: Yale University Press, 1967), describes the villainous declension of the satirical-picaresque protagonist, pp. 110–14.

16 Donald Davie, *The Heyday of Sir Walter Scott* (London: Routledge & Kegan Paul, 1961), p. 36.

17 See Scott's anonymous review of the anonymous first series of *Tales of My Landlord* in the *Quarterly Review*, 1817, reprinted in John O. Hayden, ed., *Scott: The Critical Heritage* (New York: Barnes & Noble, 1970), pp. 113–43; J. L. Adolphus, *Letters to Richard Heber, Esq.*, 1822; extracted in *Scott: The Critical Heritage*, pp. 197–214; Welsh, *Hero of the Waverley Novels*, pp. 30–57, 149–74, etc.

18 '*He was a pretty man*'. Evan Dhu's words are echoed, poignantly, in Scott's Canongate tale 'The Two Drovers': once more, applied by a Highlander to an Englishman. But now the murmured sentence of admiration is an epitaph, as Robin Oig (like all non-Sassenach,

dark, slim, passionate and prone to stabbing) gazes at the body of the friend he has killed for honour, the name of an intransigent cultural difference.

19 In some later versions, e.g. *Rob Roy*, the social motive is made more explicit: the hero's romance sensibility measures his revulsion from a middle-class destiny.

20 Cf. Harold Bloom, 'The Internalization of Quest Romance', in *The Ringers in the Tower* (Chicago: Chicago University Press, 1972), pp. 13–36. Jay Macpherson, *The Spirit of Solitude: Conventions and Continuities in Late Romance* (New Haven: Yale University Press, 1982), pp. 75–96.

21 Daiches, 'Scott's Achievement'. Hart, *Scott's Novels*. Gordon, *Under Which King?*. Robert Kiely, *The Romantic Novel in England* (Cambridge, Mass.: Harvard University Press, 1972). Shaw, *Forms of Historical Fiction*. Millgate, *Walter Scott*. Moretti: *Bildungsroman* narrates the teleology of a 'new' domain of bourgeois everyday life, *The Way of the World*, pp. 15–74.

22 Welsh, *Hero of the Waverley Novels*, pp. 114–26.

23 *Ibid.*, pp. 120–5.

24 Harriet Martineau saw Scott as a strong, albeit unconscious, advocate for 'the rights of woman' in an 1833 article in *Tait's Edinburgh Magazine* (reprinted in *Scott: The Critical Heritage*, pp. 340–2). In the context of 'demonization', Nina Auerbach describes two Victorian idealizations of Scott heroines, T. E. Kebbel's 'Diana Vernon' and J. E. Millais's 'Effie Deans': *Woman and the Demon: The Life of a Victorian Myth* (Cambridge Mass.: Harvard University Press, 1982), pp. 190–8.

25 Welsh, *Hero of the Waverley Novels*, pp. 70–82. Frye, *The Secular Scripture: A Study of the Structures of Romance* (Cambridge, Mass.: Harvard University Press, 1976), pp. 83–5.

26 Scott, letter to J. B. S. Morritt, 1816; cited in Edgar Johnson, *Sir Walter Scott: The Great Unknown*, 2 vols. (New York: Macmillan, 1970), I. 522.

27 Such scenes of healing dominate the medieval romances, *Ivanhoe, The Betrothed* and *The Talisman*. They evoke the author's own autobiographical myth of a loss and recovery of self. Scott's childhood convalescence from the polio that lamed him for life (disabling him from the military career he claimed to covet) took place in a maternal and female idyll of romance reading: source of that energy of imagination by which, and no martial or political exertion, he would gain estate and rank. See Johnson, *Great Unknown*, I. 8–17.

28 The account of the novel most alert to the play of romance

allusion is Millgate's, although 'romance' tends to remain a monolithic category: *Walter Scott*, pp. 38–57.

29 Burke, *Reflections on the Revolution in France* (Harmondsworth: Penguin, 1968), p. 159.

30 Both Millgate (*Walter Scott*, p. 52) and Kerr (*Fiction Against History*, pp. 33–4) read this passage in terms of a perspectival shift in which the romantic picturesque dissolves into historical realism.

31 Wilt reads Donald, motivated by 'pure playful self-expression', as Scott's metanarrative figure of romance plotting: *Secret Leaves*, pp. 31–3.

32 Cf. David Quint, 'The Boat of Romance and Renaissance Epic', in *Romance: Generic Transformations from Chretien de Troyes to Cervantes*, ed. K. and M. S. Brownlee (Hanover: University Press of New England, 1985), pp. 178–202.

33 See Parker, *Inescapable Romance: Studies in the Poetics of a Mode* (Princeton: Princeton University Press, 1979), pp. 16–39. For Scott's own descriptions of his youthful reading: Hewitt, ed., *Scott on Himself*, pp. 26–33, 246; he relates his 'audacity' in writing a student essay preferring Ariosto to Homer, p. 31.

34 For this version of Spenser, see Parker, *Inescapable Romance*, pp. 54–113; James Nohrnberg, *Analogy of 'The Faerie Queene'* (Princeton: Princeton University Press, 1976).

35 For Flora's context in contemporary poetics: Macpherson, *Spirit of Solitude*, describes Flora in terms of an 'elegiac romance' typology of deserted scenes whose geniuses reflect only the melancholy isolation of the onlooker, 107–8. Geoffrey Hartman, 'Romantic Poetry and the Genius Loci', in *Beyond Formalism: Literary Essays 1958–1970* (New Haven: Yale University Press, 1970), pp. 311–36, describes the project of 'a native poetry which would express the special destiny of the nation', grounded on a natural site and 'intrinsically related to vision and prophecy'. The most acute discussion of Flora as figure for the 'interdependence of romance and history' is by Valente: 'Upon the Braes', 252–8.

36 Shaw, *Forms of Historical Fiction*, identifies this 'symbolic ordeal' as the centre of 'Romance' in the book, pp. 180–1.

37 Millgate gives the fullest account of Waverley as 'picturesque tourist', an identity he must overcome by ethical and historical engagement: *Walter Scott*, pp. 41–52. P. D. Garside, '*Waverley's* Pictures of the Past', *ELH* 44 (1977), 659–82, describes a characteristic rhetorical pattern of an approach to a scene of romance followed by its deflation. Garside's is a subtle and precise account

of Scott's treatment of the picturesque, in the context of the novel's concern with representational mediation.

38 A glance at the *Cambridge Bibliography of English Literature*, ed. F. W. Bateson (Cambridge: Cambridge University Press, 1966), II, 156–7, shows a handful of tours grouped around the period of the 1707 Act of Union, notably Martin Martin (1698) and Daniel Defoe (1726); then nothing until a sprinkle of journals written by followers of the Duke of Cumberland's 1746 expedition, inaugurating the full spate of tours and surveys. The most thorough was Thomas Pennant's (1769, pub. 1772); the most famous Samuel Johnson's (1773, pub. 1775). The Sandby brothers, who also accompanied Cumberland's army, began the vogue for painting the Highlands. Already in 1759 Lord Breadalbane noted the fashion for Highland travel, and by 1773 he was complaining of the number of visitors (cited in Peter Levi's 'Introduction', Johnson and Boswell, *A Journey to the Western Islands of Scotland and The Journal of a Tour to the Hebrides* (Harmondsworth: Penguin, 1984), p. 12.

39 For the 'National Tale' I am indebted to the work of Katie Trumpener, who contrasts the regenerative journey to an Irish periphery, its culture remaining intact, in the novels of Owenson (*The Wild Irish Girl*) and Edgeworth (*The Absentee*), with the destruction of the archaic regional culture by the forces of modernization represented in the historical romance of Scott: 'Domestic Histories, Nationalist Plots: Scott's *Waverley* and the National Tale', MLA Convention, Chicago 1990. For cultural definitions of the Highlands and the ideology of the tour in the sixty years between Culloden and Scott: Peter Womack, *Improvement and Romance: Constructing the Myth of the Highlands* (London: Macmillan, 1989), pp. 22–5, 40–2, 61–86, 149–58.

40 The figure is Adam Smith's, from *The Theory of Moral Sentiments* (1759), where it signifies the regulation of conduct by sympathy. David Marshall, 'Adam Smith and the Theatricality of Moral Sentiments', unfolds the ambiguities and perplexities of the figure in terms very pertinent to Scott's representation of Waverley's subjectivity, *Critical Inquiry* 10 (June 1984), 592–613.

41 Although we are expected to remember the grisly particulars of English treason penalties (abolished only in the year of the novel's publication), Scott is still more explicit elsewhere about the traumatic violence of the spectacle, the painfulness of the knowledge gained. How often must a Scott hero or heroine be the helpless, immobile spectator of torture, murder, execution and

genocide: cf. Morton's attendance, marking the termination of his rebel career, at the butchery and inquisition of his comrades in arms (*Old Mortality*, chs. 35 and 36); Osbaldistone's presence at Helen MacGregor's summary vengeance (*Rob Roy*, ch. 31). The spectacle tends to get nastier in the later Scott: onlookers are sprayed with blood when the villain is trampled by an elephant in *The Surgeon's Daughter*; the pacifistic protagonist of that romance of ghastly mutilations, *The Fair Maid of Perth*, is forced twice to witness the terrific destruction of weak sons (Conachar, Rothsay) by the partriarchal forces (respectively, martial and political) they have neglected, in a savage age of military honour. She herself, the romantic object of these sons, is claimed by the obediently violent survivor. The climactic event of the novel is a genocide of rival clans, set up as spectacle by the 'civilized' power for its own political end (ch. 34). Scott's choice anecdote of tourism-in-history, recounted in the author's introduction to the *Magnum Opus* edition of *Rob Roy*, tells of a party of Glasgow students who went to watch a clan battle and got massacred in the general exuberance (London: Dent, 1906), p. 389.

42 On 'The Romance of Romance', the transvaluation of the idyll, and Callidore's vision at Acidale as an emblem of aesthetic reflection, in Spenser's Book VI: Parker, *Inescapable Romance*, pp. 101–13. Nohrnberg, *Analogy of 'The Faerie Queene'*, pp. 659–64.

43 Cf. Valente's account of Scott's representation of 'inherently unstable' geographical, historical and generic borders which are ultimately political and epistemological: 'Upon the Braes', 258–64.

44 Thus, Scott's Abbotsford was no original ancestral home: its fabric exhibits the act of restoration as its gesture of foundation. It was indeed a museum, though not in the sense of the public institutions of the nineteenth century – the word is in fact another trope for romance revival, as in the Burns and Johnson song collection, *The Scots Musical Museum* (1787–96). Scott's relics were all charged with personal meaning and feeling; they were fragments of a mythology he himself had composed, that is, collected and confected, carefully disclaiming original invention.

In a darkly personal sense, 'Sixty Years' Since' signified also for the Author of Waverley a threshold between life and death. Critics have liked to account for the superiority of the pre-*Ivanhoe* 'Scottish novels' in Scott's own terms of the limit of a live oral tradition, defined by his mother's memory. (She had spoken with someone who remembered Cromwell's entry into Edinburgh, in

1650: Johnson, *Great Unknown*, I. 31. Millgate notes the coincidence of her death with Scott's turn toward medieval matter, in *Ivanhoe: Walter Scott*, pp. 130–1.) It is striking that the first of those Scottish novels, exemplary and generic in terms of the series, should have identified the life-span Scott himself believed to be allotted to the males of his family. In his journal in 1825 he made the calculations: 'Square the odds and goodnight Sir Walter about sixty', *The Journal of Sir Walter Scott*, ed. W. E. K. Anderson (Oxford: Clarendon Press, 1972), p. 29. As it turned out he died at sixty-one.

45 Millgate, *Walter Scott*: 'although in youth the power of imagination may find its outlet in dream, narcissistic fantasy, and escapism, in the mature individual it can express itself in different ways, can be indeed the very means of achieving that release from the prison of the self into full sympathy with other men which is the mark of maturity' (pp. 55–7). But Marshall, 'Adam Smith and the Theatricality of Moral Sentiment', has traced the ways in which sympathy is a figure confirming an ontological alienation from others and from the self.

46 My sense of this topic, particularly with regard to *The Antiquary*, is indebted to David Kaufmann, 'Political Economics and Regionalism: Scott, Ricardo, Burke', MLA Convention, Chicago 1990.

47 Davie, *Heyday of Sir Walter Scott*, pp. 32–3.

48 Boswell, *Life of Johnson*, ed. G. B. Hill and L. F. Powell (Oxford: Clarendon Press, 1950), V. 187–205.

49 Wilt, *Secret Leaves*, pp. 6–17. The topos of Charles Edward's escape, in which flight signifies native identity, proliferates throughout Scott, and beyond. The 'flight across the heather' is the favourite matter of Scott's Scottish romance successors such as Stevenson, Munro and Buchan (*Kidnapped, John Splendid, The Thirty-Nine Steps*, etc.).

50 Its most elaborate versions are perhaps to be found in the novels of John Cowper Powys, cf. *A Glastonbury Romance* (1933), *Owen Glendower* (1940), *Porius* (1948): Powys calls it 'the mythology of escape'. This figure of romance revival also turns up in Kipling, Woolf, Forster, Lawrence and the Eliot of *Four Quartets*, not to mention a host of modern medievalist and Arthurian fantasies.

51 A view most scornfully expressed ('a kind of inspired folk-lorist') by F. R. Leavis, in *The Great Tradition* (New York: New York University Press, 1969), p. 5 n. 2.

52 Cf. Jameson, *The Political Unconscious: Narrative as a Socially Symbolic Act* (Ithaca: Cornell University Press, 1981), p. 102.

3 THE SUSPENSION OF BELIEF

1 Thomas Carlyle, 'Sir Walter Scott', *Essays: Scottish and Other Miscellanies* (London: Dent, 1967), p. 65. Future references to this edition will be given in the text.

2 Scott, *The Journal of Sir Walter Scott*, ed. W. E. K. Anderson (Oxford: Clarendon Press, 1972), 18 December 1827, p. 399.

3 Robert C. Gordon, *Under Which King? A Study of the Scottish Waverley Novels* (Edinburgh: Oliver & Boyd, 1969), p. 213.

4 Scott thus describes himself at the crisis of his fortunes: *Journal*, 18 December 1825, p. 40. For Hazlitt, *The Spirit of the Age* (London: Dent, 1967), pp. 224, 231–4.

5 Scott, *Journal*, 18 July 1827, p. 333.

6 James Kerr, *Fiction Against History: Sir Walter Scott as Story-Teller* (Cambridge: Cambridge University Press, 1989), reads the Waverley novels as a sustained play between contradictory impulses of history and romance. Emphasizing problems of epistemology, Kerr argues that the Waverley novels are divided by an ideological contradiction which is only resolved aesthetically when – in the later Scottish novel *Redgauntlet* – Scott raises it into consciousness as his primary topic.

7 Scott himself called the novel 'a tale of private life' (Edgar Johnson, *Sir Walter Scott: The Great Unknown*, 2 vols. (New York: Macmillan 1970), I. 466). The description is amplified in Jane Millgate's full and sensitive reading of *Guy Mannering*, to which my own is indebted: *Walter Scott: The Making of the Novelist* (Toronto: University of Toronto Press, 1984), pp. 59–84. Otherwise, although among the most popular of the Waverley novels in the nineteenth century, it has met with neglect and incomprehension from modern readers. Perhaps the most dismaying casualty of the decline of Scott's reputation and of the cultural loss of terms with which to read him, it has not even enjoyed the notoriety of the 'tushery' romances.

8 Scott, *Guy Mannering; or, The Astrologer* (London: Dent, 1906), p. 245. Future references to this edition will be given in the text.

9 Tobias Smollett, *The Expedition of Humphry Clinker*, ed. James L. Thorson (New York: Norton, 1983), pp. 206–12. T. C. Smout describes the topographical and social transformation of Edinburgh: plans for the New Town were approved in 1767, and by 1783 the migration of the gentry began to be noticeable, although not completed until around 1815 (*A History of the Scottish People 1560–1830* (New York: Scribner's, 1969), pp. 366–72).

10 For example: James Reed, *Sir Walter Scott: Landscape and Locality* (London: Athlone Press, 1980), pp. 69–88.

11 An embarrassment for modern critics. Daiches describes it as a pretext for characterizations ('Scott's Achievement as a Novelist', repr. in *Modern Judgements: Walter Scott*, ed. D. D. Devlin (London: Macmillan, 1969), p. 48), Hart as a mechanical distraction (*Scott's Novels: The Plotting of Historic Survival* (Charlottesville: University Press of Virginia, 1966), p. 265).

12 Cf. Nichol Smith, *Shakespeare in the Eighteenth Century* (Oxford: Oxford University Press, 1928). Millgate's fine discussion of Scott's 'analogical' plot structure, characterized by narrative figures of doubling, appeals to Renaissance romance and Shakespeare in particular. The chapter usefully explicates some of the particular figures and conventions Scott uses (*Walter Scott*, pp. 67–8, 77–8).

13 See (in particular) Northrop Frye, *Anatomy of Criticism: Four Essays* (Princeton: Princeton University Press, 1957), pp. 182–4; *A Natural Perspective: The Development of Shakespearean Comedy and Romance* (New York: Harvest Books, 1965), pp. 118–59.

14 Martin Green, *Dreams of Adventure, Deeds of Empire* (New York: Basic Books, 1979), usefully locates Scott in the prehistory of British Empire romance as its father (the grandfather is Defoe). He reminds us that Edinburgh was a major centre of East India Company patronage, through Dundas (Lord Melville) and others, pp. 21–3.

15 Millgate has a fine discussion of the 'artifice' associated with the Westmoreland sojourn, in contrast to the natural scenery of Scotland (*Walter Scott*, pp. 70–1). As she points out, the only literary presence allowed across the border is Bertram's pocket Shakespeare – we have seen why.

16 On the oriental origins of romance: John Dunlop, *The History of Fiction* (Philadelphia: Carey & Hart, 1842), p. 34. Scott's most elaborate – scholarly – version of the myth of the fall of a daimonic universe, in the late *Letters on Demonology and Witchcraft* (1830), will be discussed below. The anticipation here of later imperial romance themes of 'darkness' is striking. Cf. Patrick Brantlinger's informative *Rule of Darkness: British Literature and Imperialism 1830–1914* (Ithaca: Cornell University Press, 1988). 'Area of darkness' is V. S. Naipaul's phrase.

17 I am indebted for this point to discussions with Katie Trumpener, who is researching literary representations of gypsies, and with Peter Garside, whose work on the forthcoming Edinburgh edition

of *Guy Mannering* has documented in detail the novel's oriental motifs and their contemporary currency.

18 For a detailed theoretical exploration of this (basically Gothic) gender-mythology, and a description of some nineteenth-century versions: Margaret Homans, *Bearing the Word: Language and Female Experience in Nineteenth-Century Women's Writing* (Chicago: University of Chicago Press, 1986), pp. 1–39, 68–119. Judith Wilt notes in Scott 'the victory of two linked "modern" principles, male rationality and textualized language, over their progenitors, female enchantment or mystery and performative speech': *Secret Leaves: The Novels of Walter Scott* (Chicago: Chicago University Press, 1985), p. 17.

19 In Scott, *Complete Prose Works* (New York: Connor & Cooke, 1835), I. 67–9.

20 The phrase is James Nohrnberg's, *Analogy of 'The Faerie Queene'* (Princeton: Princeton University Press, 1976), p. 743. Scott himself unfolds the topos (quoting Milton's 'Nativity Ode') as a historical allegory, in the *Letters on Demonology*, pp. 12–19.

21 Cf. Dinmont, 'they say that whether her spaeings and fortune-tellings be true or no, for certain she believes in them a' hersell, and is aye guiding hersell by some queer prophecy or anither', 323. The most striking of such figures in Scott is Norna of Fitful Head, in *The Pirate*.

22 Frye, *Anatomy of Criticism*, p. 202.

23 For example by Hart, *Scott's Novels*, pp. 330–3; Harry E. Shaw, *The Forms of Historical Fiction: Sir Walter Scott and His Successors* (Ithaca: Cornell University Press, 1983), pp. 224–37.

24 Hart, *Scott's Novels*, p. 332.

25 Scott, *Letters on Demonology and Witchcraft*, pp. 12–78. In the *Magnum Opus* Introduction to *The Monastery*, Scott defended the idea of the White Lady of Avenel on the grounds that such spirits were realities within the mentality of a historical culture. A provocative discussion of the paradoxes of superstition in Scott is by Daniel Cottom, *The Civilized Imagination: A Study of Ann Radcliffe, Jane Austen, and Sir Walter Scott* (Cambridge: Cambridge University Press, 1985), pp. 148–70, who argues that it represents the persistence of 'aristocratic ideology'.

26 Millgate shows that this date was Scott's original intention, carried in the manuscript and in early editions, and summarizes the 'extensive critical debate' on the subject. In *Magnum Opus* Scott changed the date, for technical reasons, to a post-Union one, thereby increasing the sense of an abstract fatality (*Walter Scott*, pp. 171–6 and notes).

27 Scott, *The Bride of Lammermoor* (London: Dent, 1906), pp. 43–5. Future references to this edition will be given in the text.

28 Cf. John P. Farrell, *Revolution as Tragedy: The Dilemma of the Moderate from Scott to Arnold* (Ithaca: Cornell University Press, 1980), pp. 119–20: Caleb can only offer a 'parodic distortion of communal allegiance'.

29 Scott's introductory essay on Radcliffe, in the *Ballantyne Novels* edition, criticized her for rationalizing her supernatural machinery (reprinted in *Sir Walter Scott on Novelists and Fiction*, ed. Ioan Williams (New York: Barnes & Noble, 1968), pp. 115–18).

30 The principal romance analogue is no doubt Redcrosse's lethal dalliance with Duessa, midway in *Faerie Queene* Book I. Hawthorne imitates Scott's version in *The Marble Faun*, another novel which plays with ambiguous natural, sexual and demonic crossings.

31 Michael Millgate, *Thomas Hardy: His Career as a Novelist* (New York: Random House, 1971), p. 322.

32 Thomas Hardy, *The Mayor of Casterbridge* (New York: Norton, 1977), p. 254.

33 Scott, *Letters on Demonology and Witchcraft*, p. 78.

34 Sir Walter Scott, *The Heart of Midlothian* (Oxford: Oxford University Press, 1982), p. 74. Future references to this edition will be given in the text.

35 Charles Dickens, *Our Mutual Friend* (Harmondsworth: Penguin, 1971). 'Postscript in Lieu of a Preface', p. 893.

36 For complaints of unevenness, see the anonymous critic of the *British Review* (November 1818) who scorned 'the trash with which he has composed the latter part of his work' (John O. Hayden, ed., *Scott: The Critical Heritage* (New York: Barnes & Noble, 1970), p. 169), and (severest of the moderns) Dorothy Van Ghent, *The English Novel: Form and Function* (New York: Holt, Rinehart, 1961), pp. 114–15. More sympathetic critics have pronounced the ending misjudged: F. R. Hart, *Scott's Novels*, pp. 127–8; Robert C. Gordon, *Under Which King?*, pp. 95–7; Jane Millgate, who acknowledges the strategy, *Walter Scott*, pp. 162–7. Of the defences, the most persuasive have been Thomas Crawford, who argues schematic and generic as well as historical aptness: *Sir Walter Scott* (Edinburgh: Scottish Academic Press, 1982), pp. 96–7; Douglas Gifford, 'Myth, Parody, and Dissociation: Scottish Fiction 1814–1914', in Douglas Gifford, ed., *The History of Scottish Literature: Volume 3, Nineteenth Century* (Aberdeen: Aberdeen University Press, 1988), pp. 220–3; and James Kerr, *Fiction Against History*, pp. 62–84.

37 Crawford, *Sir Walter Scott*, p. 92.

38 Alastair Fowler, *Kinds of Literature: An Introduction to the Theory of Genres and Modes* (Cambridge, Mass.: Harvard University Press, 1982), pp. 186–8 and notes.

39 Millgate, *Walter Scott*, pp. 153–4. Wilt, *Secret Leaves*, p. 134.

40 Charlotte Smith, *The Old Manor-House* (1793); Robert Bage, *Hermsprong, or, Man As He Is Not* (1796).

41 Critics have argued about the exact identity of the transgression at issue in Scott's plot. Those who have taken for granted a theme of sexual conduct have been dissatisfied, because of a lack of rhetorical interest in erotic life, in the psychology of temptation and remorse, etc. Effie Deans is not Hetty Sorrel, or Hester Prynne or Tess Durbeyfield. F. R. Hart (*Scott's Novels*, pp. 133–5) and P. F. Fisher ('Providence, Fate, and the Historical Imagination in Scott's *The Heart of Midlothian*', in D. D. Devlin ed., *Modern Judgements: Walter Scott*, pp. 98–111) describe, more plausibly, a 'capricious' and 'fatalistic' characterization, bound to a (Calvinistic) unregenerate nature. Wilt, close to my reading but a bit more fanciful, interprets the threat to, and reassertion of, 'the new natural law' of a female imperative to protect male life: *Secret Leaves*, p. 126.

42 Alexander Welsh, *The Hero of the Waverley Novels* (New Haven: Yale University Press, 1963), pp. 138–41.

43 Wilt, *Secret Leaves*, pp. 123–5, 136.

44 The most precise account of the 'political fable' represented here is Kerr's, *Fiction Against History*, pp. 62–84. Kerr insists, as I do (below), on the rhetorical fictionality of Scott's last act.

45 On eighteenth-century improvement and the Campbell estates: Crawford, *Sir Walter Scott*, p. 96; Smout, *History of the Scottish People*, p. 357. Both cite E. R. Cregeen, ed., *Argyll Estate Instructions* (Edinburgh: Scottish History Society, 1964), although it documents a period later than Scott's novel (1771–1805). Smout describes the new crisis of the Highlands economy from 1815, pp. 350–9. Eric Richards, *A History of the Highland Clearances: Agrarian Transformation and the Evictions 1746–1886* (London: Croom Helm, 1982), points out that despite the progressive intentions of the Campbells, after 1806 it was clear that their experiment had failed, pp. 124–5. In Scott's generation the attempt by the Marquess of Stafford, an English millionaire, to develop his wife's vast Sutherland estates was seen as 'strictly comparable with that of the Duke of Argyll in the previous century', p. 213. The Sutherland clearances, which took place between 1811 and 1821, were notoriously violent, pp. 284–362. Scott's official attitude was melioristic, as in the *Tales of a Grandfather* (Edinburgh: Charles

Black, 1898), pp. 1190–1: 'an inevitable evil'. He defends Stafford; the Marchioness was a family friend.

46 Raymond Williams, *The Country and the City* (Oxford: Oxford University Press, 1973), pp. 17–18. St Thomas More, *Utopia*, ed. Edward Surtz, SJ, (New Haven: Yale University Press, 1964), pp. 24–7.

47 Peter Womack, *Improvement and Romance: Constructing the Myth of the Highlands* (London: Macmillan, 1989), pp. 115–31. John Gray, *Reflections Intended to Promote the Success of the Scotch Fishing Company* (London, 1788), called extravagantly for the construction of a city the size of Liverpool in the West Highlands (cited in Smout, *History of the Scottish People*, p. 360 and n. 38). More georgic, and literary: Smollett, *Humphry Clinker*, p. 237; Johnson, *A Journey to the Western Islands of Scotland*, ed. J. D. Fleeman (Oxford: Clarendon Press, 1985).

48 Johnson, *Journey*, pp. 54, 229. Smollett, *Humphry Clinker*, pp. 230–2.

49 Lockhart's account remains the best: *Memoirs of the Life of Sir Walter Scott*, 7 vols. (Boston: Otis, Broaders & Co., 1837), v. 147–63.

50 Scott, *Journal*, 18 October 1831, p. 326.

51 The boast of 'the Eidolon, or representative Vision of the AUTHOR OF WAVERLEY', interviewed by one of his creatures in the Introductory Epistle to *The Fortunes of Nigel* (London: Dent, 1906), p. xxviii.

4 SCOTT AND DICKENS: THE WORK OF THE AUTHOR

1 *The Letters of Charles Dickens*, ed. M. House, G. Storey, *et al.*, 6 vols. (Oxford: Clarendon Press, 1965–) IV. 66 and n., 77; V. 216.

2 James Hillhouse, *The Waverley Novels and their Critics* (Minneapolis: University of Minnesota Press, 1936), pp. 162, 166. Wilt, *Secret Leaves: The Novels of Walter Scott* (Chicago: Chicago University Press, 1985), pp. 1–2.

3 Richard Altick, *The English Common Reader: A Social History of the Mass Reading Public 1800–1900* (Chicago: University of Chicago Press, 1957), pp. 262–3. Jane Millgate, *Scott's Last Edition: A Study in Publishing History* (Edinburgh: Edinburgh University Press, 1987), pp. 89–90.

4 Altick, *The English Common Reader*, pp. 267–9. Millgate, *Scott's Last Edition*, pp. 90–107.

5 Millgate, *Scott's Last Edition*, pp. 109–17. The principle of the cheaper reprint series was already established by the editions brought out a few years later than the first publication ('Novels and Tales of the Author of Waverley', 1819, etc.).

6 Thomas Carlyle, *On Heroes, Hero-Worship, and the Heroic in History* (London: Dent, 1964), p. 239.

7 Carlyle reviewed Lockhart in the *London and Westminster Review* in January 1838 (see above, chapter 3), and gave the lecture 'The Hero as a Man of Letters' in May 1840. The period is also marked by the republication of Boswell's great biography in the elaborate scholarly edition of Scott's friend Croker, provoking famous reassessments from Macaulay, Carlyle and others. By the late 1830s 'Literary Lionism' was sufficiently in vogue for Harriet Martineau to write an article on the topic (1837; incorporated into her *Autobiography* (London, 1857), I. 289–92), and for Dickens to include Mrs Leo Hunter in the sixth number of *Pickwick Papers* (September 1836). The most acute recent discussion of the ascendancy of the 'man-of-letters hero' in the 1840s is by Mary Poovey, *Uneven Developments: The Ideological Work of Gender in Mid-Victorian England* (Chicago: University of Chicago Press, 1988), pp. 101–16.

8 On 'character' as a Victorian demonic figuration: Nina Auerbach, *Woman and the Demon: The Life of a Victorian Myth* (Cambridge, Mass.: Harvard University Press, 1982), pp. 185–205.

9 On Boswell, Johnson and the invention of the writer as hero in a print culture: Alvin Kernan, *Printing Technology, Letters, and Samuel Johnson* (Princeton: Princeton University Press, 1987), pp. 91–153.

10 F. R. Hart, *Lockhart as Romantic Biographer* (Edinburgh: Edinburgh University Press, 1971), pp. 236–52. For Lockhart's relation to Boswell and to intervening biographers, pp. 1–45; Ian Jack, 'Two Biographers: Lockhart and Boswell', in *Johnson, Boswell and Their Circle: Essays presented to Lawrence Fitzroy Powell in Honour of his Eighty-Fourth Birthday* (Oxford: Clarendon Press, 1965), pp. 268–85.

11 Lockhart, *Memoirs of the Life of Sir Walter Scott*, 7 vols. (Boston: Otis, Broaders & Co., 1837), VII. 294, 292.

12 Scott, 'General Preface to the Edition of 1829' (reprinted in David Hewitt ed., *Scott on Himself: A Selection of the Autobiographical Writings of Sir Walter Scott* (Edinburgh: Scottish Academic Press, 1981), p. 251). It is quite likely, however, that we owe the completion of *Waverley* to the serious financial shudder of 1813 (which drove Scott and the Ballantynes back to Constable).

Edgar Johnson, *Sir Walter Scott: The Great Unknown*, 2 vols. (New York: Macmillan, 1970), I. 412–28, 432–6. For Lockhart and Scott's death: Hart, *Lockhart as Romantic Biographer*, pp. 237–8.

13 Lockhart, *Life of Scott*, III. 109.

14 Hart, *Lockhart as Romantic Biographer*, p. 237. The power of the anecdote is evident in its citation in two recent popular studies: A. N. Wilson, *The Laird of Abbotsford: A View of Sir Walter Scott* (Oxford: Oxford University Press, 1980), p. 67; Mark Girouard, *The Return to Camelot: Chivalry and the English Gentleman* (New Haven: Yale University Press, 1981), p. 30. In 1896 Margaret Oliphant made it the basis for her great tale of female quixotism, writing and the uncanny, 'The Library Window'.

15 Jane Millgate, *Walter Scott: The Making of the Novelist* (Toronto: University of Toronto Press, 1984), pp. 59–67; Wilt, *Secret Leaves*, pp. 185–203.

16 Lockhart, *Life of Scott*, VII. 304–6. Scott, *The Journal of Sir Walter Scott*, ed. W. E. K. Anderson (Oxford: Clarendon Press, 1972), p. 40.

17 Scott, *Journal*, p. 404.

18 Cf. Lockhart, *Life of Scott*, VII. 307–8, and Wilt, *Secret Leaves*, p. 2.

19 Edward Bulwer-Lytton, *England and the English* (1833), ed. Standish Meacham (Chicago: University of Chicago Press, 1970), p. 298. Bulwer-Lytton criticized Scott, in terms analogous to Carlyle's, for being insufficiently serious about his vocation: E. Eigner and G. Worth, eds., *Victorian Criticism of the Novel*, (Cambridge: Cambridge University Press, 1985), p. 23.

20 Kathryn Chittick, *Dickens and the 1830s* (Cambridge: Cambridge University Press, 1990), pp. 18, 62–6, 77.

21 Edgar Johnson, *Charles Dickens: His Tragedy and Triumph*, 2 vols. (New York: Simon & Schuster, 1952), I. 226. Comparisons between Scott and Dickens in terms of popularity, characterization and social tone were a staple of nineteenth-century reviewing: cf. the index entries, Hillhouse, *Waverley Novels and Their Critics*, and Philip Collins, ed., *Dickens: The Critical Heritage* (New York: Barnes & Noble, 1971).

22 *Letters*, I. 54 n. 2. Johnson, *Charles Dickens*, p. 122. Fred Kaplan, *Dickens: A Biography* (New York: William Morrow, 1988), pp. 66–7.

23 To T. C. Barrow, 31 March 1836 (*Letters*, I. 144).

24 William Carlton, 'George Hogarth – A Link with Scott and Dickens', *Dickensian* 59 (1963), 78–89.

25 This pattern of affiliation and succession marked, of course, the typical transmission of power among the professional and com-

mercial classes. The distinction in Hogarth's own family, his identity as gentleman of letters, descended from *his* father-in-law George Thomson, who had collaborated with Burns to produce a genteel edition of Scots songs (with arrangements by eminent contemporary composers.) Meanwhile Dickens had given his actual father the part of 'The Great Unpaid' in private family theatricals, 1834 (Kaplan, *Dickens*, p. 57).

26 The highlight of the evening's entertainment was a comic dialogue between the Dominie Sampson and Wackford Squeers. Johnson, *Charles Dickens*, I. 339–40. Peter Ackroyd, *Dickens* (New York: Harper Collins, 1990), pp. 329–31. Wilson's *Lights and Shadows of Scottish Life*, which Dickens read in the early 1830s, is an important source of Dickens's sentimental manner (*Letters*, I. 9 n. 4).

27 On Dickens's struggles with Bentley and others: Johnson, *Charles Dickens*, I. 235–53, etc. J. A. Sutherland, *Victorian Novelists and Publishers* (Chicago: Chicago University Press, 1976), pp. 21–3, who sums up 'a successful exercise in elbowing aside the booksellers who stood between him and the reader', p. 166. Robert L. Patton, *Dickens and his Publishers* (Oxford: Clarendon Press, 1978), pp. 75–118.

28 'Scott and his Publishers': the first article, dated 2 September, is reprinted (with a note by K. J. Fielding) in *The Dickensian* 46 (1950), 122–7. The other two, dated 31 March and 29 September 1839, are collected in B. W. Matz, ed., *Miscellaneous Papers* (London: Encyclopaedia Britannica, 1908), pp. 75–89. Dickens's defence of Lockhart, thus of Scott, was unusually vehement. He wrote to Forster, 29 August 1838, 'I have thought it better not to make use of anything I know from the Hogarths' ' (*Letters* I. 428).

29 *Letters*, I. 370; II. 365.

30 To the Hon. Mrs Richard Watson, 11 July 1852; *Letters*, VI. 427. Cf. II. 41, III. 591.

31 To Forster, 24 February 1842: *Letters*, III. 82–3. Cf. also K. J. Fielding, ed., *The Speeches of Charles Dickens* (Oxford: Clarendon Press, 1960), p. 25.

32 On copyright and literary property: Patton, *Dickens and his Publishers*, pp. 18–27. N. N. Feltes, *Modes of Production of Victorian Novels* (Chicago: University of Chicago Press, 1986), pp. 2–14. Poovey, *Uneven Developments*, pp. 112–13.

33 Poovey, *Uneven Developments*, pp. 101–16. Feltes, *Modes of Production*, pp. 19–20. Ackroyd, *Dickens*, pp. 589–95, 611–12, 666–7, 629.

34 Chittick, *Dickens and the 1830s*, pp. 137–9. Dickens would finally literalize such immediate vocal presence before an audience in the

public readings that absorbed (and probably abbreviated) his career after 1858.

35 Carlyle, *On Heroes and Hero-Worship*, p. 391.

36 On the relationship between Carlyle and Dickens: Michael Goldberg, *Carlyle and Dickens* (Athens: University of Georgia Press, 1972); William Oddie, *Dickens and Carlyle: The Question of Influence* (London: Centenary Press, 1972). For a succinct account of the Carlylean prophetic persona and its diffusion in Victorian literary culture, Walter E. Houghton, *The Victorian Frame of Mind 1830–1870* (New Haven: Yale University Press, 1957), pp. 148–54, remains useful.

37 The fullest account of the Dickensian mythology of the hearth, and the opposition between public and private life, is by Alexander Welsh, *The City of Dickens* (Oxford: Clarendon Press, 1971), especially pp. 141–63. See also Northrop Frye, 'Dickens and the Comedy of Humours', in *The Stubborn Structure: Essays in Criticism and Society* (Ithaca: Cornell University Press, 1970), pp. 218–40.

38 Charles Dickens, *Nicholas Nickleby* (Harmondsworth: Penguin, 1978), p. 47.

39 For suggestive accounts of the operations of serial publication: Kathleen Tillotson, *Novels of the Eighteen-Forties* (Oxford: Oxford University Press, 1956), pp. 43–7. D. A. Miller, *The Novel and the Police* (Berkeley: University of California Press, 1988), pp. 81–3, 87–9.

40 Charles Dickens, *The Old Curiosity Shop* (Harmondsworth: Penguin, 1972), p. 41.

41 Poovey, *Uneven Developments*, p. 104.

42 Charles Dickens, *David Copperfield* (Harmondsworth: Penguin, 1966), p. 45. Future references to this edition will be given in the text.

43 *Letters*, III, 39 n.

44 Charles Dickens, *The Uncommercial Traveller and Reprinted Pieces* (Oxford: Oxford University Press, 1958), pp. 61–2. John Forster, *The Life of Charles Dickens*, ed. J. W. T. Ley (London: Cecil Palmer, 1928), pp. 2–3. While personally fond of Boz, Carlyle seems to have regarded the cultural achievements of the two novelists with about equal disdain: Ackroyd, *Dickens*, pp. 302–3.

45 Cf. Welsh, *City of Dickens*, pp. 130–5; Franco Moretti, *The Way of the World: The Bildungsroman in European Culture* (London: Verso, 1987), pp. 186, 199–201.

46 J. Hillis Miller, *Charles Dickens: The World of his Novels* (Cambridge: Harvard University Press, 1958), pp. 154–9. On this kind of plot: Robert Caserio, *Plot, Story and the Novel: From Dickens to Poe*

to the Modern Period (Princeton: Princeton University Press, 1979), pp. 27–56. On 'self-elegy' as an autobiographical mode: Jahan Ramazani, *Yeats and the Poetry of Death* (New Haven: Yale University Press, 1990), pp. 134–60.

47 Cf. George Moir, in 1842: E. Eigner and J. Worth, eds., *Victorian Criticism of the Novel* (Cambridge: Cambridge University Press, 1985), p. 50.

48 Ned Lukacher identifies an allusion to Ezekiel 18:2: 'The fathers have eaten sour grapes, and the children's teeth are set on edge.' *Primal Scenes: Literature, Philosophy, Psychoanalysis* (Ithaca: Cornell University Press, 1986), p. 321. He glosses: 'The disfiguring effect of painful memories is an experience no less catastrophic than hereditary sin would be.'

49 Cf. Alexander Welsh, *From Copyright to Copperfield: The Identity of Charles Dickens* (Cambridge, Mass.: Harvard University Press, 1987), pp. 141–6. Poovey, *Uneven Developments*, pp. 116–20. For theories of character doubling and the narrative construction of desire in the nineteenth-century novel: René Girard, *Deceit, Desire and the Novel: Self and Other in Literary Structure* (Baltimore: Johns Hopkins University Press, 1965), pp. 1–112 etc.; Eve Kosofksy Sedgwick, *Between Men: English Literature and Male Homosocial Desire* (New York: Columbia University Press, 1985), pp. 21–7 etc.

50 Cf. Linda H. Peterson, *Victorian Autobiography: The Tradition of Self-Interpretation* (New Haven: Yale University Press, 1986), pp. 49–50. Dickens's principal model here is Carlyle, in chapter 9 of *Sartor Resartus* ('The Everlasting Yea').

51 Poovey, *Uneven Developments*, pp. 89–125.

52 Hillis Miller, *Charles Dickens*, p. 157; Welsh, *City of Dickens*, pp. 180–5, 194–212.

53 John Carey, *The Violent Effigy: A Study of Dickens's Imagination* (London: Faber, 1973), p. 171.

54 The importance of *Rob Roy* to *David Copperfield* is argued by David Hewitt, ' "Rob Roy" and First Person Narratives', in Hewitt and Alexander, eds., *Scott and His Influence*, (Aberdeen: Association for Scottish Literary Studies, 1983), pp. 372–81.

5 SCOTT AND DICKENS: THE END OF HISTORY

1 Percy Fitzgerald, 'Scott and Dickens', *The Dickensian* 1.1 (1905), 4–6.

2 The price of a new Scott novel, at 10 shillings and sixpence per

volume in 1822, would have come to just 5 shillings less than a month's rent for the Dickens family's house in Bayham Street. Dickens's father did not belong to a circulating library. Dickens himself procured a reader's card at the British Museum and joined a circulating library in 1830. The library at Devonshire Terrace, where Dickens lived after 1839, contained a set of the *Magnum Opus* Waverley novels, 1829–33 (*The Letters of Charles Dickens*, ed. M. House, G. Storey *et al.*, 6 vols. (Oxford: Clarendon Press, 1965–), IV, appendix). References to Scott novels in the late 1830s and early 1840s suggest eager familiarity and rereading: see *Letters*, I. 576, II. 256, III. 446 and n. 2, 550; the prefaces to *Pickwick Papers* and *Oliver Twist*; *American Notes*; and the *Master Humphrey's Clock* framework. Novels specifically mentioned are *Old Mortality*, *Rob Roy*, *The Heart of Mid-Lothian*, *A Legend of Montrose*, *Peveril of the Peak*, *The Fortunes of Nigel* and *Kenilworth*.

3 On fairy-tales: Harry Stone, *Dickens and the Invisible World* (Bloomington: Indiana University Press, 1979). On the reading list: Steven Marcus, *Dickens from Pickwick to Dombey* (New York: Norton, 1965), pp. 20–30. On popular culture: Paul Schlicke, *Dickens and Popular Entertainment* (London: Unwin Hyman, 1985), pp. 8–9, 14–32.

4 On the elements of *Pickwick's* novelty and success: Peter Ackroyd, *Dickens* (New York: Harper Collins, 1990), pp. 195–200. On advertising: Jennifer Wicke, *Advertising Fictions: Literature, Advertisement and Social Reading* (New York: Columbia University Press, 1988), pp. 19–53.

5 For a stern refusal of membership, however, see N. N. Feltes, *Modes of Production of Victorian Novels* (Chicago: University of Chicago Press, 1986), pp. 16–17.

6 Charles Dickens, *The Pickwick Papers* (Harmondsworth: Penguin, 1972), pp. 702–3. On Dickens as 'Dick': Ackroyd, *Dickens*, p. 294. 'The dickens' was the devil, furthermore.

7 On the relation between the main narrative and the interpolated tales: Edmund Wilson, 'Dickens: The Two Scrooges', *The Wound and the Bow* (New York: Houghton Mifflin, 1941), pp. 9–12; Marcus, *Dickens from Pickwick to Dombey*, pp. 41–4.

8 Scott, *Peveril of the Peak*, chapter 30. Cf. the Alsatia episodes in *The Fortunes of Nigel*. W. Harrison Ainsworth, *Rookwood* (London: J. M. Dent, 1931), pp. 3–8. Philip Collins, *Dickens and Crime* (London: Macmillan, 1962), p. 256. Keith Hollingsworth, *The Newgate Novel 1830–1847* (Detroit: Wayne State University Press, 1963), pp. 98–109. Andrew Sanders, *The Victorian Historical Novel, 1840–1880* (London: Macmillan, 1978), pp. 32–46.

9 To Dickens's embarrassment. Kathryn Chittick discusses the relation between the two novels: *Dickens and the 1830s* (Cambridge: Cambridge University Press, 1990), pp. 153–66.

10 Alexander Welsh, *The City of Dickens* (Oxford: Clarendon Press, 1971), pp. 125–6. Philip Collins, *Dickens and Crime*, pp. 196–272. Dickensian violence is described with the requisite prurient relish by John Carey, *The Violent Effigy: A Study of Dickens's Imagination* (London: Faber, 1973), pp. 18–22. Sikes's murder of Nancy might be compared with the murder of Morris by Helen MacGregor's gang at the end of chapter 31 of *Rob Roy*.

11 Dickens, *The Old Curiosity Shop* (Harmondsworth: Penguin, 1972), p. 56.

12 John Ruskin, *Fiction, Fair and Foul* (1880), in Harold Bloom ed., *The Literary Criticism of John Ruskin* (New York: Doubleday, 1965), p. 363. Marcus, *Dickens from Pickwick to Dombey*, pp. 135–42. J. Hillis Miller, *Charles Dickens: The World of His Novels* (Cambridge, Mass.: Harvard University Press, 1958), pp. 94–6.

13 On the production of *Barnaby Rudge*: Kathleen Tillotson, 'Introduction', *Barnaby Rudge* (Oxford: Oxford University Press, 1953), p. iv. Robert L. Patton, *Dickens and his Publishers* (Oxford: Clarendon Press, 1978), pp. 75–118. John Butt and Kathleen Tillotson, *Dickens at Work* (London: Methuen, 1957), pp. 76–89: Dickens's 'first projected novel'. Kathryn Chittick, *Dickens and the 1830s*, pp. 152, 166. Peter Ackroyd, *Dickens*, pp. 185, 296–7, 322–3, 327–8, 334.

14 Butt and Tillotson, *Dickens at Work*, pp. 13–14, 78. Chittick, *Dickens and the 1830s*, pp. 152–3, 165. Elsewhere, Kathleen Tillotson remarks that the authority of the form was declining through the 1840s, i.e. after Dickens actually finished the work: *Novels of the Eighteen-Forties* (Oxford: Oxford University Press, 1956), p. 142.

15 Marcus, *Dickens from Pickwick to Dombey*, pp. 131–2. Ackroyd, *Dickens*, pp. 298–300. Chittick, *Dickens and the 1830s*, pp. 176–7. Alexander Welsh, *From Copyright to Copperfield: The Identity of Charles Dickens* (Cambridge, Mass.: Harvard University Press, 1987), pp. 8–9.

16 The best account of a progression from 'linear succession' through 'simultaneous adjacency' to complex spatial patterning in Dickensian narrative is in Peter K. Garrett, *The Victorian Multiplot Novel: Studies in Dialogical Form* (New Haven: Yale University Press, 1980), pp. 30–1. Cf. H. M. Daleski, *Dickens and the Art of Analogy* (London: Faber, 1970) and Jonathan Arac, *Commissioned Spirits: The Shaping of Social Motion in Dickens, Carlyle, Melville and Hawthorne* (New Brunswick: Rutgers University Press, 1979),

pp. 1–9. Robert L. Caserio connects Dickens's reliance upon complicated, mystery- and peripety-based plots with Scott, although Fielding and Shakespeare are important models for both: *Plot, Story, and the Novel: From Dickens to Poe to the Modern Period* (Princeton: Princeton University Press, 1979), pp. 57–60, 285–6. Caserio's argument, wise as it is, perhaps rests upon an excessively classical (Fieldingesque) sense of Scott, as of plot. Scott returned the model of comic prose epic after Fielding to a non-classical, 'romance' tradition, which he transmitted from the eighteenth-century scholarly and poetic revivals. The national genius of this tradition is Shakespeare. If recent critics, from Leavis to Bloom, have liked to invoke Shakespeare as the measure of Dickens's magnitude, so did Victorian critics in the case of Scott – among them, Dickens himself: 'Foremost and unapproachable in the bright world of fiction, gifted with a vivacity and range of invention scarcely ever equalled, and never (but in the case of Shakespeare) exceeded; endowed, as never fabled enchanter was, with spells to conjure up the past, and to give to days and men of old the spirit and freshness of yesterday . . .' ('Scott and his Publishers', *Dickensian* 46, 127).

17 Marcus, *Dickens from Pickwick to Dombey*, pp. 169–212. Marcus notes Dickens's careful structural 'principle of opposition and analogy', p. 178, articulating a 'correspondence between political and personal motives', p. 172. Myron Magnet, *Dickens and the Social Order* (Philadelphia: University of Pennsylvania Press, 1985), pp. 49–172, elaborates Marcus's account to come to similar conclusions.

18 Charles Dickens, *Barnaby Rudge: A Tale of the Riots of 'Eighty* (Harmondsworth: Penguin, 1973), p. 422. Future references to this edition will be given in the text.

19 Marcus, *Dickens from Pickwick to Dombey*, in fact remarks that 'of all the sons in the novel, [Edward] seems the most depressed, violated, and hopelessly unmanned', p. 196. In short, the paradigmatic Waverley hero.

20 On *Barnaby Rudge* and *King Lear*: Marcus, *Dickens from Pickwick to Dombey*, pp. 204–5; on *Dombey and Son* and *King Lear*: Welsh, *From Copyright to Copperfield*, pp. 87–103.

21 On *The Fair Maid of Perth*, see F. R. Hart, *Scott's Novels: The Plotting of Historic Survival* (Charlottesville: University Press of Virginia, 1966), pp. 235–44.

22 For both Marcus and Magnet, these conclusions are proof of the novel's (proto-Freudian) prophetic strength: describing a 'Hobbesian' vision of the essential aggressiveness of the masculine

will (*Dickens and the Social Order*, pp. 170–2), 'a radical disorder in the individual's relation to authority, which comprehends his most intimate personal relations as well as his relation to society' (*Dickens from Pickwick to Dombey*, p. 210). For opposed views, see the note following.

23 Lukács, *The Historical Novel* (Lincoln: University of Nebraska Press, 1983), pp. 242, 244; Caserio, *Plot, Story, and the Novel*, pp. 60–4: Dickens 'wants to thematize deadlock, even though his story tells of resolution'. And the other way around, perhaps. Cf. also S. J. Newman, '*Barnaby Rudge:* Dickens and Scott', in *Literature of the Romantic Period 1750–1850*, ed. R. T. Davies and B. G. Beatty (Liverpool: Liverpool University Press, 1976), pp. 171–88: Dickens's novel 'is thematically at war with itself', failing to reproduce Scott's 'imaginative synthesis of private and public events . . . in a richly ambiguous vision of the past'.

24 Thomas J. Rice, 'The Politics of *Barnaby Rudge*', in *The Changing World of Charles Dickens*, ed. Robert Giddings (London: Vision Press, 1983), pp. 51–74, situates the novel's 'fully articulated political allegory' very precisely in its historical moment: the theme of the Gordon riots became topical again with the fall of the Melbourne Whigs, with whom Dickens's political sympathies were aligned, the ascendancy of a Peelite coalition, and an anti-Catholic bigotry shared between far-left Chartism and ultra-Tory reaction. On Dickens and Chartism: Patrick Brantlinger, *The Spirit of Reform: British Literature and Politics 1832–1867* (Cambridge: Harvard University Press, 1977), pp. 83–96.

25 Once again, this is more true of the pre-1820 Scottish novels, such as *Old Mortality* and *The Heart of Mid-Lothian*. In *Quentin Durward* and *The Betrothed* mutinous populaces are merely violent and irrational. Dickens's later historical novel, *A Tale of Two Cities*, is a more succinct and elegant reproduction of *Barnaby Rudge* as far as its representation of revolution goes. Its main difference lies in the private plot, which is charged with a positive sentimental valence.

26 G. K. Chesterton, *Appreciations and Criticisms of the Works of Charles Dickens*, 1911 (repr. New York: Haskell House, 1970), p. 168.

27 Avrom Fleishman, *The English Historical Novel* (Baltimore: Johns Hopkins University Press, 1971), p. 113, reads this passage very differently, praising both *Barnaby Rudge* and *A Tale of Two Cities* for their 'historicity'.

28 On the 'design and execution' of *Dombey and Son*: Butt and Tillotson, *Dickens at Work*, pp. 90–113.

29 Charles Dickens, *Dealings with the Firm of Dombey and Son: Whole-*

sale, Retail, and for Export (Harmondsworth: Penguin, 1970), p. 71. Future references to this edition will be given in the text.

30 'In *Dombey and Son* Dickens undertakes a comprehensive, unified presentation of social life by depicting how an abstract principle conditions all experience. That principle is change.' Marcus, *Dickens from Pickwick to Dombey*, p. 298. On romance figures: Tillotson, *Novels of the Eighteen-Forties*, pp. 174–5.

31 Tillotson, *Novels of the Eighteen-Forties*, p. 182.

32 Cf. Raymond Williams, *The Country and the City* (Oxford: Oxford University Press, 1973), pp. 155–6. Peter K. Garrett, *The Victorian Multi-Plot Novel*, pp. 31–5. Jonathan Arac, *Commissioned Spirits*, pp. 17–23.

33 Raymond Williams, *The Country and the City*, p. 163.

Index

Abbotsford, 58–9, 62, 87, 108, 152, 182–3, 185, 191, 198, 269n.44
Ackroyd, Peter, 254n.2, 279n.26, 282n.4
aesthetic, 14–15, 49, 58–9, 61–2, 68–70, 71–2, 83–4, 89–92, 117, 127–30, 150, 175–6
Ainsworth, W. Harrison, 18, 188, 213–14
allegory, 5, 7, 10, 26–7, 29–32, 80–2, 87, 114–15, 119, 125–6, 136, 143–5, 147–51, 155–61, 163, 181, 207–8, 211, 215–17, 222, 225–8, 236–9, 249, 250, 253, 260
Altick, Richard D., 179, 276n.3
Anderson, Perry, 3
anti-romance, 8, 11–12, 13, 40, 46, 59, 63, 66–8, 80, 92, 100–1, 119, 135, 186, 199
Arabian Nights, The, 122, 133, 199, 203, 210, 238
Arac, Jonathan, 283n.16
archetype, 22, 25–7, 32–3, 36, 45, 86, 101, 103–4, 113–15, 138, 140, 143–5, 157, 160, 200, 209, 214–15, 225, 238–9, 249
Ariosto, Lodovico: *Orlando Furioso*, 40, 57, 75–6, 79–82, 88, 119, 148, 212, 267n.33
Armstrong, Nancy, 35–6, 255n.9, 257n.28
Auerbach, Nina, 266n.24, 277n.8
Austen, Jane, 63
author: cultural status of, 1–2, 17–18, 177–201, 277n.7; death of, 197–8, 200, 207–8; figures of, 124, 126–32, 175–6, 177–9, 181–6, 193–206; gender of, 17–18, 35–6, 63, 107–8, 206–7
autobiography, 199–200, 204, 207

Bage, Robert, 157, 263n.16
Bakhtin, Mikhail, 5, 94, 150, 222, 257n.25
Ballantyne, James and John, 179, 185, 189, 190–1, 277n.12
Barbauld, Anna Laetitia, 262n.34, 265n.15
Beckford, William: *Vathek*, 22, 27, 33
Beethoven, Ludwig van, 149
Bildungsroman, 12, 37–8, 52, 59, 68, 95, 199–208, 214–16, 232, 262n.1
biography, 18, 51, 180–7, 199
Bloom, Harold, 266n.20
Boiardo, Matteo, 76, 81, 212
borders, 21, 60, 65–6, 80–1, 144, 179, 214
Boswell, James: *Journal of a Tour to the Hebrides*, 100; *Life of Johnson*, 180, 182, 277n.7
Brantlinger, Patrick, 278n.16, 285n.24
Bronte, Charlotte, 18
Brooks, Peter, 17, 254n.3
Brown, David, 264n.12
Brownstein, Rachel M., 260n.23
Buchan, John, 177, 181–2, 270n.49
Bunyan, John: *The Pilgrim's Progress*, 4, 31, 32, 119, 154, 160, 215, 239
Burke, Edmund, 23–5, 36, 53, 77, 95, 262n.33
Burney, Frances, 12, 37, 63, 65
Burns, Robert, 178, 190, 269n.44, 279n.25
Butler, Marilyn, 263n.6
Butt, John, 283n.13

Carey, John, 206, 283n.10
Carlton, William, 278n.24
Carlyle, Thomas: and Dickens, 194–5,

211, 280n.36, 280n.44, 281n.50; *Heroes and Hero-Worship*, 180–1, 194; on Scott, 106–7, 175, 182, 187, 198, 265n.12
Carroll, Joseph, 254n.4
Caserio, Robert, 231, 254n.3, 280n.46, 284n.16
Castle, Terry, 260n.23
Cervantes, Miguel de: *Don Quixote*, 11, 63
character, 30, 178, 181–2
Chaucer, Geoffrey, 4, 57, 181
Chesterton, G.K., 177, 181, 234
Chittick, Kathryn, 188, 193, 283n.19
city, 56, 148, 181, 213–14, 217–20, 226–27, 240–3, 249
closure, narrative, 37, 49–50, 61–2, 133–5, 145–6, 173–6, 205, 207–8, 230–1
Coleridge, Samuel Taylor, 40, 113, 123
Collins, Philip, 213
Collins, Wilkie, 130
Collins, William, 83
Constable, Archibald, 179–80, 185, 188, 277n.12
Cottom, Daniel, 60, 264n.11, 273n.25
Crabbe, George, 115
Craig, David, 263n.4
Crawford, Thomas, 149, 151, 168, 274n.36
crime, 118, 212–16, 219–20, 225, 236
Croker, John Wilson, 277n.7
Curran, Stuart, 255n.8, 264n.7

Daiches, David, 262n.3, 272n.11
Daleski, H. M., 283n.16
Damrosch, Leopold, 260n.15, 265n.15
Dante Alighieri, 31
daughters: and fathers, 16–17, 160, 162–3, 166, 229–30, 245, 247–9, 251–3; and mothers, 124, 139–42
Davie, Donald, 64, 99
Day, William Patrick, 259n.8
Defoe, Daniel, 5, 11, 88, 268n.38
DeLamotte, Eugenia C., 261n.28
desire: feminine, 12, 37–8, 66–7, 70–2, 121–2, 124, 139, 159–60; masculine, 33–5, 66–7, 80, 82–5, 120–1, 124, 128–9, 202–4, 206–7, 249–50; and plot, 38, 84–5, 120–1, 128–9, 204
Dickens, Charles: and Gothic, 16, 32–3, 39, 201, 208, 213, 219–20, 225, 252; and history, 16, 218–20, 225, 230–7, 239–44; and politics, 232–4, 246, 285n.24; and publication, 187–8, 190–8, 211–12, 221–2; and readers, 194–8, 221, 236–7, 246–7; and romance, 16, 200, 202–3, 207–8, 210–13, 216–20, 237–9, 240, 245–7, 249–53; and Scott, 15–16, 18, 177, 181–2, 188–94, 198–9, 201, 207–8, 209–15, 218–35, 237–42, 247, 253, 278n.21, 284n.16; as author, 1–2, 18, 35, 148, 181–2, 188, 192–9, 200, 206–8, 219; career and reputation, 3, 18, 187–93, 210–22, 255n.5, 278n.21, 279n.34; literary influences upon, 15, 199–200, 202–3, 209–11, 220–2, 228–32, 239, 282n.2, 284n.16; views of literature, 1–2, 16, 193, 245–7
WORKS: *American Notes*, 282n.16; *Barnaby Rudge*: apocalyptic allegory in, 225–8, as emulation of Scott, 16, 190, 220–5, 228–32, 235, 239, criticism of, 230–1, 284n.22, 285n.23, fathers and sons in, 222–5, 231, 247, 248, history in, 225, 227–8, 230–1, 232–7, 285n.24, production of, 190, 210, 220–2, 283n.13; *Bleak House*, 150, 219, 228, 240, 257n.25; *A Child's History of England*, 234; *David Copperfield*: and romance form, 201–2, 204, 207–8, author in, 193, 199–200, 202–8, doubling in, 201–2, 204–8, prefaces, 196–8, reading in, 199–200, 202–3, 209, sexuality in, 202–7, women in, 203, 205–8; *Dombey and Son*: allegory in, 150, 237–40, 244–5, 248–50, 253, childhood in, 239, 247, 249–52, economy in, 241–2, 244, 248, 250, 252, modernity in, 218–20, 240–4, 253, patriarchy in, 237, 246–9, 252–3; romance conventions in, 237–9, 245–7, 252–3, sexuality in, 247–50; *Household Words*, 193; *Little Dorrit*, 16, 150, 209, 218, 240; *Martin Chuzzlewit*, 198; *Master Humphrey's Clock*, 221, 234, 241, 282n.2; *Nicholas Nickleby*, 193, 195–6, 211, 231; *The Old Curiosity Shop*, 196, 211, 216–18, 219, 221, 237, 250, 252; *Oliver*

Twist, 201, 211, 214–16, 219, 237, 282n.2; *Our Mutual Friend*, 150; *The Pickwick Papers*, 181, 187–8, 191, 211–13, 220, 277n.7, 282n.2; Prefaces to novels, 195–8; 'Scott and his Publishers', 190–1, 279n.28, 284n.16; *A Tale of Two Cities*, 207, 285n.25
digression, 79–81, 90, 101, 120, 138, 159, 224
Disraeli, Benjamin, 239
doubles and doubling, 85–6, 138–9, 141, 159–61, 201–2, 204–8, 224–5, 238–9, 281n.49.
Dundas, Henry (Lord Melville), 171, 272n.14
Dunlop, John, 4, 258n.6, 272n.16

economy, 14, 16, 100–1, 114, 117, 169–70, 184–7, 191, 194–8, 200, 219–20, 241–2, 244, 248, 250, 252
Edgeworth, Maria, 63, 87, 174, 268n.39; *Castle Rackrent*, 138, 153
Edinburgh, 54, 58, 111–12, 117, 154, 174, 177–8, 189–90, 218–19, 271n.9, 272n.14
elegy and elegiac, 14, 44, 49–50, 83–4, 89–93, 96–9, 118, 197–9, 202, 205–8, 217–18
Eliot, George, 5, 18, 70, 113, 150, 170
Ellis, Kate, 261n.28
epic, 28–9, 75–7, 80, 170

Farrell, John P., 263n.3, 274n.28
fathers, 28, 125–31, 137–8; and daughters, 16–17, 36, 43–5, 49, 162–3, 166, 229–30, 245, 247–9, 251–3; and sons, 30, 67–8, 85–6, 99, 157, 158, 189, 191–2, 199–200, 203, 222–6, 229–31, 237–8; and writing, 30–2, 47–9, 126–30, 197–8, 206; *see also* patriarchy
Feltes, N. N., 193, 282n.5
female quixote, 12, 13, 17, 36–7, 63–9, 79, 83, 121, 124, 139–42, 159, 162, 200, 278n.14; *see also* Lennox, Charlotte
Ferrier, Susan, 171
Ferris, Ina, 17, 255n.9, 265n.14
feudalism, 22–4, 55, 97, 100–5, 112–20, 131–2, 152, 154, 165–6, 234
Fielding, Henry, 5, 8, 11, 12, 195, 284n.16; *Tom Jones*, 55–6, 62–4, 78, 119, 202–3
Fisher, P. F., 275n.41
Fitzgerald, Percy, 209
Fleishman, Avrom, 285n.27
Fletcher, Angus, 30–1
folk culture, 4–5, 57–9, 81–3, 131, 135, 142, 151, 159–60, 210, 212–13, 218–19
Forbes, Duncan, 263n.5
Forster, John, 18, 181, 254n.2, 279n.28, 280n.44
Fowler, Alastair, 256n.13, 275n.38
Frankl, Paul, 258n.4
Freccero, John, 260n.16
Freud, Sigmund, 25, 32, 84, 208
Frye, Northrop, 2, 6–8, 10, 19, 57, 71, 114–15, 134, 256n.13, 280n.37

Galt, John, 113
Garrett, Peter K., 283n.16
Garside, Peter D., 263n.5, 267n.37, 272n.17
genius loci, 14, 81–4, 144, 181–2
genre: allegory of, 14, 56–7, 63–70, 73–94, 99–101, 122–35, 237–9; and gender, 17–18, 170–1; and history, 7–9; mixtures of, 20, 75–7, 148–52; transformations of, 134, 140–1, 149–65, 203–14, 239
georgic, 14, 111, 168
Ghent, Dorothy Van, 255n.5, 274n.36
Gifford, Douglas, 149, 274n.36
Gilbert, Sandra, 257n.28
Girard, René, 281n.49
Girouard, Mark, 278n.14
Godwin, William, 64, 263n.6
Goldberg, Michael, 280n.36
Gordon, Robert C., 264n.12, 271n.3
Goslee, Nancy M., 264n.7
Gothic novel, 20–50, 58, 64, 125, 135, 139–44, 172, 184, 213; and history, 13, 23–6, 37, 213–14, 219–20, 225; and national identity, 22–5, 77; and politics, 21–7, 35–7, 46–7; and private life, 25–7, 32, 56, 225; and romance revival, 13, 20–3; and sensibility, 12–13, 37–43, 139–41, 162; and sexuality, 13, 25–7, 32–4, 36–8, 56, 72, 156, 273n.18; and women, 12–13, 27, 35–50, 139–43,

261n.28; setting of, 24–5, 34–6, 142, 144; tonality of, 27, 32, 145
Gothic revival, 21–5, 177–8
Green, Martin, 272n.14
Gubar, Susan, 257n.28

Hardy, Thomas, 5, 113, 145
Hart, F. R., 61, 103, 135, 182, 264n.11, 272n.11, 277n.10, 284n.21
Hartman, Geoffrey, 267n.35
haunting, 30, 38, 43–4, 61, 143, 183–4; *see also* supernatural
Hawthorne, Nathaniel, 10, 274n.30
Hazlitt, William, 58, 108, 113, 232
Herbert, Christopher, 255n.11
heroes: cultural, 18, 106, 180–3, 187, 196; literary, 37, 63–9, 74–6, 84, 119–21, 153, 161–2, 199, 202–3, 204–7, 214–15
heroines, 36–40, 64, 70–3, 83–4, 139–42, 153, 163–5
Hewitt, David, 281n.54
Highlands: clearances in, 88, 105, 166–9, 275n.45; culture of, 57, 74, 75, 81–3; tourism in, 14, 57, 79, 87–91, 169, 268n.38
Hillhouse, James T., 254n.4, 276n.2
historical novel, 8, 18, 24, 26, 51–4, 107–10, 210, 213–14, 220–2, 232–7, 239, 262n.1
history: and fate, 116, 135–8, 142–5; and fortune, 68, 116–17, 136–7; and Gothic, 21–6, 31, 213–14, 219–20, 225; and private life, 26, 36–7, 51–2, 53–6, 59–62, 136–7, 228–30; and romance, 7–9, 13–14, 26, 51–62, 73–9, 81–6, 88–105, 109–11, 116–19, 146, 149–57, 167–76, 181–2; and tragedy, 37, 81, 83–5, 89–93, 135–9, 151; and women, 13, 35–7, 70–3, 170–1, 229–30; versions of, 8–9, 55, 73, 107–8, 152–3, 233–7
Hobsbawm, E. J., 255n.8
Hogarth, George, 188–9, 190–1, 279n.25
Hogg, James, 15, 58, 262n.2
Hollingsworth, Keith, 282n.8
Homans, Margaret, 257n.28, 273n.18
homecoming narrative, 90–2, 103–4, 118–20
Homer: *The Odyssey*, 77, 90, 99, 118
Houghton, Walter E., 280n.36
Hume, David, 25
Hurd, Bishop Richard, 22, 258n.4, 260n.15

ideology: aristocratic, 7, 73–5, 182–3, 186, 273n.25; bourgeois, 24–7, 53–5, 186, 198–9, 200–2, 212, 232–3; protestant, 31, 194, 200; revolutionary, 8, 15
idyll, 10, 15, 33, 37, 41, 49, 55, 82, 90, 95, 100–1, 103–4, 115, 139, 156–7, 166–72, 201, 205, 213, 217–18, 241–2, 252, 266n.27
imagination, 59–60, 91–2, 124, 127–8, 205–6, 210–11, 216–20, 250
imperialism, 14, 88, 117, 121–2, 157, 167–8, 240–1, 272n.14
India, 120–5, 240–1, 272n.14

Jack, Ian, 277n.10
Jacobinism, 24–5, 56, 77–8, 102, 115
Jacobin romance, 56, 263n.6
Jacobitism, 11, 24, 52, 55–6, 73–9, 81–4, 152, 172
James, G. P. R., 18
Jameson, Fredric, 2, 6, 9, 270n.52
Johnson, Edgar, 118, 189, 221, 255n.5, 266n.26, 278n.21
Johnson, Samuel, 12, 28, 94, 113, 114, 182; *Dictionary*, 10; *Journey to the Western Isles of Scotland*, 88–9, 135, 169, 268n.38, 276n.47; *Lives of the Poets*, 4, 180; *Rasselas*, 130
Johnston, Arthur, 255n.8, 263n.7

Kafka, Franz, 31
Kaplan, Fred, 278n.22
Kaufmann, David, 270n.46
Kelly, Gary, 261n.25, 263n.6, 264n.9
Kernan, Alvin B., 255n.8, 277n.44
Kerr, James, 149, 267n.30, 271n.6, 275n.44
Kiely, Robert, 266n.21
Kliger, Samuel, 258n.4

law: Dickens and, 154, 215, 219, 230–1; in Gothic, 31, 46–7; Scott and, 54, 94, 112, 117, 130, 147, 154–5, 157–8, 160, 166
Leavis, F. R., 3, 175, 182, 255n.5, 270n.51

Lennox, Charlotte: *The Female Quixote*, 12, 37, 67–8
Lentricchia, Frank, 256n.13
Levine, George, 175, 265n.12
Lévy, Maurice, 258n.4
Lewis, Matthew: *The Monk*, 20, 25, 27, 33–4, 45, 48, 213, 225, 258n.3
Lipking, Lawrence, 255n.8
literalization, 28–34, 143–6, 228
Lockhart, John Gibson, 189, 263n.4; *Life of Scott*, 18, 180–7, 188, 190–2, 276n.49
London, 213–14, 217–20, 240–3; *see also* city
Lukacher, Ned, 281n.48
Lukács, Georg, 9, 18, 51, 53, 231, 256n.16, 262n.1
Lytton, Edward Lytton Bulwer-, 18, 187, 213, 239

MacAndrew, Elizabeth, 260n.17
Macaulay, Thomas Babington, 277n.7
Mackenzie, Henry, 195, 257n.24; *The Man of Feeling*, 64, 96
McKeon, Michael, 7–8, 256n.13, 260n.15
McMaster, Graham, 262n.2
Macpherson, Jay, 261n.26, 267n.35
Magnet, Myron, 284n.17
Marcus, Steven, 217, 222, 255n.5, 282n.3, 284n.19, 286n.30
Marshall, David, 268n.40
Martineau, Harriet, 266n.24, 277n.7
Maturin, Charles: *Melmoth the Wanderer*, 25, 27, 35, 46, 125, 213
Miller, D. A., 280n.39
Miller, J. Hillis, 206, 255n.5, 256n.11, 283n.12
Miller, Karl, 263n.4
Millgate, Jane, 60, 96, 111–12, 134, 180, 186, 264n.7, 267n.28, 271n.7, 272n.12, 273n.26
Millgate, Michael, 274n.31
Milton, John, 4, 39, 76, 273n.20; *Paradise Lost*, 29, 30, 53, 67, 78, 88, 227–8
Mitchell, Jerome, 264n.7
modernity, 4, 6, 9, 39, 111–12, 116–18, 217–20, 235–7, 239–44, 253
Moers, Ellen, 261n.28
Moir, George, 255n.9, 281n.47
More, Thomas, 168
Moretti, Franco, 3, 5–6, 262n.1, 266n.21
Morgan, Lady, *see* Owenson, Sydney
mothers, 38, 142–3, 155, 156, 157–61, 205–6
Muir, Edwin, 263n.4
Munro, Neil, 270n.49
mystery, 25, 48, 130, 219–20
myth, 6–7, 26, 86, 94, 103–5, 114–17, 128, 135–6, 181–2, 214–15, 235–6

Nabokov, Vladimir, 9
narcissism, 12,.33, 59, 65–7, 159, 200, 202, 207, 224
narrative form: of Dickens, 201–2, 205, 207–8, 210–12, 222, 238–40, 283n.16; of Gothic, 34–5, 38–40, 47–8; of Scott, 80–1, 94–5, 119, 136–7, 147–50, 284n.16
nationalism, 18; and Gothic, 21–5; and literary tradition, 3–6, 57–9, 181, 190; and romance revival, 4, 14–15, 57–9, 181–2; and Scott, 14, 54–9, 94–5, 103–4, 149, 152, 167, 235
national tale, 87–8, 268n.39
natural theology, 47, 107, 113–15, 143
nature, 27–8, 67, 103–4, 112–15, 118, 126–8, 135, 157, 160, 161, 218, 247, 253
Newgate novel, 156–7, 213–14, 219, 221, 239
Newman, Gerald, 255n.8, 258n.4
Newman, S. J., 285n.24
Newton, Isaac, 127
Nohrnberg, James, 267n.34, 273n.20
novel: and literary canons, 3, 17; and society, 2, 187, 240–7; criticism of, 2–3, 17, 63–4, 187; history of, 4–8, 11, 17–19, 55–6, 62–4, 187–8, 213–14, 239

Oddie, William, 280n.36
Oliphant, Margaret, 278n.14
organic society, 9, 59, 67, 95, 100–5, 112–17, 218–19
Orient, 10, 22, 57, 122–4, 133–4, 240–1, 272n.16
origins, 7, 22–3, 45, 81, 86, 90–1, 95, 103–4, 112–16, 118–19, 143, 157, 206, 211, 239
Owenson, Sydney (Lady Morgan), 63, 88, 268n.38

Parker, Patricia, 256n.18, 267n.33
pastoral, 14, 90, 103, 111–12, 156, 166–9, 170, 217–19, 241–2; *see also* idyll
patriarchy, 10, 12–13, 28–34, 36–8, 43–7, 58–9, 67–8, 72–3, 88, 95–105, 111, 131–2, 137–9, 152–3, 157–67, 169, 189, 197–200, 205–7, 222–5, 229–31, 237–8, 246–7, 251–3; *see also* fathers
Patton, Robert J., 279n.27, 283n.13
Paulson, Ronald, 8, 265n.15
Peterson, Linda, 281n.50
picaresque, 64, 211–16
plot, 2, 5, 30, 34, 38–40, 45–7, 63–4, 76, 84–7, 101–2, 113–17, 125–6, 128–32, 135–9, 155–61, 213, 223–5, 230, 254, 283n.16
Poovey, Mary, 193, 196, 205, 206, 257n.28, 277n.7
Pope, Alexander, 123
popular culture, 18, 210–11, 212–13, 216–19
Porte, Joel, 259n.8
Powys, John Cowper, 270n.50
Price, Martin, 6, 256n.13
private life, 12, 16, 25–7, 36–7, 51–2, 53–6, 59–62, 64, 152, 155, 166–7, 182–4, 195–6, 230, 244–7
progress narrative, 119–20, 154, 164, 200, 201, 204, 211, 215–16
prophecy, 10, 68, 70, 82–3, 107, 125–32, 142–4, 160, 194–5, 207
prospect, 41–4, 47–9, 87, 98
Providence, 47, 107, 118–21, 131–2, 173, 253
public sphere, 51–3, 55–6, 60, 67–9, 154–5, 181, 194–6, 214–20, 225–8
publishing: Dickens and, 187–8, 190–8; Scott and, 179–81, 184–6, 189, 190–3, 277n.12
Punter, David, 259n.11
Puritanism, 119–20, 152–4, 162, 164, 172, 199, 201–2

quest narrative, 10, 67, 79–80, 120, 162–3, 165
Quint, David, 267n.32

Radcliffe, Ann, 12–13, 25, 33, 35–50, 64, 71, 79, 87, 98, 123, 140–2, 143, 213; as author, 17, 27, 35–6; narrative form of, 38–40, 47–9, 84–5, 126; on terror and horror, 47–8; suspense in, 41–3, 47–50; *The Italian*, 38, 40, 45–6, 142, 258n.3; *The Mysteries of Udolpho*, 35, 38, 39–50, 67–8, 72, 165, 252, 258n.3; *The Romance of the Forest*, 20–1, 25, 36, 39, 40, 45, 46, 258n.3
Ramazani, Jahan, 281n.46
Ranger, Terence, 255n.8
Ray, Gordon N., 254n.2
reader, 11–12, 14–15, 47–50, 61–3, 65–6, 69–70, 79–80, 82–4, 180, 182, 194–8, 199–200, 202–3, 207, 236–7, 246–7
reading public, 18, 54, 178–80, 187, 194
realism, 6, 31, 62, 170–1
Reed, James, 272n.10
Reeve, Clara: *The Old English Baron*, 24, 250; *The Progress of Romance*, 20–1
regionalism, 14, 87–8, 91, 111–14
retrospect, 17, 43, 49, 87, 98, 202
revolution: in Britain, 3, 8, 11, 20–5, 52–3, 77–8, 100–5, 107–8, 155–7, 175, 233, 242–4, 252–3; in France, 21, 24–6, 36, 46, 77
Reynolds, Sir Joshua, 22
Rice, Thomas J., 285n.24
Richards, Eric, 275n.45
Richardson, Samuel, 5, 8, 11, 12, 63, 140–1, 261n.27; *Clarissa*, 36–7, 44, 144, 164, 261n.27; *Sir Charles Grandison*, 24, 64, 261n.27
riot, 25, 34, 100, 155–6, 159, 225–8, 232–3, 236, 243, 285n.25
romance: meanings of, 2, 10–11, 20–1, 39, 56–8, 62–3, 92, 181, 210–11, 220, 237–9, 250, 254n.3; and the aesthetic, 14, 26, 58–9, 61–2, 68–70, 83–4, 89–92, 127–30, 132–5, 175–6; and aristocratic ideology, 7–8, 73–5, 118–21, 152; and childhood, 16–17, 59, 199–204, 210, 216, 239, 247, 249–52; and education, 37–8, 59–60, 79–80, 202–4; and history, 6–9, 13–14, 22–6, 51–62, 73–9, 81–6, 88–105, 109–11, 116–19, 146, 149–57, 167–76, 181–2; and magic, 71–2, 103, 113, 118, 122–35, 170, 184, 200, 241; and modernity, 4, 5–6, 9, 11, 14–15, 20–7, 39, 88–92, 104–5, 126–35, 174–6, 178, 181–2, 217–20, 239,

241–2, 244–7; and national identity, 2, 4–5, 14–15, 21–5, 57–9, 149, 267n.35; and nature, 6, 103–5, 113–14, 118, 123, 126–31, 135, 196–7, 218, 247; and the novel, 2–3, 5–6, 8–9, 11, 149–51, 237–9; and popular culture, 5–6, 210, 212, 216, 218–20; and primitivism, 3–4, 5, 6, 11, 14, 88, 101–4, 131–2, 210, 218; and Puritanism, 10, 119–20, 152–4, 160, 162; and reality, 2–3, 5–6, 19, 21, 49–50, 100–2, 168–9, 240–6; and restoration, 69, 72, 73, 90–2, 104–5, 116–17, 132, 152, 163–6, 169–73, 207; and revolution, 8, 11, 26, 100–5, 252–3; and subjectivity, 12–15, 16–17, 26, 51–4, 59–60, 89–93, 119–20, 124, 127–8, 139–42, 181, 193–8, 199–208, 211, 249–52; and women, 11–13, 17–18, 36–40, 62–73, 81–4, 103–4, 111, 125–6, 131–2, 139–44, 159–65, 170–1, 203, 205–8, 247–53; as escapism, 33, 50, 79–86, 90–2, 100–2, 108, 139–40, 181; as fiction, 3–6, 15, 26, 61–2, 109–10, 129–35, 136, 169–76; as form, 5–6, 56, 91–2, 172–6, 207–8; as myth, 6–7, 86, 103–5, 114–15, 181–2; as tradition, 3–4, 8–9, 14, 57–8, 140, 151, 200, 210, 213; failure of, 26, 40, 50, 92–3, 100–2, 110, 138–42, 225, 230–1; French, 10–12; Italian, 57, 75–6, 79–82, 151; oriental, 22, 57, 122–4

romance revival, 2, 4, 7, 10, 14, 21–3, 57–9, 73–6, 81–4, 91–2, 113–15, 126–31, 212–13, 284n.16

romans héroïques, 10–11

romanticism, 9–10, 57, 124, 128

Ruskin, John, 3, 22, 209, 218

Sade, Marquis de, 259n.11

Salzman, Paul, 256n.15, 256n.20

Sanders, Andrew, 258n.29, 282n.8

Schiller, Friedrich, 6, 57, 61

Schlicke, Paul, 210, 282n.3

Scotland, 54; history, 52–3, 107–8, 111–12, 136, 152–3, 157, 167–9, 171

Scott monument (Edinburgh), 177–8, 180–1

Scott, P. H., 263n.4

Scott, Walter: and Gothic, 13, 17, 33, 37, 39, 46, 49, 50, 54, 64, 72, 87, 99, 126, 139–44, 172, 219–20, 259n.14, 262n.34, 274n.29; and history, 8–9, 13–15, 51–3, 55–6, 58–62, 73–9, 95, 107–18, 168–9, 175, 213, 224–5, 234–5, 263n.5, 269n.44, 275n.45; and materialism, 61–2, 68–70, 106, 175, 195; and national identity, 14–15, 53, 54–5, 57–9, 93–4, 98, 103–4, 147, 167, 171–2, 182, 198–9; and the novel, 3, 4–5, 8–9, 17–18, 55–6, 119, 186–7, 195, 284n.16; and politics, 52–5, 69, 78, 107–8, 152, 186–7, 232–3, 262n.2; and popular culture, 57–8, 178–80, 218; and romance revival, 4–5, 7, 8–9, 10–11, 14, 56–9, 75–6, 91–2, 151–2, 208, 211, 212, 269n.44, 284n.16; and Shakespeare, 52–3, 57, 110, 113–15, 119, 127, 134, 135, 138, 140, 142, 145, 151–2, 165, 284n.16; and women authors, 17–18, 170–1; and writing, 69, 93–5, 126–30, 175–6, 183–5; as author, 17–18, 54, 94, 107, 171, 175–6, 177–93; career and reputation, 4, 5, 54, 171, 178–87; characters of, 65–73, 95–6, 178, 181; criticism of, 3, 7, 62, 65, 68, 104, 106, 134, 135, 149, 173, 175, 182, 263n.4, 264n.11, 265n.12, 271n.6, 272n.11, 274n.36, 275n.41, 278n.19, 284n.16; publication of works, 178–80, 184–6, 189, 190–3, 209–10, 273n.26, 277n.12; ruin and death, 18, 55, 174–5, 179–80, 184–7, 189, 190–2, 270n.44; self-representation, 94, 98, 108, 115–16, 124, 171, 175–6, 178, 184–6, 266n.27, 276n.51

WORKS: *Anne of Geierstein*, 46, 121, 219; *The Antiquary*, 95, 96–7, 98, 109, 184; *The Betrothed*, 266n.27, 285n.25; *The Bride of Lammermoor*, 18, 183, and ballads, 57, 135, 142–3, and Gothic, 57, 142–4, as tragedy, 61, 135, 145, failure of romance in, 110, 138–42, 229, fatality in, 110, 135, 143–4, female power in, 72, 139–43, 161, formal unity of, 135, 145, history in, 136–8, 145–6, supernatural in, 135–6,

142–4, textuality in, 145–6; 'Essay on Romance', 10, 264n.7; *The Fair Maid of Perth*, 229–30, 269n.41; *The Fortunes of Nigel*, 95, 184, 276n.51, 282n.2; *Guy Mannering*, authorship in, 121–31, fiction in, 109, 122–31, genre, 7, 14, 57, 122, 235, 239, imagination in, 124, 127–8, magic and prophecy in, 122–35, modernity in, 111–12, 116–18, narrative closure in, 131–5, nature in, 112–15, orientalism in, 57, 121–2, plot of, 113–21, 124–6, 129–32, 156, 253, regional representation in, 111–14, sexual and parental allegory in, 125–32, 139; *The Heart of Mid-Lothian*: allegory in, 147–51, 155–67, crisis of patriarchy in, 150, 153–4, 157–67, 169–72, fiction in, 151, 169–76, folk-culture in, 151, 154, 159–60, history in, 152–5, 166–9, 171–6, idyll in, 95, 150, 156–7, 167–72, the law in, 147, 151–2, 154–8, 160, 166, maternity in, 155, 156, 157–61, mixed genre of, 57, 110, 147–52, 155–7, 167–76, narrative closure in, 173–6, Puritanism in, 152–4, 160, 162, society in, 147–8, 153, 170–1, 225, 239, textuality in, 154, 156–7, 172–6, Victorian novel and, 110, 149–51, 154, 166, 167, 176, 229, 239, 247, 282n.2, women in, 150, 153–4, 155, 157–65, 170–1, 247; *Ivanhoe*, 235, 266n.27, 270n.44; *Journal*, 86–7, 185–6, 270n.44, 271n.4; *Kenilworth*, 179, 229, 282n.2; *The Lady of the Lake*, 87, 169; *A Legend of Montrose*, 95, 282n.2; *Letters on Demonology and Witchcraft*, 127, 135–6, 272n.16, 273n.20; *Life of Napoleon Buonaparte*, 185; *Lives of the Novelists*, 4, 180, 265n.15; 'Memoir', 59, 267n.33; *Minstrelsy of the Scottish Border*, 58, 212; *The Monastery*, 273n.25; *Old Mortality*, 51, 60–1, 75, 95, 102, 103, 108–9, 110, 153, 170, 175, 179, 223, 228, 269n.41, 282n.2; *Peveril of the Peak*, 184, 213, 228, 229, 282n.2; *The Pirate*, 142, 273n.21; *Quentin Durward*, 121, 285n.25; *Redgauntlet*, 95, 99, 110, 138, 156, 223, 271n.6; *Rob Roy*, 95, 109, 110, 169, 266n.19, 269n.41, 281n.54, 282n.2, 283n.10; *St Ronan's Well*, 170; *The Surgeon's Daughter*, 269n.41; *Tales of the Crusaders*, 184–5; *Tales of a Grandfather*, 234, 275n.45; *Tales of My Landlord*, 98–9, 171, 221, 265n.17; *The Talisman*, 121, 266n.27; 'The Two Drovers', 265n.18; *Waverley*: aestheticism in, 8, 14–15, 68–9, 83–4, 88–92, 100, anti-romance in, 13, 62–8, 92–3, digression in, 79–82, 120, education in, 13, 52, 79, 96–7, 230–1, elegy in, 82–4, 88–93, 98–9, gender and sexuality in, 13–14, 52, 54, 63–73, 81–4, 86, 139, genre and, 56, 57, 63–70, 73–94, 99–101, heroism in, 63–9, 71–3, 78–80, 84–5, 88–9, 96–9, history in, 8, 13–14, 51–2, 72–105, ideology of, 73–5, 103–5, patriarchy in, 67–73, 88, 97–105, place in, 14, 81–3, 87–8, 91, 100–4, politics in, 67–9, 73–4, 76, 78–9, 84, 88–9, production of, 183, 277n.12, reading in, 63, 66–7, 69–70, 79, 83–4, 91–2, 199–200, 202, revolution in, 77–8, 102–5, sympathy in, 89, 96–7, 270, tourism in, 14, 87–91, 100–1; *Woodstock*, 228

Scottish Enlightenment, 9, 10, 26, 55, 57–8, 94, 112, 257n.24

Sedgwick, Eve Kosofsky, 259n.13, 281n.49

sensibility, 12–13, 37–9, 41–2, 47–9, 64, 67, 72, 139–42

sentiment, 89–92, 96–7, 99–100, 195–8, 207, 218

serial narrative, 188, 195–7, 201, 210–12, 221

sexuality, 12–13, 25–7, 36–8, 45, 64–6, 70–3, 129, 141, 202–7, 247–8

Shakespeare, William, 4, 14, 39, 57, 119, 181, 218, 228–9, 284n.16; comedies and romances, 10, 50, 113–15, 134, 151–2, 165; histories, 52, 53, 222; tragedies, 32, 135, 145; *Hamlet*, 138; *King Lear*, 67, 284n.20; *Macbeth*, 142; *Measure for Measure*, 151; *Othello*, 247; *The Tempest*, 90,

127, 140, 152; *The Winter's Tale*, 78, 151–2, 175, 249
Shaw, Harry E., 265n.12, 267n.36
Sherbo, Arthur, 255n.8
Showalter, Elaine, 257n.28
Smith, Adam, 107, 184, 257n.24, 263n.5, 268n.40
Smith, Charlotte, 27, 64, 157
Smith, Nichol, 272n.12
Smollett, Tobias, 11, 172; *Ferdinand, Count Fathom*, 64, 78–9; *Humphry Clinker*, 64, 88–9, 112, 169; *Roderick Random*, 202–3
Smout, T. C., 263n.4, 271n.7
Spacks, Patricia Meyer, 254n.3, 257n.28, 261n.30
Spencer, Jane, 257n.22
Spenser, Edmund: *The Faerie Queene*, 4, 14, 26, 31–2, 40, 57, 76, 77, 79–82, 86, 90, 91, 103–4, 119, 140, 239, 249, 274n.30
Stafford, Marquess of, 275n.45
Sterne, Laurence, 64, 206
Stevens, Wallace, 226
Stevenson, Robert Louis, 19, 270n.49
Stewart, Dugald, 178, 263n.5
Stone, Harry, 282n.3
Stuarts, 76–9, 100, 154, 157, 166
subject, 25–7, 30; formation of, 89, 91–8, 119, 195–8, 199–207; and gender, 13, 33, 35–6, 36–42, 54, 63–73, 202–4, 206–7; and history, 13–14, 52–4, 56, 59–62, 91–2; and romance, 12–13, 47–9, 58–62, 83–4, 91–2, 119–20, 127–8, 139–41, 207–8
Summers, Montague, 258n.4
supernatural, 29–31, 49, 113, 127–35, 135–6, 143–4, 146; *see also* haunting
Sutherland, J. A., 279n.27
Sutherland, Kathryn, 263n.5
sympathy, 89, 96–7, 104, 195–8, 230, 247

textuality, 83, 93–5, 106–7, 124–6, 127–35, 145–6, 154, 156–7, 160, 174–6, 195–8, 206–7, 239–40
Thackeray, W. M., 3, 18, 254n.2
Thomson, George, 279n.25
Tillotson, Kathleen, 220, 239, 280n.39, 283n.14
Tompkins, J. M. S., 259n.9, 262n.34
tour narratives, 14, 41, 57, 87–91, 169, 212, 268n.38
tragedy, 32, 83–4, 88–93, 134, 145, 151
tragi-comedy, 151–2
Trumpener, Katie, 268n.39, 272n.17

Utopia, 3–7, 41, 168

Valente, Joseph, 264n.11, 267n.35, 269n.43
Varma, Devendra P., 259n.8
violence, 12, 33–4, 36–7, 45, 66, 72, 141, 214–15, 223–8, 230, 268n.41
Virgil: *Aeneid*, 80, 99; *Eclogues*, 167–8

Walpole, Horace: *The Castle of Otranto*, 20, 27–32, 45, 48, 213
Warton, Thomas, 260n.15
Watt, Ian, 256n.15
Welsh, Alexander, 53, 65, 70–1, 85, 200, 206, 214, 280n.37
Wicke, Jennifer, 272n.4
Williams, Ioan, 257n.20
Williams, Raymond, 168, 252
Wilson, A. N., 278n.14
Wilson, Edmund, 255n.5, 282n.7
Wilson, John ('Christopher North'), 189, 279n.26
Wilt, Judith K., 103, 163, 191, 259n.8, 264n.11, 267n.31, 273n.18
Wolff, Cynthia Griffin, 261n.28
Womack, Peter, 268n.39, 276n.47
women: and history, 37, 70–3, 229–30; and the law, 155, 157–61, 162–3; and the novel, 17–18, 35–6, 63, 170–1, 257n.28, 261n.28; and power, 12, 27, 38, 44–9, 71–3, 131–2, 142–3, 161–6, 230; and romance, 11–13, 36–40, 63–6, 70–3, 81–4, 103–4, 131–2, 139–44, 159–65, 170, 203, 205–8, 247–53; and writing, 27, 35–6, 63, 273n.18, 278n.14
Woolf, Virginia, 35, 61
Wordsworth, William, 53, 115, 123, 142

Lightning Source UK Ltd.
Milton Keynes UK
UKHW012153180821
389073UK00002B/585